The Business of Healthcare Innovation

The Business of Healthcare Innovation is the first wide-ranging analysis of business trends in the manufacturing segment of the healthcare industry. In this leading edge volume, Professor Lawton R. Burns focuses on the key role of the "producers" as the main source of innovation in health systems.

Written by professors of the Wharton School and industry executives, this book provides a detailed overview of the pharmaceutical, biotechnology, genomics/proteomics, medical device, and information technology sectors. It analyzes the market structures of these sectors as well as the business models and corporate strategies of firms operating within them. Most importantly, the book describes the growing convergence between these sectors and the need for executives in one sector to increasingly draw upon trends in the others. It will be essential reading for students and researchers in the field of health management, and of great interest to strategy scholars, industry practitioners, and management consultants.

Lawton Robert Burns, Ph.D., MBA is the James Joo-Jin Kim Professor, Professor of Health Care Systems and Management, and Director of the Wharton Center for Health Management and Economics at the University of Pennsylvania.

Never has the need for a reasoned analysis of the business of healthcare innovation been greater. The costs of innovation have been escalating steadily for decades and the willingness and ability of society to fund ongoing innovation is under strain. At the same time, as healthcare becomes increasingly complex those participating – basic and discovery scientists, product developers, providers, and those involved in regulating, managing, and funding the system – become more specialized and find it harder to understand the industry as a whole. Yet the components of the system are not independent of one another and we ignore the interrelationships at our peril. This badly needed volume will be a compelling read for those directly involved in healthcare, for students aspiring to enter the system, and for the rest of us who one way or another collide with the system more often than we might like.

Peter A. Tollman, Ph.D., Vice President and Director, Boston Consulting Group

The healthcare sector of the developed world's economies has become one of the most significant in terms of both cost and human benefits created. The authors have done an excellent job of providing a clear understanding of the basic industry platforms that create both the product innovation and their associated benefits and costs. This book offers valuable insights in to how the diverse segments converge to create a rapidly changing healthcare experience impacting both patients and payors.

James Vincent, Chairman and CEO (ret.), Biogen

All sectors of the healthcare products industry are not the same. *The Business of Healthcare Innovation* provides an interesting primer on the various product categories while framing key questions regarding the future evolution of this fascinating industry.

Arthur D. Collins, Jr., Chairman and Chief Executive Officer, Medtronic, Inc.

This book presents a concise analysis of the factors influencing innovation in the health supplier sector. It is highly recommended for programs in health services management and will also be of interest to healthcare executives seeking to obtain a deeper understanding of the supplier side of the industry.

Stephen M. Shortell, Ph.D., Blue Cross of California Professor of Health Policy and Management Dean, School of Public Health, University of California – Berkeley

This book is an up-to-date and authoritative description of innovation in the healthcare industry. While there is substantial change in how healthcare services are delivered and reimbursed, the focus here is on innovation in products. This is appropriate as new pharmaceuticals and devices generate the greatest new benefit to patients and value to our economy. In addition to related subject matter, the book provides a comprehensive discussion about the biotechnology industry, in particular those companies devoted to the healthcare sector: their innovations, financing, development, evolution, and how they are regulated on a global basis. The profound impact biopharmaceuticals are having on serious diseases is effectively illustrated by cogent examples of breakthrough medicines and the companies that developed them. This book presents compelling evidence that the pharmaceutical industry, with its productivity gap, has become ever more dependent on the biotechnology industry as its engine of innovation for new products.

L. Patrick Gage, Ph.D., Venture Partner, Flagship Ventures

This timely and well-written volume provides a much needed analysis of the healthcare sector that delivers technological innovation. I am particularly impressed with both the breadth and depth of coverage that Lawton Burns and his colleagues achieve here, given the expansive topic.

Edward J. Zajac, Ph.D., James F. Beré Distinguished Professor of Management and Organizations,
Kellogg School of Management

The business of medical technology is virtually ignored in most academic books, despite the sector's substantial size, growth rate, complexity, and promise. *The Business of Healthcare Innovation* ably fills this gap. It couples authoritative, complete descriptions of each of the major components within medical technology – pharmaceuticals, biotechnology, medical devices, and information – with cogent analyses of how adept managers gain and sustain competitive advantage.

Regina Herzlinger, Ph.D., Nancy R. McPherson Professor of Business Administration,
Harvard Business School

The Business of Healthcare Innovation

Edited by

Lawton R. Burns, Ph.D., MBA

The Wharton School, University of Pennsylvania

CAMBRIDGE
UNIVERSITY PRESS

CAMBRIDGE UNIVERSITY PRESS
Cambridge, New York, Melbourne, Madrid, Cape Town, Singapore, São Paulo

CAMBRIDGE UNIVERSITY PRESS
The Edinburgh Building, Cambridge CB2 2RU, UK

Published in the United States of America by Cambridge University Press, New York

www.cambridge.org
Information on this title: www.cambridge.org/9780521547680

First published 2005

Printed in the United Kingdom at the University Press, Cambridge

A catalogue record for this book is available from the British Library

Library of Congress Cataloguing in Publication data

The business of healthcare innovation / [edited by] Lawton R. Burns.
    p.   cm.
Includes bibliographical references and index.
ISBN 0-521-83898-3 (hdk) – ISBN 0-521-54768-7 (pbk)
1. Medical care – Technological innovations.   2. Medical technology – Economic aspects.
3. Business forecasting.   4. Economic forecasting.   I. Burns, Lawton R.
R855.3.B87 2005
610'.28–dc22   2005046981

ISBN-13 978-0-521-83898-6 hardback
ISBN-10 0-521-83898-3 hardback
ISBN-13 978-0-521-54768-0 paperback
ISBN-10 0-521-54768-7 paperback

To my two sets of parents,
Dr. and Mrs Robert K. Burns and
Dr. and Mrs Dimitri G. Polydefkis

Contents

Part II   Devices and information technologies

Figures

Contributors

Lawton R. Burns is the James Joo-Jin Kim Professor and Professor of Health Care Systems at the Wharton School, University of Pennsylvania. He is also the Director of the Wharton Center for Health Management and Economics. He sits on the Board of the Institute of Medicine (Health Services Section). He earned his doctorate and MBA from the University of Chicago. He is author of *The Health Care Value Chain* (Jossey-Bass, 2002).

John Evans is returning to McKinsey after just completing his MBA from the Wharton School and a Masters of Biotechnology from the University of Pennsylvania. He has a BA from Yale University. Professionally, he worked for two years in McKinsey & Company's Pharmaceuticals practice and one year in Bayer's Biologicals group.

Jeff C. Goldsmith is President, Health Futures, Inc. and Associate Professor of Medical Education at the University of Virginia. He earned his doctorate in Sociology from the University of Chicago in the 1970s, and has worked in health services management and policy for thirty years.

Kurt H. Kruger followed the medical device industry as a Wall Street analyst for sixteen years working for Banc of America Securities, Montgomery, and Hambrecht & Quist. Before that he spent over five years working in the medical products industry, first as a biomedical engineer developing devices used in open heart surgery for Sarns, now Terumo, then as a marketing manager for pacemaker/defibrillator leader Guidant. He holds an MS in business from the Massachusetts Institute of Technology, an MS in Bioengineering from the University of Michigan, and an Sc.B in Biomedical Engineering from Brown University.

Sean Nicholson is Assistant Professor in the Department of Policy Analysis and Management at Cornell University and Faculty Research Fellow at the National Bureau of Economic Research. He is currently conducting research in three areas: innovation in the biotechnology and pharmaceutical industries; determinants of whether and how quickly physicians and hospitals adopt new medical technologies and treatment methods; and measuring the benefits to employers of investing in their workers' health.

Jon Northrup is currently CEO of Horizon Biotechnologies, LLC, a company devoted to helping client biotechnology companies utilize outsourcing to lower costs and increase productivity. Previously, Jon spent almost thirty years in the pharmaceutical industry, at Eli Lilly and Company, holding positions including: Director, Corporate Strategy and Business Development; Director, Marketing; Director, Strategic Asset Management; Director, Corporate Business Development; Manager, Sales; Manager, Marketing Research; Manager, Economic Studies; New Product Planning; International Marketing; and Financial Manager, ELANCO. He is also the author of "Prescription Drug Pricing in Chain and Independent Pharmacies," University of Pennsylvania Press, 1976.

Dr. Cary G. Pfeffer is founder and head of The Pfeffer Group, working as an independent business advisor to biotechnology companies and their executives, leading business development and other strategic business efforts. Prior to this role he spent over ten years at Biogen, Inc. where he was most recently Vice President, Global Medical Affairs; Director, International Distributor Operations (based in Paris, France); and Director, Business and Market Development. He held other senior leadership positions in Program Management and Business Development as well. Earlier in his career he spent two years at Shearson Lehman Brothers, where he focused on investment banking for health care companies. While attending the Wharton School and the University of Pennsylvania School of Medicine, he initiated and led the effort to develop the Wharton elective course, *The Management & Economics of the Pharmaceutical Enterprise.*

Stephen M. Sammut has a dual career. He is Senior Fellow, Wharton Entrepreneurial Programs and Health Care Systems, through which he teaches a variety of courses including healthcare entrepreneurship and private enterprise approaches to global health needs. He is also Venture Partner, Burrill & Company, a global life sciences venture capital fund.

Preface

This book has been in the making for the past ten years, since I arrived at the Wharton School at the University of Pennsylvania. Located in Philadelphia, geographically Wharton is surrounded by pharmaceutical, biotechnology, and medical products companies. Our MBA student cohorts are filled with former and future employees from these companies, and our classrooms are continually filled with their executives, who visit Wharton to teach and recruit students. Increasingly, our course offerings in the Department of Health Care Systems have necessarily encompassed these sectors of the healthcare industry, and our faculty's academic agenda has adopted them as research topics.

A few years ago I published a four-year investigation of the flow of products, information, and money between the manufacturers of healthcare products, the distributors and organized buyers of these products, and institutional customers. That investigation, published as *The Health Care Value Chain* (2002), examined the trading relationships between (a) the providers of healthcare services such as physicians and hospitals (a traditional focus of scholarly inquiry) and (b) their upstream suppliers (a nontraditional focus for scholars). The book was the first formal analysis of supply chain relationships in the healthcare industry. It included separate chapters on three sets of manufacturers (or "producers") of healthcare products: pharmaceuticals, medical devices, and medical-surgical supplies. In writing it, I realized there was no central source of information about the producer side of the healthcare industry. Most textbooks on the industry either ignored producers or focused on the regulatory side of the industry (e.g., the Food and Drug Administration).

This volume seeks to fill this gap in our understanding. The book is intended for two different audiences. First, it is designed to teach students (and their faculties) in graduate programs of health administration about a major portion of the healthcare industry that gets neglected. It provides a detailed overview of the pharmaceutical, biotechnology, genomics/proteomics, medical device, and information technology sectors. In addition, because these are for-profit sectors, the book also examines the business models and corporate strategies of firms in these sectors. As a result, the book may be more at home in health administration programs located in business schools, but may still be useful for programs in schools of public health and public administration.

Secondly, the book is intended for practitioners in each of the sectors covered – not so much to educate them about their own sphere of activity, but rather to educate them about the other sectors that are increasingly interdependent with their own. For example, there is a clear trend for the pharmaceutical and biotechnology sectors to align with each other in drug discovery, development, and commercialization efforts. There are also trends for pharmaceutical firms to partner with medical device and information technology firms in order to facilitate drug development and deliver new patient care therapies.

Many of the chapters in this volume are quite long by necessity. The sectors covered in each chapter are research-intensive and technologically complex. They are also dynamic competitively, despite their very different market structures (e.g., some are fragmented markets, others are oligopolistic). The authors of the respective chapters have done an excellent job of distilling all of this complexity (for the first time in one volume) into as few pages as they have, without sacrificing scope or relevant detail. As editor, I beg the reader's indulgence in confronting the detailed analyses of these fascinating sectors of healthcare. They comprise the only truly global portion of the healthcare industry.

Lawton R. Burns
The Wharton School
University of Pennsylvania

Acknowledgments

I have taught an introductory MBA-level course on the healthcare system since 1984. Originally, my view of the healthcare system was shaped by my Ph.D. and MBA training, which emphasized the *providers* of healthcare services (e.g., physicians and hospitals) and the *payers* for these services (e.g., governments, employers, insurance companies). It was not until my arrival at the Wharton School in 1994 that I began to be heavily exposed to an entirely new portion of the industry: *the producers* of healthcare products such as pharmaceuticals, biologicals, medical devices, and information technology (IT).

At Wharton, I assumed responsibility for the core introductory course, Healthcare Management (HCMG) 841, "The Health Services System." This particular course, more than any other course I have ever taught, has challenged me to broaden my view of what the healthcare industry really consists of. A large percentage of the first-year MBA students taking the class come from the producer side of the industry or from investment and consulting firms dealing with the producer side of the industry. They come to Wharton seeking deeper knowledge of these firms, along with the financial and strategic tools to manage them. In response to their interest, a faculty colleague and former instructor of HCMG 841, John Kimberly, developed a tripartite course structure that examined "payers, providers, and producers." I have adopted this structure and elaborated it over time to develop my own view of the entire healthcare value chain.

I thus owe a great deal of gratitude to the students of this class, who I have had the privilege to teach and learn from over the past few years. Their desire to know more about the producer side of the healthcare industry has pushed me to learn it myself, although I am certainly no expert yet. I am also thankful to my academic colleagues, who have helped to reorient the Wharton MBA curriculum to encompass the producers.

During the years I have taught HCMG 841, I have relied on industry experts to teach much of the course content on producers. I have been fortunate to draw on the expertise of several Wharton School graduates who have worked in the pharmaceutical, biotechnology, medical device, and IT sectors and possess a far deeper understanding of them than I. These individuals have graciously agreed to return to Wharton each fall semester to teach the incoming MBA class about their particular sector. Over time, they have honed their presentations, and these form the basis for the chapters contained herein. I thank Jon Northrup (formerly with Eli Lilly) and Cary Pfeffer (formerly with Biogen) for broadening the students' understanding of the pharmaceutical and biotechnology sectors. They have contributed chapters 2 and 3, respectively.

For other producer sectors, I have called on long-time friends and colleagues to teach the course content. Kurt Kruger, formerly a top medical devices analyst with Hambrecht & Quist, Montgomery, and Banc of America Securities, has been a close friend for nearly three decades. Jeff Goldsmith, originally my instructor at the Graduate School of Business at the University of Chicago, is now a valued colleague and part-time faculty member here at Wharton, teaching information technology. Kurt and Jeff have contributed chapters 6 and 7, respectively.

I have also had the privilege of being surrounded by first-rate scholars and colleagues in the Department of Health Care Systems here at Wharton. Patricia Danzon and Mark Pauly are two of the nation's top health economists and have spent much of their time analyzing pharmaceutical pricing. Although not authors in this volume, both have lectured in HCMG 841 and raised my understanding of these issues. Sean Nicholson has cowritten (with Patricia Danzon) some of the best recent work on pharmaceutical mergers and strategic alliances with biotechnology companies. Sean has collaborated with me and one of my students in HCMG 841, John Evans, to coauthor chapter 5, on mergers and acquisitions in the pharmaceutical sector. Another colleague in the department, Steve Sammut, lives a double life as a venture capitalist in the life sciences industry. At Wharton, Steve teaches courses on entrepreneurship and new ventures, and also teaches a session in HCMG 841. For this volume, he has contributed chapter 4, on genomics and proteomics technology companies, and has helped me to make sense of all the chapters by coauthoring chapter 8.

Several people have enabled me to produce this volume. I wish to thank my administrative assistant, Sylvie Beauvais, and her assistant Erica Garvey, for their help in preparing the manuscript. I also wish to thank Richard Barling, Chris Harrison, and Karen Matthews at Cambridge University Press, for their enthusiastic support of this project. Lastly, I wish to thank my precious wife Alexandra and our son Brendan for their continuing love and support, and for having helped me to reorient my priorities in life.

Finally, let me reiterate: this book represents a major slice of the Wharton core MBA curriculum on the healthcare industry. It represents a fascinating portion of the industry, which is research intensive, technologically complex, and heavily focused on innovation. My hope is that we have done justice to the enormous complexity here. I trust readers will find the volume as useful to read as we found in assembling it.

Lawton R. Burns
The Wharton School
University of Pennsylvania

1 The business of healthcare innovation in the Wharton School curriculum

Lawton R. Burns

Innovation and the value chain in healthcare
The technological imperative in healthcare
The innovation challenge
Why study the producers of healthcare products?
Convergence of technologies across sectors
Impact of technology sectors on local and national economies
Similarities and differences across producer sectors
Overview of the volume and of chapter content

Innovation and the value chain in healthcare

All first-year MBA students at the Wharton School who major in healthcare systems take a required course during their first semester. The course, Healthcare Management 841, analyzes the entire value chain in healthcare (see figure 1.1). The structure of this chain is straightforward: there are three key sets of actors and two sets of intermediaries between them. The three key sets of actors are the individuals and institutions that purchase healthcare, provide healthcare services, and produce healthcare products (purchasers, providers, and producers). Two sets of intermediaries separate these key actors: those firms who finance healthcare (offer insurance to the purchasers and handle reimbursement to the providers) and those who distribute products (from the producers to the providers).

The logic of this chain is a bit more interesting. All of the money that gets pumped into the healthcare system starts on the far left side of figure 1.1 and flows to all of the boxes to the right. Conversely, much of the innovation in healthcare starts on the far right side and flows to the adjacent boxes on the left. The two flows collide in the middle, in the provider side of the industry, that is, doctors and hospitals who then

Purchasers	Fiscal intermediaries	Providers	Product intermediaries	Producers
Government Employers Individuals Employer coalitions	Insurers HMOs Pharmacy benefit managers	Hospitals Physicians Integrated delivery networks Pharmacies	Wholesalers Mail order distributors Group purchasing organizations	Pharmaceutical & biotechnology manufacturers Medical device makers Medical suppliers Information technology firms

Figure 1.1   The US healthcare value chain.

Source: Lawton R. Burns, *The Health Care Value Chain* (San Francisco, CA: Jossey-Bass, 2002).

have to determine how much of the innovation from the right side they can afford to utilize in patient treatment given the limited supply of funds received from the left side. This is the point at which much of the spending on healthcare and the consumption of healthcare products takes place.

In a prior book, the Wharton faculty examined the flow of money, products, and information between producers, providers, and their intermediaries (wholesalers, distributors, group purchasing organizations).[1] The current book examines the producers of the innovative products in the healthcare industry – the major sectors of innovation within the manufacturing side of the industry – on a global basis. These sectors include:

- Pharmaceutical sector
- Biotechnology sector
- Genomics and proteomics sector
- Medical device sector
- Information technology sector

The book aims to educate the reader about the structure of each of these industry sectors, the competitive dynamics among firms in these sectors, and the push for technological innovation that distinguishes them from other sectors of healthcare. The book also highlights the growing convergence among these sectors, as innovations in one sector are utilized by another. Chapters contained in this volume are written by faculty, executives, and analysts from these sectors who teach in the Wharton School as part of Healthcare Management 841.

The technological imperative in healthcare

The five industry sectors listed above are responsible for supplying a majority of the innovative products utilized by physicians and hospitals and which are increasingly demanded by consumers. This supply and demand logic has exerted both positive and negative effects.

On the one hand, technology is commonly cited as being the major driver of rising healthcare expenditures worldwide. Scholars have characterized this trend as the "technological imperative" – that is, innovative treatments and equipment are demanded by patients and their (physician) agents on the grounds of quality, and are reimbursed by payers and their fiscal intermediaries. Indeed, empirical evidence from the United States documents that the cost of new technology, and the intensity with which it is used, consistently accounts for anywhere from 20 percent to 40 percent of the rise in health expenditures over the past forty years (see figure 1.2).

Particularly disturbing to many, given these costs, is evidence that high levels of spending on technology, particularly in the US, do not translate into added value and better outcomes on a host of other measures.[2] The problem here may be twofold: the overutilization of technology in the US (which increases spending without added benefit) and market-based competition among provider organizations to have the latest equipment (which increases

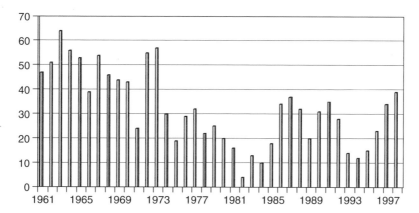

Figure 1.2   Technology and intensity of service as share of annual percentage increase in US personal health expenditures, 1961–1998.

Source: Center for Medicare and Medicaid Services (CMS).

the diffusion and utilization of expensive technology at the expense of older, less expensive alternatives).[3]

Governmental efforts in the US to contain spending on medical technology (e.g., certificate of need laws enacted in the 1970s, the Prospective Payment System enacted in 1983, the threat of presidential-led health reforms in 1978/79 and 1993/94) exerted only short-term effects, followed by a resumption in spending. Governmental restrictions on access to this technology have been a favored method of controlling healthcare costs in other countries.

On the other hand, there is growing public recognition, based on recent scholarly evidence, that such products contribute to increases in longevity and mobility, reductions in disease and pain, improvements in worker productivity, and improvements in quality of life – especially for patients with particular conditions.[4] Another recent report argues that increased health spending is "worth it": over the past twenty years, each additional dollar spent on healthcare services in the US produced health gains valued at $2.40–$3.00 (e.g., in terms of increased life expectancy, reduced disability, improved overall health).[5] Based on this recognition, there continues to be public pressure for more healthcare spending and access to new technology worldwide.

This book does not seek to attack or defend the technological imperative in healthcare. It takes the position that technology does not increase costs by itself, but rather must be viewed as part of the health systems in which they are used. What is critical are the payment structures and incentives established within a given healthcare system that promote or retard the use of technologies for given patients (and their diffusion to other patients). The book also takes the position that analyses of increased spending on technology must be combined with an analysis of the benefits achieved by using these technological resources.[6] Finally, the book takes it as a given that technological innovation will continue to drive the dynamics of the healthcare industry into the future, as it did during the past century.[7] The book seeks to analyze the push for innovation through the lenses of the companies that produce it.

The innovation challenge

All of the healthcare sectors studied here are considered "high-technology."[8] Like other high-tech industries, innovation is the key driver of competitive advantage and commercial success. Analysts at the Boston Consulting Group (BCG) report that research and development (R&D) investments can account for up to one-third of a medical technology firm's stock price, and are correlated with the firm's gross margins four to five years down the road.[9] At the same time, innovation is also the continuing challenge facing firms in these sectors. The high price-to-revenue multiples for many of these firms suggest that financial markets expect these firms to grow revenues and sustain gross margins above and beyond other investment sectors, all of which necessitate continued innovation.[10]

Successful innovation hinges on many factors, including serendipity of discovery, wise paths taken in the past, wise investment decisions in the present, and access to new technologies via mergers and acquisitions (M&As) and strategic alliances. These factors manifest themselves in terms of favorable market structures, the possession of key resources and capabilities, and fruitful ties with other organizations upstream and downstream in the value chain. However, successful innovation also rests largely on the process skills or the art of management practiced inside of a firm.

This book examines the source of technological innovation in the healthcare industry. Specifically, for the firms in each of the innovative sectors listed above we ask the following set of questions:

- What products do these companies make and what is so innovative about them?
- What are the different business models of innovation pursued by firms in this sector, and how do they finance them?
- What are the strategies pursued by firms in this sector?
- What are the key success factors for innovative firms in this sector?
- How have firms in these sectors, and the sectors themselves, grown over time?
- What impact have these firms had on the organization and delivery of healthcare?
- What are the important competitive and regulatory forces shaping these sectors?

To answer these questions, the book adopts multiple, related perspectives: industrial organization, the resource-based view of the firm, value chain analysis, and organizational innovation and change. These perspectives help to focus on the many determinants of successful innovation. They are outlined below.

Industrial organization perspective

Industrial organization (IO) is a branch of economics that examines the number of competitors in a market (or industry), the size and distribution of these firms and their respective market shares, the degree of concentration (i.e., how many firms account for the majority of the market share), and the strategies pursued to broaden the horizontal and vertical boundaries of the firm (e.g., horizontal consolidation, vertical integration into input and output markets). In the last two decades, the IO perspective has been popularized in Michael Porter's "Five Forces" framework, which analyzes five sets of factors that shape an industry's competitiveness and the ability of firm within it to earn above average profits.[11] These forces include: degree of internal rivalry among incumbent firms; threat of entry by new firms; degree of substitution by new products/technologies; bargaining power of suppliers (input side); and bargaining power of buyers (output side). Viewed in this perspective, a firm's competitive advantage derives from the structure of the industry in which it finds itself, as well as its position: for example, small number of large-sized firms, presence of scale economies that serve as an entry barrier, competitive input and output markets, and so on.

The IO perspective is used here to assess the corporate strategies of firms in these sectors. Thus, the chapters discuss the use of M&As to build scale, access new technology and products, and erect barriers to entry; the pursuit of economies of scale and scope to achieve efficiencies; the degree of vertical integration into upstream and downstream markets; and the pursuit of product and market diversification in order to expand.

Resource-based view

The resource-based view (RBV) of the firm suggests that competitive advantage in an industry lies not only in a firm's position within a favorable industry context (i.e., among the five forces above). Advantage also derives from the distinctive capabilities a firm possesses. Capabilities are based on assets and resources that firms harness and coordinate in productive ways. Capabilities become distinctive, strategic, and valuable when a firm can coordinate these resources to provide superior returns in ways that other firms cannot duplicate.[12]

The RBV perspective is used here to discuss the distinctive abilities of different life sciences firms to create new products. Thus, the next two chapters examine the differential capabilities of large pharmaceutical firms versus smaller biotechnology firms in developing small and large molecules, respectively. The perspective is also used here to analyze the strategic alliances that develop among different life sciences firms to broaden their total set of capabilities. Finally, the RBV perspective is utilized in order to describe the types of integrative processes and learning mechanisms needed to help mergers and acquisitions succeed.

Value chain perspective

The value chain perspective analyzes the entire sequence from raw materials (input) markets to final customer (output) markets.[13] The sequence is labeled a "value chain" because each link in the chain adds value to its inputs. Each link also seeks to maximize its contribution to the total product's value added, thereby capturing as much profit as it can. This may involve focusing on only those links that add the greatest value (and let other firms focus on links that add less value), or encompassing as many links as possible in order to maximize the total profit captured (and leave as little as possible for other firms to divide up).

The value chain perspective is used here to assess the business models of firms in these sectors. Thus, the chapters discuss the key steps in the value chain in that sector (e.g., research and development, manufacturing, sales and marketing), how much value is generated within each of those steps, trends in the scope of these activities that firms elect to focus on (e.g., broad versus narrow range of steps), and the use of the strategies above to broaden a firm's business model.

This perspective is also used to assess the trading relationships between adjacent firms in the value chain of healthcare (e.g., producers who supply drugs and devices to providers, payers who reimburse providers for these supplies). A value chain view suggests that firms can develop strategic advantage as they develop long-term, collaborative alliances with adjacent firms that benefit both sides and address problems of information exchange between trading partners.[14]

Organizational innovation perspective

The organizational innovation perspective draws on management theory and research in order to examine some of the key managerial practices and organizational conditions needed to sustain strategic change. The findings from this literature are so diverse as to warrant a separate volume to summarize them.[15] Nevertheless, ingredients for successful innovation include:

- the need to balance divergent and convergent thinking
- the need to balance top-down strategic initiatives with bottom-up experimentation
- the need to balance a focus on short-term efficiency and shareholder value maximization with long-term exploration
- the ability to source new ideas from anywhere inside and outside the firm
- the need for integrative structures to coordinate the contributions of multiple disciplines (silos) within a firm
- the benefits of organizational slack (e.g., dedicated resources for innovation, latitude for long-term thinking and commitment to projects)
- a focus on the process of change and not just the structure of change
- the need to conduct integrative programs of change that recognize the importance of articulating changes in one part of the firm with changes in other, related parts of the firm

Some common themes emerge from this list: balance, sourcing of ideas, integration, latitude and slack, and process.

In partial validation of this list, Boston Consulting Group consultants have identified their own list of "process" skills based on recent field research and have labeled them "high science." These skills include: R&D governance (e.g., using milestones as learning exercises, analytical tools, and decision-making criteria), the use of measurement systems that balance short-term and long-term perspectives and integrate the efforts of the entire R&D team, and the use of incentives that keep innovators motivated.[16]

The organizational innovation perspective is used here to highlight the different managerial skills required in the development of a start-up firm in the biotechnology sector and in the coordination of the internal and external activities of a large pharmaceutical firm. It is also used to explain why M&As within the pharmaceutical sector often fail to achieve their intended results. The perspective is helpful in understanding why new technology often fails to be widely adopted by the intended end user (e.g., the physician) by virtue of neglecting how it disrupts the work routines of professionals.

Why study the producers of healthcare products?

Ignored in traditional curricula of health administration

The producers of innovative products in the healthcare industry are virtually ignored in most graduate-level courses in health administration taught in schools of business and public health. A quick perusal of the most popular introductory texts reveals few, if any, chapters dedicated to the product sectors of the industry.[17] The handful of texts that do include some discussion typically offer a cursory examination of the pharmaceutical sector (e.g., the role of the Food and Drug Administration, the price and value of drugs), but few discuss industry dynamics and company business models.

Similarly, there are few graduate programs in health administration that include dedicated courses on these industry sectors. The Wharton School is one of a very small number of business schools that include courses on pharmaceuticals and devices (at both undergraduate and graduate levels), as well as dedicated lectures on each of the product sectors in the introductory MBA-level course.

The failure to understand these sectors can foster a limited and narrow view of the overall industry on the part of academic researchers and executives of health provider organizations. Graduate curriculums of health administration devote considerable attention to the purchaser and provider sectors of the industry, along with the fiscal intermediaries that separate them (see figure 1.1). This is understandable, given that (a) healthcare policy focuses heavily on governmental regulation and reimbursement of health services, and (b) the bulk of academic research is conducted on these sectors of the healthcare industry. With a handful of exceptions, most researchers have not considered the implications of developments in the "producer" side of the industry for the purchaser and provider sectors. Consequently, the majority of graduates of health administration programs receive little formal training on the healthcare industry sectors that manufacture the products utilized by providers and consumed by patients.

Failure to fully appreciate the technological imperative

Why might this be of concern? As an illustration, one cannot fully understand the technological imperative in the US healthcare system unless one understands the relationship that vendors of new products have with individual physicians. The failure to understand this relationship can undermine efforts by health provider organizations to control their own costs. Executives of provider organizations may not fully appreciate that their physicians often develop closer alliances and attachments to the manufacturing firms than to their own organizations. These attachments have as much to do with the innovative features of the products made as with the intense sales and marketing support that goes with them. Indeed, vendors and physicians have developed a two-way exchange of mutual benefits that executives and purchasers may have trouble modifying. For their part, vendors offer clinicians access to the latest technology, information about the product, assistance and training in its use, involvement in clinical trials, training of the clinician's residents and nursing team, donations and honoraria, and opportunities for "naming" rights on new equipment. For their part, clinicians offer to vendors thought leadership, avenues for influencing colleagues to use the product, feedback on the product to assist with next generation product development, leaders for clinical trials, and access to patients.

Payer and provider difficulties in controlling the diffusion of technology

Countries such as the United States lack centralized allocation of capital by the government, and are witnessing the dismantling of regulation surrounding the allocation of capital (e.g., the gradual demise of "Certificate of Need," or CON programs in the fifty states). Moreover, a recent two-year review of competition and regulation by the Federal Trade Commission in the US calls for the abolition of CON laws.[18] Given this state of affairs, providers will become even more responsible for controlling the diffusion of new technology.

However, based on the preceding section, purchasers and providers will thus likely face difficulties in controlling the diffusion of new technology. Moreover, provider organizations may face unforeseen difficulties in developing "integrated delivery networks" (IDNs) to partner with their physicians, and launching "value analysis committees" with their clinicians to control the selection, prices, and utilization of high-cost supplies. In both instances, the physicians' loyalty lies elsewhere.

Lack of provider focus on upstream supply costs

To aggravate this problem, many provider organizations have concerned themselves primarily with the "downstream" portions of the value chain – that is,

Hospital market basket	Percentage
• Labor (wages, salaries, benefits)	61.7
• Professional fees	5.4
• Utilities	1.4
• Malpractice insurance	0.8
• Other products	19.5
• Other services	11.2
• TOTAL	100.0

Figure 1.3   Composition of hospital expenses.

Source: Medical Payment Advisory Commission (MedPAC).

public purchasers in the government and fiscal intermediaries who reimburse them. They have largely ignored the "upstream" players in the value chain, such as the producers/manufacturers and the distributors of their products. This lack of attention is important for several reasons. Healthcare supplies (e.g., drugs, medical devices, medical–surgical supplies, etc.) account for 19 percent of a hospital's total expenditures, according to US government figures. If one includes the costs of handling and distributing these supplies internally, as well as the cost of all services contracted from the outside, the percentage of hospital expenditures may reach as high as 30 percent (see figure 1.3). These are portions of the hospital's cost structure that historically have been undermanaged and now represent a major area for cost containment and improved supply utilization. Without appropriate training at the level of the chief executive officer (CEO), chief operating officer (COO), chief financial officer (CFO), chief medical officer (CMO), chief nursing officer (CNO), and the newly emergent chief resource officer (CRO) – what some pundits refer to as the new O-zone layer – provider organizations may be unable to achieve improvements.

Within this large bucket of supply expense, the two biggest categories of spending are drugs and medical-surgical supplies, including medical devices (see figure 1.4). Costs for these supplies have been rising quite rapidly. Retail pharmaceutical costs as a percentage of national health expenditures are predicted to increase in the US from 10.7 percent (2003) to 14.5 percent (2014). This represents an average annual growth of 12.3 percent, contrasted with hospital expenditure growth of 6.3 percent, physician expenditure growth of 7.0 percent, and national health expenditure growth of 7.5 percent.[19] Trend data over the past thirty years reveal that pharmaceutical costs alone are approaching shares of total spending by

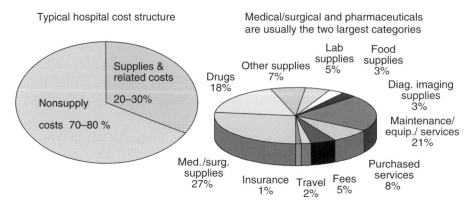

Figure 1.4   Composition of hospital supply costs.

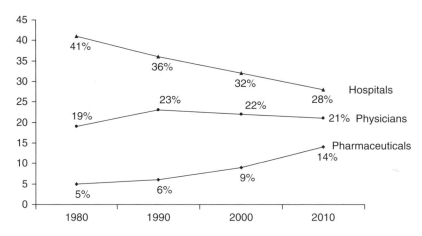

Figure 1.5   Spending by category, 1980–2010 (as percentage of US national health expenditures).

hospital and physician services – areas that historically have accounted for the majority of health spending (see figure 1.5). These cost figures do not include pharmaceutical products shipped to hospitals, which are embedded in hospital cost figures and which may account for 10–15 percent of total prescription drugs costs.[20]

Medical devices costs have also been rising, but are harder to document since they too are embedded in inpatient hospital cost figures. Medical device spending in the US reached $55–65 billion at the turn of the millennium. Much of this rise is due to the technological imperative noted above. As an illustration, executives at one GPO reported that despite their successful efforts to secure a lower contract price with a device manufacturer for its products, the overall costs of the contract rose 25 percent in one year due to increases in new product introductions (primary reason) and utilization (secondary reason).[21]

New producer–provider strategic alliances forming

Recently, some provider organizations have correctly recognized the value of forming strategic alliances with producers. Hospitals across the US and a handful in Europe have developed symbiotic partnerships with vendors of operating room and imaging equipment. In some partnerships, the hospitals receive lower-cost capital, equipment, and training from the vendors to upgrade their surgical and ancillary services. In return, the vendors either convert a new customer from a rival vendor's business or develop deeper penetration of the local hospital market. More importantly, the hospitals may serve as alpha and beta test sites for new innovative equipment developed by the vendors, which allows the vendor to gather real-time, first-hand information on equipment performance that subsequently helps them improve their next generation product development.

These new alliances follow long-standing alliances between the manufacturers of innovative products and one of their primary customers – the physician. They will also be accompanied by another set of new alliances between the physician and the platform technology firms that enable the clinician to selectively apply therapies and treatments to those subsets of patients who greatly benefit from their application.

Reinforced stereotypical views of manufacturers

The lack of understanding of producer sectors may reinforce stereotypical views of firms within these sectors. For example, pharmaceutical companies are often viewed as charging high prices for their products and earning unseemly high levels of return, without understanding the risks in their business models that might counterbalance these returns. Casual observers of the life sciences industry may fail to perceive the high failure rates associated with product development and technological innovation that necessarily increase the costs of the products that do succeed and make it on to market. In a similar vein, pharmaceutical companies are increasingly criticized for charging higher prices in the US than they receive in foreign markets, thus requiring US citizens to subsidize the rest of the world.[22] A global perspective on pharmaceutical pricing and innovation might suggest, however, that part of the problem rests with foreign national governments that create welfare losses – for example, lower levels of R&D investment, job losses, lower tax revenues – in their own countries by regulating prices. Price caps limit the ability of foreign-based companies to earn sufficient returns to support their research and development efforts, which subsequently get moved to the US (see chapter 5).

It must be stressed that this volume has not been compiled to defend these industry sectors. Rather, the intention is to offer a balanced view of what is occurring within them, and to prepare future healthcare executives to transact with them. The editor acknowledges, however, that several chapters have been prepared by executives and analysts from these industry sectors, who present their own views of the contributions made by firms in their sectors.

Growing prominence of product sectors in the economy

Finally, these product sectors are important in their own right, comprising a major part of the corporate world. Nine pharmaceutical firms and four medical device firms are listed among the Fortune 500, based on 2003 revenues (see figure 1.6). This list does not include the large foreign-based pharmaceutical firms that do a lot of business in the US (see chapter 2, figure 2.4). Worldwide, firms in the pharmaceutical, biotechnology, and medical device industries generated over $600 billion in revenues in 2003.

Manufacturing firm	2003 revenues (billion $)	Fortune 500 rank
Pfizer	45.9	25
Johnson & Johnson	41.9	30
Merck	22.5	83
Bristol-Myers Squibb	20.7	92
Abbott Laboratories	19.7	96
Wyeth	15.8	125
Eli Lilly	12.6	156
Amgen	8.4	246
Schering-Plough	8.3	247
Medtronic	7.7	263
Guidant	3.7	453
Stryker	3.6	465
Boston Scientific	3.5	478

Figure 1.6   US healthcare manufacturing firms: revenues and rank in Fortune 500.

Product sector margins support other parts of the value chain

The profit margins earned within these sectors are the envy of other parts of the healthcare industry, which frequently look to the producers for help with their own margins. Thus, for example, pharmaceutical wholesalers have relied in the past more on upstream drug manufacturers than on downstream hospital customers for the bulk of their ever shrinking margins. Similarly, group purchasing organizations (GPOs) have earned the bulk of their revenues from contract administration fees (CAFs) paid by the manufacturers in order to do contracted business with the GPOs' hospital members. Hospital efforts to partner with manufacturers (described above) represent the most recent example of less profitable portions of the healthcare industry seeking assistance and relief from the more profitable sectors. Indeed, the middle three blocks of the value chain in healthcare (providers and the two sets of intermediaries) enjoy much lower returns than does the producer sector. Faced with governmental pressures to restrain increases in provider reimbursement and employer concerns over rising healthcare outlays for their employees, providers and their intermediaries will increasingly (be forced to) look to the manufacturing sectors for financial assistance.

Convergence of technologies across sectors

Not only are these manufacturing sectors important in their own right, they are also increasingly important to one another. Several new innovations in research, product development, and healthcare delivery rely on the joint use of technologies from multiple sectors. For example, a drug-eluting stent (DES) combines a bare metal stent made by a device manufacturer coated with a pharmaceutical to reduce narrowing of the heart vessels due to postsurgical scarring (restinosis). Johnson & Johnson's Cordis Corporation used Wyeth's drug sirolimus to develop the first DES called Cypher. Boston Scientific quickly followed with its own Taxus DES, coated with the drug paclitaxel. Such products have reduced the incidence of restinosis from over 25 percent to 9 percent. They have also spurred the sales of stents.

Another device manufacturer, Medtronic, has merged one of its standard tools in orthopedic surgery (a graft-holding titanium cage) with a biological agent (bone morphogenic protein-2, or BMP-2) to develop a new product called Infuse. The "convergent product" promotes bone fusion following back surgery, and obviates the need to take a bone graft out of a patient's hip. Results suggest an increase in surgical success from 89 percent to 95 percent, along with less pain to the patient and lower cost to the payer (by virtue of avoiding the autograft).[23]

Clinicians have found that biotechnology drugs may work on only specific subsets of patients that express certain proteins. Some manufacturers have developed *in vitro* tests to identify the appropriate genetic subgroup in which a drug is effective. Illustrations include Genentech's drug Herceptin and the diagnostic test PathVysion developed by the Vysis division of Abbott Laboratories. In the future, such genetic tests will likely be employed to determine which patients are best suited for medical devices such as defibrillators and spinal fusions.

Of course, there are many other examples of technological convergence now and in the likely future. These include:

- Pharmaceutical firms are using imaging equipment and techniques to study the human body's processing of drugs.
- Medical device firms are using imaging to guide the proper insertion of implants into patients' joints.
- Medical device firms see their future in catheter-based systems to deliver biological products locally to the patient via the vascular system.[24]
- Medical equipment firms (e.g., General Electric) that make positron emission tomography (PET) scanners are seeking to partner their products with "passive pharmaceuticals" (e.g., contrast agents) and radiopharmaceutical tracers. Such product convergence can serve to illuminate diseases at a molecular level before they become fully manifest.[25]
- Pharmaceutical and biotechnology firms have been using information-based platform technologies such as high throughput screening, rational drug design based on computer-based molecular modeling, and systems biology (see chapter 3).
- Pharmaceutical firms are utilizing a host of other information technologies, such as web services that allow drug discovery scientists to access data, handhelds that allow clinical investigators to capture patient information in clinical trials, and radio frequency identification (RFID) to track drugs.[26]

Still other examples of convergence include radiation and smart implants, implantable drug pumps, targeted cell/gene therapy delivery, image-guided surgery, and remote monitoring and therapy management.[27]

The future of innovation in healthcare may thus involve leveraging a greater number of product combinations across manufacturing sectors. The development, utilization, and reimbursement of these combined technologies will require a greater understanding of the component products and the sectors that produce them. Payers and clinicians will find this opportunity for convergent development very attractive, since it leads to higher efficacy rates of treatment. Nevertheless, there are some barriers to technological convergence, and many of them are found among the manufacturers themselves. Pharmaceutical firms, for example, have not yet embraced this convergent development with diagnostics, since it may lead to smaller market sizes for their products.[28] Another barrier is the difference in culture and business models as one goes from one sector to another. Biotechnology and medical device firms focus on different elements of the value chain – research in the former, development in the latter – with very different product development cycles (i.e., long-term versus short-term). Convergent product development will require enormous skills in alliance formation and management.

Impact of technology sectors on local and national economies

Product sectors are also playing increasingly important roles in national and local economies. At a national level, governments are protecting their pharmaceutical industries against foreign competition and the threat of foreign takeover (see chapter 5). Such moves are undertaken for reasons of national pride as well as the desire to maintain highly skilled labor (e.g., scientists in research and development). National governments are also actively developing biotechnology sectors in order to attract skilled workers, develop an R&D base in a growing industry, and become a regional hub for such activity. Countries such as the United Kingdom are making major investments in information technology in order to improve the efficiency of their national health systems and their levels of customer service.

Similar developments are occurring at local government level. Cities in the US, such as San Diego, San Jose, Boston, Philadelphia, and Raleigh-Durham, are seeking to develop technology clusters in pharmaceuticals and biotechnology in order to foster economic development and investment.[29] Other cities have developed clusters of medical device firms (e.g., Warsaw, Indiana). These areas are leveraging the advantages that physical proximity affords scientists in the life and medical sciences to generate, transmit, and share knowledge. Such clustering also serves to attract and retain scientific talent and companies in search of this talent, and also permits other businesses and the local economy to reap the benefits of the innovation that is locally grown.

In this manner, cities develop crucial interactions among scientists, entrepreneurs, and venture capitalists.

Michael Porter has argued that proximity of specialized companies leads to unusual competitive success. This is partly based on increased productivity by ensuring better access to employees and suppliers. It is also partly based on superior access to new and specialized information. Finally, it is partly the fact that proximity generates both competition and cooperation (e.g., vertical linkages in the value chain between manufacturers and the suppliers of inputs and specialized infrastructure). Such clustering serves to increase local firms' ability to innovate and compete both nationally and globally.[30] Not surprisingly, the current strategy of many countries is to emulate the local clusters found in the US, particularly in biotechnology.[31]

Similarities and differences across producer sectors

In studying the chapters in this volume, the reader might keep in mind several themes that highlight the commonalities in the innovation process across the above producer sectors. Five such themes are: risk, capital, time, space, and scale. Most of the healthcare sectors examined here are characterized by high risk. Failure rates in the life sciences are especially high, as are the failure rates of new ventures in all of the sectors studied here. Indeed, small firms account for much of the innovation across these sectors, and firm survival rates here are notoriously low. Firms in these sectors require success with the technologies they develop and early success in order to survive. They also require heavy injections of capital from venture capitalists and the public (in the form of initial public offerings or IPOs, secondary offerings, etc.) in order to sustain themselves through the innovation process, especially as this process may take years. Capital and time often interact in the form of "boom and bust" cycles in some of these sectors (e.g., biotechnology), as a sector goes in and out of fashion with venture capitalists or as the window for IPOs periodically opens and closes.

Time is also important in studying these sectors for three other reasons. First, the products developed in these sectors have development cycles that can be either long in duration (e.g., pharmaceuticals and biologicals) or short in duration (e.g., medical devices). Second, the sector itself may be either youthful (e.g., biotechnology) or older (e.g., pharmaceuticals). These time dimensions dictate much of the strategic behavior of firms within these sectors, and also their capabilities to innovate. Third, there is a tendency for analysts and observers (as well as investors) to overestimate the impact of new technology on these sectors in the short-term, and to underestimate the impact of new technology in the long-term. Thus, the technological innovations mentioned in this volume may take longer to play out but may have a more profound impact than was originally anticipated.

A fourth important theme is space. Some of the sectors analyzed below are truly global businesses, such as pharmaceuticals. Other sectors, such as biotechnology, are found in many nations with a common aim to become global businesses. Still other sectors, such as medical devices and information technology, are largely domestic (medical devices are heavily based in the US), although they too are trying to penetrate foreign markets. The Cerner Corporation's recent effort to win a national contract from the National Health Service in the UK for "e-bookings" is a recent illustration of the nascent globalization of IT.

Lastly, firm scale and scope are important dimensions. All of the sectors are growing. They all face issues of managing large size and diversity of operations, and thus face the need to coordinate their complex operations. They also all pursue strategies of mergers and acquisitions, while some simultaneously pursue strategies of vertical integration and diversification. Due to the common avenues of growth pursued, these firms are ripe for strategic analysis along the perspectives outlined above.

Overview of the volume and of chapter content

This volume is organized into two parts. The first part is devoted to the life sciences industry. Chapter 2 analyzes the oldest product segment here – the pharmaceutical sector. The chapter distinguishes the small molecules developed by pharmaceutical firms with the large molecules developed by biotechnology firms. It then describes the size and growth trends in the pharmaceutical market, the high risk and long development and return periods, and the regulatory environment in which drug development takes place. A major section of this chapter describes the internal value chain of a large pharmaceutical firm (research, discovery, development, manufacture, and commercialization), as well as its growing need to source innovation from outside firms.

The remainder of chapter 2 focuses on key business and competitive issues within the pharmaceutical sector. These include the focus on blockbuster products, the value proposition of pharmaceuticals and the growing need to

develop "affordable innovation," portfolio management, business development and alliances, mergers and acquisitions, the questionable value of large
scale, and the need for integrated management. The chapter reveals that
despite a decade of consolidation, the sector is still somewhat fragmented
and very competitive. The chapter also discusses the twin issues of innovation
(focus of R&D) and adoption of that innovation (the focus of commercialization), as well as the key resources and capabilities needed to manage these
issues.

Chapter 3 analyzes the therapeutics side of the biotechnology sector. As in
the pharmaceutical sector, biotechnology companies face the key challenges
of harnessing complex science and new technology in order to develop new
products, as well as the issues of high-risk and long-term development cycles.
Unlike pharmaceutical firms, biotechnology companies face these challenges
as a youthful sector comprised of a lot of small start-ups with limited capital,
cumulative losses, and periodic cycles of investor enthusiasm. There are only
a handful of large biotechnology companies that have approached the scale of
big pharma.

The chapter also reviews the various business models used historically in
this sector and describes the common desire to emulate the model of the large
pharmaceutical firms. A key firm asset in this sector is the ability to manage
the transitions from a small research-based start-up firm to a large integrated
company. Other critical assets are sustained financing in order to grow and
remain independent, entrepreneurial cultures, and effective systems for
resource allocation. In particular, these smaller firms need to balance their
nascent pipeline development activities with the need and/or desire to commercialize their own products. Finally, the chapter chronicles the changing
relationship between pharmaceutical and biotechnology firms from licensing
technology to licensing products, thereby increasing the survival chances of
both firms.

Chapter 4 expands a portion of the content of chapter 3 by examining the
firms employing platform technology business models (e.g., in genomics and
proteomics). The chapter describes the historical progression of business
models, the limited opportunities for fully integrated firms that can compete
with pharmaceutical companies, and three of the options facing these firms:
specialty drug development, systems biology, and personalized medicine. The
chapter also describes in detail how genomics and proteomics technologies
are applied to the drug discovery value chain, the high degree of specialization
of roles here, the resultant need for strategic alliances, and the variety of
strategic alliances thus structured. Finally, the chapter highlights the critical

need to manage the knowledge and information generated by these technologies, and how to transfer this knowledge from discovery to development and commercialization.

Chapter 5 examines the trend in consolidation over the past decade and the rationales for mergers and acquisitions in the pharmaceutical sector. The chapter distinguishes motivations based on defense against hostile external forces versus motivations to proactively generate value. The chapter then reviews all known empirical research, both from academia as well as consulting firms, on the benefits reaped from M&As. The evidence consistently points to few documented benefits. The chapter then describes at length some of the managerial processes needed to extract value and synergies from M&As, and the capabilities that pharmaceutical firms need to build to integrate their internal silos of activity and their external acquisitions. Finally, the chapter discusses the future of M&A in the pharmaceutical sector, and argues that pharmaceutical firms need to develop value chain alliances with multiple players in the healthcare industry beyond physicians and patients, including the payers of healthcare services.

The second part of the book analyzes two other sets of technology companies. Chapter 6 analyzes the medical device sector. As in the life sciences industry, firms in this sector have been growing at fast rates and earning high margins. Many of the key success factors in life sciences are also present here, such as access to financial and intellectual capital and access to new innovative products. Also like the life sciences, firms in this sector need to balance technology development with marketing and commercialization activities. Unlike the pharmaceutical sector, the medical device sector has managed to combine both continued high innovation with high earnings. Also unlike the pharmaceutical sector, firms here focus more on development than on basic research, and spend more of their time marketing to a small number of specialists rather than to a large number of primary care physicians. This has enormous implications for their relative spending on R&D, their channel activities, and the efficiency of these activities.

Chapter 7 analyzes the information technology (IT) sector. Like many of the sectors above, IT firms have enormous potential to transform the efficiency and clinical delivery of healthcare. Specifically, like medical devices, there is a developing opportunity to harness together electronics and decision-making systems to complement the work of healthcare providers. There are also numerous areas where IT developments converge with innovations in other sectors. Unlike other sectors, however, IT has achieved much less demonstrated performance. Part of the problem has been the technology itself; another part is the high cost of replacing legacy systems; and still another part of the problem has been the need for significant change management by providers in order to utilize innovations in IT. Thus, unlike other sectors, IT is not necessarily welcomed by providers (hospitals and physicians).

Finally, in chapter 8 we summarize the technological developments across all of the above sectors and what can be learned about the business of innovation in healthcare. We revisit many of the themes outlined earlier – such as the changes in market structure occurring in each sector, the major business models used in each sector, the key success factors and distinctive capabilities of firms in each sector, the convergence between sectors and the formation of value-adding alliances, and the managerial skills needed to sustain innovation and change in each sector.

NOTES

1. Lawton R. Burns, *The Health Care Value Chain: Producers, Purchasers, and Providers* (San Francisco: Jossey-Bass, 2002).
2. Peter Hussey, *et al.*, "How Does the Quality of Care Compare in Five Countries?," *Health Affairs* 23(3) (2004): 89–99.
3. Cinda Becker, "The Best Care Money can Buy?," *Modern Healthcare* (August 9, 2004): 26–29.
4. "The Health of Nations: A Survey of Health-Care Finance," *Economist* (July 17, 2004): 3–19. David Cutler and Mark McClelland, "Is Technological Change in Medicine Worth it?," *Health Affairs* 20(5) (2001): 11–29.
5. Value Group, *The Value of Investment in Health Care: Better Care, Better Lives* (http://www.aha.org/aha/value/index.html), accessed August 24, 2004.
6. Penny Mohr *et al.*, *The Impact of Medical Technology on Future Healthcare Costs* (Bethesda, MD: Project Hope, 2001).
7. Rosemary Stevens, *In Sickness and in Wealth* (New York: Basic Books, 1989); Paul Starr, *The Social Transformation of American Medicine* (New York: Basic Books, 1982).
8. "High technology" firms are those engaged in the design, development, and introduction of new products and innovative manufacturing processes, or both, through the systematic application of scientific and technical knowledge. They also typically use state-of-the-art techniques, devote a high proportion of expenditures to R&D, and employ a high proportion of scientific, technical, and engineering personnel. Compare Daniel Hecker, "High-Technology Employment: A Broader View," *Monthly Labor Review* (June 1999): 18–28.
9. Peter Lawyer *et al.*, "High Science: A Best-Practice Formula for Driving Innovation," *In Vivo* (April 2004): 70–82.
10. Ibid.

11. Michael Porter, *Competitive Strategy* (New York: Free Press, 1980).
12. Birger Wernerfeld, "A Resource Based View of the Firm," *Strategic Management Journal* 5 (1984): 171–180; Jay Barney, "Firm Resources and Sustained Competitive Advantage," *Journal of Management* 17 (1991): 99–120.
13. Michael Porter, *Competitive Advantage: Creating and Sustaining Superior Performance* (New York: Free Press, 1985).
14. Jeffrey Dyer, *Collaborative Advantage* (Oxford: Oxford University Press, 2000); Lawton R. Burns, *The Health Care Value Chain* (San Francisco, CA: Jossey-Bass, 2002).
15. Michael Beer and Nitin Nohria, *Breaking the Code of Change* (Boston: Harvard Business School Press, 2000); Andrew Van de Ven, H. L. Angel, and M. S. Poole, (eds.), *Research on the Management of Innovation* (New York: Ballinger/Harper & Row, 1989); Andrew Van de Ven, and M. S. Poole, "Explaining Development and Change in Organizations," *Academy of Management Review* 20 (1995): 510–540; Van de Ven *et al.*, *The Innovation Journey* (Oxford: Oxford University Press, 1999).
16. Lawyer *et al.*, "High Science."
17. Stephen Williams and Paul Torrens, *Introduction to Health Services*, 5th edn (Albany, NY: Delmar Publishers, 1999); Phoebe Barton, *Understanding the US Health Services System* (Chicago: Health Administration Press, 1999); Anthony Kovner and Steven Jonas (eds.), *Health Care Delivery in the United States*, 7th edn (New York: Springer Publishing, 2002).
18. Federal Trade Commission and the Department of Justice, *Improving Health Care: A Dose of Competition* (July 2004), Available at http://www.ftc.gov.
19. Center for Medicare and Medicaid Services (CMS). Office of the Actuary.
20. Burns, *Health Care Value Chain*.
21. David Ricker, personal communication.
22. Anna Wilde Mathews, "FDA Chief Targets Europe's Controls on Drug Prices," *Wall Street Journal* (September 25, 2003): A3, A8.
23. Ashish Singh, Chris Zook, and Norbert Hueltenschmidt, "Healthy Convergence," *In Vivo* (July/August 2004): 61–68.
24. David Cassak, "Convergent Calling: An Interview with Medtronic's Stephen Oesterle," *In Vivo* (September 2003): 35–43.
25. Anita Raghavan, and Kathryn Kranhold, "GE May Offer $8.31 Billion for U.K.'s Amersham," *Wall Street Journal* (October 10, 2003).
26. David Shiple *et al.*, "Five Information Technologies Vitalize Life Sciences," *Forrester Research TechStrategy Brief* (August 19, 2003).
27. Singh *et al.*, "Healthy Convergence."
28. Ibid.
29. Ross DeVol, *America's Biotech and Life Science Clusters* (Milken Institute, 2004); Kerry Dolan, "San DNAgo," *Forbes Magazine* (May 26, 2003): 122–126.
30. Michael Porter, "Clusters and the New Economics of Competition," *Harvard Business Review* (November–December 1998): 77–90.
31. Des Dearlove, "The Cluster Effect: Can Europe Clone Silicon Valley?," *Strategy + Business* 24 (fall 2001): 67–75.

Part I

The life sciences

2 The pharmaceutical sector

Jon Northrup

Overview of the pharmaceutical sector

Before a study of the pharmaceutical sector can begin, it is necessary that a definition be made of a pharmaceutical.

What is a pharmaceutical?

It has been suggested that *a drug is any substance that a scientist uses in a rat to create a scientific paper!* A more stringent, and believed more accurate definition is that a pharmaceutical is a drug for human consumption, specifically developed to impact a disease, which goes through the regulatory process designed to approve prescription medications for marketing to physicians.

Thus not included are drug-coated devices, over-the-counter medications, nutritional supplements, generic drugs, or herbs. This is not to imply any attributes, positive or negative, to these categories, but rather to allow focus on the complex and specific business model of discovery, development, manufacture, and marketing of new chemical entities (NCEs) and bioproducts (proteins, peptides, monoclonal antibodies, vaccines, etc.) designed to enhance human health.

New chemical entities

NCEs are small molecules that typically bind to a target and cause a biological process to stop or start. These chemicals are called "small" because they need to be much smaller than proteins in order to be able to be taken orally, then survive the stomach and/or colon, pass into the blood, survive or be appropriately metabolized by the liver, and reach their target in an organ or tissue successfully. For a centrally acting drug, such as an antidepressant, anxiolytic, or many pain medications, the NCE must also cross the blood–brain barrier and achieve central nervous system concentrations. For most patients, a medication that can be taken orally, once a day, as a pill or tablet, is enormously preferred to any other route into the body. Small molecules are able to deliver this convenience and compliance advantage.

Biologicals/bioproducts

The body's natural chemistry is not limited to small molecules, although some processes depend on chemicals such as nitrous oxide, molecular oxygen, and so on. The body is heavily reliant on proteins. And proteins can do things that man just cannot induce small chemicals to do for a number of diseases. Most small molecules inhibit processes in the body. For example, Prozac (fluoxetine) and other SSRIs (selective serotonin reuptake inhibitors) inhibit the process of serotonin being destroyed in the neuronal synapse. This in turn increases serotonin concentrations. But what about diseases where one wants to add or supplement a protein because of an organ's failure to produce an important molecule? This requires a bioproduct such as insulin, growth hormone, Erythropoietin, Growth Colony Stimulating Factor (G-CSF), and others. Sometimes a disease problem might require hitting more than one target or designing an especially complex inhibitor. All these areas and more are often better served by using proteins, peptides (protein fragments or sections), monoclonal antibodies, and other biological approaches.

These molecules all share one major handicap. They are all big relative to most small molecules and are therefore chewed up and destroyed in the stomach and poorly absorbed through other routes. Consequently, another approach is required to allow them to achieve their site of action in the body with therapeutic activity. These approaches include intravenous injection, intramuscular injection, subcutaneous injection, depot (long-acting) injection, inhalation, patch and other, more exotic approaches being experimented with in development. Current experimental technologies include oral systems designed to protect and facilitate transport, buccal (absorption through the mouth), implantable, and enhancements to transdermal, inhalation, and injection technologies.

The pharmaceutical market

Market size

In 2003 the worldwide pharmaceutical sector was just shy of one-half trillion dollars in size. Almost one-half of that business was in the USA, at $220 billion, with the next largest chunk of 27 percent spread out across the European Union.[1] In twenty-five years the distribution of world business has changed dramatically, as Europe and Japan have declined in their overall prominence and the USA has almost doubled from 23 percent of the world to 45 percent by sales. Although the increasing importance of the USA has been a continuing theme during the last quarter of a century, it was especially pronounced in the five years from 1996 to 2001. During this time, world pharmaceutical growth in dollars expanded by $103 billion. The bulk of that, $87 billion, was in the USA, while Europe grew only $1 billion, as exchange rates on the strengthening dollar offset almost all the local currency growth in Europe.

Over the last five years growth in the USA has been trending down toward 10 percent per annum, while the EU has seen local currency growth rates fairly close to 10 percent across the period. China, now one of the top ten markets, has become a strong growth contributor to the pharmaceutical business, as its economy expands. Many believe that by 2010 China could be one of the top five world pharmaceutical markets.

	2003		1980	
	sales (billion $)	% of world	sales (billion $)	% of world
USA	220	45	14	23
Europe	135	27	24	39
Japan	59	12	10	16
ROW	78	16	14	22

Figure 2.1   2003: heavily about the USA.

Source: 2004 and previous IMS World Reviews.

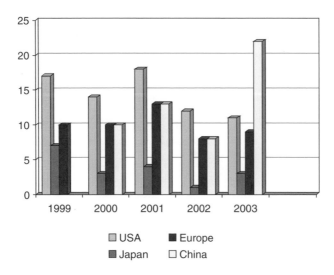

Figure 2.2   Growth of key markets (year-to-year percent in local currency).

Source: IMS World Review.

Japan, on the other hand, continues to deal with a challenging problem in funding its national healthcare program while the Japanese population ages. As a result, the country has been enacting stricter pricing policies for new drugs and more aggressively cutting prices on older drugs. This has caused Japan, still the number two pharmaceutical market, to continue to shrink as a percentage of the world market, as well as to create difficult economic pressures on much of the Japanese pharmaceutical sector. India, although significant as a market for other industries, has yet to fully provide intellectual property protection, so it is primarily a generics marketplace for pharmaceuticals.

The largest companies

American companies fill nine of the top fifteen pharmaceutical company slots, five companies are European, and one is Japanese. Pfizer, through its own organic growth and with acquisitions of Pharmacia and Searle, is over 50 percent larger than the number two company. GlaxoSmithKline through AstraZeneca forms a group of the largest pharmaceutical companies after Pfizer, while Bristol Myers Squibb through Lilly forms a middle tier. Year-over-year growth has been divergent by company, with the extremes represented by Schering-Plough's 20 percent decline and Amgen's 40 percent growth.

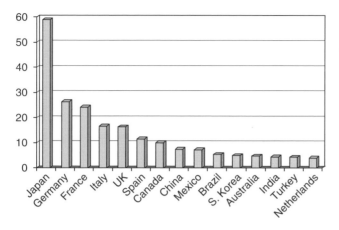

Figure 2.3   Top worldwide countries (except USA) over $4 billion country sales.

Source: IMS World Review.

Rank	Company	Sales (billion $)	% growth 02/03
1	Pfizer	47	14
2	GlaxoSmithKline	31	9
3	Sanofi-Aventis	25	22
4	Merck & Co	23	11
5	Johnson & Johnson	22	16
6	Novartis	20	24
7	AstraZeneca	19	5
8	BMS	15	9
9	Roche	15	20
10	Abbott	13	15
11	Wyeth	13	11
12	Lilly	12	17
13	Amgen	8	40
14	Takeda	8	15
15	Schering-Plough	8	− 20

Figure 2.4   Sales of top companies, 2003.

Source: 2004 IMS World Review.

Over the rest of the decade to 2010 pharmaceutical companies aggregately will likely see a slowing of growth after 2007. The hiatus is caused by a number of important patent expirations in the middle of the decade that will impact the sector significantly. Of course, this is difficult to forecast, because

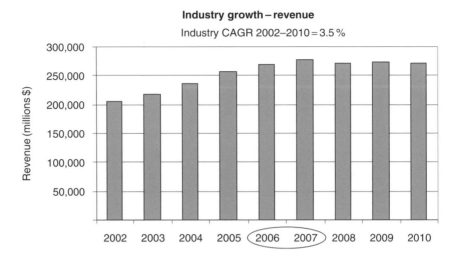

Figure 2.5   Twelve largest pharmaceutical companies grow to 2007, slow to 2010.

Source: Internal Analysis by Northrup & Associates.
Notes:
• Decline in industry growth due to blockbuster* patent expirations in 2006 and 2007.
• > 50% of the industry comprised of twelve top-tier pharmaceutical companies.
* Blockbuster drug defined as sales >$1 billion.

although patent expirations and their impact are clearly foreseeable, the strength of new products and their adoption curves cannot be as well understood.

Therapeutic areas

As patent expirations and new products flow through the marketplace, we can anticipate that major therapeutic areas will change in their economic importance as well. Figure 2.5, showing therapeutic growth from 2002 to 2010, just represents branded therapies from the largest pharmaceutical companies, which is over 50 percent of the pharmaceutical business. The cardiovascular marketplace, long the largest therapeutic area in the business, should decline as lipid lowering agents and hypertension medications are increasingly generic. The key question in cardiovascular (CV) will be the adoption of high-density lipoprotein (HDL) raising and other atherosclerotic approaches, but overall many CV therapies will be generically available. Neuroscience therapies will also see many new generically available antidepressants, antinauseants, and antimigraine agents that may more than

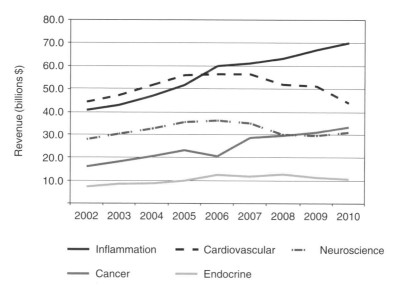

Figure 2.6   Therapeutic area growth, 2002–2010.

Source: Internal analysis by Northrup & Associates.

offset the advances in Alzheimer's therapy in this time frame. Two bright spots for new pharmaceutical therapies are oncology and inflammation. Therapies for arthritis and new cancer agents should both contribute substantial new business to the pharmaceutical marketplace, with inflammation becoming the largest therapeutic area in the time frame.

Generic drug companies

Generic drugs are a major benefit to consumers that flows from the innovation created by the pharmaceutical sector. Once a product's patent protection lapses, any specialty chemical producer is able to make the product with access to all the published patent data and the know-how that have been created. For most pharmaceuticals, this is about twenty years after discovery, which often translates into ten years after initial marketing. For some bio-products, this can be considerably longer, because additional development and manufacturing patents can be filed that are important to the production of these complex molecules. Minimal, if any, clinical work past the establishment of bioequivalence is required in order to register and sell a generic product. And as multiple generic companies enter the market, prices may eventually drop to 10–15 percent over cost. In 2003 generic sales increased in double digits in all major markets except Japan, and grew between 20 and 40 percent in the USA and major Europe.[2] Some generic companies are focused on the generic model as a way to become a future pharmaceutical company. Examples include the Indian companies Dr. Reddy's Laboratories and Ranbaxy, who have first developed production and chemical expertise and are now researching new compounds in existing therapeutic areas in order to try to create best-in-class therapies.

What defines the industry and what is outside of it?

Risk, time, and return

The overriding business model that defines the pharmaceutical sector is the interplay of high *risk*, long *time* lines for development, and the investment *returns* required to motivate stakeholders to engage in the business model. The stakeholders include scientists, physicians, shareholders, executives, and universities on the supply side and government, employers, healthcare providers, and consumers on the demand side. Although there are wonderful and unusual tales of expedited development and governmental review for the few AIDS and cancer drugs that receive highly accelerated review, the historical reality is much different for most drug projects. The typical time span for a drug is:

- from concept to optimized lead candidate: 2–5 years
- two more years for two or more of these optimized leads to have one that has clinical success (achieves a positive efficacy trial – phase II): 4–7 years total
- three to five more years for required safety studies (phase I) and efficacy studies (phase II), for a combined time line of between three to five years or more: 7–12 years total
- an additional three to five years in definitive multicenter registration studies (phase III) and their review: 10–17 years total

It is quite typical for the bench-to-bed program to span at least a dozen years before the first sale is earned. In addition to a time to sales of twelve years, the risk of having a registered product is roughly two out of a hundred projects that are conceived. This translates to a research and development (R&D) model where of the overall fully loaded cost, the cost of "dry wells" (projects that die) is greater than the cost of "wet wells." Of the roughly $800 plus million in R&D it costs to bring a drug to market, two-thirds of the cost may be attributable to dry well efforts that have to be funded by the successful few.

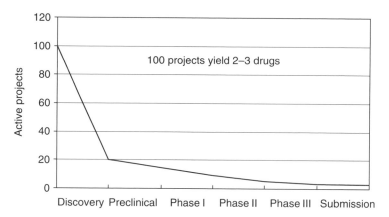

Figure 2.7   Drug development attrition rate.

Source: KMR Pharmaceutical R&D Benchmarking 2001.

Because it is high risk, time lines can only be approximate. For example, the Food and Drug Administration (FDA) added eighteen months to two years to the development time line of peroxisome proliferator activated receptor agonists (PPARs), products useful for diabetes, obesity and cardiovascular indications.[3] The FDA took this action because of concerns that toxicities in rodents could translate to humans. This is a concern that developed during research and development, and could not have been known at the initiation of the discovery program.

A challenging business model

So, looking forward at twelve years to market and 2 percent probability that the project makes it to market, one has a very challenging business model to fund competitively. Compare this business proposition to all the other industries and business models that investors have to choose from. This is the challenge that faces the sector, from a small biotechnology company pursuing its dream of a fully integrated pharmaceutical company (FIPCO), to the large pharmaceutical company with a portfolio of projects stratified over time, and working to deliver a steady increasing stream of earnings that are reportable on a quarterly basis. Looking backward at the successes that then drive the winners at this economic endeavor are all of the industries' critics. They see the fruits of a decade or more of effort, and cannot understand why one product should cost so much relative to its overall project cost or the per unit manufacturing cost. It becomes a challenging discussion to explain that ingredient cost and processing charges (manufacturing) are the small part of the economics driving the business. Rather than tangible infrastructure that you can see in the product (such as the steel in a railroad car), the majority of the money is going into intangibles such as intellectual capital (discovery, experimentation, analysis, and scientific review) and communication to healthcare providers and patients (marketing). A small white powder has been uniquely studied with complex tools and highly skilled and educated scientists and physicians to do one special thing, and then proven to do it in a very predictable fashion through highly monitored and carefully controlled human experiments. The final drug was engineered for its activities, and only a little effort was put into the things we normally use to judge value – taste, appearance, and smell.

And if the critics accept the long time lines, they then claim the industry is less than innovative, merely creating multiple analogs of a very few significant inventions. Again, this lacks a real understanding of the business. Multiple companies do strive for their version of a particular therapeutic class to be the best product, and this competition can be neck and neck. Rarely is it clear which product is best until the end of the development race or sometimes until the products are marketed for years. As a result, there are typically several alternatives, which may turn out to be therapeutically very close, or so distant that the lesser molecules are terminated in development. Companies will then strive to produce better molecules distinguished by better dosing convenience, a wider window between efficacy and side effects, or better formulations. Although these products may or may not achieve their objectives, they are efforts to enhance choice and therapy.

Biotech companies and pharmaceutical companies

Biotech company evolution

Biotechnology companies, typically started after the discovery of the structure of DNA, generally focus first on an important biology involved in human disease. Chemistry typically comes later in their evolution to a FIPCO, and they may focus only on protein chemistry. Many biotech companies were started as a way for leading scientist-academicians to enjoy more risk and reward in the development of their inventions.

A hypothetical example of a biotechnology company's evolution might be as follows. The owning university would license promising work done in the scientist's academic lab to a fledgling biotech company (NEWBio). The discovering scientist might become the Chief Scientific Officer of NEWBio.

Venture capitalists (VCs) would finance the first milestones of the company's business plan toward its long march to profitability. Additional financing rounds (mezzanine financing) would occur as and if the company made progress on its drug concept. After four years or so, enough work on the drug would occur to interest pharmaceutical companies to try to in-license the molecule as a preclinical opportunity. After a carefully orchestrated auction, a deal with one company would emerge around the molecule.

NEWBio might then work to take the next program a stage farther down the value chain. After one strong deal, and additional promising technology in the wings, NEWBio might consider an initial public offering (IPO) and go public. This could allow a rotation of investors and possible monetization of some of the investment of the founding VC partners. Each time, with each new program, NEWBio adds to its downstream capabilities and eventually is able to move to the status of a specialty pharmaceutical company. Achieving this, NEWBio could now enjoy the synergies of research, development, and marketing of its own compounds. If successful as a specialty company, NEWBio can commence to broaden its infrastructure and capabilities and begin to build itself into a retail pharmaceutical company, capable of a global primary care marketing reach.

Pharmaceutical companies

Pharmaceutical companies tend to be older and typically chemistry-based, focusing on small molecules that can be taken orally. They vary quite widely in their roots, philosophies, and emphasis. The breakout section below briefly describes a few of these companies and attempts to characterize the sector by showing how the histories of the companies have created differences in corporate philosophy and capabilities.

The history and beginnings of pharmaceutical companies

Johnson & Johnson[4]

J&J grew out of the Johnson family business that was started in 1886. The business introduced its first surgical dressings in 1887. In 1905 one of the family members, Mead Johnson, decided to leave the family business and strike out on his own to the western frontier. He settled in Evansville, Indiana, and started Mead Johnson. Mead Johnson evolved into a successful baby food and related products business that Bristol Myers acquired in 1967. In 1921 J&J launched the Band-Aid brand and became known in every household. In 1932 R. W. Johnson, son of the founder, set out the decentralization policy for which J&J has become distinctively known in the pharmaceutical sector. Today, J&J's business model appears to be similar to a large healthcare investment company.

Acquisitions of companies that are small but have a proven technology and substantial upside are purchased. J&J funds their expansion to realize their potential sooner and more fully. As they become mature, their cash is pulled back and used to fund other acquisitions, and so the cycle continues. J&J thus brings into itself a healthy share of external technology, which it attempts to commercialize optimally. The challenges of this model are the internal pharmaceutical R&D at J&J and the inability to synergize across the businesses. For example, the R. W. Johnson research laboratories and Janssen-Cilag have yet to be optimally integrated and coordinated, even though the Janssen acquisition occurred in 1961.

J&J illustrates a pharmaceutical company that is a diversified healthcare conglomerate. The strength of J&J's business model is its ability to attract external innovation across medical devices, bioproducts, surgical products, over-the-counter products, and pharmaceuticals.

Bristol-Myers Squibb[5]

BMS is fascinating because its dominant side came from the consumer and cosmetics industry. In many ways, this explains BMS's historical reputation to be heavily focused on the marketing and commercial side of the business, and less deep on the scientific side. Bristol Myers started with the acquisition of Clinton Pharmaceuticals by William Bristol and John Myers in 1887. In 1943, the company acquired Cheplin Laboratories, a manufacturer of acidophilus milk. Cheplin's fermentation efforts were put toward penicillin for the war effort, and represented BMS's first major pharmaceutical product.

In 1959 Clairol was acquired and with it a number of members of the eventual senior management team, the Gelb family. By 1976 Richard Gelb, the elder son of Clairol's founder, became Bristol's CEO. In 1989 Bristol merged with Squibb, creating the second largest pharmaceutical company of its day and bolstering its research ability. Established in 1856 by Edward Squibb, Squibb discovered and marketed the first angiotensin-converting enzyme (ACE) inhibitor, Capoten, in 1975. Squibb brought Bristol a great cardiovascular franchise and a strong research orientation, and Bristol brought Squibb the sales firepower to better compete against Merck's Vasotec, which had stalled Capoten's market share with its introduction. BMS went on to develop strong businesses in human immunodeficiency virus (HIV) therapy, cardiovascular, diabetes, and cancer. BMS's cancer franchise was the envy of the rest of the industry until 2000 – and it was created entirely through licensing agreements. In 2001 the company spun off Clairol to Proctor & Gamble (P&G) and purchased DuPont Pharmaceuticals.

BMS illustrates a pharmaceutical company that at first succeeded because of its strong business orientation, building itself almost entirely through the research of other houses and external scientists. But this lack of an historical scientific strength may have hurt BMS in 2000–2004. During key patent expirations, and despite enormous investments, Vanlev, its neuroendopeptidase inhibitor for hypertension, was not approved. UFT, its oral 5-FU-like cancer therapy did poorly in the marketplace, and a pivotal head-to-head study designed to show the value of Pravachol versus Lipitor in fact showed the opposite.

Sanofi-Aventis[6]

Sanofi and Aventis is the product of quite different cultures and events. Aventis was created in 1998 when Rhone-Poulenc-Rorer merged with Hoechst-Roussel-Marion. Given that both are "triple barreled " names, one can see that this is a corporate entity created by a number of separate entities that have been purchased through time.

Hoechst started in 1863 as a German dye and explosives company and became one of the largest chemical and pharmaceutical companies in Germany by World War One. During the twentieth century Hoechst was the ubiquitous pharmaceutical organization in Germany, with its name advertised in virtually every pharmacy. Its chemical facility on the River Rhine by Frankfurt-on-Main was at least a square mile in size, with a water purification capability that could power a city of a million inhabitants. It purchased a majority interest in the French company Roussel Uclaf in 1974, and the "triple barreled" American company of Marion-Merrill-Dow in 1995. Dow purchasing Merrill had created Merrill-Dow. Then Merrill-Dow came together with Marion. Marion had successfully licensed diltiazam (an important calcium channel blocker for hypertension and other cardiovascular diseases) marketing rights in the USA. Marion developed into a great marketing organization, but had no pipeline to sustain it when diltiazam lost patent protection in the USA.

The Hoechst stock price languished in the 1980s and 1990s as Europe's restrictive pricing environment held profits down and the protective labor laws kept employment high. By 1995 Hoechst was pushing hard to develop its presence in the US market and revitalize its European operations. Hoechst went through great turmoil in Europe, especially in Frankfurt, as it spun out of a number of chemicals areas, turned its large facilities into a more open industrialization zone, and reduced employment. Throughout this time, Hoechst pharmaceutical remained a division of the larger chemical concern. In order to do business development, sometimes up to twenty contracts would need to be created to account for all the corporate relationships and minority stakeholders between Hoechst, Roussel, and MMD.

During this time, Rhone-Poulenc-Rorer faced similar European challenges. Rhone Poulenc was created in 1928 when the Société Chimique des Usines du Rhône merged with the Établissements Poulenc Frères. In 1968 Institute Merieux A. was acquired, with its strong vaccine base and lineage from Dr. Louis Pasteur. A company with a market share oriented to French and French-speaking markets, Rhone-Poulenc (R-P) purchased Rorer for its USA presence in 1990. In an interesting managerial maneuver, the head of Rorer and the head of R-P shared the Office of the President in the joint company for a few years post merger.

Aventis was created in 1998, Richard Markham from Merck was recruited as President, and pharmaceutical headquarters set up in New Jersey at the previous offices of Celanese, an earlier Hoechst chemical acquisition. Aventis was created only three years after the acquisition of MMD. The quickness of these major moves caused a number of employees to relocate from New Jersey to Kansas City, MO, previous headquarters of MMD and the initial site decided on for the Hoechst-Roussel-Marion company, and then back to New Jersey within two years or less with Aventis. Post merger, Aventis worked to de-merge its animal and agricultural group and build focus on pharmaceuticals.

Sanofi was started in 1973 by the Société Nationale des Petroles d'Aquitaine. In 1999 Sanofi acquired Synthelabo. In 2004 Sanofi, with the blessing and intersession of the French government, made a hostile bid for Aventis and succeeded in creating Sanofi-Aventis. Sanofi-Aventis represents a pharmaceutical company created from many smaller, regional or even just national players. As such, it has enormous market share in France and Germany from its history of regional in-licensing, substantially more employees than its American counterparts, and a very broad cultural heritage.

Summary

Pharmaceutical companies can be quite diverse in their heritage and approach. Today it would be hard to imagine a sustainable business model that did not include both capable business/marketing and cutting edge scientific discovery, both bioproducts and NCEs, and a global marketing presence. Pharmaceutical companies are typically a century or more in the making, started as chemical, consumer, or regional companies, and have over time divested most nonpharmaceutical or related areas and grown through internal products and external licensing and acquisition.

The broad environment

Healthcare innovation environment

It is also important to understand the metaenvironment in which healthcare innovation is delivered. To a large extent, biotechnology companies, pharmaceutical companies, universities, the National Institutes of Health (NIH), and other sources of scientific effort act together in very complementary ways. Universities and the NIH fund and deliver the basic research that discovers new mechanisms of disease and new scientific tools of value, in the hunt for therapeutic molecules. Typically, a biotechnology company is the translation vehicle for showing how these discoveries can be harnessed for commercial value and the commercial vehicle to allow the university to participate in the risk and reward of the process. A pharmaceutical company (including the largest biotechs that have become pharma companies) is where the literally hundreds of scientific disciplines can be harnessed to make the invention suited for people (oral, once a day, stable, soluble, consistently reproducible, etc.) and taken forward through technical and clinical development, worldwide registration, and availability.

Role of the USA

The USA has become increasingly dominant in healthcare innovation because of this broad healthcare interest and support. This can be seen in the increasing proportion of patents coming from the USA, the migration of scientists in biochemistry and biology to the USA, and the initiatives by most states to attract life science companies and jobs.

Pharmaceutical innovation is sensitive to the environmental variables required for success. Nowhere can this be seen more clearly than in the financing roller coaster that biotechnology companies have faced over the last twenty years. From one perspective, many biotechnology companies are focused on one technology or one key innovation. As such, they are examples of the pharmaceutical model with a reduced long-term portfolio of opportunities in multiple stages of development and commercialization. Europe, with its more restrictive pricing environment and more difficult access to capital, boasts far fewer biotechnology companies. Japan, India, and China also have very few companies indeed.

In the USA spending on prescription drugs, while increasing as a percentage of total healthcare costs, is currently less than 10 cents of the healthcare dollar. But prescription drugs are almost one-fourth (23%) of American's out of pocket medical expenses, because of differences in what is insured across different types of healthcare.

The USA also has very different concepts for medical liability than the rest of the world. This has a significant impact on pharmaceuticals. For example, in the Wyeth (American Home Products) situation around the inappropriate promotion of their in-licensed drug Redux (dexfenfluramine) with the OTC drug phentermine, called "fen-phen," Wyeth has taken $18 billion to date in charges, adding an additional $1.3 billion in the seventh amendment to its proposed 1999 settlement, and it is still quite possible that that amount could be insufficient. Contrast this with the roughly $100,000 settlement given to each hemophiliac and others who contracted the HIV virus from contaminated blood in France prior to 1985. Even though HIV testing was available to screen the blood supply, those responsible elected not to use the test.[7]

Yet, healthcare customers are loudly and emphatically stating that prescription costs are too high. And pharmaceutical companies are often considered to be major culprits in the cause. For a robust future, pharmaceutical companies will have to find ways of being more efficient in order for these critical health innovations to continue to flow, but be less burdensome to the ultimate payers.

The regulated marketplace: national approaches for healthcare

There is great diversity in the way nations provide healthcare to their populations. In many countries healthcare is considered a basic service provided for the great majority by a national authority with a desire to maintain a no-increase budget. As population ages and more and better pharmaceuticals become available at higher price points, considerable pressure comes to these agencies to provide more and better drugs at minimal new cost.

United States of America

The USA has a mostly free pricing system for pharmaceuticals, subject to a number of constraints. Drug prices are established by list prices set by the manufacturer and then negotiations between manufacturers and large purchasers. In order to access Medicaid patients (about 10 percent of the population), manufacturers must have their products on the Federal Supply Schedule (FSS). FSS prices are by law at least 24 percent lower than an average manufacturer price, and are intended to be the best price a manufacturer offers in the country. Also, under separate law, drug manufacturers must provide essentially their best price to state Medicaid programs, regardless of FSS listing.

France

France has statutory health insurance (Caisse Nationale d'Assurance Maladie) covering virtually everyone and their prescription expenses. Although a pharmaceutical company is technically free to set its own price, in order to be reimbursed it must negotiate an acceptable price with the Comité Economique du Medicament. That price becomes the single price for the country. Historically, France has been a tough pricing environment for pharmaceuticals.

Germany

Germany's evolution from a free-pricing market to one of experimentation with a number of approaches is a story in itself. Today, the German government, through a complex reference price system, reimburses pharmaceuticals. The reference pricing system will limit reimbursement to the lowest cost product among several. For example, in 2004 Germany considered reference pricing all statin drugs (including Lipitor and Crestor) to a generic pricing scheme. In addition, an explicit negative list of drugs not eligible for reimbursement is maintained. If the prescription budget is exceeded, German physicians are also asked to limit prescribing and can have their fees reduced.

Japan

The Japanese are covered by virtually universal health insurance via several systems, which provide taxes to fund the National Health Insurance (NHI). Drug prices are fixed for the NHI by indication. In the 1970s and 1980s Japan had some of the highest drug prices in the world. Prices were initially set based on the Japanese evaluation of innovation and therapeutic benefit. As they aged on the market, the initial high prices were reduced every two years. Physicians in Japan received a dispensing fee and a professional fee for their services, and more aggressively prescribed new drugs. In the mid 1990s, Japan's NHI expenditure went into deficit. As a result, Japan has been revamping its system. Between 1996 and 1998 prices were revised downward every year. Physician incentives are being moved from dispensing toward professional fees. Initial prices are referenced to Europe and elsewhere, and now are typically below US prices and closer to European prices.

Conclusion

The models used around the world for controlling pharmaceutical prices are varied and unique in each country with a national health insurance system. Most systems seem to outstrip their ability to pay for innovation over a few decades. Most operate to limit choices and deny or slow access to new drugs in addition to the pressure put on new product prices.

The value proposition and potential demand for pharmaceuticals

The value proposition

Individual healthcare status has been estimated to be primarily determined by behavior and lifestyle choices (up to half of total status), about a fifth by environmental factors, a fifth by human biology (i.e., the genes you are born with), and only about 10 percent by the medical care you receive. Of the medical care an individual receives, only a fraction is determined by pharmaceutical therapy.

Yet pharmaceutical therapy is capable of yielding tremendous productivity improvements and tremendous care gains. Examples are the difference between the constant care required for a debilitating disease, and the

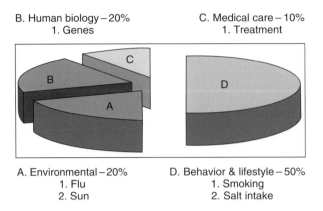

B. Human biology – 20%
   1. Genes

C. Medical care – 10%
   1. Treatment

A. Environmental – 20%
   1. Flu
   2. Sun

D. Behavior & lifestyle – 50%
   1. Smoking
   2. Salt intake

Figure 2.8   Individual healthcare status.

potential to have that disease controlled sufficiently such that it is not the cause of an individual's mortality or lack of ability to function normally. In one study of heart attack sufferers, new pharmaceuticals increased life expectancy by eight months.[8] In another study, new drugs saved $127 per patient when overall costs were considered.[9] On a considerably broader level, prescription drugs are part of an overall biomedical effort that has helped to increase the life span of an American from 47 years to 77 years over the course of the twentieth century.[10] Part of the increase in overall lifespan comes from rising cancer survival rates, which have moved from less than 50 percent in 1975 to an estimated 65 percent in 1999.[11] Rates of disability have also dropped dramatically for the elderly.[12] Dr. Manton and his colleagues have reported that disability in the elderly US population dropped at an accelerating rate between 1982 and 1999. One reason cited is that "Stroke, heart disease, and crippling arthritis as events leading to chronic disability and dependency have also been sharply reduced, since their effects can now be much better controlled with medication."[13]

New drug technology versus older drug technology

How is it that new drugs might be better than existing drugs? If we take a brief look at the history of drug discovery we can understand this phenomenon.

First in class drugs

One aspect of new drug technology is that it may treat a disease that previously did not respond to a therapy. Or, it may treat an aspect of the disease that previous medications did not. Over time, this ability to conquer totally new frontiers is very important. For example, an early 1930s symposium listed only seven diseases amenable to drug treatment.[14] The situation today is far more hopeful.

Newer drugs for diseases that already have treatments

The first drugs were extracts, powders, and elixirs of natural products. These are still often important products that can be found in health food stores. But they typically share a big flaw – they are often less potent and broadly active across many body processes. Any effect outside the desired effect is an adverse effect. Most early discovery was empirical chemistry, which attempted to simplify and distill biologic activity in order to reduce adverse effects and increase the therapeutic effect. As human biological processes were understood, chemicals could be screened, and leads were found that were more and more specific to the biological system. Natural products, a "shotgun approach," were replaced by synthetic products. These provided a "rifle approach," hitting the target with a minimum of additional effects and with greater potency. As biological understanding increased, scientists aimed at cells, then cell surface receptors, then targets within the cell, and finally at the gene–protein and protein–protein interactions within cells. As a result, newer drugs often have fewer side effects, less interactions with other drugs, and better efficacy and time duration than older drugs. Hence, a popular expression for the World War Two generation is, "the fewer the drugs, the better" (because this generation saw many drugs with as many adverse effects as therapeutic effect). Baby Boomers tend to use more drugs and to be more actively involved in their healthcare because they have many more "rifle" drugs that can be used without troublesome adverse effects or incompatibilities with other therapies.

Drivers for advancements in healthcare

As a society, we have a great need for advances in healthcare and, therefore, in pharmaceutical therapy. There are several drivers for advances in healthcare. First, as we are able to deal effectively with the diseases that kill the young and middle-aged population, humanity ages and new diseases come to the forefront. As we age, we gradually lose many organ functions, immune system functions, and some organs may become overactive (thyroid). These changes may subject us to a variety of ailments. Our prescription usage often goes up dramatically. Look at the movement of population by age group across the world. The US population over 65 years of age is expected to grow to 46 million people by 2015. The average compound growth rate of over 65 years

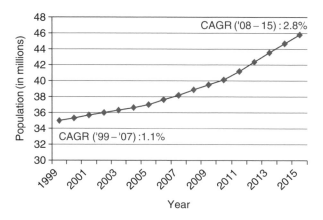

Figure 2.9   USA population over 65 years of age.

Source: Matteson Jack Epi Database.

of age more than doubles in the period 2008 to 2015 (2.8%) compared to a similar preceding period (1.1%).[15] As we age, we typically deal with more than one medical problem. Our medical issues increase, and newer therapies with the "rifle approach" discussed earlier are needed in order to circumvent interactions among drugs and to manage our care. Thus as we age so our prescription bill goes up both by the number of prescriptions we take and because we are taking newer, more expensive therapies. A 2002 survey of Americans over 45 years of age found on average that respondents took four prescription medications per day, and that the incidence of prescription use increased with each age category studied.[16]

The aging effect is not limited to the US. Japan leads the age wave and most European Union countries are net declining in population because of the aging effect. World population, accountable in large part to the growing prosperity of China and India and to the effect this is having on birth rates, is forecast to peak in 2050, and then to begin to decline. Only in the poorest countries of the world is the population continuing to grow and the average age remaining young. Even in these countries, the need for medicines is high. The lack of basic hygiene, the disruptions caused by war or strife, famine and political instability, create two enormous issues. First, this is a robust breeding ground for plague and infectious disease. HIV, emergent polio, tuberculosis, malaria, SARS, and other infectious agents start in these areas and spread to the rest of the world via human, animal, and insect travelers. Second, the often very difficult and physically stressful childhoods of the poor create weaker adult bodies that suffer hypertension, diabetes, arteriosclerosis, arthritis, obesity, and

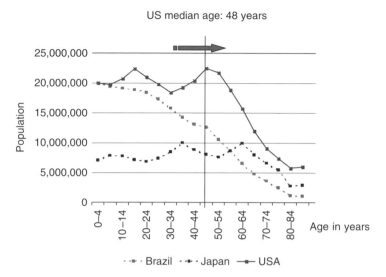

Figure 2.10   Age profile in major markets, 2010: Brazil, Japan, US.

Source: Matteson Jack Epi Database.
Note: Notice the "age wave " in the US over the next ten years, leading to a large increase in Rx growth and demand for innovative therapies.

other diseases associated with aging in wealthier societies. However, these people may start their disease one to two decades before it would be seen in a body with a more protected childhood. As a result, even in the poorest nations such as Sierra Leone in Africa, more people suffer from obesity than from starvation. And therefore, the incidence of disease in the world is shifting toward chronic and degenerative conditions and away from acute infectious diseases as a general trend. Infectious diseases of concern tend to be either new diseases such as SARS or HIV, or resistant diseases created from casual or intermittent use of existing therapies. For example, the substandard confinement and inability to properly treat multiple resistant tuberculosis (TB) in the Russian prison system has created a resistant TB problem that is slowly spreading across the world today.

The potential demand for pharmaceuticals

Many estimates of pharmaceutical product demand rely on worldwide estimates of disease sufferers, or diagnosed and treated patients, or simply raw numbers of prescriptions sold. None of these approaches is very satisfactory.

A realistic appraisal of potential demand needs to be based on (a) people who are afflicted by the disease a pharmaceutical may help and the likelihood that they will be diagnosed, seek treatment, and be able to afford that treatment, and (b) the price for therapies for that disease.

Population

The potential demand for pharmaceuticals is a function of the number of people in the world who have access to and can afford prescription medications. A look at population, its growth, gross domestic product (GDP), and its anticipated future growth, provides a sense of how many people might be able to afford sufficient medical care to utilize pharmaceuticals. Work conducted at Eli Lilly suggests that by 2010 over 1.25 billion people may be the size of the world pharmaceutical market in consumers. This estimate counts only eleven major markets and notably does not include India or most of Eastern Europe. It is anticipated that China will surpass the USA in market size in terms of pharmaceutical consumers (352 million compared to 309), although the USA will still be substantially bigger in dollars because of the

	% population growth 1998–2015	Average % GDP growth rate 1995–1999	2010 pop. brand eligible	
USA	0.7	3.7	309	
France	0.2	2.1	59	
Germany	−0.2	1.5	83	
Italy	−0.3	1.8	58	
Spain	−0.2	3.3	39	
UK	0.0	2.7	60	
China	0.7	8.8	352	(26%)*
Japan	−0.1	1.1	127	
Australia	0.8	4.4	19	
Brazil	1.1	2.2	66	(34%)*
Canada	0.6	3.3	33	
Poland	0.0	5.7	39	
Able to purchase pharmaceuticals			_1,240_	

Figure 2.11 Worldwide prescription consumers – 2010.

Source: 2000 World Development Indicators, World Bank.
*% of population Rx brand eligible.

prescription intensity and higher price level per person of the USA compared to China.

Determinants of pharmaceutical pricing

Pharmaceutical pricing is determined by a multitude of variables. First, what is the level of capability of drugs to impact the various diseases that afflict man? At best, it is highly variable across disease states. Some diseases, like most bacterial infections, are very well treated. Others have no treatment, only palliative or symptomatic treatments (ventricular arrhythmias, many cancers, and Alzheimer's). Some medicines can slow the progression to worse disease, positively impact a patient's quality of life, and even have a dramatic effect in lowering the mortality with the disease. Typically, pricing is often set by comparison with preexisting agents that treat the disease in question. If robust treatments exist (bacterial infections), new treatments are likely to have small up-charges even though they affect a complete cure. On the other hand, if current treatments slow disease progression slightly (Alzheimer's) and are considered expensive relative to antibiotics, new treatments that are better but still far from ideal will also be in a similar pricing range.

What is the pricing level of the therapeutic category as well as the relative level of enhancement a new drug would deliver? Therapeutic areas that found their first good treatments early in the twentieth century have low pricing while therapeutics that had no precedent until more recently have higher prices. For example, estrogen/progestin and insulins were first produced in the 1920s, so these therapeutic areas have efficacious historical precedents with low prices. New entrants tend to price lower because of the otherwise larger gap in price between new products and previous standards of care. In certain geographies, the governments who set the pharmaceutical prices at which they will reimburse, specifically "reference" the older products in determining the price they will allow.

What is the customer enthusiasm for the product and what it offers? For a pharmaceutical product to be priced higher than others and still used, healthcare professionals, regulators, thought-leading and academic physicians (all are important customers) must feel it is a valuable contribution to a patient's health and well-being. "Customer enthusiasm" is expressed when physicians feel strongly that their patient needs access to a particular treatment, when formularies and pharmacists quickly adopt the product on to their unrestricted list, and when the organizations that are looked to for setting the standards of care (centers of excellence, key medical publications, thought-leading physicians) include the new product in their regimens.

Other factors are also important. If the medicine is for a very small population, a higher price can often be justified because of the small market opportunity and the limited impact on healthcare expenditures for most payers.

Pricing will often have a lower bias if the medicine is useful mostly for elderly patients. This segment of the market impacts government more directly, especially in the USA, with the Medicare program. Although Medicare is focused on the poor in society, the elderly represent a group that are well represented and for which prescriptions may represent a significant expense. Pricing tends to have an upward bias if the drug is a biotechnology drug. These products have often been developed on higher risk funding, and have greater manufacturing complexity.

Market demand equals price-times-population

In order to try to understand the future potential of the pharmaceutical business, I undertook a project to see if all these variables could be roughly measured. I interviewed thousands of physicians in over a dozen specialties on the relative need for new therapy across hundreds of diseases. Information on each disease's mortality, progressivity (how likely and quickly it leads to more severe disease), and quality of life challenges was collected. This was used to create a pricing algorithm to price over 300 existing products. When this one algorithm gave consistently good answers compared to the product's actual prices, this question was posed: "If there existed a pharmaceutical in every major disease that did what the best drugs today do, how big would the pharmaceutical market be?"

In order to understand the meaning of "what the best drugs do," take the example of hypertension. Virtually no one is cured of hypertension from drug therapy today. Also, there are still difficult-to-treat subsets of patients that do not benefit adequately from existing therapies. Yet many consider hypertension a satisfied and well-treated disease. The reason is that the multiple therapeutic classes available for hypertension can adequately treat the vast majority of patients. Although their disease will continue to progress over time, drugs may be added to their regimen and doses increased to maintain control. Most patients will be able to manage their disease such that hypertension is not the cause of their death. For most diseases today, this is the definition of pharmaceutical success.

Contrast this disease state with a diagnosis of nonsmall cell lung cancer (NSCLC), which typically cannot be treated with curative intent. The best that can be hoped for is up to an extra two years of life over the natural progression of the disease. This in no way suggests that those two years are of low value – they are extremely important to the NSCLC patient. But, what would be the relevant value proposition and appropriate price if a pharmaceutical therapy could be discovered that changed the treatment of NSCLC from its current paradigm to that of hypertension? In other words, therapy where one could live the rest of one's life, not dying from lung cancer but rather holding it at bay until something else is the cause of mortality. Given that patients are paying in the region of $50,000 in the USA for that extra two years, a therapy that would give twenty to thirty years of life should be worth a great deal.

The result is a potential pharmaceutical market, given that the technology is discovered, of $1.6 trillion. The amazing finding is that so few diseases have the impact of creating this figure. If ordered by size, one-half of the value of the market lies in just thirty-three diseases. It takes only 116 diseases to cover 90 percent of the value of this potential market. The blockbuster target area of the pharmaceutical space, and the enormous burden of disease, is surprisingly focused, considering there are tens of thousands of diseases.

This provides the first step in an overall firm plan and strategy for therapeutic areas. Pharmaceutical companies should focus on disease issues where three key variables come together to make their research efforts viable. First, have a plan to work in valuable areas (the worth dimension). Second, work where the technology has the potential of providing new solutions now (is it real?). Finally, work where a company has competitive advantage and believes it can succeed.

Research and development: the key steps in the value chain

The pharmaceutical value chain is two very different businesses "welded" together to create a profitable and sustainable business model. The first business is the *business of scientific innovation* – that is finding the molecule, optimizing it, and proving that it is real innovation. This is called discovery and early clinical development. The other business is *an innovation adoption business* – that is, creating the information regulators and customers desire to see and communicating it to them so they can use the product everywhere it is truly a best choice. This is called phase III clinical development, registration, marketing, phase IV studies, and selling.

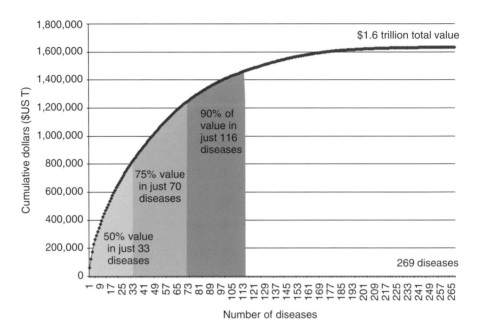

Figure 2.12   Worldwide disease potential.

Source: Northrup Analysis.

Disease name	Value (billion $)	Disease name	Value (billion $)
Obesity (BMI>30)	61	Psychoses	26
*Chronic hypertension**	60	HIV	24
*Atherosclerosis**	53	*Alzheimer's**	23
Ventricular arrhythmias	53	*COPD**	22
*Cancer, lungs and bronchus**	36	*Osteoarthritis**	22
Chronic sinusitis	29	Migraine prophylaxis	22
Migraine	28	Cancer, breast (prev)	21
*Diabetes type II**	27	*Second prevention of AMI**	20
*Frailty in the elderly**	26	Epilepsy	20
*Colorectal cancer**	26	*Age associated memory impairment.**	19

Figure 2.13   Top twenty future diseases in 2010.

*Diseases more common in an older adult population

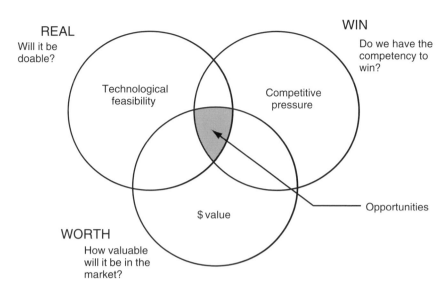

Figure 2.14 Three dimensions of pharmaceutical strategy.

Discovery

Pharmaceutical discovery research is often confused with basic or academic discovery research on the one hand, or with pharmaceutical development on the other. Pharmaceutical discovery is an applied science. Everything done has a molecule in its gun sights as the end point. There is no research just for understanding unless that understanding can be applied to creating or finding a drug candidate. It is called research because it is so risky, and it is very different than the academic research of understanding for the sake of understanding. Even with this unitary focus, on average it takes a hundred discovery research projects to see two to three drugs enter the pharmaceutical market. Discovery also differs from development in that discovery is about creating the molecule, and development is about creating the knowledge and processes around the molecule to make it a pharmaceutical product.

Discovery generally includes the phases of target identification, target validation, lead generation, and lead optimization and candidate selection.

Target identification

Today, the pharmaceutical sector is target rich. It seems as though every month scientific researchers in academia and industry are publishing results of a discovery of a novel gene, protein, or receptor and its relationship to a

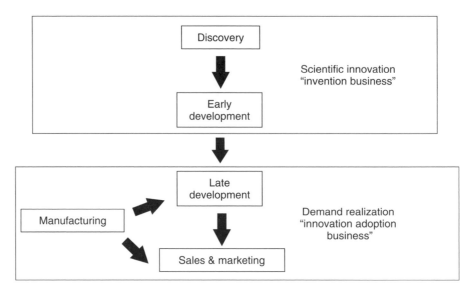

Figure 2.15 The value chain.

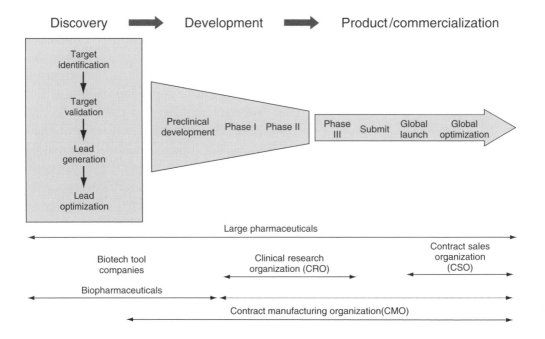

Figure 2.16 Varying scope of pharmaceutical business models.

disease pathology afflicting man. With the strides that have been made mapping the human genome, it seems likely that this will continue for the foreseeable future. Target identification is a pharmaceutical discovery scientist picking a target that is hypothesized to have an improved therapeutic effect on a human disease state. Usually this is based on some provocative findings that tie the target to the potential modification of the course of the disease.

First example   The incretin hormones are produced by the gastrointestinal tract in response to food intake and have a role in causing the body to release insulin.[17] This observation, well-known today, created a pharmaceutical target for diabetes when it was first discovered. The hypothesis would have been that adding an incretin hormone-like glucagon such as peptide 1 (GLP-1) or an analog (related compound) might promote better glycemic control in diabetes.

Second example   A team of researchers at the Whitehead Institute for Biomedical Research led by Dr. Robert Weinberg have discovered a new mechanism that enables the process of tumor metastasis.[18] Reported in detail in the June 25, 2004 edition of the journal *Cell*, the Whitehead team discovered a gene regulator protein, Twist, which is active in early embryonic development to enable cells to move around the embryo, and then typically becomes dormant. Some tumor cells are able to reactivate this protein, and hijack its process in order to move cancer cells to other parts of the body. This could be a very exciting pharmaceutical target, which perhaps some companies are considering or experimenting with. Yet, it is a high-risk, nonvalidated target. This is because it is not known (today) whether turning off Twist will successfully defeat metastasis. There may be mechanisms where the cancer can use other gene regulator proteins or other mechanisms to still successfully metastasize.

Target validation

The target needs to be validated. Additional proof is required that success in finding a molecule that will block or trigger the target should have a beneficial effect on the disease in discussion, and that this can be done in a way that will be acceptable to patients and physicians. Also, there must be the potential that it will be preferred over other approaches for some desirable aspect of the therapy. This is often done with a disease model such as knock-in or knock-out mice, where genes have been added or deleted to allow a reproducible and predictable model of the disease. Some diseases have great predictive models – antibiotics, hypertension, and diabetes, for example – and some diseases have no or no good models – sepsis, stroke, many mental diseases, and many cancers, for example. Not being able to validate a target at this early stage

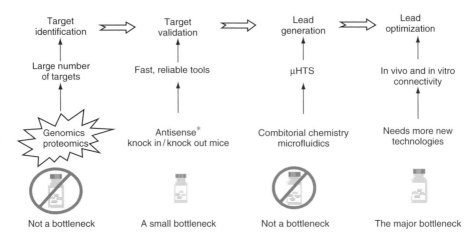

Figure 2.17   Stages in the discovery research process.

*Antisense obigonucleotides are small, modified DNA segments designed to bind to mRNA and thereby prevent the creation of a specific protein.

greatly increases the risk of pursuit and the cost of a dry hole, because it will likely take an additional \$25–50 million of studies and effort and four more years to accomplish and then complete the phase I and II studies required to answer this question.

Example   Following our earlier example, researchers in the incretin area created and found different analogs to GLP-1 and studied them in animal models of diabetes to see if they would help glycemic control. When they did, GLP-1 analogs became a partially validated target for diabetes.

Target validation is a bottleneck, although not the worst, in drug discovery. Tools available for target validation exist for many targets, but they could be faster, more reliable, and cover more of the targets of interest.

Lead generation

Lead generation is a term used to describe the creation of molecules through chemistry that can lead to the ultimate molecule that will become the drug developed to go to market. Lead generation covers the areas of assay development, screening, and early medicinal chemistry, which finds compounds that may be efficacious.

The conceptual foundation of lead generation is seen in what is called structure–activity relationship (SAR). A chemist synthesizes a small quantity of a new molecule, which is given to the biologist. The biologist puts the chemical into his or her disease-related model. Upon observing the molecule's performance in the model, the biologist tells the chemist that this latest molecule was either better or worse than the previous one. The chemist uses this information to speculate on how the molecule might be changed to create a new chemical, slightly modified. The new chemical is created and the process recycles. Over time, the two scientists test their beliefs about the relationship of chemical structure to the desired activity in the disease model to develop the best drug candidate.

Today the SAR process is still used for very tough discovery problems. In addition, industrial systems have been created that allow massive parallel processing and quicker answers. This is assay development and ultra high throughput screening (μHTS). Assay development is the "signal light" of drug discovery. An assay is a way of determining if the molecule in question has the desired activity in the disease model. Assays can be labor intensive and highly dependent on technique initially, but to be useful in the μHTS systems that are available, they have to be highly standardized, reproducible, and durable.

It is typical for assays to undergo substantial rework over a number of months to be acceptable for μHTS. μHTS began in the early 1990s as an attempt to industrialize and make massively parallel a very serial and slow industrial process. μHTS is the approach of doing the SAR all at once. Instead of a serial process, up to a million molecules are tested with a standardized assay that mimics a disease process. A number of different approaches have been tried. Some companies have tried to gain advantage by screening thousands of multiple compounds in solution at the same time. Others have tried to go directly to in-silica approaches. In retrospect, the more successful approaches have been to screen a single compound against a single assay. And to do this using robotics and microfluidics such that only tiny amounts of solution are needed in tiny wells that look more like microscopic cavities than test tubes. Also, considerable progress in in-silica approaches has been made. For example, some companies today are able to create chips where many thousands of genes reside and can be studied for how they react and bind to DNA from tissue test samples. Information about which genes are turned on and which turned off in various disease states can be correlated and potentially matched to treatments.

The result is that once a good standardized assay is developed, discovery scientists can look at the best compounds out of a million compound library to find leads and understand the SAR around a disease problem.

Even though the industry now has access to this advanced screening technology, sufficient diversity does not always exist in compound libraries to find a good lead. In this case, or even before screening, protein-imaging techniques such as X-ray crystallography are used to view the binding target and to develop strategies for medicinal chemistry to populate a newly created library of possible leads. The first HIV protease inhibitors, for example, could not have been created by HTS alone. Crystallography was used to solve the structure of the protease and to inform scientists about the chemistry required to interact with the binding site (the site to which a small molecule can attach to a human cell or protein in order to create the desired effect). It is theorized that the molecular diversity in nature is 10^{30}. Even a screen of a million compounds is a very small sampling of this diversity. Add to that the bias that exists in chemical libraries. Screening becomes a science much like looking at the night sky – seeing dense star areas such as the Milky Way and also open areas with no stars and then trying to rebalance it so that all the stars are equidistant.

Lead optimization

Once a lead is achieved, it needs to be optimized into something that can be potent, orally active, soluble, and once-a-day. In other words, once a researcher has an active compound, it may still not be a great compound for human therapy – it may not dissolve in the stomach or intestine and thus make it to the blood, or it may have a short half-life that requires it to be taken every hour. Additional chemistry and additional studies on how the compound behaves in animal systems similar to the human system are critical to this step. Lead optimization continues to be a relative bottleneck, an area of art in pharmaceutical discovery. Although new technologies and industrialization continue to be explored, it is a labor-intensive and time-consuming job to consider what might work to solve the various challenges the lead has, and to optimize it into a winning pharmaceutical.

Candidate selection

After a strong effort in lead optimization, a few compounds are worthy of further development. The scientific team needs to pick one to be the lead compound and one or two others to back up the lead, should it fail. It is quite common for the lead compound to fail in further testing, and the scientific team to go back and pick an existing compound out of the previous SAR. There may even be years of work in translating the early failure in the clinic into biological understanding and new chemistry to achieve a success. For example, in the case of an especially difficult target, Lilly's antifolate program for cancer, Alimta (launched in 2004) is the third-generation compound out of the program but the only compound out of the program to make it to market.

Intellectual property – patents

Patents may be generated at any time throughout the discovery process. Often there are patents around the biology of the disease process, around the structure of the human proteins involved, around the disease models used to try to find molecules, and around the chemical classes and structures that may have utility as a therapeutic. Additionally, there can be patents around product/process development and manufacturing processes. As a general point, patents around the composition of matter of the NCE and related compounds are considered the most valuable.

It is important to understand that it takes typically at least two years to receive a patent from an application. During those two years the patent is under review, it is confidentially held and not a matter of public record. Additionally, a patent is not a right to proceed with the development of the NCE. It is a right to exclude others from the scope defined and granted. The reason this is important is that several patents may be required to protect an exclusive position for an NCE. For example, one company may have a patent around the compound and its ability to modulate the biological target. Another company might have a patent on the biological target and its role in human disease. Both may be required to develop the compound for that disease. None of these may be sufficient to protect the company from a competitive compound that works through different chemistry at a different site of action in the body to treat the same disease.

Development

Preclinical and medical development

Preclinical development focuses on the need for good animal and toxicological work in order to show that a new experimental compound is worthy of testing in human subjects and that every reasonable precaution to find, a priori, a toxicity that might harm a clinical volunteer has been explored. The Food and Drug Administration (FDA) stipulates certain tests, and depending on the compound and the disease, additional work may be done. All preclinical work is submitted to the regulatory authorities for investigational new drug (IND) approval. Since no clinical (in humans) testing may proceed until the IND has been approved, this is a rate-limiting and serial process. Starting preclinical

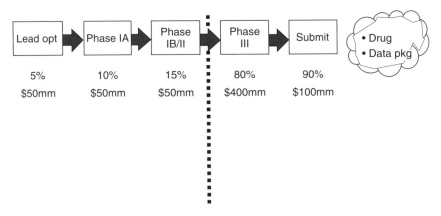

Figure 2.18 The investment inflection point: addressing early attrition.

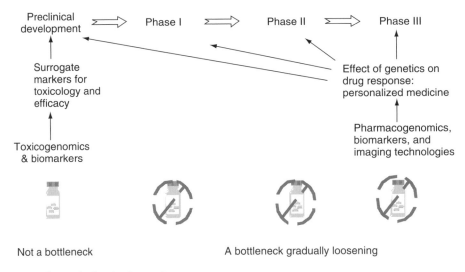

Figure 2.19 Stages in the development process.

development gives a probability of success of 10 percent. Successfully completing preclinical development does step up probabilities to about 20 percent.

Phase I testing: first studies of safety in humans

Phase I testing is the next step. This involves placing minute amounts of a drug in healthy volunteers in order to answer key questions, such as:

- Where does the drug go in the body? It is important that the drug goes to the target organ and does not concentrate in nontarget pockets in the body.

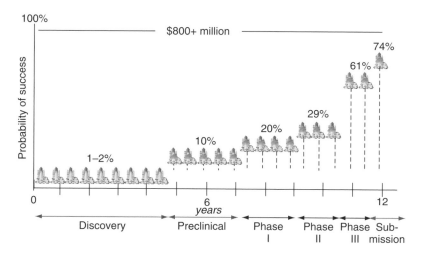

Figure 2.20   Pharmaceutical business model – long cycle time and high risk.

Source: J. A. Dimasi, "Uncertainty in Drug Development: Approval Success Rates for New Drugs," in *Clinical Trials and Tribulations*, 2nd edn, ed. A. E. Cato, L. Sutton, and A. Cato (New York: Marcel Dekker, 2002), 361–377.

- What is the time activity (the half-life, the concentration of drug in sera over time, etc.) in humans? Will the drug be dosed once a day or once an hour?
- Are there any unexpected developments, side effects, or concerns in the drug's performance and safety margins?

Sometimes a drug, by its mode of action or composition, is so safe that hints of efficacy can be seen in phase I. Some drugs are so highly specific or nontoxic that phase I dosing will turn out to include an efficacious dose. Most typically, this is not the case. As a result, successful completion of phase I rules out untoward toxicology issues and many safety concerns, but does not establish the efficacy profile of the drug. Preclinical testing has been affirmed in humans and probabilities step up close to 30 percent.

Phase II testing: first studies of efficacy

This is the *major fulcrum of value* in the development part of the value chain. Successfully completing phase II means the probability of success goes from one in three to about 60 percent or more. With successful completion of a well-done phase II study, there is more than a one in two chance that the molecule will be a product. In the pharmaceutical business model, the probability of success of the project is one of the most important value drivers. The purpose of phase II testing is to see how the drug performs in diseased individuals at therapeutic doses. When completed, the study will allow informal comparisons to the other drugs in the category and some assessment of how the drug could perform in the phase III setting.

Pharmacogenomics, biomarkers, and new imaging technologies

The potential

A discussion of clinical trials in the pharmaceutical sector would not be complete without some time spent on imaging and biomarkers. This is a subject of great interest to the FDA and throughout industry because of its potential. Although biomarkers have the potential to enhance many parts of the pharmaceutical value chain, most believe their greatest impact will be in clinical development and in the way human trials are conducted. A biomarker is a test that provides information about suitable patients for treatment, the extent of the disease, and/or other important clinical information, such as potential toxicity. A biomarker can be a gene, a protein, a metabolite, or even the profile of an image in some form of scan. Biomarkers are used across the drug discovery and development chain. In discovery, they are used and sought after to define whether the drug is reaching its target site, reaching it in sufficient concentration, and having a biological effect. In preclinical development, they are used to answer safety and toxicology questions. Biomarkers can show that new drugs penetrate the tissue of interest, hit their intended targets, and produce the expected change in the biological process of interest. Biomarkers can help select the proper dosage of a drug before a clinical trial, so that if the clinical trial is a failure, it is clear that the failure is caused by a failure in the drug hypothesis as opposed to an incorrect dosage. In development, where possible, biomarkers may direct the right patient into the right clinical trial, and may help predict outcomes.

Surrogate end points

A biomarker that the FDA feels has been validated as a predictor of a disease is a surrogate end point. Examples of surrogate end points are blood pressure readings for hypertension, low-density lipoprotein (LDL) readings for atherosclerosis, glycosalated hemoglobin (HBA1c) readings for diabetes, and liver enzymes for possible toxicity. The FDA accepts effect on surrogate end points as a true reading of the effect on the disease. Marketing approval may be granted based on the surrogate end point without lengthy trials showing effect on mortality with the disease. This is only possible because previous molecules have shown a strong correlation between effect on the surrogate end point and the disease in prospective, blinded, many-year clinical efforts.

Human biology is being better understood every day, and with this understanding comes the hope that we shall know the molecular basis of disease. If we can, then we can theoretically test for a particular and specific abnormality, and be rid of the empiricism that causes clinical trials to be done on thousands of people. Instead of recruiting

Design:
- Over 100 patients assigned to three groups
- 3-month follow-up

Therapy:
- LDL and HDL compared for three statins: Baycol, Pravachol, and Lipitor

Method:
- Identify genetic markers (HAP™)in multiple genes and correlate to drug response and definitions of active population

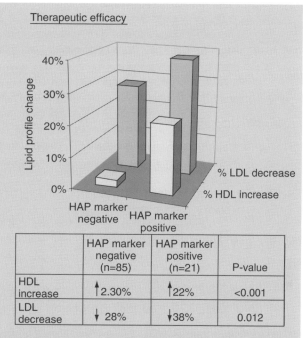

Therapeutic efficacy

	HAP marker negative (n=85)	HAP marker positive (n=21)	P-value
HDL increase	↑2.30%	↑22%	<0.001
LDL decrease	↓ 28%	↓38%	0.012

Figure 2.21 Personalised medicine: genaissance example.

"all-comers," perhaps the day will come when we can test for admission, select just those patients who will benefit, and show the drug's profile in precisely the appropriate population. This is an appealing paradigm for clinical medicine and for drug development. The promise is to heighten efficacy and minimize adverse events for patients. It is even being realized in specific diseases and specific therapies, such as Gleevec for chronic myelogenous leukemia. Oncology, in most cases a molecular disease, has great promise to be changed by such agents and capabilities.

Successes and challenges

Example   Gleevec for chronic myelogenous leukemia (CML). This is one of the more powerful examples of the potential to understand biology and to affect human suffering. CML is an example of a disease where science actually fully understands the molecular basis causing the disease. A translocation between two chromosomes known as the Philadelphia chromosome is the basis of the disease. There are highly specific tests to determine the presence of the Philadelphia chromosome, which equals a positive diagnosis of CML. In some patients, Gleevec has the ability to cause the Philadelphia chromosome translocation to completely disappear, and this is strongly correlated with length of disease-free survival in that patient. From a biomarker perspective, in CML there is a specific test that determines disease diagnosis, and there are predictive markers (response to Gleevec) that determine patient prognosis.

But many other diseases are far more difficult. In some cases the molecular abnormalities are small variations across dozens of genes, or seem to take place downstream in protein interactions. In other diseases, biomarkers can help predict response, but therapeutic choices are too few to make the information very relevant. An example is the HAP marker from Genaissance. Those who are positive have a greater benefit from LDL lowering statins. For example, in figure 2.21, those who were HAP marker positive had a 22 percent increase in HDL and a 38 percent decrease in LDL – very good therapeutic changes. But those who were HAP marker negative had a 2 percent increase in HDL (nominal change) and a 28 percent decrease in LDL. Because of the beneficial LDL change, those who are negative to the test have enough benefit that they should probably still receive a statin. Therefore, what is the clinical benefit of the test? How different is it than a short course of statin therapy to see the individual patient response? As the therapies expand for arteriosclerosis, tests such as the HAP marker may find a place by helping to differentiate patients between therapies.

Imaging technologies are also providing hard end points to diseases that were hidden to us before. Intravascular imaging can show plaque volume in arteries over time; some scanning technologies can show tumor growth or shrinkage and potentially define changes in tumor biology.

These tools can reduce the number of patients required in clinical development by increasing the signal from better patient choice. However, the cost of additional testing per patient will increase the cost of each patient in the trial. For example, in some oncology trials, per patient cost may increase from $3,000 to $5,000 to pay for the extra testing of sera, tumor, and tissue off a base cost of typically $7,000 per patient. Recruitment has to decline by a third in order for clinical trial costs to even stay identical, much more for costs to decline.

Undoubtedly, we will see biomarkers and imaging technologies become more and more relevant. It is likely that scientists will make the associations between certain drug mechanisms and disease pathologies one at a time. The process will take longer and be more piecemeal than we would hope, but it holds great promise.

Phase III: definitive multicenter trials

Phase III is a major change in development psychology for the pharmaceutical company. Although there is still risk and the possibility of failure, being in phase III means you are betting on success and acting like you have a marketable drug. In many ways, phase III is really the first phase of commercialization rather than the last phase of development. The probability of success after a positive phase II experience with a drug is usually above 60 percent, and it is finally more likely that the drug will make it to market than not.

This phase is all about your customers – the regulatory bodies around the world, physicians and other healthcare professionals, and consumers. The phase III plan is the plan of execution to show them the proof of what this new drug can do, and to explore any areas of caution so that they are clearly understood to practitioners and consumers. Phase III will often contain head-to-head studies versus current standards of care, so that customers can understand what benefits they will have with the new drug, and where they might need to be careful or more closely monitor the new therapy. What phase III gains in enhanced probability of success it gives away in sheer cost. Generally, the costs of clinical development will be in an order of magnitude that is higher in phase III than it was in phase II. This is required in order to achieve the numbers of patients required for statistical significance, and to support the different comparator arms of these studies. Head-to-head studies are clinical studies where the patients in the study receive different competitive drugs or the new drug. Each arm of the study (comparator arm) is a group of patients receiving one of the drug regimens. At completion, the new drug can be directly compared to the other drug regimens with a high degree of statistical confidence, hence the "head-to-head" terminology.

Preregistration

After the last patent has been seen for the last visit of the phase III studies, all clinical analysis and write-up has to be performed. This is combined with all other aspects of preclinical, process, and product development, and is submitted to the regulatory bodies in a New Drug Application (NDA). There is a great deal of work in preparing the submission and in making ready to answer all the reasonable questions expected from the regulatory agency. Submissions today are typically electronic and require integrated software, search engines, and statistical packages. Computers on which the data reside have to be guaranteed to be "in control," and the source data to be accurate and secure. The FDA has copious regulations on what being "in control" means. A general description is that this means the NDA sponsor can show that all data on the trial could not be altered, that everything has been checked, locked down, and is as secure and unchanged as if it had been written on paper, signed, dated, and locked up at the independent investigator site.

Registration

Each nation's regulatory body has a slightly different approach. In the USA, the FDA will accept or reject an NDA submission within ninety days. Once accepted, the FDA will give the submission a priority based on the medical need seen for the therapy. FDA experts will study the submission for typically six to twelve months. After this time, they are likely to pull together an advisory committee of physician scientists prominent in the study of the target disease. The advisory committee will meet toward the end of the registration period and receive a presentation from the inventor company and from the FDA about the drug. The committee members vote on approval, and there is a high correlation between their vote and the agency's final position.

Generally the FDA will conduct preapproval inspections at the key plant sites for manufacture of the product. If the committee is positive on the new drug, and the agency feels its concerns (clinical, technical, and manufacturing) have been generally met, it may issue an approvable letter as opposed to a "not approvable letter." The approvable letter states the drug is approvable (but has not yet been approved), subject to a list of concerns that the agency has. The FDA may wish to have label revisions, indication revisions, additional warnings, additional inspections of facilities or trial data, and other actions. Post 2000 the FDA has also issued approvable letters that request additional trials for the drug. If additional clinical trials are not requested, usually two to five months of negotiations between the company and the FDA ensue, and if the FDA's concerns are met, then approval may be granted. If clinical trials or major manufacturing changes are requested, several years could ensue between approvable and approved letter. Whatever the length of time, these final discussions between approvable and approved can often have very significant impacts on the initial sales and use of the drug.

In 2004 the FDA considered a revision of the approvable letter and approved letter process to a "complete response letter" process.[19] Complete response letters would combine input from all branches of the agency and classify the letters into Class 1 or Class 2 resubmissions. Class 1 resubmissions would be minor changes that could be accomplished in a few months, while Class 2 resubmissions would be everything that is greater.

Phase IV studies

Phase IV studies are clinical trials that begin after regulatory approval has been granted. The purpose of phase IV is to answer important questions to practicing clinicians that go beyond the primary interests of the regulators. Phase IV studies are usually head-to-head comparisons with competitive drugs, and are designed to prove superiority in an attribute of the drug important to stakeholders in the marketplace. These studies can also more fully test for economic benefits, such as advantages in fewer sick days for patients, a quicker return to work, fewer ancillary therapies or high-cost episodes (emergency room visits, etc.). Some phase IV studies are enormous undertakings, which test long-term differences in outcomes. For example, Eli Lilly has had five-year trials of Evista (raloxefine) ongoing, which examine Evista's role in fracture reduction, breast cancer prevention, and cardio-vascular health. Other phase IV trials might be small investigator studies designed to test a hypothesis of interest to the investigator, or to try to optimize dosing regimes, or to explore subpopulations of patients.

The challenge of affordable and innovative medicines

Problem statement

Over the last three decades the drug discovery process has continued to be more expensive and just as, maybe even more, risky. Pharmaceutical R&D is highly variable and mostly unproductive. The enormous challenge facing the industry is how to make this process more cost-effective and yet still deliver the march of innovation that is the envy of the world.

The fact is that pharmaceutical discovery, development, manufacturing, and marketing are no more efficient today than they were twenty-five years ago. Why is this? Efficiency has been sacrificed to tackle tougher and more arduous problems, and to better refine the understanding of the molecule when and if it makes it to market.

For example, twenty-five years ago Eli Lilly was a company with an animal insulin extraction and purification business, an antibiotic business, and some additional therapies. The antibiotic business virtually disappeared over time, because making new antibiotics became relatively easy and was therefore relatively unrewarding. It was supplanted by a neuroscience business that was more novel, with higher risk, but also more rewarding. The animal insulin extraction and purification business morphed in a biotechnology fermenta-tion and purification business, and then into a sophisticated protein modification and discovery business.

In the same time frame, human biological science has moved from early understandings of cell surface receptor biology, to protein biology, intracel-lular signaling biology, and DNA/RNA biology. The challenges of working at the boundaries of knowledge and smaller and smaller atomic worlds are why the time lines remain unchanged and discoveries do not become less risky.

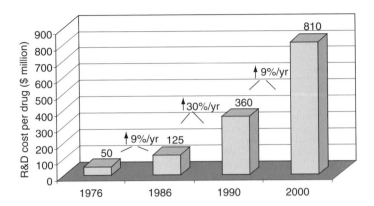

Figure 2.22   Drug development cost.

Source: US Congress, Office of Technology Assessment, Pharmaceutical R&D and KMR
Pharmaceutical R&D Benchmarking 2001
Notes: Includes both wet well and dry well costs.
Growth rates are CAGR.

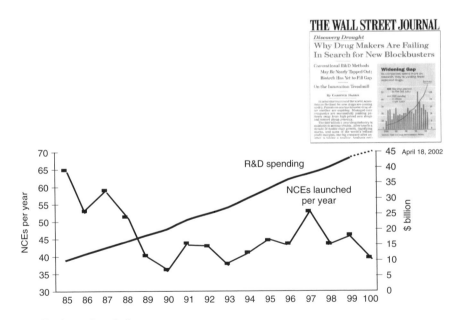

Figure 2.23   The innovation challenge.

Source: IMS Health, Pricewaterhouse Coopers 2000.

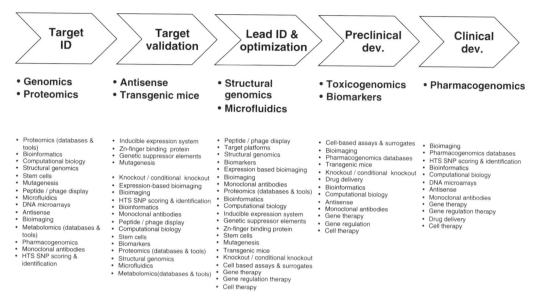

Figure 2.24   Technology applied to drug development.

The tools of the discovery researcher have increased, but so has the overall cost of deploying them. For example, the basic discovery paradigm, the structure–activity relationship, is now automated to allow for the testing of a million compounds against one industrialized assay in a day with robotics and microfluidics. The *per compound* screening cost has dropped dramatically. This cost differential allows for more screening but does not translate into cheaper research costs.

In development, the scientific standards involved in going to the next phase step up as our knowledge of potential pitfalls expands. Development has to be a very serial process – phase I and phase II cannot be done concurrently. There is hope that the ability to correlate biological changes with disease results through biomarkers, diagnostics, and imaging will provide benefit. The ultimate biomarker is the FDA's surrogate end point. Very few exist today, but when they do, they can be very powerful. These end points are able to reduce by as much as five years some registration time lines, because without them, mortality studies would be required to prove efficacy.

Biological understanding and productivity

The key to meeting the above challenge is to have the biological understanding to make better informed choices and then to run a development process that is efficient at its portfolio choices stage. The biological under-standing that we now have is an enormous leap from prior years. But still, what is not understood about the human body and how it functions is far greater than what is understood. The biological system we are exploring is extremely complex. Additionally, the tools that we have to understand it with are less than adequate to the challenge, as sophisticated as they may be. On the "spectrum of understanding" we sit midway between empiricism (finding out by trial and error) and engineering. Compare this to aviation, and the enormous body of knowledge that allows us to simulate with great accuracy the variables of flight. Our lack of biological understanding results in low productivity and high variability in pharmaceutical research and develop-ment compared with many other human endeavors.

Key levers of productivity–success rates in development clinical trials, and total time for drug research and development (synthesis to approval) – are moving in the wrong direction. Clinical trials are becoming more complex and data-intensive, as a result of (a) more competition for patients globally, (b) more tests and medical procedures, and (c) greater focus on health outcomes to meet payer needs.[20] Although the promise of biomarkers may push this in a favorable direction, for most products this has yet to happen. Time lines are increasing, not diminishing, as the industry takes on more difficult diseases with more novel targets. One study noted that in 1990 the average pharmaceutical target had a hundred references in the scientific literature.[21] Today eight references are typical.

What can be done? Doing the process better, through the development of higher biological understanding and creating superior biomarkers and ima-ging techniques, may allow better and quicker choices to find the best candidates for a given therapy. Ways need to be found to pull the risk forward and fast fail in development. With modeling technologies that allow for fast-fail approaches, the attrition rate at each stage of development could be enhanced. The result could be a strong benefit over all stages and multiple projects. Figure 2.26 shows how "fast-fail" techniques could theoretically increase early failure and therefore decrease late and expensive failures – allowing greater system efficiency. Figure 2.27 shows a Monte Carlo simu-lation of two companies, each with a pipeline of twenty compounds. Running the analysis for a thirty-year time frame and comparing usual development approaches to a "fast-fail" approach shows a faster time to first submission and more products emerging from the "fast-fail" company than from the company utilizing the typical development approach. In essence, this suggests that anything that can be done to test the research

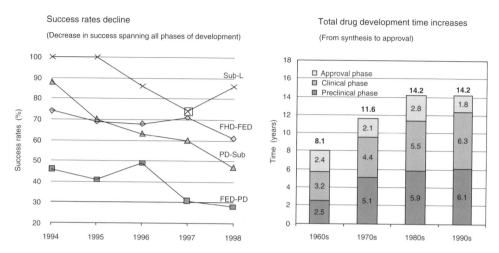

Figure 2.25 Key innovation levers are moving in the wrong direction.

Notes: Sub-L: NDA submission to lead found

FHD-FED: First human dose to first efficacy dose (Phase I start to Phase II start)

PD-Sub: Product decision to submission (Phase III start to NDA submission)

FED-PD: First efficacy dose to product decision (Phase II start to Phase III start)

Sources: Centre for Medicines Research International, "Challenging Issues for the Future of the Pharmaceutical Industry: Pharmaceutical Investment and Output in 2000," August 2001, available at http://www.cmr.org, publication; J. A Dimasi, "New Drug Development in the United States 1963–1999," *Clinical Pharmacology & Therapeutics* 69(5) (May 2001): 286–295.

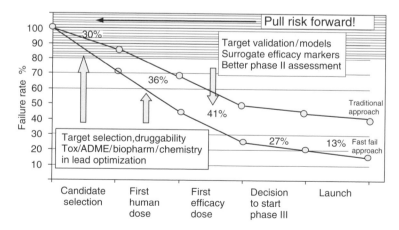

Figure 2.26 Drug candidate attrition: pull risk forward.

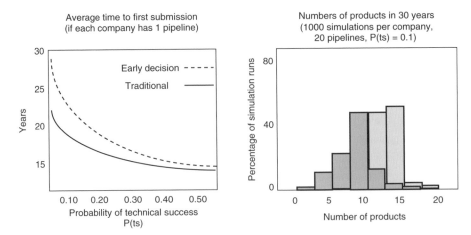

Figure 2.27   Fast fails: comparison of two companies (early decision and traditional development).

hypothesis as quickly and as early as possible has tremendous cost savings for pharmaceutical discovery.

Organizational structure

One of the major challenges for a modern pharmaceutical company comes from the need to be flexible and able to integrate a vast number of disciplines and expertise into the discovery and development process. A company needs experts in disease and discovery involved in its own research programs, but these experts also need the flexibility to switch to alliances around external programs if those programs are superior. It is a challenge to do the best discovery, wherever it is located, and to harness the best technologies for a given effort, whether they are protein- or small-molecule-oriented.

Have organizational structures fully kept up with technology innovation in the modern pharmaceutical company? This may be one of the biggest issues facing the largest companies that have come together through merger and acquisition activity. The inability to have a continuous steady stream of work come from research requires a company to be flexible. In addition, in today's skeptical clinical trial climate, having arm's-length relationships with third parties who independently do the clinical trials and report on the trial outcomes enhances the credibility of the results.

One important trend is the growing cross-functional team approach many pharmaceutical companies are using. Teams may be organized by phase of drug development and have differing configurations for each phase. Also, technology advancements have made it easier for networked organizations to collaborate on projects across corporate entities and geography. Taking advantage of networks for surge capacity, and owning only basal capacity, allows a company to leverage its asset basis more and thereby increase its efficiency. Building a culture that is flexible, quick to adapt, able to succeed at risk-taking – in short, a learning organization that embraces change, will be a key organizational advantage in the pharmaceutical business.

An important current example is that of translational medicine. This focuses on diseases where the biology is known, and *"discovery clinical"* can quickly focus resources to explore initial hypotheses of researchers, biomarker development, and clinical validation to evaluate new drug candidates in the early clinical and preclinical stages.

Manufacturing and process development

Introduction

Recently, manufacturing has been "in the spotlight" for the pharmaceutical sector. Typically, the perception had been that sales and marketing drive top-line growth and deliver the short-term financial return for the firm, while robust pipelines determined by R&D productivity ensure sustainable long-term growth. To a large extent, this strategy has been rational and effective and there are often good reasons why manufacturing should take a backseat to these two critical functions.

However, a closer look reveals that manufacturing often accounts for one-third of a company's human resources and consumes more expenses than R&D. Even though no major pharmaceutical company has stated publicly that building its core competencies around manufacturing is a key priority, effective manufacturing operations may go a long way to optimize the performance of a pharmaceutical company.

Events continue to highlight the importance of manufacturing management. First, the FDA has reinvigorated its efforts on current Good Manufacturing Practices (cGMP) compliance, and as a result several major US pharmaceutical companies have either received consent decrees or have been forced to hold back key product launches. This has led to huge fines (such as $0.5 billion to Schering Plough) and/or loss of the revenue that could have been realized. Second, in some situations, misjudgment of capacity requirements to ensuing demand has resulted in product shortages. The company suffers lost revenue, diminished customer confidence, and lower market share.

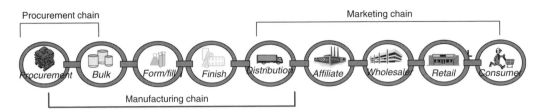

Figure 2.28 Pharmaceutical supply chain.

The value chain within manufacturing

How far does the manufacturing operation span? It entails both making the medicine and supplying the medicine.

Making the medicine

There are two major phases in "making the medicine" – bulk manufacturing and form/fill/finishing (F/F/F).

Bulk manufacturing

Active pharmaceutical ingredient (API) is manufactured in bulk through a series of chemical or biological reactions. In this phase, the operation is typically technology-driven. Yet different companies take quite different approaches to bulk manufacturing. Bristol Myers Squibb outsources their entire bulk operation. Although this approach has the advantage of avoiding capital investment and keeping a lean workforce, it also adversely impacts on cost of goods sold (COGS) and overall profit margins, especially since tax benefits often link to the bulk operation.[22] AstraZeneca engages in internal manufacturing operations only to the last few steps of bulk synthesis, in order to capture the tax benefit. Typically, top operational priorities for bulk manufacturing are increasing yield, maximizing asset utilization, and minimizing any and all adverse health, safety, and environment impacts.

Form/fill/finishing (F/F/F)

APIs will be further processed at F/F/F sites. For example, for tablets, excipients such as starches and lactose will be added to the bulk chemical and coated, compressed, and dispensed in pills, which will be subsequently packaged in bottles (the most common form in the USA) or blisters (each tablet individually sealed) for world markets. Excipients help to process APIs more efficiently (through lubrication, manageable sizes, etc.) and also enhance drugs' pharmacokinetics – particularly for absorption and distribution. In the F/F/F phase of the operation, complexity rather than technology is the major concern. Just imagine a single product made in three different strengths and supplied to one hundred countries with different packages. The explosion of the number of SKUs (stock-keeping units or individual package presentations) for the one product will demand efficient operations management at a site.

Also, given the close interaction with local regulatory agencies and distributors of a site, customer service toward these stakeholders becomes a key aspect. F/F/F sites are typically not outsourced for pharmaceutical companies. This is because these facilities control the final appearance and packaging of the product, and because many of these facilities may figure in pricing discussions for new pharmaceuticals. It is common for countries with a national healthcare system that set a reimbursable price to favorably consider the employment and facilities that a pharmaceutical company has in the country when determining what price they will grant for reimbursement. Since F/F/F sites are less complex and more flexible, they are more likely to be dually used in this way.

Supplying the medicine

Medicine is provided to patients through channels depending on its therapeutic use and administration method. For instance, hospital drugs (intravenous infusion, etc.) are typically supplied directly to healthcare providers from the manufacturer. On the other hand, retail drugs such as tablets and capsules will go through wholesalers and pharmacies before patients receive them. Due to the low profit margin associated with the drug distribution business, pharmaceutical companies typically see little benefit in vertical integration. Many drug distribution companies make their money financially, working with capital float, while their physical distribution business essentially breaks even. Given this very specialized business, it is rare for a pharmaceutical company to own retail distribution operations. It should be noted that the inventory management strategy for pharmaceutical companies is quite different for the two types of medicine. For retail drugs, because of the number of "middlemen" in the system, there is more inventory in the supply chain. Supply and demand disequilibria caused by surge demand, supply shortages, or arbitraging possible price increases, can be absorbed more readily. The buffer for hospital drugs is often significantly less, forcing manufacturers to carry more inventories.

What determines a reliable pharmaceutical supplier? Three key factors can influence customer service responsiveness:

1. *Manufacturing performance*   A company with production, scheduling, and quality problems could rarely be a dependable supplier.
2. *System integration*   System compatibility and integration with wholesalers and retailers allow you to have real time demand signals that will synchronize your production plan with customer needs.
3. *Customer-focused culture*   Due to the criticality of the products pharmaceutical companies provide, it is essential to have a culture of urgency and responsiveness. A good manufacturing plant always pushes to satisfy customers both internally and externally.

Key inputs that determine manufacturing excellence

Three key external variables have a significant impact on manufacturing operations: forecast accuracy, process robustness, and compound potency.

Forecast accuracy

Forecast accuracy influences medicine supply in both the long term and the short term. Sales and manufacturing operations planning is the process that matches demand and supply. If the near-term forecast for sales is far from the actual need, both manufacturing operations and the rest of the company will be stressed trying to deal with the result.

Underforecasting a product's potential may cause rationing of the market to occur. Some patients may not receive potentially life-saving drugs, or may be started but then continued on competitors' medicines. Peak market share will suffer. Overforecasting a product's true demand causes a company to carry too much inventory, which hurts the balance sheet by chewing up working capital, and typically increases variances, which deteriorate COGS, driving down earnings.

An accurate long-term forecast will drive appropriate capacity planning. Since the lead time of manufacturing facility delivery is typically long (between two and five years), it is critical to have a relatively accurate demand picture. Immunex (later acquired by Amgen) and Wyeth underestimated the demand for Enbrel, a breakthrough rheumatoid arthritis drug. As a result, a significant portion of Enbrel's market opportunity was compromised. This opened the door for greater market share to competitors, such as JNJ/Centacor's Remicade and Abbott/Knoll's Humira, and had a long-term impact on the anti-TNF alpha Rheumatoid Arthritis market segment. The same situation also happened to Eli Lilly's insulin product Humalog, slowing the conversion from Humalin to Humalog in the United States.

Compound potency

Compound potency also influences manufacturing operation and economics. For instance, antibiotics often require over 500 mg/day of therapy (DOT). On the other hand, small molecule compounds such as cardiovascular and neuroscience drugs are typically in the range of 1–50 mg/DOT. Thus, in order to serve a patient's need for one-day therapy, manufacturing needs to produce ten to one hundred times more active ingredient for antibiotics. In combination with often not so favorable prices, the cost of goods sold for antibiotics could be as high as 40 percent.

Potency for a company's product portfolio tends to move up and down over time. This has as much to do with the natural serendipity associated with an innovation-driven discovery approach as to corporate pressure to bring pipeline products to market at a fastest pace. Sometimes these forces cause candidates to be selected that are not the compound with the best potency. Companies that pay close attention to optimizing the potency of their research compounds will find many advantages in the marketplace. This is because potency is a key determinant of cost and therefore eventually of profitability and marketing spend flexibility.

Process robustness

Some people believe that manufacturing is no more than an extension of the pilot study in development to a larger scale. It has been a common challenge in the industry to proceed in this fashion and not fund and research a robust manufacturing process that is capable and in control. "In control" is a concept that means all steps in the process are being monitored, producing expected results, and providing expected outputs. It also means that operations can prove that this is so to the relevant regulatory bodies. It is sometimes a challenge to keep operations in control because of the pressure of "speed to market," and also the lack of investor interest in spending extra money in an area taken for granted by many.

The development group in a pharmaceutical company too often does not have an opportunity to optimize their chemical or biological processes before handing the project over to manufacturing. In most pharmaceutical companies, R&D is two parts of the same function. Manufacturing typically is seen as a different function. Because of this, the development group and the manufacturing group often possess different scorecards and report to different senior executives. Many times, the best "bang for the buck" fix in product quality issues is to improve yield and gross margin. This is typically most effective when done in the process development stage. A careful calculation needs to be considered, because the earlier in development the process optimization is done, the more effective it is likely to be. But the earlier the process optimization, the more risky the effort will be because the molecule will have a smaller chance of ultimate success. Later stage fixes are substantially more costly than development fixes, but the relative success – and therefore the capacity needs of the molecule – is much clearer.

Current good manufacturing practices and compliance

The main objective of enforcing current good manufacturing practices (cGMP) on drug manufacturing and testing is to provide patients with a product that has equivalent identity, safety, strength, quality, and purity to the one used to establish the clinical database.[23] The FDA establishes cGMPs through regulations and guidance. It is the pharmaceutical companies' responsibility to set up and maintain quality systems to assure product quality. Despite its significance, many companies do not put corporate priorities on cGMP. For instance, the PhRMA 2000 Annual Survey shows a significant reduction of production and quality control personnel since 1980.[24] In 1980, 43 percent of domestic pharmaceutical sector employees were engaged in production and quality control activities, as opposed to 30 percent in 1990 and 26 percent in 1999. Part of the reduction results from equipment automation and process improvement; another part may be attributable to a lack of sufficient priority on the part of manufacturing. By comparison, marketing and sales employees increased from 23 percent to 34 percent during the same period. Since the late nineties the FDA has sent repeated loud messages to the industry. The FDA has typically used the approach of the Consent Decree as a severe method of bringing companies into compliance. The costs of a Consent Decree can be very large. They may include consultants, revamped systems, explicit fines, and many years of follow-up and scrutiny by the FDA. In 1999 Abbott suffered a fine of $100 million for quality system nonconformance, and total costs at Abbott from this Consent Decree have run much higher. It is estimated that the total cost of the 1993 Warner-Lambert (now part of Pfizer) Consent Decree, with an initial fine of $10 million, actually approaches $1 billion because of facility costs, delays, product terminations, and additional requirements.[25] A few of Lilly's new products, such as Cymbalta, were delayed in launch due to FDA findings of cGMP issues at its Indianapolis plants in 2001.

In light of these highly publicized FDA actions, pharmaceutical firms have started to emphasize regulatory compliance. Efforts have been put into process validation, equipment qualification, quality system design, operator and quality training, and documentation. Although these activities will help to fill gaps in the short run, they also make manufacturing more expensive and often even less efficient. Many companies have seen the cost of goods sold increase in recent quarters because of cGMP compliance issues. Coupled with worldwide price pressure on pharmaceuticals, this has caused some firms to suffer the pains of a profit squeeze.

A new approach

Visionary companies have begun to adopt another approach. First, cGMP compliance is by nature reactive as opposed to proactive (sometimes to the FDA's 483 observations – which are the agency's format for describing the significant deficiencies it has found). Also, cGMP compliance is often the minimum that needs to be done. The most important concept is to embed quality into daily operations and then to drive for continuous improvement. Specifically, firms need to focus on quality in design (in the process development stage), quality in product (making the products), and quality monitoring (customer feedback – particularly complaints). By fostering a culture of "quality starts from me," a company can establish a closed-loop quality system to drive continuous improvement. The real compliance is constantly being in a state of control. Processes are validated, equipment is qualified, and people are trained and competent. The FDA is working with PhRMA and a group of pharmaceutical companies to develop a science-based risk management approach to cGMP. The objective is to take the perspective of patients' health and with it to focus on control of critical points in the manufacturing process. This may generate a paradigm change in the future. The companies that are truly in a "state of control" will be at the forefront of manufacturing excellence in the future.

Biotechnology products

Biotechnology products are large-molecule drugs that include several different classes, such as therapeutic proteins, antibodies, peptides, and DNA and RNA molecules. These products receive their name because most of them have been discovered and marketed by biotechnology companies. However, one of the most "ancient" and well-known biotech products is insulin. Typically, biotech products are more expensive to make. This is because the bulk process relies on cells' biological reaction to produce a large quantity of API and the form/fill operation requires a sterile (no microorganisms) operational environment. However, helped by higher prices, and often high potency, the gross margin of these products is typically very attractive.

There are multiple cell systems and platforms to manufacture biotech products, such as bacterial (e.g., e. coli), fungal (e.g., yeast), mammalian cell, and other hybrid systems. The platform chosen and the process development invested will have a significant impact on the overall manufacturing efficiency and COGS for a given molecule. In addition, the first biotechnology products were so unique that dedicated plant capacity had to be built to make them (one plant, one product). A dedicated facility for large molecules could cost hundreds of millions of dollars in capital investment – and be required to be built before regulatory approval. A late stage clinical development failure could translate into a significant asset write-off. Today, with the help of genomics research and the advancement of biotechnologies (such as humanized antibodies), the industry is starting to see a portfolio of biotechnology molecules in the development pipeline. Pharmaceutical companies have begun to formulate strategies to build flexible platforms that may be used for multiple products. For example, a yeast platform facility could be used for human therapeutic proteins, and mammalian cell systems might be ideal for multiple antibody products and provide significant cost savings over other approaches.

Commercialization

Marketing across the value chain

Marketing can help an organization throughout the entire value chain. The molecule determines the potential of the medication, but marketing "unlocks" the potential. First, in picking biological targets for disease, marketing can inform discovery on what clinicians and patients are most looking for over current therapies and those in development. Efforts that show where the needs exist in the marketplace and where pharmaceuticals can provide value-added benefits to current treatment practices could point discovery research in the areas most viable. At candidate selection, knowledge of what customers most want may help researchers pick among molecules to decide on their lead candidate. During early clinical work, clinicians can best understand what clinical protocols will both inform them about the candidate and those that will be the most meaningful to opinion-leading investigators. All of this is the role of new product planning (NPP). NPP will also structure many of the communication forums with opinion leaders during early development, and will try to develop broad interest in the clinical community about the new drug.

After a pivotal and successful phase II trial, prelaunch marketing will start. This involves input into the phase III clinical plan to help that effort answer key questions of clinicians around the world as well as thought leaders and regulators. Marketing will also begin to communicate with all stakeholders about the development program in order to understand the need for symposia, presentations on the evolving clinical profile of the drug, the need and design of compassionate use programs, medical education for the relevant therapeutic area, health economic and managed care requirements for reimbursement, and pricing studies to try to understand the potential value of the medication and the determinants of that value. Market research works to understand appropriate commercial expectations in sales, and financial research develops the likely cost and expense picture for the product.

The focus on blockbusters

For the majority of products a pharmaceutical company launches, the product will be a "base hit" in baseball terms. Most products do not become blockbusters simply because along the long journey from conception to market the bright concept in the laboratory becomes marginalized by issues discovered in development. A side effect is found or efficacy is less than hoped for, or only a segment of the diseased population responds to the therapy. These drugs still provide help for patients and are needed, and are usually launched with all the preparation of larger products, but on a smaller budget. Occasionally, the drug does not have these problems and looks like it can meet the vision of the discovery scientist. Then, maybe, it is a blockbuster.

Why is the industry so fixated on blockbusters? It is because so much cost and expense is involved in bringing a product to market, and in the "dry holes" or nonproductive research and development that has to be done in

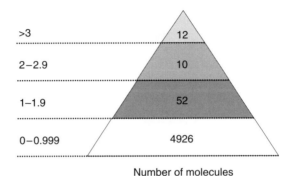

Figure 2.29   Top 5,000 molecules by 2001 revenue ($ billion).

Source: IMS: Sergeant Database.

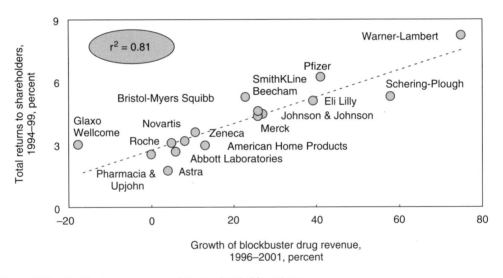

Figure 2.30   Blockbuster revenue correlates to shareholder returns.

Source: Sumit Agarwal *et al.,* "Unlocking the Value in Big Pharma," *McKinsey Quarterly* 2 (2001).

order to find a productive product. It takes a blockbuster (a product that sells $1 billion or more per year) to make money. That is why studies of the industry continue to show a strong correlation between blockbuster sales and shareholder return.[26]

If it might be a blockbuster, then things are going to become expensive. To find out if a drug is a blockbuster, it will take $1–1.5 billion in prelaunch and

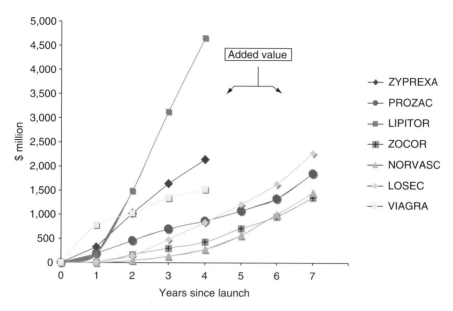

Figure 2.31   Increasing rewards from new launch standards.

Source: IMS Health, 2001.

two-year postlaunch marketing and sales expenses. The reason for this is that large products have the potential to dramatically affect the business. By better communicating with customers and other stakeholders in order to help them understand how and when to use the product, you may be able to change the speed of uptake of the product and perhaps even its total eventual utility in the market. Lipitor and Zyprexa have demonstrated this through a steeper launch curve than previous blockbusters.

But to have a chance at that kind of launch success, prelaunch and early postlaunch activities are required. These activities must be appropriate from the viewpoint of all stakeholders – clinicians, regulators, and disease sufferers. And such near-to-launch activities are higher risk than activities undertaken two or more years postlaunch, because there is little or no sales feedback to tell if the effort will be rewarded and if stakeholders are responding. So efforts begin early to prepare the market for as successful a product introduction as the utility of the molecule allows.

Over 20 percent of marketing expenses may be prelaunch expenses across the three years of one year before launch and two years after launch – the high-risk period. Once the product is launched, sales representative promotion and direct-to-consumer promotion of the product may begin. Typically,

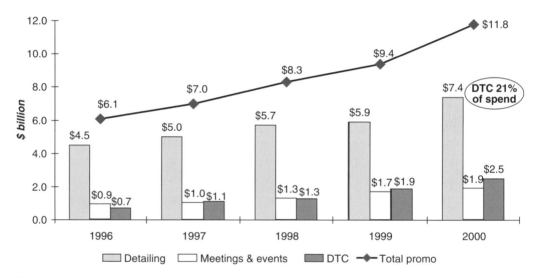

Marketing spend for blockbusters

Over 20% of spending prior to launch

Categories	Prelaunch*	Postlaunch*
Patients	$90	$445
Physicians	17	290
Clinical trials	80	100
Payors	33	60
Market research	40	40
Advocates	20	50
Advisory boards	10	15
Total	**$300**	**$1,000**

Figure 2.32 Spending begins early and aggressively.

Source: McKinsey & Company.
*3 year: 1 year pre-Launch, 2 years post-Launch

Figure 2.33 Total pharmaceutical promotional spend.

Source: Scott Levin.

sales representative efforts are complemented with educational symposia, information booths and presentations at scientific and clinical meetings, journal advertising and communications aimed at informing consumers about the new choice that exists for sufferers of the relevant disease.

Adopting an innovation in the pharmaceutical sector is complex. A patient must be motivated to seek an appointment with a physician, the physician needs to be able to diagnose the condition successfully, and the patient and the physician must agree on a treatment plan, which is improved because of the new drug innovation. Then the patient has to carry that prescription to a separate store, decide to have it filled, and of course the store has to have the drug in order to dispense it. At each one of these decision points, patients who would benefit from the therapy are lost.

Communicating with customers

The industry has been experimenting with new technologies to enhance communication with key stakeholders and customers. Multichannel access (e.g., email, call centers, websites), customer relationship management (CRM), and e-detailing are all helping to make these efforts more effective and efficient.

The sales organization

Traditionally, the primary means of communication about branded pharmaceuticals, and the most expensive method, has been one-to-one selling by pharmaceutical sales representatives ("detail reps"). Companies have generally augmented their sales forces' efforts by spending on journal advertisements and educational symposia. But the industry has had a near universal belief that the number and frequency of "details," or selling encounters with physicians, is the primary driver of sales growth. This has resulted in an "arms race" among companies competing to deliver the highest "share of voice" for their products within the therapeutic categories in which they compete. As a result, the number of "detail reps" in the US doubled between 1995 and 2000, rising from 37,000 to 75,000, and this expansion has persisted.

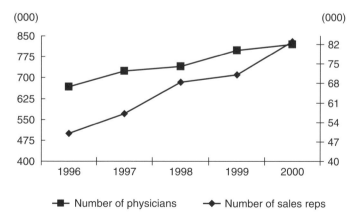

Figure 2.34 US sales representatives "arms race."

In the 2002–04 time period sales organizations appear to have leveled out, with companies focusing more on targeting the right physician, making sure the sales representative–physician interaction is one that is effective and supportive, and seeing the physician with a frequency such that the message is remembered. For sales representatives, Lilly utilizes the "sales productivity process" to help representatives focus on the key variables of selling: talk to the right doctor, with information of interest and important medical content, and with a frequency that appropriately reinforces your message.

Multichannel access to customers

With the emergence of technology-based alternative means of communicating with physicians and other prescribing influencers, many pharmaceutical companies have experimented with supplementing, or replacing, the sales person's details with invitations to access websites and call centers for answers to commonly asked questions concerning a company's drugs. These alternative channels allow important questions to be addressed in a more timely fashion than via monthly or bimonthly representative visits. For high-prescribing or highly influential physicians, access to websites that provide more detailed information or that guarantee that individual questions are answered by the company's own medical experts have been offered. These special customers receive passwords that allow them to access these and other medically appropriate, value-added services. Conversely, for low-prescribing physicians who do not represent enough potential business to be visited regularly by an expensive sales representative, a website supplemented by periodic e-mails can be a highly cost-efficient way to maintain a modest but beneficial relationship with the customer.

Customer relationship management

The process of using customer information (including such data as their prescribing behavior, their preferences among communication channels, and their responses to prior marketing messages), analyzing this information to segment the customers by behaviors and beliefs, and developing and implementing targeted communications (created to motivate each discrete segment to change, especially increase, their prescribing behaviors), is called customer relationship management (CRM). The pharmaceutical sector has borrowed from the experiences of the financial services industry in attempting to differentiate its customer base according to value, and then to focus the highest-impact programs toward those customers who are likely to respond in the most positive way.

Unfortunately, the acronym CRM has acquired a highly negative connotation among pharmaceutical companies, due to its adoption by technology vendors and consulting firms to sell expensive information technology systems that pledge to transform any company into a closely integrated and efficient marketing machine. That machine supposedly stores and links all customers' contacts, evaluates promotion response rates, and automatically delivers personalized messages to each customer when and where they wish to receive it. The reality is that technology is not the key to channel management and CRM. It is changing the behavior of each employee that "touches" the customer in his or her job that is the essential first and most difficult step along the CRM journey to success. What good is it to purchase a computer-based system that connects a company's call center operators with the sales force, if the sales representatives do not input accurate information on their physicians (such as address, medical specialty, or visit frequency), or do not bother to follow up on a promise made to the customer by the call center (for example, to have product samples delivered at the physician's request)? The potential of CRM to better serve the needs of each customer is significant, but the barriers to successful implementation require a thorough change management program to ensure the employees affected see the value of, and therefore contribute to, the new integrated approach.

E-detailing

Other methods designed to gain access to physician customers more efficiently than via in-person selling include e-detailing, telephone detailing, and video detailing. Each of these methods involves obtaining a physician's agreement to participate in a detail at a time and place of his or her preference. E-detailing involves a physician logging in to a website, or being directed to a website via an e-mail, and working through an audiovisual presentation, supplemented by the opportunity to ask questions. This can be done at any time that is convenient to the doctor. E-detailing does not require the pharmaceutical company to have a sales representative involved at the time of the physician's activity. Telephone and video detailing, however, require scheduling a mutually satisfactory time in order to conduct a live interaction between a company's representative and a physician. Because visual aids can be helpful in communicating scientific information, a company may send out through ordinary mail or e-mail a set of promotional literature to be used during the telephone call. An advantage of the video detail is that the promotional material can be shown on the screen, with another advantage being the opportunity to establish a "face-to-face"

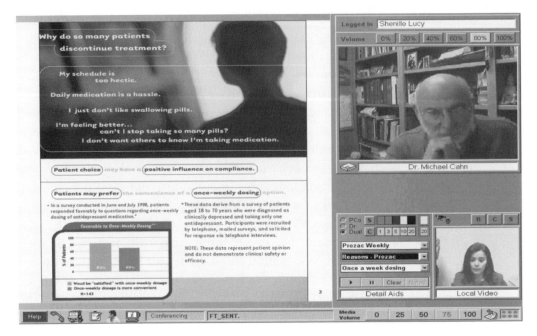

Figure 2.35   E-detailing.

rapport, similar to the rapport that can be established by a sales representative visiting the office. A typical telephone or video detail can last 8–10 minutes, and usually commands the customer's full attention.

Contrast this with the sales representative that attempts to call on a busy doctor during working hours – and may receive only thirty seconds of time, and not always with the customer's undivided attention. Therefore, there can be both quality and the cost-effectiveness advantages to these alternative selling methods.

Requirement: coordinated implementation, implementation, implementation

Once on the market, operations and coordination of all parts of the marketing and selling functions of the business need to work together and to consistently refine their efforts with new information on where customers are having success or challenges with a new therapy. It becomes all about implementation, planning based on new learning, and redirecting marketing based on the new insights received from stakeholders and customers. Affiliates, corporate staff, sales representatives, and marketers need to see themselves as one team and should communicate well and frequently.

Strategic alliances and mergers & acquisitions

Pharmaceutical portfolios: the internal development approach

All businesses would like to see a steady growth in business and opportunities that provides both a smooth increase in dividends over time and steady progress in achieving business and financial goals. Yet rarely is it the case that this can be done. For pharmaceuticals, no matter how hard the companies in the industry try to have a steady stream of innovation in the "pipeline," pharmaceutical R&D is just too risky and too long to make that a common reality.

Can it really be a smooth-flowing pipeline?

The reason that discovery will never be smoothly and continuously delivered to market are: (a) drug fallout occurs all along the discovery and development time line; (b) the later drug fallout occurs, the less a company can compensate for that fallout; and (c) even runs of success, where higher probabilities of success occur, exacerbate the problem. Of course, when runs of low success projects occur, it clearly hurts the ability to deliver innovation. But high success hurts smooth and continuous delivery as well, because later development is very expensive, and this high late stage burn rate causes a company to constrain early development and discovery in order to pay for the extra late stage burden, and then cyclicality is increased. In the future, those constraints will eventually cause a drop in development project load.

The discovery and development process is a long one. Each project is different, but most NCEs marketed today were probably in the neighborhood of 5,000 days or more from conception to global launch. Should a development project fail, the later it is in development the greater the problem it creates. First, the resources expended accelerate as clinical testing moves into phase III. Hence, a bigger financial dry hole has to be managed. Second, the tougher it is to substitute a second project "waiting in the wings" for the discontinued project. A new discovery lead going into preclinical testing will not fit the time line needed to compensate for a failed phase III development project. The only way to cushion the blow from these inevitable failures internally is to frontload the system with additional opportunities at every level: have more viable phase II candidates than are taken into phase III, have more viable phase I candidates than are taken into phase II, and so forth on

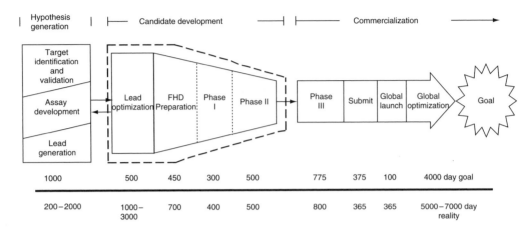

Figure 2.36   Cycle times.

down the line. This way, it is possible to reach back just one level in order to start a new opportunity.

The role of risk

In addition to the concern over flow of projects there is the concern of risk. Pharmaceutical projects can vary greatly in risk. If a project is around a new, first-in-class mechanism of action, it may have great potential, but it will also have great risk. This will be especially true if the development path is also very risky. One development path can be where there are no preclinical models that are predictive of success in the disease; risk will not be greatly reduced until a phase II pivotal trial is successfully completed. On the other hand, projects that are best-in-class but which follow other first-in-class products may be much less risky in development and commercialization. Lipitor, for example, benefited from previous statin drug efforts to understand and educate patients and healthcare professionals about lowering LDL cholesterol and its benefits. Lipitor could simply show better cholesterol lowering, and have that communicate as a powerful message. Often, good preclinical animal models have a high degree of predictive value in these diseases, thereby lessening risk in development.

For a portfolio, it is important to monitor the mix risk of the different projects in their development and commercial uncertainties. Too many "moon shots" and no "second and better" projects can exacerbate the potential of a rocky future, as the probabilities play out over time. Commercial uncertainty flows from the product archetype of the project. Eli Lilly classifies

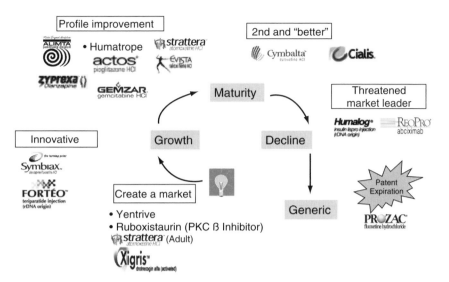

Figure 2.37   Lilly's product archetypes.

products as to whether, among other things, they are a new concept in therapy or a "create a market" product, a new approach or mechanism in a disease with existing treatments, an "innovative" product, a product with an "improved profile" or a second but better product, both which are potentially best in class, or after a product is on the market and has aged, a threatened market leader or generically available product.

By optimizing the internal portfolio a company can efficiently use its resources in the most impactful way. NCEs need to be optimized, but also new indications for existing products and new line extensions (formulations). All of these can be developed either (a) typically with the normal solid approach, (b) with an accelerated or "heavyweight" approach, (c) with a skinny, "no frills" approach, or (d) internal development can end and the product can be outpartnered for adoption. The best portfolio approach will maximize return to the firm, provide for a continuous flow of innovation and sales, and reduce portfolio risk.

The business development approach

In addition to relying on internal innovation, virtually all companies actively participate in in-licensing and acquisition activities in order to enhance the flow of innovation. In fact, with Merck dramatically increasing its business development activity in 2003, there is no remaining company espousing that "going it alone" is a viable strategy. External opportunities can "plug in" to the portfolio at exactly the right time in order to deliver a replacement development project for a company. There are often natural synergies that can be taken advantage of.

For small biotechnology companies that have a great research capability, partnering with a larger pharmaceutical company may provide access to development and regulatory skills that the smaller company does not have and may or may not want to build. For regional pharmaceutical companies, access to a company with expertise in another global arena may allow it to start and build operations in the new region with the help of a capable and experienced partner. Finally, even two large pharmaceutical companies may partner when one discovers an exciting product or develops a product indication in an area where it does not have expertise or additional products. Partnering may be the best way to realize the full potential of the molecule without creating duplicative development and sales organizations in a nonstrategic therapeutic area.

Not only does in-licensing make sense, but more and more companies have come to understand that outpartnering is also a viable activity in order to help a firm. Many companies have thought that if a product was not

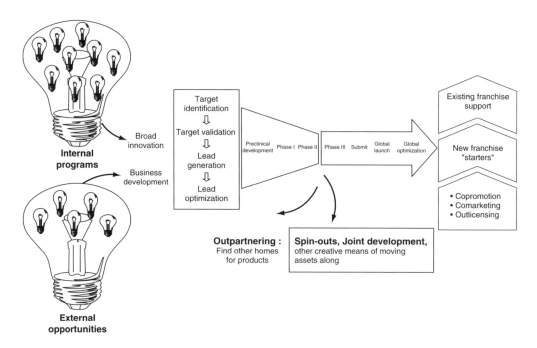

Figure 2.38 Goal – strong, steady innovation matched to franchise engines.

exciting to them, then it could not be valuable to others. There has also been the potential of an embarrassment factor – what if my company does not realize the potential and someone else does? But if through in-licensing and internal development a company constantly tried to up-average its portfolio, then there will be good value-enhancing projects that drop out because other projects are just higher value and the firm's resources are limited. Outpartnering becomes a viable way of realizing the value of projects that would otherwise stall in development. Pharmaceutical projects are like fresh fruit – they depreciate quickly if they are not being tended to, and they do poorly sitting on the shelf with long periods of inactivity.

In addition to simple outpartnering, there are a number of creative ways of keeping pharmaceutical assets moving that an industry will undoubtedly attempt. Instead of trying to be bigger, most of these approaches focus on being small, more virtual, and more focused, and through that, accessing a larger development capability. One example is spinning out assets into a company. Novo-Nordisk spun out Zymogenetics, and Biovitrium was spun out of Pharmacia. Both companies have had some success and the parent companies have been rewarded in the spinout through their continuing equity position.

The ability to access capabilities without building or owning the infrastructure those capabilities require is a tremendous benefit that continues to drive partnering activity in modern business today. And it is at the center of the debate over whether bigness is valuable in and of itself and whether big mergers pay in the pharmaceutical sector.

Anatomy of a strategic alliance

Strategic alliances (SAs) are key to the industry. There is just no way that one company can access all the technology it needs if it is restricted to internal efforts. SAs are also very instructive, because they provide a meaningful way to consider value creation from the earliest aspects of discovery to patent expiration, when the value left is virtually only the brand equity in the trade name. SAs are done for research tools and manufacturing technology as well, but this discussion will focus on molecule deals. The economics of sharing a molecule are divided into up-front payments, milestone payments, royalties (payments based on a percentage of sales), and sometimes success payments (milestone payments for hitting certain levels of annual sales). Although each individual circumstance can vary, some general ranges tend to exist at each stage of development. Additionally, there are always a few deals done at very high price points. For example, Burrill & Company note six preclinical deals

Deal type	Signing payments ($ million)	Milestone payments ($ million)	Royalty % of sales	eNPV value split to seller at time of deal (%)	eNPV value split to seller in total if successful (%)
University to biotech technology concept	1–3	0–5	1–4	~75	~5
Biotech to Pharma					
Preclinical	5–15	25–50	6–10	~75	~15–25
In phase I	15–25	60–100	10–14	~75	~25–45
In phase II	40–60	80–120	15–20	~85	~45–60
In phase III	100 or >	200–300	50/50 profit split in USA, ~10 royalty elsewhere	~90	~65–80

Figure 2.39 Pharmaceutical deals between 2002 and 2004.

Source: Analysis by Northrup.

that have been done over $50 million and five phase I deals that have been done over $100 million.[27] In considering the value of royalties, each 1 percent of sales is equal to about 1.75–2 percent of value and profits.

Figure 2.39 is based on approximate values as computed by the author for average deals in 2002–04, for their primary indication. It attempts to strip out higher reported numbers in deals where payments relate to nonprimary indications, back-up molecules, or other less likely scenarios.

The most significant fulcrum in pharmaceutical deal-making is when phase II is successfully completed (equivalent to in phase III). Because of the substantial change in risk, a strong phase II can yield the seller an enormous step up in value.

Pharmaceutical molecules can vary quite a bit depending on their sales potential (Lipitor at over $10 billion to small specialty products at a few $100 million or less), phase III investment, synthesis costs, and so on. Prices for the seller have steadily increased over the past fifteen years, and as a result, today the innovator can realize the great percentage of the overall value simply by completing the phase II experience. Pharmaceutical SAs have also had their fair share of noneconomic deals, where the seller received a deal well beyond what seems to make sense. All of this suggests that it is the innovation side of the equation that is the most valuable, and the large infrastructure of sales/marketing/manufacturing that is losing value as a percentage of the total over time. This again casts doubt on whether size is really of great value in pharmaceuticals.

Making the strategic alliance work

Once the deal is struck, the real work begins. An SA is created with both companies planning for value creation – but that value often goes under-realized. The reason is that alliances are very difficult. They require the equivalent of grafting a foreign body part on to a host, and all kinds of rejection stimuli are triggered. Each company has an identity and a perspective, and so does the alliance. So, to be great at alliances, companies need to put time and talent into the relationship, and need to understand that alliances more typically fail than succeed.

Alliances go through the process that all teams experience, but with the added complication of reporting to different owners.[28] First, the team is formed ("forming") and the group tentatively starts working together, then the team hits some major disagreements ("storming") and becomes dysfunctional. If the team responds well, it goes on to "norming," where it begins to function in a reasonable manner. Then, as conflicts have been resolved and trust developed, the team can move to "performing" and achieve the hoped-for goals. The role of alliance management is to lessen the "dip" and shorten the "storming."

It is important to communicate frequently and attempt to work out differences all the time and point the alliance toward achievement of mutual

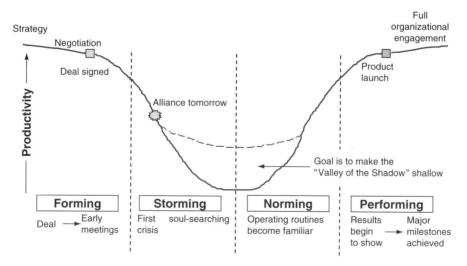

Figure 2.40   Alliance life cycle – breakdowns are normal.

Source: Andersen Consulting.

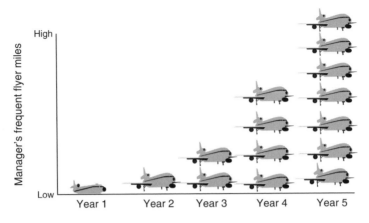

Plot of manager's frequent flyer miles

Figure 2.41   Key element of successful alliance management.

purpose. Eli Lilly actively monitors the health of its alliances and proactively tries to intervene if one falls on rocky ground. In this way, it hopes to be excellent in alliances and alliance management in order to reliably deliver value to the company and its partners.

Mergers and acquisitions (M&A)

M&A is a term that really encompasses two very different types of activity. The acquisition of one company by another of somewhat similar size is commonly called a merger; the acquisition of one company by a company of larger size is commonly called an acquisition. Both are happening at a fast rate in the pharmaceutical and biotechnology business, but there is considerable controversy over whether mergers make sense, whereas many acquisitions clearly make sense (see chapter 5). In fact, one might suggest that the successful Johnson & Johnson company business model is built on healthcare acquisitions as a way to renew internal R&D.

Acquisitions often make sense when a pharmaceutical company needs a particular technology or product and wants to fully participate in the positive risk of that opportunity. Only acquisition gives a company 100 percent of the opportunity. So, for example, J&J acquired Scios and picked up a small but innovative hospital product for congestive heart failure called Natrecor and an exciting new oral arthritis platform called p38 inhibitors in early clinical development. One can wonder if the executive conversations at J&J might have been involved in something about the acquisition with Natrecor enabling near self-funding over the product's life cycle, with new delivery systems to expand use, and that with the p38 platform, J&J would have a home run opportunity if the technology worked. Secondly, acquisitions can be the only tool to access a technology that will favorably impact a firm in the short term. This is because in-licensing is usually driven to happen earlier in development, when one partner needs capabilities to successfully make it to market. If a pharmaceutical company wants to enhance its earnings in the near term, in-licensing is unlikely to be available – firms with products have either decided to keep them entirely or they have made their licensing choices earlier in development.

Mergers have been controversial in the industry, especially the mergers among the largest pharmaceutical companies. It is not controversial that the industry is consolidating. That is clear from any analysis. Eight of the top fifteen and all but two of the top nine pharmaceutical companies today have been built by merger activity. In the top nine, the two that have not are J&J and Merck. Since J&J could be considered a healthcare conglomerate, with its decentralized company structure, that leaves only Merck, and Merck is now in difficult times, with three recent projects having crashed in late stage development.

Mergers have been controversial because analyses of the Bristol–Squibb and GlaxoWellcome–SmithKline mergers have not shown growth in share-holder value beyond what the separate companies could theoretically deliver. There are issues that make mergers more difficult than acquisitions.

First is the question of whether economies of scale can be realized by the new entity. Since both companies were fully integrated before the merger, it is hard to see where the economies will come from. Less corporate overhead, keeping just the best projects, and streamlining all departments are primarily cost savings. Although that can help, it is hard to save your way to success. There are inevitable costs in morale and shifted emphasis as employees wonder if they and their project will be continuing with the new entity. And there are different corporate cultures, which have to come together.

Economies of scale is a concept that suggests that the larger the company, the more it can benefit from an advantage of size. For most large pharma-ceutical companies that already have multitherapeutic discovery efforts, global development, and sales, the concept of critical mass might be more appropriate. Critical mass implies that there is a size which is needed in order to be competitive, but that after that size is attained the benefits to additional size are diminishing in nature. An examination of each piece of the value chain may tell which concept best fits.

In *research*, there is a therapeutic orientation that is needed for excellence in the disease state, in the models, and in connections to research done around the world. There are a host of support tools the researcher needs that are not therapeutically dependent – protein synthesis and characterization, imaging technologies, toxicology work, and so on. Further, the more industrialized approaches such as μHTS and information technology infrastructure require larger investment. Additionally, molecular targets may start out as interesting in one therapeutic area but migrate to another. Insights into one disease state may actually lead to another disease state. For example, classic cardiovascular disease is moving toward inflammation, as the role of inflammation in cardiovascular tissue becomes better understood as a critical presage to heart attack, stroke, and arteriosclerosis. Neuroscience and endocrine disciplines come together in the study of obesity, around the feedback loops between fat cells and the brain, in regulating body weight. The former, classic therapeutic orientation may be a critical mass capability and the latter, support tools, industrialized approaches, multitherapeutic connections, may enjoy some scale. But even with the latter a small company, such as a biotechnology company, can enjoy access to these technologies through alliances.

In *development*, independent investigators for ethical reasons do most of the clinical trial work. Contract research organizations (CROs) are able to handle many of these needs. Investigators and thought-leading and academic clinicians are attracted to how exciting the product may be for therapy more than who happens to own it. Critical mass to know these important individuals around the globe, and to recruit capable clinicians, seems to be the right concept in development.

In *manufacturing*, there may be benefits that respond to the scale concept. Technical development is more related to chemistry approaches and may not be therapeutically correlated.

Sales forces for primary care may handle many therapeutic areas, and the ability to "flex" these organizations across opportunities allows surge detailing and special launch programs that smaller companies have more difficulty undertaking. Large customers and consolidated payers who want integrated programs could drive benefits to consolidation. An example was the innovative program that Pfizer pioneered with the State of Florida to provide its therapies at one maximum price packaged with disease management capability. Although the State of Florida has cancelled Pfizer's contract to continue the program due to its belief it can further reduce costs, the full benefit to Florida citizens is still being understood.

Overall, the greatest benefit that responds to scale may well be portfolio challenges. Having a substantial portfolio allows smoothing out the peaks and valleys in discovery and development, keeping more projects going with varied risk, and being able to make very big bets. When one looks at the majority of mergers in the industry, they have been fostered by portfolio challenges. Squibb merged with Bristol when Merck's Vasotec stalled Capoten in the marketplace. Glaxo merged with Wellcome when Zantac was coming off patent. Glaxo and SmithKline merged when Glaxo had more of a late pipeline, but little early pipeline, and SmithKline had the reverse. Aventis succumbed to Sanofi's overtures when Aventis's pipeline was looking light. Only Pfizer merged with Warner-Lambert and then Searle out of a strength-to-strength play, primarily around securing the rest of Lipitor and Celebrex, respectively.

Barriers to entry in pharmaceuticals

Another way to consider the size question is to ask how significant are the barriers to entry in pharmaceuticals? Many would suggest that there have been few new pharmaceutical companies and therefore the barriers are steep. However, biotechnology companies need to be considered in the analysis, since they are typically trying to become fully integrated pharmaceutical companies. Amgen, Genentech, ICOS, Gilead Sciences, Ligand, Vertex, Incyte, Millennium, Neurocrine, and many others have achieved some success. All these companies have used some type of breakthrough technology, internal or purchased, to create their ascendancy into pharmaceuticals. It is not size that has been critical, but the understanding of how science could translate into a great product and a fine revenue stream. Amgen has become a global player based on two products from one technology! Coming from the other end of the value chain, Forest Laboratories and King Pharmaceuticals have achieved some success as marketers and developers. This may be tougher, but again, the recognition of what technology could be and the ability to make the vision happen has allowed Forest to take an old anti-depressant, Celexa, and make it a major player in the USA, and has allowed King to take an old antihypertensive, Altace, and do the same.

Pharmaceutical companies have three primary advantages. One is access to a lower cost of capital. Because many pharmaceutical companies have a positive cash flow, they can invest in new projects with a lower cost of money. Second is the portfolio effect of working on many projects to offset

	Goals	Shots *on* goal	Shots *per* goal
Wins	4,294	30,329	7
Ties	682	8,704	13
Losses	1,851	29,132	16

Figure 2.42 It is not the number of shots on goal – data from 2000 NHL season.

Source: http://sportsillustrated.CNN.com/hockey/nhl/STATS/2000/Team_scoring/0_by goals.html

the risk associated with a single project. Finally, pharmaceutical companies have the ability to integrate all the steps in the value chain.

Yet many mid-size and regional pharmaceutical companies are struggling, while some smaller biotechnology-oriented companies are thriving. Struggling pharmaceutical companies can be characterized by their lack of ability to come up with new technologies and products and to adapt themselves to the insights coming out of biotechnology and academia. This suggests that pharmaceutical company advantages in financing a portfolio and integration can be offset. The key to success is innovation, the access to new technology, and an understanding of its relevance. This allows smaller but capable competitors to pick a better project, focus on just a high-value piece of the value chain, and deliver good returns to higher cost venture capitalists. Like the National Hockey League, winners take shots that more often score, and do not just take more shots on goal.

Summary and conclusion

Today the USA is the largest and most diverse market for healthcare, in solutions, jobs, and spending. It has acted as a magnet to healthcare researchers, physicians, and companies, and has helped to create a more concentrated and productive pharmaceutical sector that is the envy of the world. Europe, and now Japan, has moved away from this model to a more controlled, lower priced, and potentially even innovation-hostile pharmaceutical marketplace. The difference in price for pharmaceuticals between the US and some other countries has created a large political question for the US. Price differences arise from exchange rates, different starting prices, price freezes, and, in some cases, the threat of compulsory licensing (essentially seizing the company's intellectual property) to achieve a low purchase price.

Pharmaceutical research and development is complex, time-consuming, and highly risky. Yet with it comes the potential of a better and longer life for all those who can participate in the fruits of the industry. The challenge ahead is how to routinely and efficiently create drug innovation so that these benefits can be delivered at a price that the world can afford. Some hope exists in the biological revolution presently underway and in the potential to understand disease and its biological roots. Some hope exists in informed consumers who understand the value of the intangible effort that goes into the creation of a small pill with unique properties.

NOTES

I would like to thank all the individuals who have helped with this chapter and who have supported the project. I would like to thank Eli Lilly & Company, Inc., for providing many opportunities to learn about the pharmaceutical business; David E. Thompson, for his insights through the years and endorsement of the project; my wife Melissa for her support and sacrifices; and my parents for their help and advice.

I also appreciate and recognize the efforts and contributions to the work by Richard Ding on the manufacturing section; Richard A. Brown on the marketing section; David Mozley for his review and critique; L. Michelle Klaips for research assistance at the Wharton School; and the advice and support of my editor, Lawton R. Burns.

1. IMS Health Applications, "IMS 2004 World Review Analyst," May 2004, available on http://www.ims-global.com/products/sales/review.htm.
2. IMS Health Applications – Pharmaceutical Market Intelligence, "Generics Flourish as Innovation Stalls," June 23, 2004, available on http://www.open.imshealth.com/IMSinclude/I_article_20040623a.asp.
3. Matthein Harper, "Cancer Worries Dog New Anti-Fat Drugs," *Forbes Magazine* (July 15, 2004): technology section.
4. See http://www.jnj.com/home.htm.
5. See http://www.bms.com/landing/data/index.html.
6. See http://www.aventis.com/main/home_static.asp and http://www.sanofi-synthelabo.us/index.html.
7. Robert K. Jenner *et al.*, *Transfusion Associated AIDS* (Tucson, AZ: Lawyers & Judges Publishing Co., 1995).
8. D. Cutler *et al.*, "Are Medical Prices Declining?," NBER working paper no. 5750 (September 1996).
9. Frank R. Lichtenberg *et al.*, "Are the Benefits of Newer Drugs Worth Their Cost?," *Health Affairs* 20 (2001): 241–252.

10. Arthur D. Ullian, Chairman, Task Force on Science, Health Care & the Economy, testimony before the US Senate, May 10, 2001, available on http://www.laskerfoundation.com//ffpages/ulliansen.htm.

11. National Cancer Institute and Centers for Disease Control and Prevention, *2003 Cancer Progress Report*, figure 23a, "5-Year Relative Survival Rates, all Cancers, 1975–1995."

12. "Changes in the Prevalence of Chronic Disability in the United States Black and Nonblack Population Above Age 65 from 1982 to 1999," *Proceedings of the National Academy of Sciences of the United States of America* 98(11) (May 2001): 6354–6359.

13. Ullian testimony.

14. Merrill Goozner, *The $800 Million Pill – The Truth Behind the Cost of New Drugs* (Berkeley: University of California Press, 2004), ch. 8.

15. Mattson Jack Group, "Epidemiological Data Base," available at http://epidb.com/app/fmeLayout.asp.

16. American Association of Retired Persons, "Prescription Drug Use Among Persons Age 45 +," available at http://research.aarp.org/.

17. Medscape, "The Incretin Hormones in the Treatment of Type 2 Diabetes: An Expert Interview with John Buse, M. D., Ph.D.," available at http://www.medscape.com/viewarticle/480545.

18. Whitehead Institute for Biomedical Research, "New Insight into Cancer Metastasis," available at http://www.wi.mit.edu/nap_features_twist3.html.

19. "FDA Proposes Changes to Provide Clearer Information to Drug Sponsors Concerning Reviews of their New Drug Applications," *FDA News*, available at http://www.fda.gov/bbs/topics/news/2004/NEW01092.html.

20. DataEdge, April 2001, PhRMA (Pharmaceutical Research and Manufacturer's Association); a greater than 40 percent increase in medical procedures per patient in clinical trials from 1992 to 2000.

21. Lehman Brothers–McKinsey & Company study, "The Fruits of Genomics."

22. The reason tax benefits link primarily to bulk operations is because these operations primarily take commodity inputs and step them up to the final material. As such, most tax authorities accept that these operations create a majority of the value of the final product. This allows transfer pricing within a company to reflect this value increase. If high value operations can be positioned in tax favorable locations, then a company can realize a high percentage of its value-added in low tax arenas.

23. Bruce Burlington, "Risk-Based cGMPs: Defining Risk and Quality," April 22, 2003.

24. PhRMA, *2000 Annual Survey* (Washington, D.C.: PhRMA).

25. BioPharm International, "After the Consent Decree – An Uphill Battle for Affected Companies," June 2004, available on http://www.biopharm-mag.com.

26. Sumit Agarwal, Sanjay Desai, Michele Holcomb, and Arjun Oberoi. "Unlocking the Value in Big Pharma," *McKinsey Quarterly* 2 (2001).

27. Burrill & Company, *Biotech 2004, Life Sciences: Back on Track* (San Francisco, CA: Burrill & Co., 2004).

28. Bruce Tuckman, "Developmental Sequence in Small Groups," *Psychological Bulletin* 63 (1965): 384–399.

3 The biotechnology sector – therapeutics

Cary G. Pfeffer

Introduction

The biotechnology sector was born about thirty years ago when technology zealots, investors, and entrepreneurs alike set out to utilize novel scientific discoveries around genetic engineering and a landmark court decision to create a business that would improve healthcare and agriculture in ways that before could only have been imagined. At the time, biotechnology, strictly speaking, was the use of genetic engineering techniques to create unique cells that could produce proteins that under normal circumstances would not be produced. The hope was that using this technology to modify the genetic material of a living cell, pest-resistant plant cells, and human cell factories producing large quantities of proteins with therapeutic potential could be created. As one looks back over the last thirty years, without a doubt these entrepreneurs were right, although the sector has endured many hurdles along the way. Focusing primarily on the therapeutic segment, this chapter will review the impact the biotechnology sector has had on parts of the healthcare sector, including pharmaceutical companies and patient care, the forces that continue to drive the sector, its growth globally, and the regulatory environment in which it must operate.[1]

In analyzing the biotechnology sector, the perspective of time is important. Since the product development cycle of biotechnology drug development is about fifteen years from discovery through commercialization, the sector is still in its infancy, and even the sector's earliest entrants have barely passed through two cycles. Observers of the sector who remain disappointed in its output and impact may not have been realistic about the long cycle of drug development. During the founding of the first companies, expectations of financial return and product output were irrationally high, and many claim the sector has not met those expectations. A recent *Wall Street Journal* article highlights the sector's $40 billion cumulative losses, and compares the sector to "the ultimate roulette game."[2] On the other hand, taking a longer term, perhaps more realistic perspective on this young industry, thousands of companies globally have obtained government support and financing, and the numbers continue to grow. As of 2003, at least 196 products have made it to market, 70 percent of them in just the last six years, and the impact thus far on drug discovery and development, the pharmaceutical sector and patient care has been nothing short of spectacular.[3] Even with $40 billion of cumulative losses, the sector remains as vibrant as ever.

History

In 1953, James Watson and Francis Crick identified DNA as the complete genetic code that defined all aspects of a living organism.[4] On the molecular level, it was the code that defined the structure of all of the proteins which make up a living being and are responsible for all metabolic, physiologic, and biochemical activities within that living being. The discovery of the structure of DNA began a revolution in the scientific community to understand the many interactions among proteins in the human body. Soon thereafter, a floodgate of ideas and innovation opened, and within less than twenty years the biotechnology sector was officially founded.

The initial technical foundation of the sector was to utilize the newly invented recombinant DNA techniques (rDNA) to reengineer the DNA code in cells in some rational way, to create unique cells that could produce new proteins or normal proteins in high quantity, which would be useful as therapeutics.[5] The techniques essentially allowed one to take the DNA code for a specific protein, integrate it into the DNA structure of specialized human or bacterial cells, and culture or grow those cells in mass quantity in order to produce large amounts of the specified protein. With the new genetic engineering techniques, biological molecules such as monoclonal antibodies and other natural proteins, like tissue plasminogen activator and erythropoietin, could be mass produced and ultimately used as drugs.

The founders of Genentech in San Francisco, one of the early entrants in the field, had discovered a key technology that enabled the genetic engineering techniques. In 1972 Herbert Boyer, a biochemist at the University of California, San Francisco, and Stanley Cohen, an assistant professor of medicine at Stanford University, collaborated and developed a process that enabled the cloning of specific sequences of DNA.[6] Boyer then presented the technology to venture capitalist Robert A. Swanson and the two founded Genentech. This technology breakthrough enabled the founding of the biotechnology sector, and today is the basis for the production of all recombinant protein-based drugs and vaccines (biologics).

Other genetic engineering techniques also played important roles in defining the sector in the early days (see figure 3.1). Monoclonal antibody technology created additional excitement around drug development. These specialized proteins were viewed as the silver bullets that could have significant impacts on many human diseases because of their ability to bind so specifically to other proteins. In the years that followed a host of other technologies were developed, which continue to fuel the sector.

The technology on its own, however, would not have been enough to cause substantial private and public capital to flow into the sector to support its growth without exclusive market protection afforded by patents. In 1980 the United States Supreme Court decided the landmark court case which enabled the creation of the valuable intellectual property that protects the new living organisms that have been discovered within the industry.

The developments for the court case *Diamond, Commissioner of Patents and Trademarks* v. *Chakrabarty* began in 1972, when General Electric Co. microbiologist Ananda Chakrabarty filed a patent application under Title 35 U.S.C. § 101, which provided for the issuance of a patent to an inventor of "any" new and useful "manufacture" or "composition of matter," for a bacterium that was capable of breaking down crude oil. The application was denied by both a patent examiner and the Patent Office Board of Appeals on the ground that living things are not patentable subject matter under § 101. Ultimately, the case was brought before the US Supreme Court

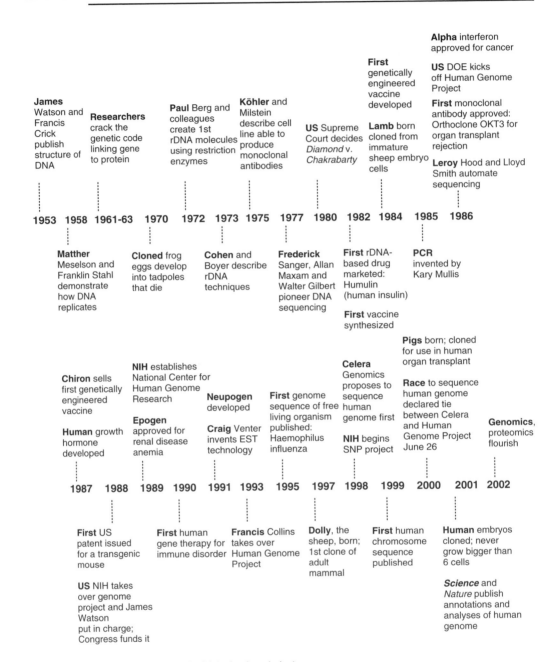

Figure 3.1   Discoveries driving the biotechnology industry.

and in a close five-to-four decision the Court explained that while things not invented by man, such as natural laws, physical phenomena, abstract ideas, or newly discovered minerals, are not patentable, a live artificially engineered microorganism is worthy of a patent. The majority opinion of the Court held that the creation by man of a bacterium that is not found in nature constitutes a patentable "manufacture" or "composition of matter" under Section 101.[7] This decision enabled new biotechnology companies to gain exclusive protection on the genetically engineered cell, which served as the miniature factory for the protein drug under production. This patent protection was tantamount to the patent protection that pharmaceutical companies obtain when they patent new chemical entities as drugs. It blocked others from copying the process to make the same protein drug, enabling biotechnology companies to obtain market exclusivity for up to twenty years on the cell lines that produced the protein drugs. Following this initial case, intellectual property law has played a critical role in the growth of individual companies and of the industry as a whole.

Although many legislative acts in the US have been important to the industry, in the early days the Bayh–Dole Act of 1980 played a key role in accelerating the industry's growth. This Act facilitates the transfer of technology from federally funded institutions to the commercial sector. Prior to the passage of the Act, universities and small businesses were not able to patent products discovered with federal funds. The Act had two purposes: (a) to permit universities, not-for-profit organizations, and small businesses to patent and commercialize their federally funded inventions; and (b) to allow federal agencies to grant exclusive licenses for their technology, originally funded with public money, to provide more incentive to businesses.[8] The Act has had a substantial impact in enabling publicly funded technology to be developed and commercialized within the private sector. Since 1980 over 2,900 new companies have been formed based on technology licensed from universities, and over 18,000 licensing agreements exist between universities and the commercial sector.[9]

Within five years of the founding of Genentech, 155 other biotechnology companies were founded in the US, most based on rDNA technology, but with eyes toward developing biological drugs for human disease, diagnostic products, or genetically engineered crops (see figure 3.2). Along with Genentech, other pioneering companies of the time were Amgen, Biogen, Genetics Institute, Cetus, Chiron, Repligen, and Centocor. With the challenges of product development in front of them, and with the additional challenges of the new technology, it is not clear that anyone at the time understood clearly the risk, time, and capital required to build these companies into the successes that some

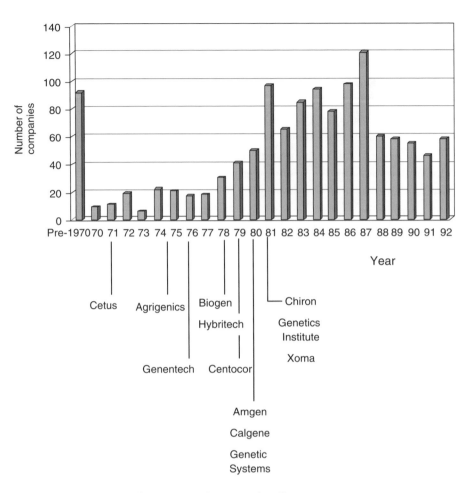

Figure 3.2   The biotechnology industry – year of company founding.

Sources: Adapted from G. Steven Burrill and the Ernst & Young High Technology Group, *Biotech 90: Into the Next Decade* (New York: Mary Ann Liebert, Inc., 1989), 130–131; and G. Steven Burrill and Kenneth B. Lee, Jr., *Biotech 94: Long-Term Value and Short-Term Hurdles* (San Francisco, CA: Ernst & Young, 1993), vi.

of them have become. In many cases the companies did not overcome the enormous technological, regulatory, and business hurdles facing them.

Overview of the biotechnology sector today

The therapeutics segment of biotechnology has evolved in many ways over the last thirty years. Even the definition of the biotechnology sector

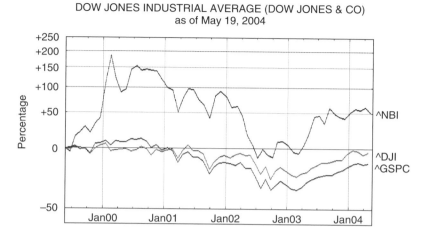

KEY: NBI = NASDAQ Biotech index
      DJI = Dow Jones Industrials
      GSPC = S&P 500 Index

Figure 3.3   Recent stock market performance.

Note: Copyright 2003 Yahoo!Inc. (http://finance.yahoo.com/)

itself has changed. Whereas in the early days most companies were based on developing biologics utilizing rDNA technology, today the sector has taken on a much broader definition, to include all entrepreneurial companies using innovative technology in the research or development of medical therapeutics, diagnostics, research tools, agbio products or even neutraceuticals.[10] The result has been a blurring of the distinction between biotechnology, biopharmaceutical, small pharmaceutical, and specialty pharmaceutical companies. The common element today is not so much the rDNA technology, but rather that all companies are founded on scientific innovation directed at developing drugs, diagnostics, vaccines, agbio products, or other closely related products with true entrepreneurialism at the core.

There have been periods throughout the last thirty years when most investors would have said that biotechnology was not delivering the expected financial returns or even acceptable returns. Even in recent times, from early 2001 through early 2003, the industry has struggled (see figure 3.3).

In addition, if one measures the parameters of the income statement of the US biotechnology sector versus Pfizer or Merck, one may conclude that the sector has performed poorly on the whole from a financial perspective (see figure 3.4). The $40 billion cumulative losses highlighted recently by the *Wall Street Journal* support this view.[11]

	1993			2003		
	Biotech	Merck	Pfizer	Biotech*	Merck	Pfizer
Sales ($ million)	10,000	10,500	7,500	46,200	22,400	45,200
R&D expense ($)	5,700	1,200	974	13,800	3,200	7,100
Net income (loss) ($)	−3,600	2,200	658	−4,300	6,800	3,900
Cash & equivalents ($)	–	829	729	39,700	5,300	1,500
Market cap ($)	45,000	40,400	18,500	342,000	135,000	243,000
Public companies	235	–	–	315	–	–
Total number of companies	1272	–	–	1,457 (342 public)	–	–
Employees	97,000	47,100	40,500	193,753**	33,200	122,000

Figure 3.4   US biotechnology companies versus Merck and Pfizer.

Source: "Customer Insights: Biotechnology Industry Seeks to Recover," *Chemical Market Reporter* 264(6) (September 1, 2003): 17.
*Public companies only; 12 mos. trailing 9/30/03.
**Year end 2002. Private and public worldwide.

However, the industry's vibrancy today can be measured in many ways. In terms of growth and investment, in the US alone as of 2003, 1,115 private companies and 342 public companies exist, and in the last five years alone $22.9 billion of private capital and $58.5 billion of public capital has been invested in biotechnology.[12–13] To put this in context, the pharmaceutical sector spent over $130 billion in research and development since 2000, and the US Government National Institutes of Health (NIH) budgeted $27.3 billion for research in 2003 alone.[14] From a global perspective, many governments have identified life sciences and biotechnology as a high priority industry providing financial and regulatory incentives in order to foster rapid growth nationally. Growth in numbers of companies and invested capital is occurring rapidly around the globe, including Asia, Australia, Europe, the Middle East, and Canada. However, a global biotechnology sector looks different than a global pharmaceutical sector. Whereas in the pharmaceutical sector many companies are truly multinational and have worldwide development and commercial capabilities, few biotechnology companies have similar capabilities across more than one continent. Rather, many small companies with more limited capabilities exist and flourish across the globe.

There has also been a substantial positive shift in the way big pharmaceutical companies view the biotechnology sector.[15] In the early 1980s most

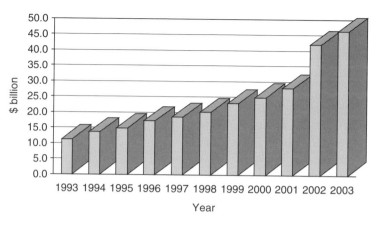

Figure 3.5   US biotechnology revenues.

Source: Burrill & Company, *Biotech 2004, Life Sciences: Back on Track* (San Francisco, CA: Burrill & Company, 2004), 51.

pharmaceutical companies took a "wait and see" attitude toward biotechnology, which was viewed mostly as a research toolbox but not as something that could produce blockbuster products. Today pharmaceutical companies are accessing increasingly more of their innovation and pipeline from the biotechnology sector. In the last five years there have been on average 14.7 deals completed annually between big pharmaceutical and biotechnology companies compared to 10.9 deals on average from 1993 to 1997.[16] In addition, although of late there has been a decline in the number of deals overall, deal values, particularly of late stage deals, have increased significantly.

Most importantly, the sector is finally producing products. Today there are at least 196 biotechnology drugs on the market (including large pharmaceutical company biologics). In 2003 US biotechnology company revenues reached $46.2 billion (see figure 3.5).[17] In thirty years the sector has come a long way from its inception, although many investors and some observers believe the successes have taken too long, cost too much and risked substantial capital.

Impact on healthcare

Perhaps the most obvious way to measure the success of biotechnology is by its impact on healthcare, which has been important and far-reaching. Biotechnology has affected many segments of healthcare, including the

Drug	Indication	2003 sales ($ million)	Manufacturer
Epogen	Anemia, cancer	2,435	Amgen
Aranesp	Anemia	1,544	Amgen
Rituxan	Cancer	1,489	Genentech / Biogen Idec
Enbrel	Rheumatoid arthritis	1,300	Amgen
Neupogen	Neutropenia	1,267	Amgen
Neulasta	Neutropenia	1,255	Amgen
Avonex	Multiple sclerosis	1,170	Biogen Idec
Synagis	RSV	1,054	MedImmune
Betaseron	Multiple sclerosis	945	Berlex / Schering AG Group
Cerezyme	Gaucher's disease	733	Genzyme
Herceptin	Cancer	425	Genentech
Integrilin	Myocardial infarction	306	Millennium / Schering-Plough
Activase / TNKase	Thrombolytic	185	Genentech
Pulmozyme	Cystic fibrosis	167	Genentech

Figure 3.6   Selected biotechnology-derived drugs.

Source: Company 10Ks / websites.

pharmaceutical sector, physicians, patients, pharmacies, employment, and academic research and technology transfer. This value is illustrated by the list of all the therapeutic products derived from biotechnology.[18] Since 1982 at least 196 drugs have been approved that were invented by biotechnology companies or are biologics developed by large pharmaceutical companies.[19] These products impact on a wide range of diseases, including renal disease, cancer, cystic fibrosis, rheumatoid arthritis, and cardiovascular disease. They also include vaccines for hepatitis B and influenza, as well as diagnostics for many diseases, including several cancers, HIV, and hepatitis. In addition, there are more than 370 new products in clinical development covering a wide spectrum of diseases.[20] Overall, with its products the industry has managed to have a tremendous impact on the healthcare of over 325 million patients worldwide, and has generated billions of dollars annually in revenue.[21] Many biotechnology products have become blockbusters (see figure 3.6). Although the number is large and growing, the total revenue generated by drugs discovered by biotechnology companies may never be known, because many of the drugs are licensed to pharmaceutical companies prior to launch.

The value of these products can also be measured in more subjective ways. As a result of the biotechnology sector, for the first time certain diseases such as multiple sclerosis, hepatitis, renal disease, leucopenia due to chemotherapy, and Gaucher's disease can be treated with significant clinical benefit. In other cases, biotechnology has brought to the market treatments that represent significant improvements over older therapies, such as Herceptin for certain breast cancers. The hepatitis B vaccine was greatly improved through biotechnology by eliminating the old process of extracting hepatitis B antigen from patients' serum; now the entire vaccine is made via recombinant DNA, eliminating all infection risk for people being vaccinated. Although there are many, three examples where biotechnology has had major impact on aspects of healthcare are highlighted in the section below in more detail: multiple sclerosis, anemia, and gene therapy.

Multiple sclerosis

Multiple sclerosis is a degenerative disease of the nervous system in which the ability of neurons to conduct electrical impulses is impaired. The disease, for which the cause remains elusive, leads to a variety of neuromuscular or other neurological symptoms, including muscle weakness, tremor, numbness, loss of coordination, and visual problems.[22] Before the biotechnology revolution, physicians had little to offer patients suffering from this devastating illness. However, a tremendous step forward was made in 1993 when the FDA approved the drug Betaseron for the treatment of multiple sclerosis.[23] Betaseron was developed using rDNA techniques to clone the beta-interferon gene. Two other beta-interferons, all slightly different in molecular structure, also made it to the market soon after: Biogen Idec's Avonex and Serono's Rebif. For the first time physicians were able to employ therapy for multiple sclerosis that targeted the disease process itself and not only the symptoms. Beta-interferons have now been shown to reduce both the rate at which patients become disabled and the annual acute relapse rate. Today beta-interferons remain the primary treatment for thousands of multiple sclerosis patients worldwide.

Anemia

Biotechnology has had a similar impact in the hematology market. During the early 1980s scientists at Amgen, the Genetics Institute, and other biotechnology companies were in a race to clone the gene that codes for the protein erythropoietin. (Typically the small segment of the DNA of a cell that codes for one protein is called a gene. The code for a gene specifically refers to the order in which the building blocks of DNA, called nucleotides, are bound together chemically.) Erythropoietin is a naturally occurring substance that triggers red blood cell production. Patients suffering from and/or being treated for many cancers, as well as patients in renal failure, often have depleted numbers of red blood cells. Clinical manifestations are diverse, but can range from fatigue and breathlessness to life-threatening for those with low blood counts. Ultimately, scientists at Amgen and Johnson & Johnson were able to take the product through clinical testing and licensure, and today both firms produce erythropoietin, improving the lives of millions of renal dialysis and cancer patients around the world.

Gene therapy

The promise of gene therapy is compelling and frightening all at once. William French Anderson, now Director of the Gene Therapy Laboratories at the University of Southern California, Keck School of Medicine, led the charge as the scientific father of this field, and he was able to demonstrate exciting early results. In September 1990 Dr. Anderson, then at the National Institutes of Health, carried out the world's first gene therapy trial on four-year-old Ashanti de Silva, who suffered from adenosine deaminase deficiency (ADA), an enzyme deficiency resulting in a severely compromised immune system. The rare disease was made famous by a Houston child who lived his life in a plastic bubble and died at the age of twelve. Following the insertion of a normal ADA gene into Ms. de Silva's T cells, her immune system strengthened.[24] She is now seventeen years old.[25] In addition, since 2000 at least twelve patients in France, Australia, and the UK have had their immune systems restored using similar gene therapy.[26]

However, this field has also had several significant setbacks, which have had a rapid chilling effect on any further advancement. One involved both serious clinical and regulatory violations. In 1999 Jesse Gelsinger, an eighteen-year-old man from Arizona who suffered from a rare genetic disorder, ornithine transcarbamylase (OTC) deficiency, volunteered to participate in a clinical study being conducted by researchers at Genovo, a University of Pennsylvania-affiliated gene therapy company. Sadly, Mr. Gelsinger died as a result of a complication from the experiment. Subsequently, gene therapy trials across the country were stopped and law suits against Genovo and the Institute for Human Gene Therapy at the University of Pennsylvania School of Medicine were filed. Scientists were accused of serious lapses in documentation and other regulatory procedures.[27] The FDA faulted the University of Pennsylvania for several serious regulatory violations related to adverse event reporting, previously agreed upon enrollment criteria and guidelines, and informed consent issues.[28] Since then, regulatory oversight has been augmented, and research and trials have resumed, albeit at a much slowed pace. A second event involved a young French patient treated with a different gene therapy who developed a leukemia-like syndrome.[29] The boy has been treated and is responding, but this again raised serious concerns about the safety of gene therapy.

Despite some notable setbacks, which are fairly typical in drug development overall, people live longer, more productive lives as a direct result of the technology and innovation within the industry. New pathways have been found to treat otherwise untreatable or difficult-to-treat diseases. Moreover, the future is bright for both the industry and patients, with more than 370 biotechnology drugs and vaccines currently in clinical trials in the US alone.[30]

The biotechnology sector is also attacking some of the more challenging areas of medicine. For example, within the neuroscience area, often called the last frontier of medicine, there is substantial activity in the discovery and development of cognition-enhancing drugs, which can be effective in a wide variety of serious diseases of aging, such as Alzheimer's disease, Parkinson's disease, mild cognitive impairment, and age-associated memory impairment. At least six companies are focused on memory enhancement specifically and each of them is taking a different molecular approach.[31] Although the path is risky, many patients will benefit, even if just one of these companies is successful.

Finally, in other facets of healthcare, biotechnology has also left its mark. The industry currently employs 142,900 people in the US and 193,753 people worldwide at publicly owned firms alone.[32] Certain states in the US, such as Massachusetts and California, now depend heavily on biotechnology sector growth to meet their employment needs. The Massachusetts state government has developed an entire strategy aimed specifically at retaining and attracting biotechnology companies. Academic institutions have many more customers for their technological innovations and have become much more sophisticated in marketing and licensing their inventions. Often entire companies are founded on intellectual property licensed from one or several academic researchers. Today many researchers dream of becoming founders of a new biotechnology venture based on their technology; these kinds of dreams were unrealistic thirty years ago. Biotechnology products have also changed the pricing paradigm in many instances. Whereas pharmaceutical drugs may cost several hundred to several thousand dollars annually for chronic therapy, it is not unusual for biotechnology drugs to cost in the range of $10,000 to $20,000 per year for chronic treatment. In one instance, Genzyme charges approximately $150,000/year to treat Gaucher's Disease with its protein replacement therapy, Cerezyme. In general, the higher cost of goods accounts for only a portion of the higher prices for biologic therapies.

Perhaps the greatest impact of biotechnology has been on the pharmaceutical sector as a whole. The biotechnology sector has become one of the most important innovation and product pipeline sources to the pharmaceutical sector. As evidence, in 2003 one-third of the pharmaceutical therapeutics launched in the US came from the biotechnology sector, as compared with 7 percent in 1998 and 0.5 percent in 1989.[33] In 2002 the top twenty pharmaceutical firms spent $6 billion on deals with biotechnology companies, which is 13.4 percent of their total research and development expenditure. Further description of the evolution of the biotechnology–pharmaceutical sector relationship is described below.

Innovation – the key driver of the biotechnology sector

One of the major driving forces of the continued growth of the biotechnology sector continues to be the invention of new technologies applicable to drug discovery and development. Over the last twenty years it seems as if the rate of innovation has increased substantially. Many technologies have become the basis of dozens of new biotechnology companies, as entrepreneurs and investors try to capture value. As expected, some technologies have had greater applicability to product development than others. A review of several technologies provides insight into how technology may drive significant value within the sector.

Monoclonal antibodies

Shortly after the invention of rDNA, in 1975 Georges Köhler and Cesar Milstein described the production of monoclonal antibodies which today are the basis of many approved biotechnology drugs. Antibodies are a key component of the immune system able to bind cells and molecules with unique specificity, thereby blocking specific molecular interactions. In the past, antibodies could be created by immunizing an animal (typically a mouse or other rodent) and purifying the antibody from its serum – in all cases, this process creates mixtures of many antibodies with different characteristics, called polyclonal antibodies. Cells that produce monoclonal antibodies are special in that they produce identical antibodies that all bind to the same specific part of a foreign cell or protein. This highly specific binding could be valuable therapeutically to block naturally occurring molecular interactions that cause a disease or unwanted symptom. Most chemically synthesized pharmaceuticals act similarly to block specific molecular interactions, but monoclonal antibodies have certain advantages: they are more specific; they may have lower risk of toxicity; and they can be used to block interactions that cannot be blocked with small molecules.[34] Later, Witner described the humanization of mouse monoclonal antibodies, which was important to enable broad therapeutic use.[35] In the end, the theory worked. Johnson & Johnson's Orthoclone OKT3 for transplant rejection was the first monoclonal antibody human therapeutic product sold in the US, and today there are at least seventeen monoclonal antibody human therapeutic products on the market, with US sales approaching $7 billion (see figure 3.7).[36]

Sponsor company	Generic name	US trade name	Therapeutic category	US approval
Johnson & Johnson	Muromonab-CD3	Orthoclone OKT3	Immunological	1986
Centocor	Abciximab	ReoPro	Hemostasis	1994
Biogen Idec	Rituximab	Rituxan	Antineoplastic	1997
Protein Design Labs	Daclizumab	Zenapax	Immunological	1997
Novartis	Basiliximab	Simulect	Immunological	1998
MedImmune	Palivizumab	Synagis	Anti-infective	1998
Centocor	Infliximab	Remicade	Immunological	1998
Genentech	Trastuzumab	Herceptin	Antineoplastic	1998
Wyeth	Gemtuzumab ozogamicin	Mylotarg	Antineoplastic	2000
Millennium/ILEX	Alemtuzumab	Campath	Antineoplastic	2001
Biogen Idec	Ibritumomab tiuxetan	Zevalin	Antineoplastic	2002
Abbott	Adalimumab	Humira	Immunological	2002
Genentech	Omalizumab	Xolair	Immunological	2003
Corixa	Tositumomab-I131	BEXXAR	Antineoplastic	2003
Genentech	Efalizumab	Raptiva	Immunological	2003
Imclone Systems	Cetuximab	Erbitux	Antineoplastic	2004
Genentech	Bevacizumab	Avastin	Antineoplastic	2004

Figure 3.7   Therapeutic monoclonal antibody products approved in the US.

Source: Janice Reichert and Alex Pavlou, "Monoclonal Antibodies Market," *Nature Reviews* 3 (May 2004): 383–384.

The market is poised to deliver as many as sixteen additional monoclonal antibody-based products by 2008, and the potential market could reach $16.7 billion in the US alone.

Genomics

In 1988 the US federal government via the National Institutes of Health embarked on the Human Genome Project. Its mission was to sequence all 3 billion individual nucleotides of the human genome. (Nucleotides are the individual molecular building blocks of the human genome.) At the time, there was a strongly held belief within the scientific community that access to this new information would unleash previously unforeseen advances in the molecular understanding of human disease. In February 2001 *Nature* and *Science*, two prestigious scientific journals, published a draft sequence of the human genome. The genomic revolution had begun.

Investor money flowed into many companies founded on the promise that genomics would change drug discovery, shorten pharmaceutical product

Company	Date founded	Market capitalization ($ million)
Affymetrix	1992	1,450
Celera Genomics	1998	1,007
Incyte Genomics	1991	488
Human Genome Sciences	1992	1,713
Millennium	1993	5,551
Lynx Therapeutics	1992	39
Myriad Genetics	1991	348

Figure 3.8   Selected genomics companies.

Source: Burrill & Company, *Biotech 2004, Life Sciences: Back on Track* (San Francisco, CA: Burrill & Company, 2004), 19.
Note: Market capitalization data from company 10Ks, data for year end 2003, finance.yahoo.com.

development cycles, and discover new, innovative human therapeutics that would treat or cure diseases which today are not well treated. (Genomics is the study of the structure and function of genes. Genomics technologies enable scientists to decipher the coding for genes quickly.) Investors and entrepreneurs alike believed that by using genomics technology, the structure of new genes could be understood, enabling their function to be easily deciphered. Once function could be elucidated for a new gene and its protein, drug discovery could proceed rapidly to develop new products.[37]

Beginning in the early 1990s, several companies were formed on the basis of using genomics to develop new products, and others were founded using gene structure information in the form of databases to sell to pharmaceutical companies (see figure 3.8). Genomics has led to the discovery of many new molecular targets and continues to be an important tool in discovering gene function. However, scientists soon recognized that determining the function of genes and their proteins was the rate-limiting step in finding new molecular targets for drug discovery, and genomics was not able to easily solve that challenge. Understanding the structure of genes, although necessary, is not sufficient to finding these new drug targets. Additional tools needed to be developed to elucidate gene function to ultimately identify new drug targets.

Proteomics

Following the discovery of genomics, a related discipline called *proteomics* was founded – the study of the structure and function of proteins. Using

Company	Date founded
Ciphergen	1993
Large Scale Biology Corp	1987
ACLARA Biosciences	1995
Caliper	1995
Illumina	1998
Luminex	1995
Lynx	1992
Nanogen	1993
Paradigm Genetics	1997

Figure 3.9   Selected proteomics companies.

Source: Burrill & Company, *Biotech 2004, Life Sciences: Back on Track* (San Francisco, CA: Burrill & Company, 2004), 19.

automation of various techniques, proteomics aims to work with proteins to learn as much about their structure and function and to discover ways they may be useful in drug discovery.[38] Ultimately, proteins are often the molecular targets against which many drugs bind. By understanding the specific function of a protein in healthy and diseased animal systems, scientists can determine whether it is an important drug target. In many ways the challenge of working with proteins is more daunting than the challenge of working with genes using genomics, because there are between 1 and 20 million proteins in the body, while there are only about 25,000 to 35,000 genes in the human genome.[39] Once again, with new techniques invented, many companies were formed to exploit this new area of technology (see figure 3.9).

Additional technology platforms to advance drug discovery included rational drug design (RDD), combinatorial chemistry, high throughput screening, DNA microarrays, gene therapy, antisense, RNA interference, and systems biology. Many of these technologies began to focus on improving methods to discover new small molecule drugs and not biologics. As these technologies advanced, the biotechnology sector began to change. Soon many biotechnology companies were discovering small molecule drugs and were competing directly with big pharmaceutical companies. Many of these technologies had such a great impact on drug discovery, especially in discovering new chemical entities, that eventually most large pharmaceutical companies have adapted them within their standard drug discovery process.

Rational drug design (RDD)

Rational drug design, or structure-based design, is an approach to discovering molecules using detailed structural information about the protein target.[40] In the past, finding out what drugs worked for any particular disease was done by trial and error. Today, however, scientists typically develop an understanding of the disease at the molecular level and develop drugs to interfere with that specific molecular process. To be successful, the drug must literally 'fit' together with its molecular target. Therefore, by understanding the three-dimensional structure of the protein target, scientists can design chemical molecules with enhanced ability to bind to the target. Using computer-based molecular modeling and other techniques to design molecules with very specific shapes, scientists create molecules to 'fit' the drug target. With these techniques, higher-quality drugs can be found more quickly than with the standard screening approaches that have been used in the past. This structure-based design has been used in discovering both small molecule and protein drugs.

Combinatorial chemistry

Combinatorial chemistry is an example of a brilliant technology that improves drug discovery but for which a self-sustaining business model could not be created because the technology could not be effectively patent protected. This chemistry technique, which creates new chemical entities more rapidly, is based on conducting chemical synthesis by putting together chemical building blocks of molecules in all possible ways. Novel, innovative chemical entities are rapidly created from a small number of components at a reduced cost.[41] Although many biotechnology companies were founded using this new approach, the process of combinatorial chemistry eventually became a commodity that most pharmaceutical companies now use to some extent. Therefore, most companies founded solely on this technology were driven to quickly find new technologies to grow, to develop their own products to create value, to sell themselves to larger pharmaceutical companies, or to liquidate.

High-throughput screening

High-throughput screening (HTS), another chemistry-based technology, is a super-efficient way of conducting the standard screening of chemical molecules against potential drug targets. HTS is an automated, robotics-based platform used to synthesize and test many chemical molecules in an assay system at very high rates. The combination of HTS and combinatorial chemistry today allows companies to screen up to a million compounds a week, in the time it used to take to screen only 100 compounds twenty years ago.[42] This efficiency greatly improves the chances of finding the next new drug for a particular disease. Today HTS is part of the standard process of drug discovery in all pharmaceutical companies.

Microarrays

DNA microarrays, or DNA chips, enable researchers to screen in a high-throughput fashion for molecules that bind to specific forms of DNA.[43] Essentially, these chips act like miniature laboratories containing thousands of DNA sequences on a single chip. These sequences can be bathed in solution containing molecules being tested for their ability to bind to any of the DNA sequences. Once again, the power of the technique is in the efficiency of the screens as well as in the small amount of material required to conduct the screening. One of the more successful companies based on this technology was Affymax, which was founded in 1988 and eventually bought by Glaxo PLC for $533 million, after a bidding war involving three other suitors.[44] That 1995 transaction alone suggests the power of the technology and the belief that biotechnology could streamline drug discovery for the pharmaceutical sector.

Gene therapy

Gene therapy, discussed previously, is the realization that one could insert a new gene into human cells to have a therapeutic effect. Since many diseases have some genetic basis, gene therapy could allow scientists to correct the fundamental defect that is causing the diseased state. The technology spawned many gene therapy biotechnology companies along with new rules at the FDA developed by the Recombinant DNA Advisory Committee (RAC), which reviewed and approved all human clinical trials using this technology. Unlike many of the other technologies, gene therapy has far-reaching implications for safety because it could alter the genetic structure of cells irreversibly and requires the use of potentially dangerous viral structures to deliver genes to the right cells. As a result, the FDA took quite seriously the review of this technology. Although companies in this area continue to move forward, progress has been particularly slow due to several significant scientific setbacks discussed previously.

Antisense and RNA interference

Antisense and RNA interference are both approaches to drug development which usually involve using RNA to block gene expression in order to provide a therapeutic benefit.[45–46] Antisense molecules are small pieces of single stranded RNA (or DNA) that prevent production with high specificity of the protein encoded by the blocked DNA. (RNA is ribonucleic acid and is utilized by the cell in several forms, primarily as an intermediary molecule to translate the genetic code [DNA] into proteins. Like DNA, it is made up of building blocks called nucleotides.) RNA interference involves using small double-stranded RNA to trigger the enzymatic degradation of the RNA template of a specific protein to cause the desired therapeutic effect. RNA interference is a relatively recent discovery and can be used to selectively deactivate genes. It is exciting because it can be used as a tool to understand what each of our 30,000 genes does, and it has the potential to deliver promising novel drugs. RNA interference is so exciting that even though it has only been about two years since *Science* magazine called it the number one scientific breakthrough, at least ten start-up companies are focusing on it (including several outside the US), and big pharmaceutical companies such as Merck and Abbott have begun to use the tool aggressively. Both of these processes involve blocking the function of single gene targets in order to provide a therapeutic benefit.

Systems biology

Systems biology is an attempt to discover drugs using mathematical and computational models to predict outcomes within the whole biological system.[47] The ultimate systems biology approach aims at using large amounts of data to predict outcomes within the human body. The idea is to incorporate data about the cellular machinery, proteins, and their interactions to predict outcomes at the whole organism level. This technology is one of the newest to form the basis of several biotechnology companies (see figure 3.10).

Business models – managing scale and scope

Biotechnology companies have used a variety of business models to build value. In the early stages these companies typically have limited resources and must determine how their technical and intellectual property assets can best

Company	Date founded
Gene Network Sciences	2000
Beyond Genomics	2000
Physiome	1994
Entelos	1996
Protein Pathways	1999
Merrimack	2000
Bioseek	2002
Akceli	2000

Figure 3.10 Selected systems biology companies.

Source: Burrill & Company, *Biotech 2004, Life Sciences: Back on Track*
(San Francisco, CA: Burrill & Company, 2004), 16.
Note: Data from D&B Million Dollar Database and company websites.

be developed in order to provide the optimal chance for business success. Over the last thirty years three primary strategies have been utilized by companies at different times in their evolution. Often companies switch from one strategy to another as events warrant, and variations on the primary strategies have also been created. The FIPCO (fully integrated pharmaceutical company) model is the "all out" strategy to become a pharmaceutical company, and requires substantial resources. The technology platform model builds a company into a contract research organization (CRO) renting its technology platform to produce revenues. The RIPCO (royalty income pharmaceutical company) approach is typically an intermediary strategy, where a company survives off a royalty stream from revenues of its first licensed products. Finally, a fourth model, which has become increasingly popular recently, is NRDO (no research development only), where a company aims to fill its pipeline solely via in-licensing and development of product candidates. Each of these models has advantages and disadvantages, but they can all be used to build value in the appropriate situation.

FIPCO

The FIPCO (or FIBCO), or fully integrated (bio)pharmaceutical company, is the model that many of the first wave of biotechnology companies pursued. The company sets its strategy to build and fully integrate most parts of the drug discovery and development value chain and to become a fully-fledged pharmaceutical company. Given the large amount of capital required to develop even one drug, and the high risk of drug development, few companies have been successful at this strategy. Amgen, however, was fortunate to be able to stay on its original course to become a FIPCO by exploiting what, in the industry, has often been referred to as "low-hanging fruit." These were proteins whose function was already well understood and which had been identified early on as likely drug candidates. It was believed that administration of certain of these naturally occurring human proteins in patients with specific disease states would cause significant and easy-to-measure therapeutic benefit. The challenge in successfully executing on these early opportunities was obvious to the biotechnology entrepreneurs of the time – whichever company was first in identifying the opportunity, cloning the gene, and patenting it would win each of these races. Amgen successfully discovered, patented, developed, and commercialized two large opportunities, erythropoietin (EPO, known as Epogen) and granulocyte colony stimulating factor (G-CSF, known as Neupogen). Initially Amgen received approval for EPO in the US for anemia in renal disease in 1989, and for G-CSF for neutropenia associated with cancer therapy in 1991. By 1993 the company reached sales of more than $1.4 billion from both of these products alone. Early success with two blockbuster biologics gave Amgen the financial resources it needed to build and grow, through internal research as well as acquisitions, into the largest biotechnology company today, with annual sales of $8.4 billion and a market capitalization of over $68 billion. In fact, today Amgen easily ranks in the top ten largest pharmaceutical companies in the world, as measured by market capitalization.

Many other companies have attempted a similar go-it-alone FIPCO-type strategy initially, with less success. Genetics Institute is a good example of a company that eventually chose a FIPCO strategy focused on therapeutics using rDNA technology but was not successful at remaining independent. Genetics Institute had determined, after eight years of research using rDNA technology for diagnostics, therapeutics, agricultural products, and research tools, to focus on biological therapeutics alone, and pursued replacement therapy protein products similar to Amgen. It pursued EPO, but eventually encountered a setback with its EPO patent. Amgen and Genetics Institute filed EPO patents within weeks of each other, creating an important court battle around what would eventually become one of the largest biotechnology blockbuster products. In the end, the Genetics Institute patent was not upheld in the US courts, resulting in a dramatic loss of value for Genetics Institute and an eventual acquisition by American Home Products.

Company	Technology platform
Alnylam Pharmaceuticals	RNA interference
Millennium Pharmaceuticals	Genomics
Incyte Genomics	Informatics
CombinatoRx	High throughput combination screening
Hypnion	High throughput, in vivo sleep animal model system
TransForm Pharmaceuticals	High throughput formulation screening and development

Figure 3.11 Technology platform companies.

Centocor is another example of a highly productive biotechnology company that, like Genetics Institute, eventually was not able to remain independent. Centocor developed its first product, *Centoxin*, to treat sepsis, a systemic blood infection. However, Centocor failed to win approval by the FDA after spending significant capital on clinical testing through phase III trials. Although Centocor had other products in its pipeline, it could not withstand the financial blow of its *Centoxin* failure and was eventually acquired by Johnson & Johnson. Today, Centocor's *ReoPro*, prescribed for cardiovascular indications, is an important Johnson & Johnson product.

Technology platform model

Platform technology companies have been built on a wide variety of types of technology (see figure 3.11). These technologies may be enabling for any part of the drug discovery or drug development process. For example, certain genomics technologies or RNA interference are useful in drug discovery to identify new molecular drug targets for specific diseases. Pharmacogenomics, on the other hand, is useful in the clinical development of a specific drug to identify patient populations most likely to be positively impacted by a specific drug. The technologies may be biologically based, such as the humanization of monoclonal antibodies, or chemistry-based, such as rapid high-throughput screening methods. They may be easily patentable or best protected as trade secrets. They may be most useful to improve already existing drugs (e.g., delivery technologies), or productively used to discover new drugs. Certain platform technologies are powerful enough to form the scientific foundation upon which a small biotechnology company can discover its own novel proprietary drugs and drug targets. These tend to be the most commercially valuable technology platforms today.

During the 1980s and 1990s many platform technology companies initially tried to build their business strategy around selling and reselling their technology through contracts with many pharmaceutical companies. They would collect research funding and other fees on a continued basis, similar to any fee for service contract research organization. In some cases, due to the highly technical nature of the business, these companies were also able to extract significant value via success fees or other large milestone payments. For certain technology platforms, this became a challenging model to implement on a sustained basis, because it was difficult to prevent the technology from becoming a commodity with reduced value. The combinatorial chemistry tools of Houghten Pharmaceuticals, and the bioinformatics databases of Incyte and others, are good examples of technologies that quickly became commoditized. In other cases, the technology initially was not valued highly enough by big pharmaceutical companies and the business had to change its strategy because it could not raise enough capital in order to succeed.

Ultimately, the true commercial value of the technology platform is defined by the perceived value the technology has in producing novel proprietary drugs and the ability to protect, in the long-term, the technology in the marketplace via patents. As a result, the technology platform model has evolved substantially over the years such that few pure technology platform companies access start-up capital today, because most investors do not believe that a pure technology platform company can build enough value as a contract research organization. The evidence is clear in that the deals done by large pharmaceutical companies today with technology platform companies typically have low payments and royalties associated with them. Instead, the technology platform companies that are founded today are those that can utilize their technology effectively to quickly move toward discovering and developing their own proprietary products. This comes from investors' and entrepreneurs' understanding that the superior value is in the patent protected product, with less value residing in the technology itself. As one venture capitalist in the field has explained, venture capitalists who invest in technology platforms today invest primarily in those that can quickly be translated into proprietary products in the clinic.

Millennium Pharmaceuticals is a good example of a company that was initially founded on a broad platform technology, but which eventually managed to transform itself into a product company and which now has two products on the market. Millennium was founded on a genomics platform where its goal was to discover new genes that would ultimately become new novel drug targets. Once these new drug targets were identified, new

Partner	Date	Deal terms	Committed capital and equity in deal
Bayer	1998	5-year R&D deal with splitting of costs and future revenues	$465 million payments
Abbott	2001	5-year R&D deal in metabolic disease; development, marketing, manufacturing costs worldwide split; deal terminated in 2003	$250 million equity investment
Aventis	2000	Joint development and commercialization of drugs for the treatment of inflammatory diseases; joint development of new drug discovery technologies; transfer of key elements of the company's technology platform to Aventis to enhance its existing capabilities; and purchase of an equity interest in the Company by Aventis	$450 million equity investment and payments

Figure 3.12   Selected Millennium pharmaceutical alliances.

medicines could be created. The company followed several paths in order to maximize the value of its platform. First, it took advantage of the excitement and promise of the technology as well as, perhaps, the fears of the pharmaceutical sector that it might be excluded from the next game-changing technology that could be responsible for the next wave of innovative therapeutics. If ever there was a technology since rDNA that looked like it could change drug discovery in significant ways, genomics was it. Over several years Millennium translated this into a few major pharmaceutical alliances, raising almost $1.2 billion in committed capital to finance its research efforts (see figure 3.12).

Using its genomics platform, Millennium also created a family of companies focused on the different components of the healthcare industry. Millennium formed a diagnostics company, Millennium Predictive Medicine, which was responsible for using the genomics platform to build a world-class diagnostics business, and a biologics company, Millennium Biotherapeutics, to focus on developing biologics as human therapeutics. Eventually it became clear that clinical candidates would not quickly emerge from the genomics platform, so Millennium was forced to change its strategy and acquire products to sell. This resulted in another set of deals, described below, to fill its pipeline (see figure 3.13). To date, no products in clinical development or on the market have derived from Millennium's genomics platform; however, that same platform has enabled the company to become one of the most well-financed biotechnology companies.

Company	Deal size ($ million)	Date	Product	Current Product stage	Indications
COR Therapeutics	600	2002	Integrilin	Marketed	PTCA, acute coronary syndromes
LeukoSite	635	1999	Velcade	Marketed/ phases II & III	Multiple myeloma, solid tumors

Figure 3.13 Selected Millennium acquisitions.

RIPCO

Royalty income pharmaceutical companies (RIPCOs) are typically going through a transition on their way toward trying to become FIPCOs. These companies usually license their initial product(s) to a large pharmaceutical company in exchange for a royalty on sales, with the hope that the royalty they receive can financially support the company in its early years. These companies will bring their first product through early stages of preclinical or early clinical development, creating as much value as possible, and then license the product to a large pharmaceutical or biotechnology company in order to complete the development and to commercialize the product. The royalty on sales received by the biotechnology company is typically in the range of 5–14 percent but can be quite variable depending on how much value the biotechnology company brings to the deal. The royalty rate also depends on the specific market conditions. Even if the revenues are substantial, and the royalties significant, often they take too long to arrive to be of immediate financial help, due to the long-term nature of the drug development cycle. Companies that utilize this strategy almost always need other methods of financing in order to support themselves in the early years.

One example of a company that used the RIPCO model successfully was Biogen, now Biogen Idec as a result of a recent merger. Biogen, founded in 1978 by a group of European and US scientists including Phillip Sharp and Walter Gilbert, both Nobel Laureates, clearly transformed its business model over time. Once Biogen went public in 1983, like all companies, it faced Wall Street pressures to produce products and revenues fast. Although the science in the company was top-rate, it did not have the business focus that Wall Street investors were demanding. By the end of 1985 a new CEO was brought on board with a proven track record in the business world. James Vincent, the new Chairman and CEO of Biogen, made important business decisions over his first few years, which, for the short term, converted Biogen into a RIPCO. He completed sublicensing deals during the 1980s with SmithKline French and Merck on hepatitis B antigen for the development of the recombinant hepatitis B vaccines (Engerix B and Recombivax HB). He renegotiated a previously signed deal with Schering Plough on alpha- and beta-interferons to recapture the rights to beta-interferon and to improve the royalty rate on alpha-interferon, which Schering Plough eventually developed for various cancers including malignant melanoma and renal cell carcinoma. Once these deals were completed, Biogen was looking like a company that had licensed off its most promising near-term technology (alpha-interferon and hepatitis B antigens) to big pharmaceutical companies in exchange for a future royalty. Ultimately, both of these technologies were transformed into two of the most valuable products derived from the biotechnology sector; alpha-interferon became a $1.8 billion drug for the treatment of various cancers, and the recombinant hepatitis B vaccine became the largest selling vaccine to date posting total annual sales of $2 billion at its peak. Biogen collected approximately $150 million annually from royalty streams related to these products.

Vincent also prepared Biogen for the long term to take bets on a few proprietary programs. The royalty stream enabled Biogen to develop two of its proprietary clinical programs, beta-interferon for multiple sclerosis and bivalirudin for cardiovascular syndromes, which had the potential to become valuable drugs, as well as several preclinical stage programs. Although several of these programs failed, including bivalirudin, which was licensed out to The Medicines Company, in 1996 Biogen launched Avonex (interferon B-1a) for the treatment of relapsing remitting multiple sclerosis. Avonex became a billion-dollar product within about six years and was launched in the US, Europe, and over forty other countries worldwide.

In hindsight, the Biogen strategy of mortgaging its first products early in order to provide later revenue to fund and launch its follow-on products was very successful. Without the initial royalty revenue stream it is not clear how Biogen would have survived to launch its first and second proprietary products and eventually merge with IDEC. Few other biotechnology companies have managed to execute a similar strategy as successfully.

NRDO

More recently, as the biotechnology sector has come to include venture-backed pharmaceutical companies that are developing small molecule-based drugs, some of these companies have chosen the NRDO strategy. These small

Group	2000	2001	2002	2003	Q1 2004
NRDO ($ million)	41.3	208.8	404.9	395.5	517.7*
NRDO avg ($ million)	8.3	23.2	22.5	23.3	64.7*
Total NRDO rounds	5	9	18	17	8
R&D ($ million)	202.5	883.6	1,010.0	1,053.8	570.4
R&D avg ($ million)	10.1	16.7	13.6	16.2	22.8
Total R&D rounds	20	53	74	65	25

Figure 3.14   Venture funding trends for NRDO companies versus R&D companies.

Source: "Deconstructing De-risking," *BioCentury: The Bernstein Report* 12(25) (June 7, 2004): A2.
*Includes the $250 million series B round of venture financing raised by Jazz Pharmaceuticals.

Group	Number founded since 2000	Percentage of total	Capital raised by all companies ($ million)	Percentage of total	Average per company ($ million)
NRDO	32	16	1,702.9	30	53.2
R&D	163	84	4,006.0	70	24.6
Total	195	100	5,708.9	100	NA

Figure 3.15   NRDO versus R&D company financings (public and private).

Source: "Deconstructing De-risking," *BioCentury: The Bernstein Report* 12(25) (June 7, 2004): A3.

companies have set out to license from big pharmaceutical companies products that are already in preclinical or clinical testing with potential peak sales of only $50–$300 million. Many large pharmaceutical companies have grown so big, via mergers or growth, that products with peak sales in this range are not valuable enough for them to develop. However, they are highly valuable to small companies with 50–300 employees and limited revenues. In addition, certain therapeutic areas have become less interesting to large pharmaceutical companies because of limited growth and peak revenue potential, such as antibiotics. Venture capitalists claim that the movement to this model is a swing of the pendulum to the opposite pole after the failure of the genomics model to deliver on products. As a result, venture funding for these companies has increased substantially over the last few years (see figures 3.14, 3.15).

The Medicines Company, founded in 1996, was one of the early entrants based on this strategy, and today it has revenues of $85 million annually.

Since then, many companies have taken a similar route, including Pharmion, Jazz, Oscient, Vicuron, and Cubist, the last three of which are currently focusing on the antibiotics market. Gilead Sciences is an example of a company that had been doing research for some time, but then licensed in compounds from Bristol–Myers Squibb and switched its strategy to focus on development. Most business development professionals in biotechnology and pharmaceuticals agree that finding new product opportunities to in-license can be difficult, especially on an ongoing basis, and it remains to be seen whether these companies can turn their recent success at raising money into a successful strategy for building small pharmaceutical companies.

Summary

As a company grows and matures its business strategy changes. Many biotechnology companies have utilized more than one of these strategies over several years, and sometimes a combination of two or more simultaneously, depending on the technology and other factors. As mentioned, many RIPCO companies eventually aim toward becoming a FIPCO, if possible. Today almost all technology platform companies work toward developing proprietary drugs in order for them to become FIPCOs or at least develop their own products.

In reality, most companies do not successfully become FIPCOs because they run out of capital, their technology does not produce products early enough, or their technology fails to deliver on its promise. Within the context of a venture-backed biotechnology firm, where the board of directors consists primarily of venture investors seeking a high return on their investment, any such event will cause a shift in strategy. Under these circumstances, typically the investors look to salvage their return on investment within a short period of time, while the management of the company may be more willing to weather the storm and continue to build a company. The result depends on many factors, including the ability of management to get the technology back on track. Ultimately, although few, if any, biotechnology companies are founded with the stated business strategy of being acquired, the stark reality of the requirements for investor returns causes many venture-backed biotechnology companies to look carefully at multiple options, including sale of the company, merger, or acquisition of additional technology or products. The end result is often a deal of some sort that enables the investor to extract his or her return.

Financing and the capital markets

To execute any business model successfully in biotechnology, substantial financing is required because of the large amount of capital and time required for a relatively high-risk chance at building a successful company and obtaining a financial return. Although reports differ, all studies agree that it is expensive and time-consuming, at least in the range of over $300 million (some report as high as $800 million) and ten to fifteen years on average, to develop one drug.[48–49] Because of these factors, most biotechnology industry CEOs rank raising capital to fund their businesses as top priority. Most financial advisors recommend that CEOs of biotechnology companies access capital whenever it is available because, as with many other markets, there is a cyclical nature to financing in the biotechnology sector (see figure 3.16). These cycles can occur over one to several years, and can be driven by many factors, including broad market events such as the September 11 terrorist attacks in the US, regulatory approvals of biotechnology products, biotechnology deals, intellectual property issues related to companies in the industry, and government policy affecting biotechnology. For example, a string of several FDA product approvals or positive clinical trial results might cause the initial public offering (IPO) market for biotechnology companies to open. In addition, a positive government policy statement about stem cell research funding

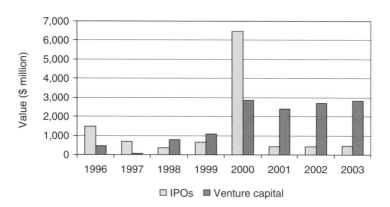

Figure 3.16   IPOs versus venture capital funding.

Source: Burrill & Company, *Biotech 2002, Life Sciences: Systems Biology* (San Francisco, CA: Burrill & Company, 2002), 294; Burrill & Company, *Biotech 2004, Life Sciences: Back on Track* (San Francisco, CA: Burrill & Company, 2004), 351.

might also impact biotechnology markets positively. Moreover, events related to other industries can also have significant impact on the availability of capital for the biotechnology sector. For example, during the late 1990s, when technology venture capital was flowing into internet, information technology, and telecommunications companies as part of the "high-technology bubble," much less private capital was available to biotechnology companies. Once the information and computer technology bubble burst and investors were moving their capital out of these technology investments, significant amounts of private capital became available in 2000 to biotechnology companies.

The large and incessant need for capital has forced the industry to become creative in order to adequately fund its research and development activities, especially during times when the more traditional routes of accessing capital are not available. In the very early phase of a company, private funding in the form of seed funding and venture capital plays a primary role. Even in later-stage companies, venture capitalists conduct mezzanine financings and provide bridge financing when additional capital is required but where a company is looking to go public in 12–24 months. As the industry has matured, public funding, which is the least expensive, has played a more significant role for later-stage companies. To access public investment for the first time in an IPO, the company must meet certain minimum criteria:[50]

- outstanding science and technology of high interest
- products in human clinical testing stage
- one or more strategic alliances with major pharmaceutical companies to validate the technology
- strong patent position
- experienced, high-quality management
- impressive board of directors and scientific advisory board

Other types of financing have also been used, depending on market conditions. Figure 3.17 reflects the mix of financing alternatives that have been used by the industry over the last thirty years. Some are no longer used.

Private placements

Private or public companies raise money from a limited number of private high net worth investors when the venture community and public markets are least receptive. These placements are often led by boutique merchant or investment banks, which apply lower valuation pressures than the venture capitalist or public markets.

Type	Amount ($ million)	Company stage	Advantages for company	Disadvantages for company
Government grants	0–5	Seed to early clinical	Free money	Limited availability
Venture capital	1–50	Seed to clinical stage	Availability; substantial VC involvement	Low valuations; high equity cost
Private placements	1–70	Preclinical to advance clinicals	Higher valuations	Limited availability
PIPEs	10–50	Preclinical to market	Lower valuation pressure	Dilution-stock sold at discount
IPO	15–100	Clinical to market	Large financings possible	Markets cyclical; public valuation not predictable
Secondary public offerings	25–150	Clinical to market	Large financings possible	Requires infrastructure
SWORDs	20–50	Preclinical to clinicals	Off balance sheet to avoid dilution	Costly repurchase
R&D partnerships	1–50	R&D	Off balance sheet to avoid dilution; tax leverage	Costly repurchase; no longer available
Convertible debt	10–100	Clinical to market	Lower "cost"; based on convertibility, not yield	Debt service requirements
Asset-based debt	1–50	Development	No dilution	For buildings, equipment, receivables, inventory

Figure 3.17 Financing alternatives.

Source: G. Steven Burrill and Kenneth B. Lee, Jr., *Biotech 93: Accelerating Commercialization* (San Francisco, CA: Ernst & Young, 1992), 33.

PIPEs

A special kind of private placement may be conducted when private investors are allowed to purchase public common stock in a company, typically at a discount of 5–20 percent of the public price. These offerings are referred to as PIPEs (private investment in public equity) and have advantages in that the investor purchases shares at a discount to the public price, the investment becomes liquid within three months, and the companies who conduct them are usually more mature and closer to profitability. On the other hand, shares issued are unregistered initially, the investor has limited ability to affect change in the company, and because of the discount the offering causes a share price dilution.[51]

Recently, concerns have been raised about PIPEs because they exclude the small investor, which creates market inefficiencies. In addition, PIPEs can cause downward pressure on the stock and large investors can manipulate prices. Because of these issues, in 2004 the Securities and Exchange Commission (SEC) began an investigation of several specific PIPE offerings. These investments continue to be popular across industries, however. In 2002 and 2003 over $12 billion was invested in all PIPEs, and the trajectory of investment for 2004 appeared to be at least as substantial.[52]

R&D limited partnerships and SWORDs

R&D limited partnerships emerged as a key resource for the industry in the 1980s when the law provided tax incentives for investors. Genentech was the first to adopt this financing vehicle to the biotechnology sector in order to fund specific clinical stage projects, which were most attractive to investors. The company "spun out" its technology and the investor received a unit, consisting of an ownership right in the limited partnership and warrants to purchase common stock of the offering company, a future royalty on sales of products being developed, a potential buy-back payout by the company of the partnership interest if the technology was successful, and a federal tax break on the research investment. The company received project funding and a right to buy back the technology from the partnership at a later date and at a fixed price.

Once R&D limited partnerships were no longer viable due to changes in the tax law that eliminated the attractive federal tax incentive to investors, a similar investment vehicle called a SWORD (stock warrant off-balance sheet R&D financing) was used in its place to fund similar types of later stage projects within companies. In this case, the specific project is spun out into a new company through similar units offering in the public market. Via the units, the investor receives certain valuable rights to the new technology, with investment downside protection via the warrants to purchase common stock in the more mature parent company, and the company can fund exciting new projects via public investment.

Convertible debt securities

Debt is issued by biotechnology companies when the equity markets are not available. Convertible debt does not cause any near-term dilution of the equity share price, and there is no need to register the notes with the SEC, which saves time. On the other hand, the debt can be converted into equity after some period of time, saving the cash-poor biotechnology company many years of debt service. The investor is essentially paid an initial fixed return to wait for a much bigger potential upside on the stock.

Government grants

Many young biotechnology companies have received SBIR (Small Business Innovative Research) grants from the US federal government to fund various research projects. This is nondilutive funding that has enabled some companies to survive as they work toward important value-creating milestones that would enable them to access other types of financing. Certain top-tier biotechnology companies such as Biogen Idec, Amgen, Genzyme, and Immunex made use of federal grants to support early research, at a time when other financing was not easily available.[53] In 2003 alone the NIH provided over $500 million in health-related grants. In addition, in 2003 the Department of Defense funded over $1 billion in health-related support grants, and a new Project Bioshield law, described later, will enable the Department of Homeland Security to provide federal grants for the development and procurement of vaccines and treatments to protect Americans against biological, chemical, and radiological threats.[54]

Summary

In the US alone, in the last six years (1998–2003) over $85 billion has been invested in the biotechnology sector, excluding any funding from the federal government, nonprofit organizations, or major pharmaceutical strategic alliances. However, the sources of this financing have shifted (see figures 3.18, 3.19). In 2000 venture capital financing grew dramatically, as funds shifted their investing energy from information technology to biotechnology. All other markets responded similarly, and over $32 billion was invested into biotechnology that year. Since then, markets have cooled. Venture capital has continued to invest well over $2 billion annually, but the public markets for biotechnology IPOs have been virtually closed, with no more than a handful of companies per year entering the public market; the only companies to go public in 2003 have had either marketed or late stage clinical products. As a result, public debt and PIPEs have played an important role in funding young

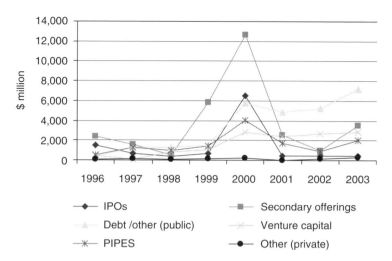

Figure 3.18 Biotech financing trends, 1996–2003.

Source: Burrill & Company, *Biotech 2005, Life Sciences: Systems Biology* (San Francisco, CA: Burrill & Company, 2004), 294; Burrill & Company, *Biotech 2004, Life Sciences: Back on Track* (San Francisco, CA: Burrill & Company, 2004), 351.

companies. In addition, companies have been forced to modify their research plans and reduce their annual expenditures. The year 2004 proved to be a bit more exciting for biotechnology: by May, sixteen companies had already completed IPOs, although most of them at lower valuations than expected.[55]

Although similar shifts in financing alternatives have occurred throughout the thirty-year history of the industry, investors and analysts in biotechnology are far more discerning and well informed about the risks today. In addition, as described in the next section, alliances with major pharmaceutical companies have evolved to play a major role in financing. In general, the biotechnology companies that deliver on products will continue to have access to capital from a variety of sources; those that have an exciting scientific story, but with products years away, will find access to capital much more restricted.

The biotechnology–pharmaceutical company alliance

Fundamental market forces have driven the biotechnology and pharmaceutical industries to work closely together via hundreds of alliances. Before examining the evolution of these inter-industry relationships, it is important to understand the challenges organizations face in making these complex

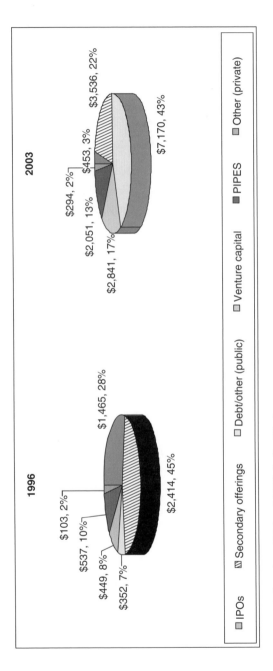

Figure 3.19 Biotech financings 1996 and 2003 (in $ million).

Source: Burrill & Company, *Biotech 2005, Life Sciences: Systems Biology* (San Francisco, CA: Burrill & Company 2004), 294; Burrill & Company, *Biotech 2004, Life Sciences: Back on Track* (San Francisco, CA: Burrill & Company, 2004), 351.

collaborations work successfully. Although the two industries are both focused on developing new medicines for human illness, and work very closely together, in many ways they do business very differently. The similarities are few and far between in terms of management, culture, business strategy, and methods across the drug discovery and development value chain (see figure 3.20).

At a high level the differences can be summarized in the following way. The pharmaceutical company is a large, multinational, fully integrated, multi-layered, well-resourced, public company that has been in business for many years, has many products on the market and in the R&D pipeline, and has put in place appropriate management structures and processes in order to function effectively given its size and geographic presence. On the other hand, the biotechnology company (excluding the few top-tier companies that fall somewhere in between the two poles of this spectrum) is typically a much smaller, resource-limited private company (or newly public company), highly influenced by its investors, with a limited management structure and core technology or product base and with a fast-paced, entrepreneurial culture and few processes. Consequently, these two types of organizations function very differently, and effectively managing alliances between them can be challenging for the management of both organizations.

To make a collaborative alliance work between a large pharmaceutical company and a small biotechnology company, it is critical that both parties view the collaboration as important to their business and that both have a significant stake in the outcome. In addition, incentives must be aligned so that the parties are working toward a common goal. Figure 3.21 outlines more specifically what makes alliances work. Without one or more of the listed components, it is very easy for a working collaboration to unravel in a way that diminishes the benefits to each.

The relationship between biotechnology companies and large pharmaceutical companies has evolved over time, and today both sides reap significant benefits and value from strategic corporate alliances. Biotechnology companies and pharmaceutical companies enter into many types of research and development collaborative relationships for a variety of reasons. Through these partnerships, biotechnology companies are able to access capital in order to fund research; in 2003 alone in the US, biotechnology companies raised almost $10 billion from pharmaceutical alliances.[56] In addition, biotechnology companies gain validation of their products or technology by the more experienced large pharmaceutical partner. This type of validation adds substantial credibility when a biotechnology company is looking to access the

	Pharmaceutical company	Biotechnology company
Management & governance		
Management structure	Large senior management team; multiple layers; increased bureaucracy	Small senior management team; flat structure
Management personnel	Seasoned business executives; many years experience in large company management; grown up through big pharmaceutical industry	Younger entrepreneurs; less business experience; highly technically qualified; many first time CEOs and senior managers
Board of directors	Seasoned business executives from a variety of industries; all publicly held	Venture capitalist investors; scientific founders; most not publicly held
Compensation	Cash with modest stock option component at higher levels of organization	Cash with significant stock option component at all levels of organization
Employees & Culture		
Number of employees	20,000–120,000*	10–2,500 largest 10,000*
Sales reps in US (total)	100,000**; Top 20 range 1,000–8,000	<5,000*; Top few range 200–450
Corporate culture	Technically oriented on research side only; commercially oriented otherwise; process oriented; bureaucratic; high level of expertise in all functions	Technically oriented throughout organization; less commercially focused, except in larger companies; less process and less bureaucracy; entrepreneurial, fast paced; mixed levels of expertise across organization
Products & Pipeline		
Products	Mostly chemical drugs; some biologics licensed from biotechnology companies	Originally protein-based drugs in form of monoclonal antibodies, fusion proteins, cytokines, naturally occurring proteins (biologics); now also chemical drugs similar to pharmaceuticals
Pipelines	In general, scores of programs at all levels of R & D, and many marketed products with complex commercial organizations	In general, few programs, and fewer clinical stage programs (<10 in most companies); limited to no commercial infrastructure except in top-tier biotechnology companies; even largest companies have <500 US sales reps
Financials & Financing		
R&D expense	$25.7B (2002)***	$12.5B (2002; publicly held only)****
R&D expense/ revenues	18% (2002)***	40% (2002; publicly held only)****

Figure 3.20 Comparison of pharmaceutical and biotechnology companies.

	Pharmaceutical company	Biotechnology company
Financing	Self-sustaining; dependent on revenues and earnings to put back into R&D and commercialization	Most not self-sustaining; dependent on periodic infusions of private or public capital, or capital from strategic alliances or government grants
Intellectual property		
Patent issues	Composition of matter patents on chemical structure of new drugs is dominating intellectual property creating market exclusivity; "patent busting" or designing NCEs around patented drugs to develop "me too" products with slightly different characteristics is common practice; use patents afford some protection	Composition of matter patents are important, and most powerful intellectual property; but patents on manufacturing process and use of molecules also creates reasonable protection; "patent busting" to design similar proteins to develop "me too" products with similar characteristics is more difficult due to various technical issues and is not common practice (although a few examples exist); for biotechnology NCEs, exactly same as pharmaceutical patent issues
Value chain (R&D, commercialization)		
Drug development process	Typically conduct at least several phase III studies with large numbers of patients; strategy is to cover all possible technical risks and issues to satisfy regulatory agencies	Typically conduct two phase III studies (sometimes one); often use minimum number of patients; strategy is to cover most important technical issues, but to take more risk, save money and reduce time
Integration of R&D and commercial functions	Most fully integrated across all segments of R&D and commercialization value chain	Most focused on only segments of R&D value chain, outsourcing other functions and not yet ready or able to build commercial infrastructure
Manufacturing	Chemical synthesis for pills and capsules	For biologics based on cell culture fermentation for vials of powder or liquid; chemistry manufacturing for NCEs outsourced always
Markets	Focus on large markets with large physician and patient customer bases	Focus on large or smaller markets with more focused physician customer bases; this is starting to change such that larger companies are targeting markets with larger customer bases

	Pharmaceutical company	Biotechnology company
Regulation	Until 2003, CDER section of FDA for chemical entities; CBER section of FDA for biologics; Today CDER for most chemical and biologic drugs, except for vaccines, gene therapy	Until 2003, CBER section of FDA for biologics; CDER section of FDA for chemical entities; Today CDER for most biologic and chemical drugs, except for vaccines, gene therapy

Figure 3.20 (cont.)

*Author's estimate.
**Michelle Goldberg, Bob Davenport, and Tiffany Mortellito, "The Big Squeeze," *Pharmaceutical Executive* 40(l) (January 1, 2004).
***PhRMA 2004 Industry Profile.
****Standard & Poor's Biotechnology Industry Surveys (June 10, 2004): 14 & 15.

Aligned incentives	Deal should be set up so that both parties have incentive to accomplish their goals; the "prize" should be important to both parties, including financial rewards; intellectual property should be treated fairly
Priority	The joint project should remain a priority for both parties so resources are appropriately applied
Relationship	The people who have to work together on the project should have mutual respect and confidence in each other's abilities
Senior management	Senior management, at the appropriate level, should be involved in the collaboration, remain interested and excited throughout
Dispute resolution	Process for handling any disputes should be simple to execute and reasonable for both parties, and should have clear endpoints
Contract	Contract should clearly define how decisions are made on key issues, including process

Figure 3.21 What makes alliances work.

public markets via an IPO. Biotechnology companies are also able to access capabilities that they otherwise do not have in order to complete the development and commercialization of their own products, such as manufacturing, development, regulatory, and marketing and sales. Big pharmaceutical companies, on the other hand, gain access to product opportunities to fill their pipelines. Additionally, they can acquire or access innovative technologies that can support drug discovery and development at lower risk than the cost (in time and money) of building them from scratch. Moreover, pharmaceutical companies can also access some of the culture of scientific innovation that big companies often struggle to replicate within the context of their complex management structures. A review of the evolution of these inter-industry alliances is instructive for an understanding of the forces that drive them and of the value they bring to both parties today.

In the late 1970s and early 1980s, at the inception of the biotechnology sector, the pharmaceutical sector did not see substantial value in the biotechnology sector. Few pharmaceutical companies viewed the biotechnology sector as much more than a "toolbox" – a set of scientific tools that might enhance productivity in drug discovery. A minority of pharmaceutical companies believed that biologics which could not be delivered orally in the form of capsules or tablets, and which had to be injected, would produce important medicines. Moreover, most pharmaceutical companies believed that if, by chance, valuable therapeutic products were to come out of the biotechnology sector, the products could be purchased at a later date with the risk substantially reduced. This perspective drove the structure and value of the alliances that pharmaceutical companies entered into at the time. Arrangements often consisted of arm's-length licenses to products with a future royalty on potential sales and little economic value to the licensor at the front end of the deal. For example, in 1978 Biogen licensed all development and commercial rights to its interferons to Schering Plough for a royalty and limited additional cash payments, and in 1979 Genentech struck a similar licensing deal for human insulin with Eli Lilly.[57] In the 1980s, as the value of biotechnology was becoming clearer, biotechnology companies began to have increased leverage in these corporate partnerships. They often sought additional financing that would supply near-term research funding in addition to a future royalty on eventual product sales in exchange for the development and marketing of their products.

As the first biotechnology products were approved by the FDA and demonstrated their significant market value, the structure of the biotechnology–pharmaceutical alliance began to change dramatically in size and scope. Evolving global trends in transaction numbers and values between the two industries tell part of the story of the changing relationship. As early as the late 1980s industry experts reported a continued trend toward increasing numbers of strategic alliances between biotechnology companies and pharmaceutical companies (see figure 3.22).[58] In 1990 Burrill reported that of the biotechnology companies developing therapeutic products, 48 percent had an alliance involving research, 61 percent had one involving a technology license, and 57 percent had one involving a marketing arrangement. From 1986 to 1991 strategic alliances clearly showed an increasing trend.[59–60] Moreover, through 1997 numbers of pharmaceutical–biotechnology alliances increased, reaching 228 deals that year. Although the total number of

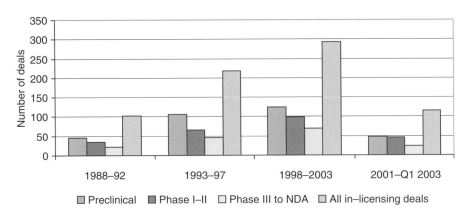

Figure 3.22 Licensing deals by phase 1998–2003.

Source: Licensing Insight, Wood Mackenzie Multiclient Study (April 2003)

Deal	Year	Purchase price($ million)	% equity purchased
Roche/Genentech	1990	2,100	60
American Home Products/Genetics Institute	1991	666	60
Lederle/Immunex	1993	350	54
RPR/Applied Immune Sciences	1993	113	37
Ciba Geigy/Chiron	1995	2,100	50

Figure 3.23 Selected early partial acquisitions in biotechnology.

Sources: Elizabeth S. Kiesche, "Immunex and Lederle Complete a Merger," *Chemical Week* 152(22) (June 9, 1993): 8; "Applied Immune Stake Sale," *Wall Street Journal* (September 23, 1993): A5; Ralph T. King, "Drug Discovery: Pharmaceutical Giants are Eagerly Shopping Biotech Bargain Bin – They Step up Investment to Find Novel Products for Managed-Care Era – The Arrows and the Targets," *Wall Street Journal* (April 11, 1995): A1.

deals involving the top twenty large pharmaceutical companies declined from 1999 through 2003, from 256 to 195, cumulative deal value increased by over 40 percent, from $4.9 billion to $6.9 billion, indicating a substantial increase in the average deal size.[61] In general, throughout the 1990s and into the twenty-first century more deals were being done at higher valuations.[62]

In addition to the high-level trends, a few specific events in the evolution of biotechnology–pharmaceutical alliances demonstrate the changing perspective of the major pharmaceutical companies and are worth noting. In 1990, when Roche bought 60 percent of Genentech for $2.1 billion, both industries took notice.[63] This was one of the first examples of a pharmaceutical company placing substantial value on a biotechnology company's ability to deliver important therapeutic products to its pipeline over time. Genentech was purchased and maintained as a separate research and development arm of Roche in order not to disrupt its productive research efforts. The Roche deal was followed by several other similar partial acquisitions of biotechnology companies by large pharmaceutical companies, as outlined in figure 3.23. It was now clear to the pharmaceutical sector that biotechnology could deliver products to its pipeline.

In addition to the partial acquisition activity, certain technologies pursued by biotechnology companies caused a flurry of deal activity because of the perceived power and value of the technology. In the case of genomics technology, the deals created were ground-breaking for biotechnology, from the perspective of value. During the genomics era, major pharmaceutical companies were concerned that they could be excluded from hundreds of novel targets and products that would derive from genomics if they did not participate early in the development of the technology. Pharmaceutical companies were specifically concerned that they would be blocked from using the novel targets that would be discovered by the biotechnology companies because these entrepreneurial companies would own all of the new intellectual property claiming these novel targets. Eventually, it turned out that the biotechnology companies were not so easily able to lock up all the intellectual property around the novel targets very rapidly. However, at the time these concerns drove deal-making. In 1993 SmithKline French paid Human Genome Sciences $125 million to access exclusive novel targets, even though the biology behind most of the targets remained unknown at the time.[64] In addition, as described previously, Millennium Pharmaceuticals was able to access over $1 billion of capital from three pharmaceutical companies who wanted to access the power of genomics in order to discover new drug targets. Few other individual technologies, aside from the original rDNA technology, have had a similar impact on biotechnology–pharmaceutical alliances.

In the last few years the dynamic between the two industries has continued to change, so that the biotechnology–pharmaceutical industry relationship has become truly symbiotic, a relationship that is important for the survival of both industries. On the one hand, more sparsely resourced biotechnology companies continue to deliver clinical candidates and products to the market, while on the other hand, large pharmaceutical company mergers have created additional need for late stage products to meet their requisite growth rates. Market demand has quickly outstripped supply of late stage products, and has driven strategic alliances between the two industries, especially as blockbuster pharmaceutical product patents have begun to expire (see figure 3.24).

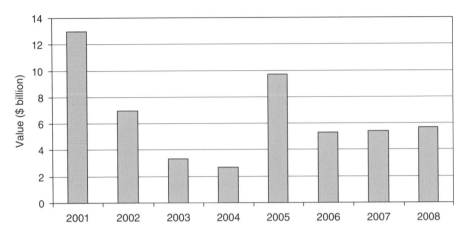

Figure 3.24   Value of prescription drugs coming off-patent.

Source: SG Cowen Health Care Group, "Asia's Biotechnology Dawn" (November 2001): 9.

By the turn of the millennium, strategic alliances began to take on a different format – those biotechnology companies with late stage clinical products were able more easily to structure co-development/co-promotion deals that allowed for substantial profit-sharing and for the biotechnology company to retain limited commercial rights to its products, at least in the US. For example, in 2002 Pfizer entered into an agreement potentially worth nearly $750 million with Eyetech Pharmaceuticals for the development and commercialization of Macugen, Eyetech's product for age-related macular degeneration and diabetic macular edema. The structure of the deal involved $100 million upfront with the remaining money being paid upon the realization of development and commercialization milestones.[65] Also in 2002, Pfizer and Neurocrine Biosciences entered into a $400 million collaboration to develop and commercialize Indiplon, an insomnia therapy. Again, the deal involved a $100 million up-front payment, with the remainder of the financing to be paid upon completion of various milestones.[66] Although both of these deals involve substantial payments to the biotechnology companies, even more noteworthy is the fact that in each one, the biotechnology company retained rights to build its own sales force and co-promote the product in the US. In the Neurocrine deal, Pfizer is obligated to support the creation of Neurocrine's commercial infrastructure.[67] In addition, in both deals the biotechnology company gains the right to sell one of Pfizer's related products in the short term, which will assist the biotechnology company sales force in establishing the appropriate sales relationships with customers. Retaining these commercial rights demonstrates the increased leverage biotechnology companies now have in late stage product deals with major pharmaceutical companies.

By 2003 even big pharmaceutical companies that were notorious for not doing many deals began to take note. Merck, for example, did ten research collaboration deals in 1999 and forty in 2003.[68] Interestingly enough, most of these were discovery deals, demonstrating that some major pharmaceutical companies have begun to access much of their innovation from the biotechnology sector as well. With industry experts today suggesting that over 65 percent of the clinical pipeline of all pharmaceuticals exists within the biotechnology sector, at least 50 percent of which are novel therapeutics with substantial market potential, large pharmaceutical companies are likely to maintain their interest in biotechnology product deals at high valuations. This remarkable statistic has created a powerful mutual dependence between these two industries.

One other event in biotechnology deal history had an opposite chilling effect on alliance formation throughout the industry. In September 2001, when Bristol–Myers Squibb(BMS) announced its deal to pay $1 billion up-front, pay an additional $200 million on signing, and to purchase a 20 percent stake in Imclone, all to access *Erbitux*, a potential blockbuster cancer therapeutic, Wall Street was excited. This was a huge deal for Imclone, which would keep 60 percent of the US sales. Then in December the FDA did not accept the application for approval of Erbitux, calling it incomplete. Imclone's stock lost 70 percent of its value upon publication of the news, BMS wrote off more than $735 million of its investment, and Imclone was soon under investigation by the SEC for insider trading issues. In the end the FDA reviewed additional clinical data and approved the drug for the treatment of advanced colorectal cancer in February 2004, BMS restructured its arrangement with Imclone, and the CEO of Imclone pleaded guilty to securities fraud and related charges. Given the negative publicity surrounding one of the largest deals in biotechnology history, major pharmaceutical companies became more cautious in their diligence process and structuring of late stage product deals.

Over the years mergers and acquisitions have also played an important role in shaping the industry and defining the biotechnology–pharmaceutical relationship landscape. Perhaps large biotechnology companies have learned from their pharmaceutical counterparts how to use acquisitions to fuel growth and build scale. The pharmaceutical sector has a long history of mergers and acquisitions (see chapter 5 below). Pfizer is an example of a company that was built in recent years through its acquisitions of Wyeth and Pharmacia. GlaxoSmithKline (GSK) is another example of a company built through mergers – initially of SmithKline French and Beecham, followed by Glaxo and Wellcome, followed by the third merger to form today's mammoth organization, GSK. In part, the driver for this consolidation has been the need to place a substantial amount of resources into all aspects of drug development research in order to maintain a continuous pipeline of new, profitable products. Pharmaceutical mergers have also occurred to build sufficient capability in marketing and sales and also in other areas. Since drug discovery and development are such high-risk activities, the more projects one can have in place at any given time, the more likely it is that one is able to maintain a flow of products to market.

Although mergers and acquisitions involving biotechnology companies are used to fuel growth as well, pharmaceutical or top-tier biotechnology companies usually purchase biotechnology companies in order to acquire one or several products or technologies, but rarely to enlarge scale. The Roche–Genentech deal in 1990 brought a new product pipeline to Roche. In figure 3.25 one can see that Johnson & Johnson, Millennium, Amgen, and others all bought companies for products. Pfizer demonstrated its intentions when at the end of 2003 it acquired Esperion, a company with a novel product impacting cholesterol levels, for $1.3 billion. In mid-2004 the large pharmaceutical company affirmed its strategy when it announced that it would fill out its pipeline via acquisition of biotechnology companies, as it faced patent expirations of several important drugs.[69] Increasingly, big pharmaceutical companies are outsourcing their discovery innovation to biotechnology companies, perhaps admitting by their actions that these large development and commercial engines struggle to create an environment that is conducive to the true scientific innovation required for the creation of novel medicines.

Finally, in the last few years there have been a few examples of biotechnology company mergers that have been executed in order to increase scope or scale, and not only to acquire a product. These are most likely to occur between two biotechnology companies. The recent IDEC–Biogen merger was a combination of two companies, each with two marketed products, that were looking to diversify their revenue bases and broaden their research funding. The combined entity has four marketed products, a more diverse research pipeline, and can take advantage of some savings by eliminating redundant infrastructure. The Millennium–Leukosite acquisition is another example of a biotechnology

Acquiror/acquiree	Date	Price($ million)	Primary rationale
Genzyme/GelTex	2000	1,000	RenaGel
Millennium/ LeukoSite	1999	635	Velcade, portfolio of cancer, inflammatory and autoimmune products
Millennium/COR Therapeutics	2002	2,000	Integrilin
Elan/Neurex	1998	700	Pain management products
Gilead/NeXstar	1999	550	HIV therapies
Amen/Immunex	2002	16,000	Enbrel
Merck/Rosetta Inpharmatics	2001	540	Data-mining software for microarray data
MedImmune/Aviron	2001	1,290	Flumist vaccine
J&J/Scios	2003	2,400	Natrecor
Novartis/Idenix	2003	612	Hepatitis B/C therapies
Lilly/Applied Molecular Evolution	2003	400	Anti-TNF alpha AB, drug development tools
Pfizer/Esperion	2003	1,300	ETC-216, for coronary artery plaques and atherosclerosis
J&J/Centocor	1999	54,900	ReoPro
IDEC/Biogen	2003	6,800	Diversify, broaden pipeline, complementary capabilities

Figure 3.25   Selected M&A transactions involving biotechnology companies.

Sources: "The Genzyme Corporation to Acquire GelTex Pharmaceuticals Inc. for 60.98 Times Revenue," *Weekly Corporate Growth Report* 111 (Santa Barbara, CA: Sept 25, 2000): 10975; "Millenium Pharmaceuticals to Acquire LeukoSite for 52.48 Times Revenue," *Weekly Corporate Growth Report* 1066 (Santa Barbara, CA: Oct 25, 1999): 10434; "K. A. Strassel, Elan Corp. Agrees to Pay $700 Million for Neurex, whose Stock Climbs 44%," *Wall Street Journal*, Eastern edn (April 30, 1998): 1; Business Brief – Gilead Sciences Inc., "NeXstar Purchase is Set for $550 Million in Stock," *Wall Street Journal*, Eastern edn (March 2, 1999): 1; "Deals & Deal Makers: Biotech Could be Game for Big Mergers," *Wall Street Journal*, Eastern edn (March 2, 1999): 1; Health Care Brief – Novartis AG, "Controlling Stake is Bought in Biotechnology Firm Idenix," *Wall Street Journal*, Eastern edn (March 27, 2003): B3; "Lilly Snags AME in $400 Million Deal, Anonymous. *Chemical Market Reporter* 264(19) (December 1, 2003): 2; "Pfizer Bags Esperion Therapeutics for $1.3 Bn," *Chemical Market Reporter* 265(1) (January 5, 2004): 2; "J&J to Merge with Centocor for $4.9 Billion," *Medical Marketing and Media* 34(8) (August 1999): 8.

acquisition that was completed not only to acquire a product but also to increase scope and scale. Although Millennium did acquire Velcade, which is now a marketed product, in this transaction it also greatly enhanced its clinical development infrastructure, which Millennium needed at the time. This development infrastructure became important when Millennium began to evolve from a research and discovery company to one focused more on the development and commercialization of its products. Changes in the types of biotechnology mergers are likely to continue as the industry matures, producing additional large biotechnology companies.

Managing a biotechnology firm

Without question, effective management of a biotechnology company is one of the critical factors for success, along with access to capital and high-quality science. Growing from start-up to an operational company is challenging in any industry, but perhaps even more so in biotechnology, where the time, cost, and probabilities of success involved in creating and marketing new medicines are so important. Statistics from the pharmaceutical sector, flush with resources, demonstrate the challenges of drug development: first, the number of new molecular entities approved annually by the FDA has fallen by 60 percent since 1996, and NDAs have dropped nearly 40 percent; and second, Merck, which devotes over $3 billion annually and about 10,000 employees to research and development of new drugs, has introduced only three new drugs since 2000.[70] When you add the complexities, existing in most biotechnology companies, of severely limited financial and human resources and a limited technology platform, the challenges of building a drug company become almost daunting. Hence, most venture capitalists investing in the biotechnology sector consider the selection of management as one of the most important decisions they make for a company.

Often, management in a biotechnology company goes through a set of necessary transitions. Initially, an entrepreneur is often selected to lead the start-up biotechnology firm as Chief Executive Officer (CEO). This person must be prepared to do everything. Most important is having a leader with the will and energy that can excite others about the company, either to join or invest. The CEO must be able to recruit the best talent, create a winning strategy, execute corporate alliances, raise capital, manage investors, understand the science well enough to sell the company story successfully, manage multiple projects, and allocate and manage resources effectively. In addition, the CEO must create and maintain an entrepreneurial culture and retain flexibility within the company in order to change or adjust strategy when necessary. Successful biotechnology start-up CEOs are unique individuals who have experience in drug development and/or research as well as business acumen. CEOs of biotechnology ventures should be people with high levels of energy, enthusiasm, and optimism, because they are often required to keep the company moving forward as it struggles to meet time lines with limited resources.

Once a company reaches a point where several projects are running simultaneously at clinical or later stages, it often needs to become more operational in nature. It must put in place effective processes at the research level to make objective decisions about which programs to continue as the programs meet key milestones. It must also put in place functioning multi-disciplinary teams responsible for leading program development. Once a company has a product on the market, it must be able to effectively balance sustained earnings growth with funding research and development of its pipeline. Moreover, it must be able to successfully build a commercial infra-structure and compete in the marketplace for customers. This level of opera-tional complexity often requires a manager with different traits than the start-up entrepreneur. The CEO of the later-stage biotechnology company must maintain the entrepreneurial culture, but also must bring a more disciplined, operational approach to the business in order to balance the new competing priorities of research, development, and marketing.

From another perspective, the transitions the CEO must manage through can be viewed as chasms the company must traverse, since they are often periods of substantial financial stress for the organization when resource allocation decisions are critical. During the first chasm, in the start-up phase of the organization, the company is spending significant resources on building its early pipeline and bringing it to the point of having at least one, or several, clinical development candidates. The length of this period is directly dependent on how quickly the CEO can translate the technology base of the company into clinical product candidates that may one day be therapeutics. The longer it takes, the more severe the period of financial stress the company must endure. As a result, venture investors today work to identify technol-ogies that they believe have the potential to create clinical candidates quickly. Once a company has developed clinical candidates, the next chasm occurs when it must invest large amounts of capital in the clinical development of its lead programs, but must still manage to support its early research engine. Companies often falter here and, essentially, starve their early research efforts because the advancement of clinical candidates creates more immediate value. The clinical development expense is often so large that it is one of the reasons companies enter into corporate alliances with large pharmaceu-tical companies for their first clinical compounds.

The final chasm occurs when a company launches its first product on to the market. Once again, the company has to manage resources and balance its commercial expense against its research and development funding. At this point in a company's growth, the magnitude of its revenues from its first products often determines how successful it will be in this balancing act. Three examples are informative. First, Amgen eventually had two blockbuster drugs on the market, with sales reaching $3.3 billion by 2003, and has been able to continue to fund its research and development pipelines over the years.[71] However, even Amgen suffered from a pipeline drought several years ago, when it was unclear what its next novel marketed product would be. As a result, it acquired Immunex to access another potential blockbuster product, *Enbrel*. As a second example, Biogen's first marketed product was also a blockbuster, *Avonex*, for multiple sclerosis, which now sells over $1 billion worldwide. Even with sales at this level, Biogen struggled to fund its research and development pipeline optimally, and eventually merged with IDEC in 2003 in order to broaden its revenue base and further fund its research and development efforts. Finally, Genentech launched tPA, its first product, with unfulfilled revenue expectations. The product reached only approximately $200 million in revenues, and Genentech had already built a research organization that required a much larger revenue base to support it. The result was the Roche buyout of 60 percent of the company, which eventually enabled Genentech to survive and not reduce its research efforts. Although there are many others, these three examples demonstrate the magnitude of resources required to fund both research and development efforts and also a commercial infrastructure in this industry. Without a sufficient revenue base, companies may be forced to merge or to significantly alter their strategy in other ways.

Building a culture of flexibility is, perhaps, another key element of managing a biotechnology organization. Many companies start with a technology that in some ways may not perform as expected. In this situation, the CEO must be creative and pragmatic in adjusting the strategy of the company in a way that will enable it to continue to build value. In some cases, when the technology fails, the right answer is to liquidate; however, often there are other options, including selling the remaining value of the company or changing strategy completely. As a company matures, often product failures drive changes in strategy that the CEO must lead. Biogen is a good example of a company that was on track to complete its phase III studies for its lead program, bivalirudin, a novel blood-thinning medicine, and build commercial infrastructure to market it. When the phase III studies did not reach their primary end point, the company dramatically changed direction. Vincent, the Chairman and CEO at the time, made the decision to stop the program, license it out, and press ahead at full speed with Biogen's other phase III program, beta-interferon for multiple sclerosis, which was ultimately successful. At a time when the morale of the company was low due to the failure of bivalirudin, Vincent's decisiveness was important in keeping the organization on a solid footing.

Some CEOs agree that if a manager is successful on three fronts – building the right culture, allocating resources effectively, and hiring the best people – then he can make a lot of mistakes and still have a good result. However one defines what the senior management of a biotechnology company must do to be successful, there is no question that management is a critical success factor for these companies. Recruiting for top management positions remains important for biotechnology companies of all sizes.

The global structure of the biotechnology sector

The US has clearly been the leader in the initiation and growth of the biotechnology sector. Several factors have contributed to this: exciting technology coming out of US academia in large part funded by the $27 billion annual NIH budget; the existence of substantial venture capital; entrepreneurs ready to run small, high-risk ventures; the already high density of large multinational pharmaceutical companies based in the US willing to form alliances with young biotechnology companies; and an effective intellectual property rights legal system. All of these factors are important to other nations looking to develop leadership in this area as well.

On a global scale, it can be seen that judging by a variety of different measures the US continues to lead in industry growth and comprises about 73 percent of the global industry among public companies (see figure 3.26). The data and history also demonstrate that the industry in the US is far more mature than in Europe, Asia, and other parts of the world – companies have existed for longer, are larger, and have advanced more products through later stages of the pipeline in the US than elsewhere worldwide. Over 50 percent of the world's public biotechnology companies are in the US. However, the rest of the world is starting to grow and nurture a biotechnology sector of its own; of the world's 3,749 private biotechnology companies, only 31 percent are in the US. Moreover, Europe has recently shown substantial growth of its biotechnology sector and boasts over 47 percent of the world's private biotechnology companies.

In the last ten years developed countries around the world have decided to support the growth of life sciences industries, and specifically biotechnology,

	Global	US	Europe	Canada	Asia
Public company data					
Revenue ($million)	41,369	30,266	8,262	1,466	1,375
R&D expense ($million)	22,012	16,272	4,989	555	197
Net loss ($million)	12,483	9,378	2,763	262	79
No. of employees	193,753	142,900	33,304	785	9,764
Number of companies					
Public	613	318	102	85	108
Private	3,749	1,148	1,776	332	493
Total	**4,362**	**1,466**	**1,878**	**417**	**601**

Figure 3.26 Comparing the domestic biotech industry with the rest of the world.

Source: "Customer Insights: Biotechnology Industry Seeks to Recover," *Chemical Market Reporter* 264(6) (September 1, 2003): 17. Financial data through 2002.

as a major industry of their future economies. Consequently, governments have made substantial changes in policy and regulation to support such growth. The two most common initiatives taken by governments have been (a) to commit significant capital to early stage companies, even when the private sector is unwilling or unable, and (b) to put in place a legal system that protects both innovators and outside investors, including one that strictly enforces patent protection. Germany, and more recently Singapore, have demonstrated how a government's commitment can support the growth of the biotechnology sector. Although the UK has traditionally been the leader in European biotechnology and still enjoys the most mature market, the number of biotechnology companies in Germany has soared and Germany now leads Europe in the number of biotechnology companies, although most are small, very young companies. Regarding intellectual property law, the two dominant nations in biotechnology, the US and the UK, both have established strong legal precedent for protecting the innovations of the sector. Let us now turn to the international biotechnology scene, with an eye toward the recent changes governments have made to support biotechnology sector growth, and look at their success so far.

Europe

Europe has a large and growing biotechnology sector. In terms of total sales, it is second only to the United States, with sales approaching $9 billion in

Country	Pre-clinical	Phase I	Phase II	Phase III	Total
UK	65	50	56	23	194
Switzerland	45	12	11	11	79
Sweden	14	8	10	–	32
France	16	8	6	1	31
Denmark	14	5	5	4	28
Italy	9	–	4	3	16
Germany	7	4	3	1	15
Norway	8	2	2	3	15
Netherlands	9	1	1	–	11
Finland	9	1	–	–	10
Ireland	2	0	2	3	7
Belgium	2	0	1	–	3
Total	**200**	**91**	**101**	**49**	**441**

Figure 3.27 Biotechnology products in development across Europe.

Source: Ernst & Young/Biocentury, "Biotech: A New Horizon?," *European Venture Capital Journal* 48 (November 2003).

2003.[72] The future for European biotechnology looks promising, given the variety of products in development across the Continent (see figure 3.27).

Nevertheless, Europe has not been immune to the troubles facing the industry globally, and valuations are still off all time highs. In fact, in 2002 alone, Europe's 102 publicly traded biotechnology companies lost half of their market value as the entire technology sector struggled, bringing the total market capitalization to $27 billion.[73] This has had profound implications on the industry, and predictably financing for biotechnology endeavors has become increasingly difficult as exit strategies for early stage investors are limited. Evidence of this is apparent in the UK biotechnology financing market (see figure 3.28).

With the IPO market diminishing in 2001 and 2002, total investments were at a fraction of previous levels, and subsequently venture capital funding has become the primary source of capital for many European firms. Moreover, dollars invested are going toward later stage products as venture capitalists are becoming more risk-averse.

United Kingdom

Despite advances in Germany and Switzerland, the UK continues to be the most mature of the European markets, with 331 biotechnology companies,

	Type of financing ($ million)				
Year	Venture	IPO	Follow-on	Other	Total
1998	93.5	172.2	130.4	203.3	99.4
1999	135.0	1.6	136.4	179.5	452.5
2000	236.3	368.7	610.3	461.2	1,676.5
2001	479.0	35.7	391.1	424.1	1,329.9
2002	246.9	34.7	32.4	71.8	385.8

Figure 3.28   UK biotechnology financing.

Source: Burrill & Company, *Biotech 2003, Life Sciences: Revaluation and Restructuring* (San Francisco, CA: Burrill & Company 2004).

46 of which are public, nearly 40 percent of the entire European pipeline, and over 20,000 employees.[74–75] In addition, by 2002 the UK biotechnology sector had produced at least thirty-eight marketed drugs with at least seven more awaiting approval and thirteen in the final phase of clinical testing.[76] The government has proven its commitment to biotechnology through a friendly regulatory process and the investment of over $2.5 billion to facilitate life sciences research.[77] Two government advisory commissions, the Agriculture and Environment Biotechnology Commission and the Human Genetics Commission, serve to minimize regulatory burdens on the industry while maintaining appropriate safeguards.[78] In addition, the Bioscience Unit of the Department of Trade and Industry acts as a lobbying organization of sorts, to ensure that the industry has a voice within government. The results of these governmental actions are obvious when one compares the state of the biotechnology sector in the UK to that of neighboring countries (see figure 3.29).

However, the UK regulatory environment has created certain challenges for the biotechnology sector, which may begin to occur elsewhere in Europe as more of these medicines find their way on to the markets. The UK's National Health Service (NHS) plays a significant role in regulating drug prices, and since biotechnology products have entered the market at relative high price points, the NHS has taken steps to regulate prices, especially with regard to careful examination of risk–benefit ratio to the patient. Probably the most publicized example of this in the last several years has been the market entry of certain multiple sclerosis (MS) biotechnology drugs. In the mid-1990s three beta-interferon products for MS were approved by the European Agency for the Evaluation of Medicinal Products (EMEA), and in 2000 glatiramer acetate was also approved.[79–80] All of these products cost in

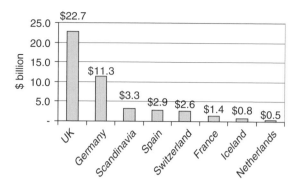

Figure 3.29   Aggregate market capitalization of biotechnology companies across Europe.

Source: "Pan-European Biotech – A Guide to the Landscape by Lehman Brothers," *Market Letter* (November 13, 2003), tablebase.

the range of $8,000–$14,000 per year. In August 1999 the Department of Health asked the advisory agency NICE (National Institute for Clinical Excellence) to appraise the MS therapies and recommend a path forward. The process went on for several years and included many submissions by the drug manufacturers and discussions with the NICE committee specifically focused on the cost-effectiveness of the therapies. Finally, on February 4, 2002 NICE issued its guidance that "on the balance of their clinical and cost-effectiveness neither beta-interferon nor glatiramer acetate is recommended for the treatment of MS in the NHS in England and Wales."[81] As a result of this guidance, the NHS reached agreement with the manufacturers on a risk-sharing scheme for the supply of the medicines, which would be available to all appropriate patients. The scheme meant that the cost of the drugs to the NHS was significantly reduced and that information would be collected to determine the real benefit of the therapies.[82] For the biotechnology and pharmaceutical companies involved, the process caused a delay of about five years before most eligible MS patients had access to the products in the UK.

Germany

Germany, led by its federal government, has made a significant effort to build a dominant national biotechnology sector (see figure 3.30). Approximately five hundred firms have emerged, however most are early stage and only thirteen companies are publicly traded. As yet, no products have advanced to market. Historically, the German government, under the Green Party, has not looked upon biotechnology favorably. The regulatory framework that was in

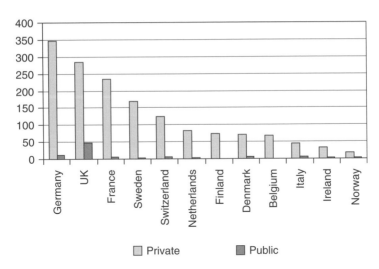

Figure 3.30   Number of companies by European country.

Source: Ernst & Young/Biocentury, "Biotech: A New Horizon?," *European Venture Capital Journal* 48 (November 2003), telebase.

place until the mid-1990s limited research and development of genetically engineered products. In 1993 this began to change, with a revision to the Genetic Engineering Act that facilitated seeking governmental approval of biotechnology products for both pharmaceutical and agricultural purposes. In addition, the government has modified intellectual property law to allow university scientists to retain the rights to their work if they elect to leave a university for the private sector. Subsequently, the government committed over $500 million to fund research and develop infrastructure for the industry, in part under the BioRegio program, which awards $50 million grants to regions for the purpose of developing the biotechnology sector.[83] As a result of these changes in policy and regulation, the industry is growing and investments into the region have increased over the last several years.

Canada

The biotechnology sector in Canada is large and growing, ranking third in terms of revenue, second in the number of companies in existence,[84] and first in R&D expenditure per employee.[85] According to BIOTECanada, the national biotechnology industry organization, annual revenues in 2002 were about $2 billion from 417 different companies.[86] More recent reports document 454 Canadian biotechnology companies.[87] Of these, about

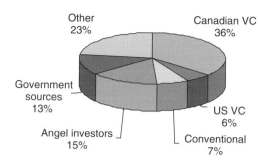

Other
23%

Canadian VC
36%

Government
sources
13%

US VC
6%

Angel investors
15%

Conventional
7%

Figure 3.31 Canadian biotechnology: sources of funding.

Source: "The Canadian Biotech Scene: Nurturing Success," available on http://www.biotech.ca.

eighty-five are publicly traded and the largest firms include QLT and Biovail, with 2003 revenues of $147 million and $823 million and market capitalizations of $1.6 billion and $2.8 billion, respectively.[88] The industry also boasts having over 9,000 products in the market and over 18,000 products in the pipeline; additionally, Canadian products account for 5 percent of the global market.[89] It is likely that most of these products are not drugs, but rather research tools, diagnostics, and other types of products. Despite this progress, Canadian biotechnology is in its early stages: 80 percent of the biotechnology companies in Canada have fewer than fifty employees.[90]

Funding for Canadian biotechnology companies is derived primarily from venture capital funds, and in light of the recent market weakness Canadian firms have been short on capital (see figure 3.31). Beyond the typical private sources, the Canadian government has devoted significant resources to funding the industry, committing over $300 million annually to various industry initiatives. Beyond that, the government has created Networks of Centers of Excellence (NCEs) to facilitate the transfer of technologies from academic centers to the private sector. Since its inception, the NCEs have led to the creation of thirty-three new biotechnology companies.[91]

Despite these steps, however, in late 2002 the Canadian legal system struck a blow against the biotechnology sector, when the courts overturned a previous decision that enabled the patenting of transgenic mice. In *President and Fellows of Harvard College* v. *Canada (Commissioner of Patents)*, the Supreme Court of Canada ruled that the so-called oncomouse developed at Harvard was not protected under Canadian patent law. This overturned an earlier decision by a lower court, despite protests from industry officials. According to one Canadian industry expert, because of this court decision Canada has suffered a competitive disadvantage in attracting funding for biotechnology due to its reluctance to allow animal patents. He believes that Canada will continue to face difficulties in attracting biotechnology investment due to this legal result.[92]

Asia

The Asian biotechnology sector is diverse in terms of company size, governmental support, therapeutic focus, and financing structure. In 2002 the region's six hundred public and private biotechnology companies earned $1.4 billion in revenues and employed nearly 10,000 people.[93] Despite a promising outlook, the region has been plagued by weak governmental support in some regions, an unwilling local venture capital industry, and untested or effectively nonexistent intellectual property laws, especially in China and India.[94] However, the postgenomic era has motivated many Asian governments to pursue technology and drug discovery more aggressively due to the explosion of information now available. Consequently, today many countries in the area, including China and India, are taking action to build biotechnology nationally. As a result, several bright spots in Asia and competition for investment dollars have triggered a race to become the biotechnology hub of Asia. Although Asia's biotechnology sector is in its nascent stages, Asian governments are hard at work building and putting in place incentives for biotechnology growth.

Asian governments have recently focused on accelerating their entry into knowledge-based industries following the 1997/98 Asian economic crisis in order to raise their level of competitiveness. Rising labor costs have led to reduced foreign investment, causing the need for change. The recent focus on biotechnology has been incorporated in the national strategic plans of many countries (see figure 3.32). Countries such as Taiwan, China, and Korea have developed specific programs and plans to support the growth of the biotechnology sector in substantial ways. In almost all of the programs across the area, government is playing a major leadership role. In addition to patent law issues and access to capital, another important challenge that most Asian countries will have to overcome is access to human capital skilled in the area. Governments seem to be addressing this problem via improving education as a long-term solution, but also by recruiting foreign talent as a near-term solution to jump-start industry growth. Thus far, Singapore and Taiwan seem to be taking the lead in terms of meeting the challenges these countries face in building the drug discovery sector of this industry base.[95]

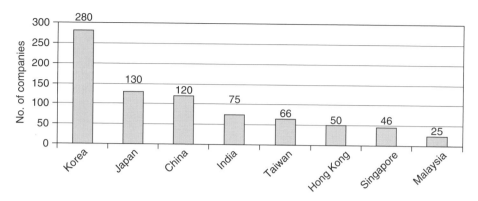

Figure 3.32   Number of Asian biotechnology companies (public and private) by country.

Source: Burrill & Company, *Biotech 2003, Life Sciences: Revaluation and Restructuring* (San Francisco, CA: Burrill & Company, 2004).

Japan

Despite being the Asian leader in pharmaceuticals, Japan has been slower to embrace biotechnology as an independent industry (see figure 3.33). As a result, many of the successful biotechnology firms in the country are affiliated with the nation's large pharmaceutical and chemical corporations.[96] Part of the reason the start-up model of biotechnology firms employed around the globe has not been as successful in Japan is because many biotechnology companies in Japan start within these larger companies. In addition, the venture capitalists that fund the majority of biotechnology around the world are based in the US, and venture capitalists like to be close to their investments since they spend significant time with senior management.[97] Moreover, the substantial cultural gap between the US and Japan makes it more difficult for the US-based venture capitalists to invest in Japan's biotechnology companies.

However, the market for biotechnology products in Japan is substantial (see figure 3.34). Therefore, the Japanese government has begun an effort to encourage biotechnology investment. In 1999 five governmental ministries concerned with biological research set up the Life Science Council, which devised a set of recommendations covering research, nurturing new enterprises, strengthening patent applications, and raising public awareness.[98] In addition, the government has committed capital in partnership with private venture capital funds in order to funnel money to earlier stage companies. Finally, the Millennium Project was started in 2001, with representatives from industry, academia, and the government, the purpose of which was the distribution of $550 million to the biotechnology sector. Today the

Industry	Number of companies	Total investments ($ million)
Consumer-related	80	171.9
Industrial/energy	27	25.6
Semiconductor/other	21	68.2
Computer software	19	85.9
Manufacturing	17	66.7
Construction	13	113.9
Other	14	3.8
Computer hardware	13	10.3
Business service	10	66.5
Finance/insurance/real estate	10	20.1
Communications	6	13.3
Transportation	4	0.4
Biotechnology	2	0.6
Agricultural/forestry/fisheries	1	21.2
Computer other	1	3.1
Utilities	1	0.2
Internet	1	11

Figure 3.33 Top industries for Japanese venture capital investment.

Source: "American VCs Land in Japan: New Laws, Cultural Changes fuel Western Interest," *Venture Capital Journal* (May 2000), tablebase.

Biotechnology product	Japanese domestic market in 2003 ($ billion)
Erythropoietin	1.18
Human growth hormone	0.56
Insulin products	0.47
Therapeutic antibodies	0.23
Imported GMO crops	2.78
Research reagents, DNA synthesis, bioinformatics	4.37

Figure 3.34 Selected biotechnology products in Japan in 2003.

Source: Burrill & Company, *Biotech 2003, Life Sciences: Revaluation and Restructuring* (San Francisco, CA: Burrill & Company 2004), 293.

government has made reinforcement of biotechnology part of the national policy, budgeting almost $3 billion for biotechnology in 2004.[99]

Taiwan

Taiwan's biotechnology sector has been growing of late, with twenty-one publicly traded companies and the creation of 108 start-up firms since 1997. Many of these new companies are small- and medium-sized businesses that largely focus on biotechnology, pharmaceuticals, testing reagents, health foods and traditional Chinese medicine, agriculture and biochips, which together account for 71.8 percent of the total business generated. To promote private business involvement in biotechnology research activities, the government has adopted several measures to support the biotechnology sector, offering businesses investment funds to engage in ground-breaking new product development. In addition, various tax relief measures and other financial incentives to create a favorable investment climate have been put in place, such as five-year tax-free operation, low shareholder investment tax, and tax incentives on company mergers, as well as preferential land tax treatment, assistance with enlisting the services of overseas specialists, the setting up of training classes, and assisting with technology transfer and R&D subsidies. Also, regulations for the public listing of biotechnology companies on both the Taiwan Stock Exchange (TSE) and over-the-counter (OTC) markets have been relaxed by the Securities and Futures Commission, allowing these firms to readily raise more investment funds.[100] Finally, Taiwan has in place an effective intellectual property protection system. Critics of the government measures and many academics in the region argue that the universities should form the backbone of the research-based biotechnology sector in Taiwan; however, to date the government has not offered these institutions sufficient resources to build the industry.[101]

Singapore

Singapore is a particularly bright spot in the Asian biotechnology universe, investing tremendous amounts of capital in recent years. The government has earmarked $7 billion over the next four years to invest in biotechnology. This commitment has triggered many multinational pharmaceutical firms, including Merck, Pfizer, Schering Plough, GlaxoSmithKline, and Eli Lilly to move portions of their operations to the region. However, one of Singapore's biggest hurdles is its small population and few natural resources. A population of 3.5 million people is probably not sufficient to supply large numbers of local, highly skilled researchers; thus it is likely Singapore will still have to rely heavily on foreign expertise.[102–103]

Singapore's government, however, is serious about this effort. In 1999 life sciences (medicine, pharmaceuticals, and biotechnology) were designated one of the country's four "industrial pillars."[104] To attract the right talent, the government has provided significant funding to set up two university faculties, five new research centers, and a series of funds designed to promote research and build biotechnology businesses. The government continues to find specific areas where it can create a national competitive advantage. At its $286 million Biopolis biomedical research complex it has built a vivarium that can house up to 250,000 mice for research.[105] In addition, Singapore actively encourages work on stem cells, unlike other governments, including the US, which limit stem cell and embryo research due to bioethical concerns.[106] Overall, the aim is for the biotechnology market to grow by 50 percent annually through 2006, creating a market worth over $300 million.[107]

China

Although China is behind its Asian competitors in becoming the most attractive country in the region for biotechnology drug development, its potential is enormous. The government has identified the biotechnology sector as a key driver for its future economic and social development. The government's focus in biotechnology will be oriented to meet its population's nutritional and health needs, and there is evidence of that already. Today the majority of China's biotechnology sector is focused on genetically modified crops and other agricultural products. On a land-use basis, China ranks among the world's top four growers of transgenic crops.[108] However, China is moving to develop its biotechnology science for drug development as well.

China today has substantial resources upon which to build its biotechnology sector. Of all the Asian nations, China's scientific base is by far the largest, and is employed at low cost – it has about 600,000 R&D scientists, of which 20,000 (in 2001) work in biotechnology, about 300,000 research scientists studying abroad, 500 government-established research institutes, 53 science parks, and 800 universities.[109–110] In addition, its massive domestic market (about 1.2 billion people) is attractive for firms in order to gain market access, and provides a substantial patient base for clinical research.

To supplement China's resources, the government has put in place incentives, mostly financial, and policies to support the industry. The government provides important tax exemptions for biotechnology companies as well as low interest rate loans and R&D grant support.[111] In addition, it has built many science parks and national laboratories as bases for research, and provides incentives to enhance a nascent but growing venture capital community. In 1996 the government created the State Drug Administration (SDA) to regulate pharmaceuticals and medical devices, and new regulations were developed to encourage research in innovative areas.

China still has important challenges to face in reaching its goals in biotechnology. Available venture capital remains inadequate and the government must find additional ways to create new venture funds and provide for exit strategies for venture investors. In addition, China's intellectual property rights system is inadequate to protect drugs in the market from premature generic competition. The China–US agreement on Intellectual Property Protection in 1996, and China's entry into the World Trade Organization (WTO) and agreement to implement its Trade Related Intellectual Property Rights (TRIPS) has afforded increased protection. However, enforcement of these rights in China has remained weak, as evidenced by the continued infringement and counterfeiting of pharmaceutical products. Until this problem is substantially resolved, drug companies will remain cautious about developing and selling proprietary medicines in China. Finally, productivity in China remains low as well, because the drug pricing scheme imposed by the government discourages private sector R&D by companies. Under the pricing policy that has been in place since 1998, drugs are allowed a fixed profit margin of 15–35 percent above production cost.[112] This is quite discouraging to pharmaceutical and biotechnology companies, because in the US and western countries drugs are not priced according to cost (which is generally low), but rather according to perceived value and what the market will bear.

Australia

The Australian biotechnology sector is smaller than those of the other regions studied, with 370 public and private firms and over $770 million in annual revenue.[113] Of late, Australian firms have had difficulty securing financing from international sources, so the government has provided a great deal of funding for firms (see figure 3.35). To further aid the development of the industry, the Australian government has established a Biotechnology Task Force to act as an advisory body for government officials. Similarly, many state governments have established similar organizations to act as a conduit between the industry and government. Beyond this, the Australian government has established the Innovation Investment Fund, which partners

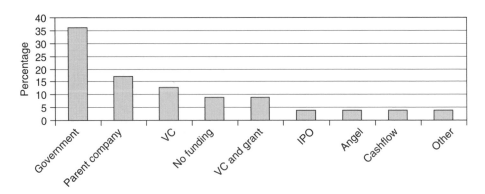

Figure 3.35 Funding sources for Australian biotechnology firms, 2001–2002.

Source: Burrill & Company, *Biotech 2003, Life Sciences: Revaluation and Restructuring* (San Francisco, CA: Burrill & Company, 2004).

government dollars with private sector investments in order to support technology firms with annual revenues less than $4 million.[114] Also, the capital gains taxes in Australia have been altered to encourage longer-term investments.[115]

The unique drug approval regulatory process plays an important role in the growth of biotechnology in Australia. Faced with ever-rising pharmaceutical costs, in 1993 Australia implemented a system that compels drug companies to prove the cost-effectiveness of new products in a strict formulaic manner. The process, which continues to be revised, compares any new treatment or modality with an existing treatment in terms of efficacy and cost. Ultimately, the Pharmaceutical Benefits Advisory Committee issues a recommendation to the Minister of Health, who has the power to include or exclude a drug from the national formulary.[116] Such a policy can be devastating for the biotechnology sector, whose products typically are on the more expensive side of the cost spectrum. Genentech's cystic fibrosis product Pulmozyme was rejected twice in the early 1990s by the Pharmaceutical Benefits Advisory Committee, who cited its cost ($13,500 per year) and the failure of the manufacturer to "provide data on how to target patients who would respond to the drug."[117] In 1996, after several years of market exclusion and in response to public outrage, the Australian government ultimately approved Pulmozyme for subsidy.

Global companies

Although most of the biotechnology sector outside the US is composed of many public and private small local enterprises, the top-tier companies are

- Understanding medical therapy and patient and physician preferences
- Understanding the payment and distribution system for the drug
- Learning how to most effectively market the drug
- Building relationships with physicians, payors and pharmacies
- Educating physicians about the product, which is especially difficult if no clinical trials were conducted in the country; Physicians usually become familiar with a new drug through participation in clinical studies
- Language differences
- Navigating through an unknown and often complex regulatory approval process
- Hiring effective sales representatives in a foreign country; integrating them into the company culture
- Navigating through national pricing negotiations with government authorities
- Learning and navigating through cultural differences in doing business

Figure 3.36   Selected challenges of commercializing drugs in foreign markets.

developing into traditional global companies. Amgen, Biogen Idec, Genzyme, and a few others commercialize, and in some cases manufacture, drugs in major countries outside the USA, such as Western European countries and Japan. In other cases, major biotechnology firms have put in place marketing and distribution agreements to sell their products in markets such as South America, Central and Eastern Europe, the Middle East, and Asia. In general, in many of these markets the cost in time and resources of building infrastructure, gaining marketing approval from the local regulatory authorities, and marketing pharmaceutical products is prohibitive, and the individual national markets are not large enough to support this cost. Moreover, the cultural and regulatory differences are often dramatic and make it difficult for a small foreign company to navigate in a cost-effective and timely manner (see figure 3.36).

Regulation

Navigating through the drug approval regulatory process is a substantial challenge for small biotechnology companies. Unlike large pharmaceutical companies that have many resources available in order to work through regulatory issues, small biotechnology companies are often not well prepared for the duration and extent of the complex process. On the other hand, the larger top-tier biotechnology companies are usually fully equipped to deal

Regulatory authority	Products regulated
Food and Drug Administration	
Federal Food, Drug, and Cosmetic Act	Human drugs
	Human diagnostics
	Human foods and food additives
	Animal drugs
	Animal feed additives
	Cosmetics
	Color additives
Public Health Service Act	Human biologics
US Department of Agriculture	
Virus-Serum-Toxin Act	Animal biologics
	Transgenic animal health issues
Federal Plant Pest Act	Plants and microorganisms that may be plant pests
Plant Quarantine Act	
National Environmental Policy Act	
Environmental Protection Agency	
Federal Insecticide, Fungicide, and Rodenticide Act	Microbial and plant pesticides, insecticides, and Fungicides
Toxic Substances Control Act	Chemical and environmental uses of microorganisms not covered by other authorities

Figure 3.37   Federal biotechnology regulatory framework.

Source: Office of Science and Technology Policy, Executive Office of the President, *Coordinated Framework for the Regulation of Biotechnology.*

with the process. The regulatory agencies governing biotechnology make policy decisions that on the one hand strive to protect the safety of the population, and on the other attempt to foster the growth and competitiveness of this young industry. Recognizing the complexity of overseeing an industry with a wide variety of products and processes, the US federal government employed a multidisciplinary approach beginning in 1986 with *The Coordinated Framework for the Regulation of Biotechnology* (see figure 3.37). This document sought to clearly define the governmental parties involved and their responsibilities regarding biotechnology. The three agencies charged with regulating the emerging technologies were the Food and Drug Administration (FDA), the US Department of Agriculture, and the Environmental Protection Agency.

Dating back to the 1980s, industry and public health officials have expressed concern that the lengthy drug approval process denies Americans immediate access to the latest technologies. The FDA argued for greater resources to help expedite drug reviews. In 1992 Congress passed the first Prescription Drug User Fee Act (PDUFA) to expand FDA resources. The Act authorizes the FDA to collect fees from companies that produce human drug and biological products. Once the Act was passed, companies applying for a marketing license from the FDA for a new drug or biologic were required to submit, along with the application, a fee to support the review process. In addition, companies now pay annual fees for each manufacturing establishment and prescription drug product marketed. Previously, taxpayers alone paid for product reviews through budgets provided by Congress. In the new program, industry provides the funding in exchange for FDA agreement to meet drug review performance goals, which emphasize timeliness.[118] Since 1993 standard drug approval times have been cut in half, and in 2002 the FDA collected $57 million in fees.[119] Critics of the law cite the fact that the number of new molecular entities (NMEs) withdrawn from the market for safety concerns after FDA approval rose from 3.10 percent before the original PDUFA Act to 3.47 percent since then. They believe that the new focus on timeliness has allowed more unsafe drugs to pass through the FDA than before 1992.

Within the FDA, the Center for Biologics Evaluation and Research (CBER) and the Center for Drug Evaluation and Research (CDER) monitor all aspects of drug development, including safety and efficacy, labeling, marketing, and advertising.[120] In 2002 the roles and responsibilities of these two centers were changed in response to industry complaints that the processes in place were not responsive. The CBER was widely criticized for its record of longer approval times relative to that of the CDER (see figures 3.38, 3.39, 3.40). As

	BLAs approved*	Priority BLAs approved	Median review time
2001	16	NA	13.8
2002	21	6 (29%)	12.9
2003	22	5 (23%)	12.8

Figure 3:38 FDA biologics approval times, 2001–2003.

*BLA: Biologic Licensing Application.
Sources: Food and Drug Administration, "FDA Sees Rebound in Approval of Innovative Drugs in 2003," press release 1/15/2004; Food and Drug Administration, "New Innovation Initiative Anticipated to Speed Approvals in Years Ahead," press release 1/15/2004; Burrill & Company, *Biotech 2004, Life Sciences: Back on Track* (San Francisco, CA: Burrill & Company, 2004), 244.

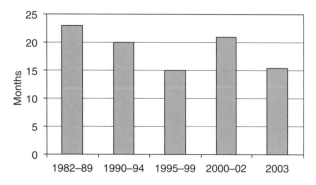

Figure 3.39   Trend of FDA biologics approval times.

Source: Tufts Center for the Study of Drug Development, *Outlook 2003.*

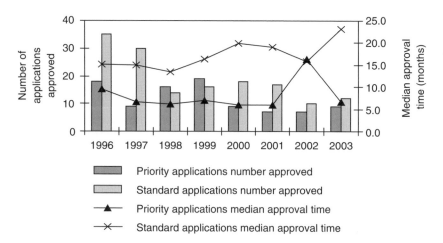

Figure 3.40   New product approvals (NMEs) 1996–2003.

Source: Burrill & Company, *Biotech 2004, Life Sciences: Back on Track* (San Francisco, CA: Burrill & Company, 2004), 240. Food and Drug Administration.

a result, in a major reorganization of the FDA the evaluation of therapeutic biologics was transferred from the CBER to the CDER. Today the CBER regulates vaccines, blood and blood products, gene therapies, somatic cell products, tissues, and other cutting-edge technologies. Under the new structure, chemical, protein, and monoclonal antibody drugs all fall under the authority of the CDER.[121] The FDA claims it is focused on encouraging manufacturers to develop innovative medicines by insuring that its research requirements are more clear and predictable and by reducing delays in bringing new biotechnology therapies to market.[122]

Critical differences exist between the biologics and new chemical entity approval processes because of the sensitivity of biologics to the manufacturing process. Whereas with traditional chemical drugs regulators focus on the pharmacologic profile of the end product, with biologics every step of the process may have unpredictable yet significant ramifications. A change in the protein manufacturing process can alter the glycosylation pattern on the surface of the protein or other aspects of the protein structure.[123] This occurred when the manufacturing process of tissue plasminogen activator (tPA), one of Genentech's early products, was changed from the original roller bottle technique to the more sophisticated large bioreactors (tanks). The resulting product showed some of these differences in protein structure and, more importantly, differences in pharmacokinetic profile. This change altered the way the drug should be dosed in patients to have its optimal effect.[124] Such occurrences necessitate thorough examination of all biologic drug products, including their manufacturing processes. Because small changes in the production process can change the product in important ways, the introduction of generic biologics has been fraught with complications (see below).

Special regulatory issues

Over the past few years a handful of topics have emerged as being particularly challenging regulatory issues from political, ethical, and scientific viewpoints.

Embryonic stem cell research

Stem cells are unique in two critical ways: they are unspecialized cells capable of renewing themselves for extended periods through cell division; and under certain conditions the cells can develop into any specialized cells of the body (nerve cells, muscle cells, etc.).[125] Such properties make the cells attractive to scientists looking to devise new ways of treating virtually any disease. The theories suggest that given a line of stem cells, scientists could replace any damaged cells in the body, thus restoring health. Although such benefits are still in the future, the use of stem cells has generated tremendous controversy because of the source of the cells.

Embryonic stem cells, as the name suggests, are derived from human embryos at the blastocyst stage (six to seven days after fertilization). Alternatively, adult stem cells can sometimes be used with significant constraints. During the late 1990s much work was being done on stem cells in the commercial and public sectors. However, the field was dealt a blow in 2001 by the Bush administration, which prohibited the federal funding of any work on stem cell lines that had yet to be developed. As a compromise, the President offered that the sixty or so lines already apparently in use could continue to receive federal aid.[126] However, by mid-2004 only nineteen lines were actually available according to the National Institutes of Health. Many pro-life organizations criticized the compromise as being disrespectful of human life, and many scientific organizations accused the Republican administration of using its ideological conservative agenda to impede important scientific research that could one day offer treatment for and cures to many serious illnesses. Since 2001 there has been increasing pressure from the scientific community and even from many pro-life advocates to allow stem cell research to continue. In mid-2004 the political pressure to change the law continued to increase as a majority of senators and House representatives signed a letter to the President requesting that he change his position on support for embryonic stem cell research. Pressure continues to mount as other influential groups get involved.

During this time, outside the US stem cell research has advanced. In Korea many new stem cell lines have been created and are readily available to scientists.[127] In addition, Singapore is attracting top scientists in this area due to its less restrictive policies and available funding. Indeed, so much work has been done overseas that scientists from various countries, including the US, have moved to countries such as Singapore in order to pursue this line of work. Alan Coleman, head of the team of researchers that cloned Dolly the sheep in Scotland, recently joined ES Cell International, an Australian firm lured to Singapore by government funding, and a leading National Cancer Institute researcher, Edison Liu, now heads Singapore's new Genome Institute.[128–129] This progress outside the US will continue to put pressure on US authorities to change the current policy to enable research in the US to keep pace with the scientific advancements elsewhere around the globe.

Human cloning and germline gene therapy

Cloning describes the process by which an organism is created based solely on the genetic material of one existing organism. In 1997 the world became familiar with cloning when Ian Wilmut at the Roslin Institute in Scotland used the technique to create a clone of a sheep.[130] News of the scientific success sparked debate as to the ethical and scientific implications. Currently, there is no federal regulation banning human cloning, although regulations prohibit federal funding of human cloning research. The practice is under the regulatory watch of the CBER.[131] Debate surrounding the cloning of humans has focused primarily on the moral and ethical propriety of altering the human genome, as well as on the possible social and physical damage that may result to the clonal child and gestational mother.[132] Despite these risks, some in the scientific community argue that further research is needed before any definite regulations are put in place.

Similarly, germline gene therapy has generated much controversy. Germline gene therapy involves the genetic manipulation of a human embryo. Potential applications include correcting single gene genetic disorders such as cystic fibrosis. Opponents argue that such practices are inherently dangerous and would lead to a eugenics movement. Again, no federal regulations are in place. However, the science in question is not yet mature enough to merit extensive regulations.

Generic biologics

The Hatch-Waxman Act of 1984 put in place the basic rules governing accelerated New Drug Application (NDA) submissions by generics producers and the pioneering manufacturers' countervailing rights of market exclusivity, patent term extensions and patent Orange Book listing,[133] and infringement litigation prior to accelerated NDA approval.[134] When the Act was first conceived, it was designed with traditional drugs in mind, and generic biologics were not yet a critical issue. However, given the number of biologics currently on the market and the race to develop generics, the issue of generic or follow-on biologics will need to be handled in the immediate future. With traditional generic drugs, the FDA approval process is abbreviated by allowing generics manufacturers to reuse most of the clinical testing data gathered by the innovator company. This provides generic drug makers with a fast route to market once the patented drug comes off patent. With biologics, however, the process is more stringent, requiring a generic biologics producer to perform a rigorous clinical study program demonstrating safety and efficacy, instead of the simpler bioequivalence studies, which are more standard for generic chemical entities. Therefore, generic or "off-brand" versions of proteins will be far more complex to manufacture than chemical drugs, because the pioneer biotechnology firms have proprietary manufacturing processes, utilizing unique cell lines, which may be difficult or nearly impossible to replicate.[135] There is currently no legal or regulatory guidance on this issue.

Figure 3.41 attempts to illustrate the size of the potential generic biologic market and the need for regulatory guidelines in the short term.

Brand	Marketer	Year of approval	2003 sales ($ millions)	Generics under development
Epogen	Amgen	1989	2,400	Yes
Procrit	Ortho Biotech	1990	3,984	Yes
Neupogen	Amgen	1991	1,300	Yes
Humulin	Eli Lilly	1992	1,060	Yes
Intron A	Schering Plough	1986	1,851	Yes
Avonex	Biogen Idec	1996	1,168	Yes
Enbrel	Amgen	1998	1,300	No

Figure 3.41 Selected top biopharmaceuticals and their biogeneric status.

Source: http://www.i-s-b.org/business/bioindustry_f.htm.

Orphan drug law

The Orphan Drug Law was enacted by Congress in 1983 to provide an incentive for industry to develop drugs for so-called orphan diseases: rare diseases and conditions that affect fewer than 200,000 people in the US. There are about 6,000–10,000 diseases that fit into this category and they include cystic fibrosis, Fabry's disease, Huntington's disease, Gaucher's disease, Fragile X syndrome, amyotropic lateral sclerosis (Lou Gehrig's Disease), and many more. The law provides a product with seven years of market exclusivity from the date of market entry to enable a company to obtain a financial return on a drug that will be used by a relatively small number of patients. In general, the law has been quite successful in that prior to 1983 fewer than ten products were approved for rare diseases, and since 1983 over two hundered products have been approved for such diseases (see figure 3.42).[136]

This law has enabled many biotechnology companies to build small commercial operations in order to market and sell their own products to a more focused physician and patient population. In addition, in many cases drugs can be developed and approved more quickly in these rare diseases, because they are often severe and warrant priority regulatory review.[137] Although many of these markets may only have peak sales of $50 million–$200 million, the law provides enough protection so that small biotechnology companies can build the appropriate commercial infrastructure and become profitable. Genzyme, which is now a top-tier biotechnology company with $1.7 billion in annual revenues, has built its business around developing and selling high-value products into orphan diseases, such as Gaucher's disease and Fabry's disease.

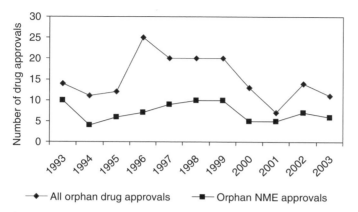

Figure 3.42   Orphan drug approvals.

Source: Burrill & Company, *Biotech 2004, Life Sciences: Back on Track* (San Francisco, CA: Burrill & Company, 2004), 369–370. http://www.fda.gov/orphan.

Bioterrorism

Because of the heightened awareness of terrorist threats in the US since September 11, 2001, Congress is in the process of allocating $5.6 billion over the next ten years toward Project BioShield. This is meant to be a comprehensive effort to develop and make available vaccines, therapeutics, and diagnostics to prepare the US against bioterrorism or other attacks using biological or chemical weapons. Although details remain to be worked out, the bill is meant to accomplish the following:

• Ensure that resources are available to pay for the "next-generation" medical countermeasures. It will allow the government to buy improved vaccines and drugs for smallpox, anthrax, and botulinum toxin, as well as other pathogens such as Ebola and plague.

• Strengthen NIH development capabilities by speeding research and development on medical countermeasures based on the most promising recent scientific discoveries.

• Give the FDA the ability to make promising treatments quickly available in emergency situations, even if the treatments have not been approved previously by the FDA.[138]

As the money becomes available, many biotechnology companies are poised to take advantage of it. This funding will be available through a grant process and will create markets for products for some companies that previously did not exist. It is likely that the biotechnology sector will play an important role in creating some of the new medicines to be funded with this new federal government appropriation.

Drug regulation outside the US

Biotechnology and pharmaceutical companies have to work with regulatory agencies worldwide in order to gain approval to market their products outside the US. In the other large pharmaceutical markets of the world, Europe and Japan, biotechnology and pharmaceutical products are approved within the same agencies. Over the last fourteen years there has been a significant effort to harmonize regulatory procedures for drug approvals across these three pharmaceutical markets – the US, Europe, and Japan. This effort has been largely the function of the International Conference on Harmonization of Technical Requirements for Registration of Pharmaceuticals for Human Use (ICH), and has been successful in bringing together the regulatory agencies of these three regions to agree on a single set of technical requirements for the registration of new drug products.

International conference on harmonization

The ICH was established in 1990 in an effort to rationalize and harmonize the regulation of drug products across the US, the European Union, and Japan.[139] The idea of having a common set of requirements that should be met internationally in order to allow a new drug to be brought to market was simple but revolutionary. It was driven by several factors, including a rapid increase in laws, regulations, and guidelines for various aspects of drug development and use, the internationalization of the drug industry as markets became more global, concern over rising healthcare and R&D costs, and a public desire to have minimum delay in getting new products to market.[140] Harmonization of the drug approval requirements was initially driven by the European Community, as Europe was becoming a single market for pharmaceuticals. Eventually, Japan and the US joined in the effort, and the first meeting occurred in April 1990. The six main participants of the ICH are, for the US, the FDA and the Pharmaceutical Research and Manufacturers of America (PhRMA), for Europe, the European Union and the European Federation of Pharmaceutical Industries' Associations (EFPIA), and for Japan, the Ministry of Health, Labor, and Welfare (MHLW) and the Japanese Pharmaceutical Manufacturers' Association (JPMA).[141]

Ultimately, industry is strongly supportive of the effort, since it has the ability to reduce development time lines and resources used to obtain approval, reduce duplication of clinical trials and regulatory activities, enable the simultaneous launch of products in the three major regions, and facilitate intracompany globalization by standardizing regulatory documents required for approvals.[142] The ICH has been successful at developing standard guidelines for efficacy, safety, and quality. It has also put in place, as of 1997, guidelines for a Common Technical Document (CTD), which allows the same technical document to be used in filings with the regulatory agencies in all three regions of the world.[143] This reduces substantial process duplication within a company and saves time and resources. Overall, the parties agree that in the interest of patient and public health, there is a need to maintain the harmonization of the technical guidelines as well as the format and content of registration applications.

Europe

As the pharmaceutical sector has become more global, the European Union has put in place a centralized organization and procedure which is applicable across all member states in the European Union, to enable companies to obtain a single approval for a drug. In 1995 a pan-European regulatory authority was established.[144] The EMEA became the first regulatory agency in the world that was empowered to approve drugs for human use across national lines.[145] The EMEA issues single marketing authorizations by the European Commission that is valid across all member states.

The EMEA was created in an effort to improve the process of drug development and approval so that safe and effective drugs could be brought to market across Europe as quickly as possible. It works to accomplish the following:

- To mobilize scientific resources across Europe to provide high-quality evaluation of drugs; to advise on research and development programs; and to provide useful and clear information to users and health professionals.
- To develop efficient and transparent procedures to allow timely access by users to innovative medicines through a single marketing authorization.
- To control the safety of medicines for humans and animals through a pharmacovigilance network, and the establishment of safety limits.[146]

The European system offers two routes for regulatory approval for drugs. The centralized procedure is compulsory for medicines derived from biotechnology, and is available at the request of companies for other innovative new products.[147] The Committee for Proprietary Medicinal Products (CPMP) conducts the scientific assessment of any human therapeutics under review via this route. Once the assessment is satisfactorily completed, the marketing authorization is given by the European Commission and applies throughout the European Union. The second route, the decentralized procedure, also referred to as the mutual recognition procedure, applies to the majority of conventional medicines.[148] Once one member state approves a drug, this procedure provides for the extension of the marketing authorization to one or more member states identified by the applicant. The EMEA plays a role in this process in arbitrating points of dispute if there are disagreements about the original national approval.

The process developed under the current centralized procedure was created, in part, in order to speed up the process by which drugs reach patients. Under the European law, the EMEA is required to complete its assessment in 210 days.[149] In addition, the procedure encourages interaction between EMEA scientific experts and the manufacturers throughout the development process in order to provide maximum scientific advice and counsel on technical issues. Furthermore, in order to encourage innovation and the development of drugs for serious rare diseases, an orphan drug law has been put in place similar to that of the US.[150] The Committee for Orphan Medicinal Products (COMP) was established to make recommendations about orphan drug designations. Under this law, market exclusivity is given for ten years to drugs for an orphan disease.[151] In addition, scientific advice is provided from the EMEA to facilitate the development of such drugs, these drugs are provided access to the centralized procedure, application fees are reduced, and in some cases financial assistance may be available to companies developing orphan drugs.

The European Commission is required to periodically review and revise these new drug regulation laws in order to continuously improve the system. The objectives of this revision process are clear:

- To guarantee a high level of health protection for Europeans by providing patients with innovative, safe, and effective new drugs as quickly as possible.
- To insure competitiveness of the European pharmaceuticals sector, taking into account the increasingly global nature of the market.
- To prepare for and meet the challenges of the European Union enlargement.
- To simplify the system, maintaining and enhancing its consistency, visibility, and the transparency of its decision-making process.[152]

Critics of the new system claim that member states have an incentive to approve drugs too quickly or work too closely with pharmaceutical companies. Under the decentralized procedure, the member state that approves the drug first becomes the reference member state, and collects most of the licensing fees from the company applying for approval.[153] This potentially creates an internal European market in which national regulatory agencies compete to approve drugs the fastest in order to maximize income from drug companies. Under the centralized procedure, an EMEA regulatory representative, called a *rapporteur,* is chosen from the member states to assist the company in its application and discussions with the EMEA. Although the rapporteur is selected by the EMEA, the company can express a preference. Critics claim that being selected as a rapporteur provides the member state with additional work and income for its national regulatory agencies, thus creating an incentive to be chosen by companies to be rapporteurs.[154] The major critique under both systems is that the public health is at risk because drugs may not be reviewed as carefully and may get to market without the full vetting of important safety concerns. To balance these concerns, the European Union has made it a point to insure that the system be as transparent about its decision-making process as possible. The debate about speed of approvals, quality assessments, and transparency of decision-making will continue as the system continues to be modified. Overall, most companies would agree that the new system is improved and enables drugs to reach the market more quickly, with appropriate safeguards in place for safety and efficacy.

Japan

For many years the Japanese process for drug approval was marked by strict national regulations that were challenging and costly for foreign manufacturers to overcome. However, in the 1990s, as Japan's economy suffered, the government was forced to open the doors to foreign producers in order to attract foreign investment.[155] The comprehensive deregulation program has put in place substantial changes in the drug regulatory process, creating growing opportunities for foreign companies.

Japan's MHLW and other organizations have undergone significant changes in order to strengthen the review of clinical trials of new drugs, improving the safety and quality of therapeutics entering the market.[156] In 1997 a new Pharmaceutical and Medical Device Evaluation Center was created as part of the National Institute of Health Science, in order to help review New Drug Applications (NDAs). Japan's Drug Organization (Kiko) has also taken on new functions, including cooperating with the Evaluation Center, advising on clinical trials, and performing data checks. In addition, several agencies have been combined to form a new Pharmaceutical and Medical Safety Bureau responsible for the safety and efficacy of drugs, cosmetics and medical devices, as well as other issues related to blood supply, narcotics, and poisonous substances. A separate division has also been created, the Evaluation/Licensing Division, to deal with important administrative functions in the NDA review process.

The Pharmaceutical and Medical Safety Bureau is working toward streamlining the approval process. A substantial effort toward reducing approval times from eighteen months to twelve months is in place.[157] In addition, efforts to accelerate the introduction of innovative drugs have been put in place via the implementation of a "fast track" review for orphan drugs. This track can be used by companies developing drugs that meet certain specific criteria demonstrating that the drugs are clearly superior in efficacy or safety to existing drugs, and are used to treat diseases that are life-threatening. The Japanese government is also working to increase and enhance the interaction with drug producers during the clinical development process, in order to provide more advice and counsel to manufacturers throughout the R&D process.

Specifically, the government has taken a number of steps to improve the clinical trial process for companies. Whereas the procedure to initiate clinical trials in Japan used to take seven to eight months, it now takes only one to two months.[158] Additionally, Japan's revised Pharmaceutical Law has put in place new Good Clinical Practice (GCP) guidelines that have dramatically improved clinical trial practice and procedures.[159] In the past the ministry's Chief Investigator had almost complete authority over clinical trials, formalities regarding trials were nonexistent, and informed consent was not standard practice. Under the new law, the sponsor of the trial is fully responsible for the clinical study, including monitoring, auditing and finalizing the data. The medical institutions that run the studies also have full responsibility for the proper performance of the studies. An Institutional Review Board (IRB) was created to review the entire clinical trial process, and new standards for informed written consent have been put in place. All of these changes have created a clinical trial process in Japan that is now more scientifically rigorous and similar to the process followed in the US and Europe. Finally, Japan is now allowing the use of foreign clinical data for domestic product approval.[160] Prior to this, companies had to repeat all clinical studies in Japan in order to register for approval in Japan. This change saves substantial costs and enables quicker approvals in Japan.

Conclusions: the real drivers of the biotechnology sector

Drug development overall is an industry fraught with challenges and risks. The highly regulated environment, long and expensive product development, and high failure rate of technology are some of the factors that contribute to the challenges of the pharmaceutical sector. These risks become compounded in the context of biotechnology companies, which have severely limited resources and constraints to diversify across multiple technologies and products. Biotechnology companies must be able to access enough capital, first and foremost, identify technologies that can be transformed into real commercial value, maintain a strong scientific foundation, and build viable business models in the face of the high level of risk that exists in order to move forward successfully. There is little question that access to capital and having a strong scientific foundation are critical elements in building a biotechnology company that can create commercial value.

Most of the biotechnology executives interviewed in preparing this chapter agree that there are certain elements that must exist within any biotechnology company in order to meet these challenges. Hiring and retaining quality people who are intelligent, passionate, and have the right experience for the job is critical. Building a culture of openness, candor, excitement, and collaboration that enhances a company's ability to be agile and make quick decisions is also very important. Some have called this an ability to "operationalize strategy"; that is, the ability to translate a strategy into action on a day-to-day basis as new data come in and the landscape changes. Additionally, allocating resources appropriately is paramount; this can be directly impacted by building a governing structure in the organization that insures a continuous review of the business model, technology, and strategy in as objective a way as possible. Objectivity increases the likelihood that the allocation of resources will lead to the creation of real commercial value. Too often biotechnology companies begin to believe their own press releases, and fail to stop or change the course of programs soon enough. Finally, in all organizations, having the management skills to manage through the transitions from a research stage to a development stage and finally to a commercial phase is very important. Many companies, large and small, have struggled on this front.

On a company by company basis, these are the critical factors to success. However, on a grander scale, what drives this industry to keep growing? After thirty years of cumulative net losses on the consolidated income statement, the biotechnology sector as a whole is as vibrant as ever, not just in the US, but also around the world; and governments in many developed nations are putting in place incentives to propel the industry forward and lead its economic growth. The forces behind this have several components. First, on the supply side, the biotechnology sector was founded by entrepreneurs with a strong passion for their work and for wanting to make a difference in healthcare. These were optimists who some have called "technology zealots." Additionally, in the model of the venture capitalists who fund these companies, the entrepreneurs' wealth is made directly dependent on the success of the companies, further enhancing the passion that drives many of the founders. Thirdly, on a more macro level, the biotechnology sector embodies dreams of improving healthcare, a topic that people in wealthy societies care a great deal about; once a society's basic needs are taken care of, treating and curing disease, saving lives, and living longer are high on the list of people's concerns.

On the demand side of the equation sits the pharmaceutical sector, where companies have grown to behemoth sizes through mergers and acquisitions. These monsters need to produce respectable annual growth rates; growing sales at a modest 10 percent rate in a company with $40 billion in top line revenues requires an additional $4 billion in sales annually. With expiring patents on billion dollar blockbusters and lower overall productivity in terms of new compounds entering the market, a substantial "product gap" has developed over the last few years (see figure 3.43).

The number of drugs coming from biotechnology companies continues to increase and the pharmaceutical sector continues to struggle to get new products to market. One can say an "innovation gap" has developed in large pharmaceutical companies, whereby most of these companies spend the majority of their R&D budgets on development, thereby foregoing real discovery and innovation work. Some executives have raised the question whether, within the context of the necessary governing and organizational structures of large pharmaceutical companies, these large firms can provide

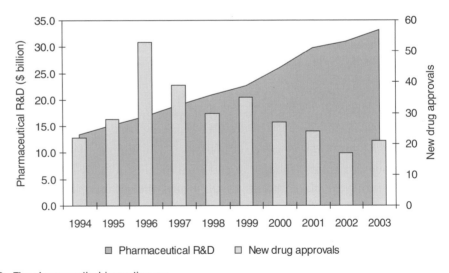

Figure 3.43 The pharmaceutical innovation gap.

Source: PhRMA, Profile: Pharmaceutical Industry Report 2004. http://www.fda.gov.

an environment where true scientific innovation can flourish and be recognized by senior management. Growing numbers of big pharmaceutical companies are depending on biotechnology companies for new products, new technologies, and scientific innovation. This has been clearly demonstrated by the deal trends in terms of deal numbers and values. The purchase prices that the pharmaceutical sector has been willing to pay for later stage products have risen dramatically; this has driven the returns to the venture capitalists who in turn continue to fund new biotechnology companies that have the next potential blockbuster product.

The laws of supply and demand in this case are working toward improving healthcare. Although one can still debate whether the financial returns in biotechnology have been worth the sizeable investment made over the last thirty years, it is more difficult to debate the impact the biotechnology sector has had on healthcare around the world. Yes, the biotechnology sector has accumulated $40 billion in losses, according to the *Wall Street Journal*, but it has also created over 196 new drugs on the market, many of which have had a substantial impact on patients' lives worldwide.

NOTES

I would like to give a very special recognition to Dr. Christopher C. Fikry, who took time away from his graduate studies at the University of Pennsylvania to assist in all aspects of writing this chapter. Without his sourcing, writing, and reviewing, this chapter would not have happened.

I would also like to acknowledge the following who were kind enough to allow me to interview them so that I might be able to understand certain events and gather certain insights that I otherwise might not have had. In addition, I thank those below who were kind enough to review the chapter and offer their advice and counsel.

Michael W. Bonney, President and CEO, Cubist Pharmaceuticals; L. Patrick Gage, Ph.D., Venture Partner, Flagship Ventures; Nicholas Galakatos, Ph.D., General Partner, MPM Capital; Bruce E. Landon, MD, MBA, Associate Professor of Health Care Policy and Medicine, Department of Health Care Policy, Harvard Medical School, Division of Primary Care and General Internal Medicine, Beth Israel Deaconess Medical Center; Mark W. Leuchtenberger, President and CEO, Therion Biologics; John Maraganore, Ph.D., President and CEO, Alnylam Pharmaceuticals; Peter Tollman, Ph.D., Vice President and Director, Boston Consulting Group; James L. Vincent, former Chairman and CEO of Biogen, Inc.

1. Agricultural biotechnology, industrial, and environmental applications, diagnostics, vaccines, and neutraceuticals will not be discussed in detail in this chapter.
2. David P. Hamilton, "Biotech's Dismal Bottom Line: More Than $40 Billion in Losses," *Wall Street Journal* (May 20, 2004): 1.

3. http://www.bio.org.

4. DNA is deoxyribonucleic acid, which is the chemical name for the genetic material of any living mammalian cell.

5. Recombinant DNA technology (rDNA) is the genetic engineering process by which the genetic material of a cell is altered to produce new proteins. These cells act like miniature drug factories and produce large quantities of the proteins that eventually become the protein-based drugs.

6. Inventor of the Week Archive, Lemelson–MIT Program, http://web.mit.edu/invent/iow/boyercohen.html (March 19, 2004).

7. Peter J. Gardner, "US Intellectual Property Law and the Biotech Challenge: Searching for an Elusive Balance," *Vermont Bar Journal & Law Digest* (Fall 2003).

8. *The Bayh–Dole Act, A Guide to the Law and Implementing Regulations*, 1999. Prepared by the Council on Governmental Relations, available on http://www.ucop.edu/ott/bayh.html.

9. Howard Bremer, *The First Two Decades of the Bayh–Dole Act as Public Policy* (November 11, 2001), National Association of State Universities and Land Grant Colleges, available on http://www.nasulgc.org/COTT/Bayh-Dohl/Bremer_speech.htm.

10. This chapter focuses on medical therapeutics, but biotechnology continues to be used to develop diagnostics, vaccines, research tools used in laboratory research, agricultural products such as genetically engineered crops, and neutraceuticals, which are subject to a different regulatory environment than drugs.

11. Hamilton, "Biotech's Dismal Bottom Line."

12. Biotechnology Industry Statistics, available on http://www.bio.org.

13. Burrill & Company, *Biotech 2004, Life Sciences: Back on Track* (San Francisco, CA: Burrill & Co., 2004), 351.

14. *2003/2004 Annual Report*, available on http://www.phrma.org.

15. Big pharmaceutical companies, often referred to as "big pharma" by industry experts, consist of larger multinational pharmaceutical companies that are focused on discovering, developing, and commercializing new chemical entities.

16. "Licensing Insight," Wood Mackenzie Multi-Client Study, April 2003, p. 3.

17. Burrill & Company, *Biotech 2004*, 51.

18. A list of all approved biotechnology drugs (1982–2003), which includes biologics developed by biotechnology companies and pharmaceutical companies, as well as small molecule products developed by biotechnology companies, can be found on http://www.bio.org/speeches/pubs/er/approveddrugs.asp.

19. http://www.bio.org.

20. Ibid.

21. Ibid.

22. Jean D. Wilson, *Harrison's Principles of Internal Medicine*, 12th edn (New York: McGraw-Hill, 1991), 2040–2041.

23. Cynthia Robbins-Roth, *From Alchemy to IPO* (Cambridge, MA: Perseus Publishing, 2000).

24. "Gene Therapy – Promises and Realities," available on http://www.biology.iupui.edu/biocourses/Biol540/genetherapy.html, accessed May 20, 2004.

25. Robert Sheppard, "Cracking the Genetic Code," *Maclean's Toronto* 116(12) (March 24, 2003): 48.

26. Burrill & Company, *Biotech 2003, Life Sciences: Revaluation and Restructuring* (San Francisco, CA: Burrill & Co., 2003), 86.

27. Sheryl Gay Stolberg, "Scientists Defend Suspended Gene Therapy," *New York Times* (February 15, 2000): A20, vol. 4.

28. Rick Weiss and Deborah Nelson, "Penn Settles Gene Therapy Suit; University Pays Undisclosed Sum to Family of Teen Who Died," *Washington Post* (November 4, 2000): A, A04.

29. Burrill & Company, *Biotech 2003*, 87.

30. http://www.bio.org

31. Companies include Helicon Therapeutics, Memory Pharmaceuticals, Cortex Pharmaceuticals, Saegis Pharmaceuticals, Axonyx, and Sention Pharmaceuticals.

32. "Customer Insights. Biotechnology Industry Seeks to Recover," *Chemical Market Reporter* 264(6) (September 1, 2003).

33. George Miller, "FDA Shifts CBER/CDER Review Functions," *Pharmaceutical Technology* 27(5) (May 2003): 18.

34. In pharmaceutical development, "small molecules" refers to chemical entities usually produced by big pharmaceutical companies, whereas proteins (antibodies, other biologics) are much larger in molecular size and weight, and were the original products of the biotechnology industry. Today many biotechnology companies discover small molecule drugs as well and some large pharmaceutical companies develop biologics.

35. Mouse monoclonal antibodies are recognized by the human body as being foreign, and often an immune response is generated over time which prevents them from being used chronically. However, humanization of these monoclonal antibodies is a process by which they are made to look more like human antibodies, and, therefore, less foreign. This often eliminates any immune response and enables chronic use of the monoclonal antibody therapy.

36. "Biopharmaceuticals – Current Market Dynamics and Future Outlook," available on http://www.researchandmarkets.com/reports/39083/.

37. Biotechnology Industry Organization, "Biotechnology Tools in Research and Development," available on http://www.bio.org/er/biotechtools.asp.

38. Ibid.

39. Gary Pisano, *The Life Sciences Revolution: A Technical Primer* (Boston, MA: Harvard Business School, 2002).

40. Ibid.

41. Ibid.

42. Ibid.

43. Ibid.

44. Ralph T. King Jr., "Glaxo Plans to Acquire Affymax For $533 Million, a 67% Premium – Pharmaceutical Concern to get Faster Methods for Discovering Drugs," *Wall Street Journal* (Eastern Edition) (January 27, 1995): B6.

45. Biotechnology Industry Organization, "Biotechnology Tools in Research and Development."

46. Natasha J. Caplen, "RNAi as a Gene Therapy Approach," *Expert Opinion on Biological Therapy* 3(4) (2003): 575.

47. Burrill & Company, *Biotech 2004*, 23.

48. Joseph A. DiMasi *et al.* "The Price of Innovation: New Estimates of Drug Development Costs," *Journal of Health Economics* 22(2) (March 2003): 151–185.

49. H. Kettler, *Updating the Cost of a New Chemical Entity*, Office of Health Economics, London, February, 1999, p. 15, table 1.

50. G. Steven Burrill and Kenneth B. Lee, Jr., *Biotech 93: Accelerating Commercialization* (San Francisco, CA: Ernst & Young, 1992), 21.

51. Burrill & Company, *Biotech 2003*, 390.

52. Riva D. Atlas, "When Private Mixes with Public," *New York Times* (June 5, 2004): B1.

53. Burrill & Company, *Biotech 2004*, 372.

54. Ibid.

55. Karen Pihl-Carey, "Alnylam, Merck Focus on Eye Disease in Second RNAi Deal," *Bioworld* (June 30, 2004): 4.

56. Burrill & Company, *Biotech 2004*, 309.

57. Arthur Young High Technology Group, *Biotech 86: At the Crossroad* (San Francisco, CA: Arthur Young, 1986), 59.

58. G. Steven Burrill, and Kenneth B. Lee, Jr., *Biotech 91: A Changing Environment* (San Francisco, CA: Ernst & Young, 1990), 63.

59. G. Steven Burrill, and Kenneth B. Lee, Jr., *Biotech 94: Long-Term Value and Short-Term Hurdles* (San Francisco, CA: Ernst & Young, 1993), 17.

60. Ibid.

61. Burrill & Company, *Biotech 2004*, 315.

62. Burrill & Company, *Biotech 2003*, 269.

63. Genentech, "Genentech Announces Third Quarter Results," press release 10/23/1990, available on http://www.gene.com/gene/news/press-releases/display.do?method = detail&id = 4328.

64. "Human Genome Plots Over 45,000 Genes in SmithKline Pact – A Wall Street Journal News Roundup," *Wall Street Journal* (Eastern Edition) (April 8, 1994): C1.

65. "Pfizer and Eyetech Sign Accord for Treatment," *Wall Street Journal* (Eastern Edition) (December 19, 2002): 1.

66. "Business Brief – Pfizer Inc.: Accord is set with Neurocrine for Funding of Insomnia Drug," *Wall Street Journal* (Eastern Edition) (December 20, 2002): 1.

67. "Neurocrine to Develop and Promote Insomnia Treatment," *Drug Week* (January 24, 2003): 45.

68. Selena Class, "Selling the Crown Jewels?," IMS Global Consulting, available on http://www.ims-global.com/insight/news_story/0312/news_story_031201a.htm.

69. Geoff Dyer and Christopher Bowe, "Pfizer to make up for Patent Losses with Biotech Purchases," *Financial Times* (May 3, 2004).

70. James Surowiecki, "The Pipeline Problem," *New Yorker* 80(1) (February 16, 2004): 72.

71. Standard & Poor's Industry Surveys, *Biotechnology* (June 10, 2004), 1.

72. Burrill & Company, *Biotech 2004*, 272.

73. Sean Milmo, "European Biotechnology Industry Faces a Severe Financing Drought," *Chemical Market Reporter* (May 12, 2003).

74. Burrill & Company, *Biotech 2003*, 289.

75. *The UK: European Location of Choice for Companies Operating in the Biotechnology Sector*, UK government document available on http://www.invest.uktradeinvest.gov.uk/Uploads/Publications/pdfs/Bio%20Feature.pdf.

76. Burrill & Company, *Biotech 2003*, 289.
77. *The UK: European Location of Choice for Companies Operating in the Biotechnology Sector.*
78. Ibid.
79. "Managing Multiple Sclerosis: One Way Through the Interferon Minefield," *British Journal of Clinical Governance* 7(4) (Bradford, 2002): 272B 1.
80. Zev Stub, "TEVA May Benefit from UK Drug Initiative," *Jerusalem Post* (January 28, 2002), on http://www.mult-sclerosis.org/news/Jan2002/UKMSDrugInitiativeImpactOn Teva.html.
81. NICE, *NICE Appraisal of Beta Interferon and Glatiramer for MS*, summary of appraisal process, on http://www.nice.org.uk.
82. Ibid.
83. John K. Borchardt, "Germany's Biotechnology Industry Takes Off," *UK Trade and Investment* (February 23, 2001).
84. Janet Lambert, "The Canadian Biotech Scene: Nurturing Success," on http://www.biotecanada.ca.
85. *BIOTECanada Annual Report 2002*, on http://www.biotech.ca.
86. "Facts, Figures, and FAQs," on http://www.biotech.ca accessed 3/1/2004.
87. Burrill & Company, *Biotech 2004*, 266.
88. Company financial statements on Morningstar.com.
89. *BIOTECanada Annual Report 2002.*
90. *Canadian Biotechnology Report 2002*. Ernst & Young.
91. "Biotechnology and Pharmaceuticals Market in Canada," on http://www.uktradeinvest.gov.uk/biotechnology/canada/profile/overview.shtml.
92. Matthias Kamber, "Coming out of the Maze: Canada Grants the Harvard Mouse Patent," *George Washington University International Law Review* (2003): 761.
93. "Customer Insights: Biotechnology Industry Seeks to Recover," *Chemical Market Reporter* 264(6) (January 9, 2003).
94. Gurinder Shahi, "The Next Big Thing," *Far Eastern Economic Review* 165(39) (March 10, 2002): 70.
95. "Asia's Biotechnology Dawn," *SG Cowen Health Care Group* (November 2001): 13–14.
96. Burrill & Company, *Biotech 2003*, 314.
97. Jim Hopkins, "More Nations Want in on Biotech Action," *USA Today* (June 7, 2004): B1.
98. Chew Li Sa and Mazlyn, Mena, "Riding Asia's Biotech Wave," *Asian Business* 38(1) (January 2002): 20.
99. Burrill & Company, *Biotech 2004*, 293.
100. "The Biotechnology Industry," on http://investintaiwan.nat.gov.tw/moea-web/InvestOpps/Type/CrrntStrngInds/Biotech/BiotechIndepth.htm.
101. Li Sa and Mazlyn, "Riding Asia's Biotech Wave," 20.
102. Ibid.
103. Wayne Arnold, "Singapore Builds a Better Scientist Trap," *New York Times* (August 27, 2003).
104. Ibid.
105. Ibid.
106. Anon., "Biotechnology in Singapore: Send in the Clones," *Economist* (August 22, 2002).

107. "Market News Express: Singapore's Biotechnology Scene Shifts Firmly to Life Sciences," on http://www.tdctrade.com/mne/it/info060.htm.

108. "Asia's Biotechnology Dawn," 45.

109. Ibid., 30.

110. David Stipp, "China's Biotech is Starting to Bloom: Made in China Clones, Plants, and Drugs?," *Fortune* 146(4) (September 2, 2002): 126.

111. "Asia's Biotechnology Dawn," 28.

112. Ibid., 30.

113. Burrill & Company, *Biotech 2004*, 288.

114. "Innovation Investment Fund," available on http://www.business.vic.gov.au/.

115. Carrie Hillyard, "The Biotechnology Industry in Australia," Australian Academy of Technological Sciences and Engineering, *Focus* 107 (May/June 1999).

116. Donald Birkett, Andrew Mitchell, and Peter McManus, "A Cost Effectiveness Approach to Drug Subsidy and Pricing in Australia," *Health Affairs* 20(3) (May/June 2001): 104.

117. A. Ochee, "Fibrosis Victims Fight Drug Price War," *Courier Mail* (June 27, 1995).

118. Food and Drug Administration, *Prescription Drug User Fees – Overview*, available on http://www.fda.gov/oc/pdufa/overview.html, accessed on May 18, 2004.

119. Paul J. Anderson, "PDUFA Draws Mixed Review from GAO," *Pharmaceutical Executive* 23(1) (January 2003): 19.

120. Office of Technology Policy, *The US Biotechnology Industry* (Washington D.C.: Office of Technology Policy, 1997).

121. Jill Wechsler, "FDA Overhauls Drug Regulation while Protecting its Turf," *Formulary* 37(10) (October 2002): 543.

122. Ibid.

123. Glycosylation refers to the structure of sugar molecules that often exist on proteins in their final natural form.

124. Christopher Webster *et al.*, "Biologics: Can there be Abbreviated Applications, Generics, or Follow-On Products?," *International BioPharm* (May 18, 2003), available on http://www.bio-pharm-mag.com/biopharm/article/articleDetail.jsp?id=73785&&pageID=2 accessed 5/18/2004.

125. National Institutes of Health, "Stem Cell Basics," available on http://www.stemcells.nih.gov/info/basics/basics2.asp.

126. James L. Dolgin, "Embryonic Discourse: Abortion, Stem Cells and Cloning," *Florida State University Law Review* (fall 2003).

127. Sheryl Gay Stolberg, "Scientists Defend Suspended Gene Therapy." John M. Border, "Limits on Stem Cell Research Re-emerge as a Political Issue," *New York Times* (May 6, 2004): 1.

128. Arnold, "Singapore Builds a Better Scientist Trap."

129. "Biotechnology in Singapore: Send in the Clones."

130. Dolgin, "Embryonic Discourse."

131. Christine Willgoos, "FDA Regulation: An Answer to the Questions of Human Cloning and Germline Gene Therapy," *American Journal of Law and Medicine.* 27(101) (2001).

132. Ibid.

133. The Orange Book is a publication maintained by the FDA that identifies the therapeutic equivalents of drugs currently on the market. It enables states as well as private organizations to identify which generic drugs can be substituted for on-patent drugs.

134. Regulatory Affairs Professional Society, *Hatch-Waxman Act and Recent Developments*, available on http://www.raps.org/.

135. Jim Kling, "Off Brand Biologics: More Questions than Answers," *Signals Magazine* (August 8, 2003).

136. FDA, "Office of Orphan Products," available on http://www.fda.gov/orphan.

137. Burrill & Company, *Biotech 2004*, 368.

138. Whitehouse, Memo on Project BioShield, available on http://www.whitehouse.gov.

139. http://www.ich.org.

140. Ibid.

141. Ibid.

142. Caroline Nutley, "The Value and Benefits of ICH to Industry," Paper prepared for the International Federation of Pharmaceutical Manufacturers (January 2000): 1, available at http://www.ich.org.

143. Ibid., 8.

144. Robin F. Harman, "The EMEA – Drug Regulation at a Supranational Level," *Pharmaceutical Journal* (269) (November 23, 2002): 752.

145. Ibid.

146. EMEA, *Ninth Annual Report on the Activities of the EMEA, 2003* (March 11, 2004): 5.

147. Ibid.

148. Ibid.

149. Harman, "EMEA – Drug Regulation at a Supranational Level," 754.

150. Ibid.

151. Ibid.

152. Commission of the European Communities, COM(2001)404 Final (Brussels, November 26, 2001), 5.

153. John Abraham, "A Licence to Print Money?," *Health Matters* 43 (Winter 2000/2001).

154. Ibid.

155. Ames Gross and Caroline Tran, "Key Asian Medical Regulatory Issues," *Food and Drug Law Institute Update* (March/April 2003).

156. Ames Gross, "Regulatory Changes in Japan's Pharmaceutical Industry", available on http://www.pacificbridgemedical.com.

157. Ibid.

158. Ibid.

159. Ames Gross, "Japan 2000. Pharmaceutical Change: New Good Clinical Practice (GCP) Requirements," available on http://www.pacificbridgemedical.com.

160. Gross, "Regulatory Changes in Japan's Pharmaceutical Industry."

4 Biotechnology business and revenue models: the dynamic of technological evolution and capital market ingenuity

Stephen M. Sammut

Overview
Technology platform companies: a turning point in biotechnology business models
Genomics, proteomics, and drug discovery
Strategic alliances and technology platform companies
Business and revenue models: an overview
Macro and micro factors affecting business and revenue models
Business and revenue models: rethinking vertical integration
Technological reintegration and the healthcare value chain

Overview

The biotechnology sector has held great promise for the alleviation of human suffering through the creation of novel protein-based drugs or drugs that mimic natural proteins. In like manner, biotechnology promises to expand the food supply with the modification of plants and animals. Biotechnology is also involved in environmental remediation and other industrial processes. During its march from origination to the present day the industry has encountered changes in social expectations and business conditions that have been far more volatile than anticipated, and this has required an agility in reconfiguring scientific, business, and financing strategy. Biotechnology companies have had to respond in kind to challenges such as:

- proving their own technologies on the complex path of preclinical research and clinical development
- navigating through an ever-expanding and evolving corpus of science and the related global base of intellectual property owned by disparate, unrelated entities, each with economic objectives of their own
- compensating for an ever-expanding competitive environment

- adapting to a regulatory process that was itself evolving to accommodate the changing nature of the technology
- responding to the volatility (and often a loss of confidence) of the capital markets
- reconfiguring relationships with initially enthusiastic but ultimately reticent pharmaceutical company partners, who were at the same time responding to these same challenges affecting their internal biotechnology programs, further compounded by a nonproductive research pipeline and a portfolio of expiring patents, all within the midst of massive pharmaceutical industry consolidation (see chapter 2)

The above challenges induced a wholesale rethinking of the biotechnology and pharmaceutical value chain, and consequently of the industry's business models. Changes in business models cascaded from the top of the chain (the fully integrated pharmaceutical companies) to the bottom (the research intensive biotechnology companies). The rethinking of the fundamental business models of biotechnology has been an ongoing process for at least two decades, but most recently the rise of so-called "genomics/proteomics platform companies" offers significant detail into the issues involved and has the added benefit of having had to evolve over a compressed time period. Platform companies therefore serve as the richest case studies and are the backdrop for the chapter's goal of offering an explication of these changes and their impact on the industry.

Technology platform companies: a turning point in biotechnology business models

The original proposed topic for this chapter was "Technology platform companies and strategic alliances between pharmaceutical and biotechnology firms." "Technology platform companies" refers to companies that were created during the period surrounding completion of the Human Genome Project (announced May 2000; published February 2001). They were largely formed from the mid-1990s through the first years of the new millennium, and bore the labels "genomics" and "proteomics," both of which will be described in due course. These public and private initiatives were perhaps the most successful assault on elucidating a base of complex information in human history, and were enabled by a convergence of biochemical techniques fused with ingenious and automated instrumentation systems, all driven by unprecedented capacity in bioinformatics. The challenge from that point on was the translation of the basic research and data accumulation into commercial products in human health. Translation demanded an entirely new way of thinking about drug discovery and strategic alliances in the biotechnology and pharmaceutical industries.

Initially, therefore, the proposed topic seemed timely, rich with material, and potentially illustrative of how a segment of the industry structures alliances. But it was clear that if left to a description of platform company alliances, an opportunity to make a critical review of one of the underlying struggles of the biotechnology sector as a whole would be lost. In the recent history of technology platform companies, their approach to doing business and their relationship to pharmaceutical companies has shifted dramatically away from the original alliance structures – some would say to the point of invalidating the original basis of the strategic alliances. The implications of this shift go beyond the technology platform companies themselves, to the biotechnology sector at large, and boil down to the issue: what is the business of biotechnology?

In order to put the platform company phenomenon into its proper context, brief digressions on the biotechnology sector are necessary. The 1990s were transitional years for the biotechnology sector. At the start of that decade there was an unprecedented infusion of capital from both private and public markets. Investment was made widely across all subsectors of the sector and was spurred by several promising drugs in phase III clinical trials. Company valuations reached levels that were detached from their underlying performance and prospects. If this sounds like a bubble waiting to burst, it was. Many of the presumed biotechnology blockbuster drugs did not survive clinical trials. Valuations tumbled for public companies across the board and the capital markets went on a biotechnology holiday. Shortly thereafter, the capital market's reaction to the proposed healthcare reform of the Bill Clinton administration brought down the market capitalization of the major pharmaceutical companies and delivered the *coup de grâce* to biotechnology companies, at least for a time. Correctly concluding that the public markets would not soon provide the capital needed for completion of drug development, the private venture capital sources could respond only by reconsidering their own investment strategies and conserving their own pools of capital for solely those companies already in their portfolios.

Through most of the 1990s the biotechnology sector languished and struggled for new capital. Indeed many pundits, including this author, forecasted two- or threefold reduction in the number of biotechnology companies operating in the United States – there were more than 1,500 at the time. Despite the scarcity of new capital, most of the companies persevered by aggressively entering license and partnering agreements with major pharmaceutical companies, albeit on terms that were less generous than in previous years. A core of some thirty or so venture capital firms that specialized in biotechnology nevertheless scouted for new opportunities, but with an eye for new business models. Highest among these were so-called "toolbox companies," that is to say, companies building products and services around providing instrumentation and bioinformatics services to universities, companies, and government programs pursuing sequencing of the human genome – commonly referred to as "picks and shovels" companies. "Toolbox companies" were something of a precursor to "platform companies" and their role in the industry provides a helpful context. Many of them – some of which forward integrated into sequencing and patenting genes – enjoyed impressive profits, thus inspiring renewed investor confidence in the industry based on a new conviction that companies could make money even if they were not bringing a drug all the way to market.

A renewed confidence could not have come at a better time. The Human Genome Project was completed far ahead of schedule and with less money than was foreseen. Automation of the sequencing process was clearly the major driver of this success, but to a smaller extent, the number of genes in the human genome proved to be less than 10 percent of what was expected (some 40,000). The elucidated human genome – suddenly rationalized on many levels – became the new foundation for commercial activity, particularly for drug discovery.

Genomics, proteomics, and drug discovery

Simply put, genome science or genomics is the study of the structure, content, and evolution of genomes. The original focus of genome scientists was the development of the tools, such as high-volume nucleotide sequencing, to characterize genomes of different species. The field has subsequently migrated into analysis of the expression and function of both genes and proteins. A look at the objectives of genomics can shed some light on how laboratories and companies fall into functional niches. They are as follows.

1. To establish integrated, web-accessible databases of gene mapping and sequence data. Initially, there were many separate databases at individual laboratories, but organizations emerged to collect and link data, manage quality control, and configure the data in usable ways. General access is

open, but there are proprietary portions owned by companies. The software needed for searches and analyses also became the basis for commercial activity.

2. To assemble physical and genetic maps of the genome for the purpose of comparing genomes of different species and for accumulating data relevant to identifying the location of genes operant in disease. Mapping methods have been developed over many decades and are in common currency, as is much of the mapping data.

3. To generate expressed gene sequences and to determine their order. The technology embedded in this objective is complex, but the bottom-line significance is that a by-product of the process results in the formation of gene fragments called expressed sequence tags or ESTs. While there is not a one-to-one correspondence between ESTs and genes, EST collections can give a good first approximation of the diversity of genes expressed in a tissue, thereby setting a basis for physiologic and pathologic studies – a necessary step in drug target identification.

4. To identify the complete set of genes encoded within a genome and annotate each gene once it is identified. Annotation is a description of a gene that links its sequence to genetic data about the function, expression, and mutant phenotypes of the protein associated with the gene. The intensity and breadth of this research has requirements that typically require a commercial tool or service. Genes encoded within the sequence must be identified using a combination of analytic tools and bioinformatics systems, as well as specialized software able to sort through massive amounts of sequence data and recognize DNA features associated with genes.

5. To compile atlases of gene expression to guide the analysis of related protein synthesis. The methods for characterizing gene expression often rely on detecting a tag corresponding to each gene in a library of hundreds of thousands of sequenced fragments. EST sequencing can be used for this purpose. Many genes are only expressed in a few tissues, so that libraries are prepared from tissues of interest, often in different stages of development or disease, or in the presence of bacteria, virus, or toxins. The ensuing collection of ESTs is subject to study by a broad array of technologies and systems, each of which have become the basis of a product or service business, such as the manufacturing and sale of "gene chips" for large-volume study and comparison of gene expression to yield clues as to gene function. Here again, companies can sell systems and reagents or they can perform their own proprietary studies in-house, either alone or as part of an alliance.

6. To aggregate data as to gene function. Under this simply stated objective are other "omics" activities:

   a. functional genomics – a variety of approaches to determine the biochemical, cellular, and physiological properties of all gene products. Among the tasks is the screening of hundreds of thousands of mutants to determine genes that affect such traits as immune response and growth and development.

   b. proteomics – the use of methods for detecting protein expression, protein–protein interaction, and protein folding. Insight into a protein's shape is important for determining which drugs bind effectively, either turning protein function on or off. In turn, proteomics requires not only the tools to identify and sequence proteins, but also the means to collect, organize, cross-check, and compare relevant genetic and physiologic data.

7. To describe and characterize DNA sequence diversity. All genomes have large numbers of sequence sites at which two or more variants are found in natural populations. These are called single-nucleotide polymorphisms or SNPs. It seems to be the case that most quantitative genetic variation – such as disease susceptibility – is traceable to SNPs, the characterization and role of which have become a commercial area of focus. The need to understand SNPs, their variations, and their role in genetically linked disease has required refinement of several analytic methods, such as microassay and microfluidics systems and phage display, with the integration of these into bioinformatics. Proteomic databases have also been assembled, and many companies have mapped the interactions of proteins in cellular and disease processes, thus creating niches for other entrants in the drug discovery services sector.

Among the major practical applications – and the basis for technology platform companies – is the creation of a new basis for drug discovery. Novel drugs were traditionally discovered by trial and error methods. The new knowledge provided by recombinant technology and genetics has essentially replaced the historical approaches with more systematic means. The foundation to this shift in discovery is that drugs act on one or more targets within cells or an organism. Drug targets are typically enzymes, receptors on the surface of native cells or foreign antigens, or biochemical pathways or ion channels. The revolutionary impact of genomics as a means of identifying drug targets is best appreciated by the research reported in many publications by Jürgen Drews and his colleagues during the late 1990s. According to Drews, the entire armamentarium of drugs developed over the preceding fifty years were directed at just over 400 targets. Indeed, at the dawn of the

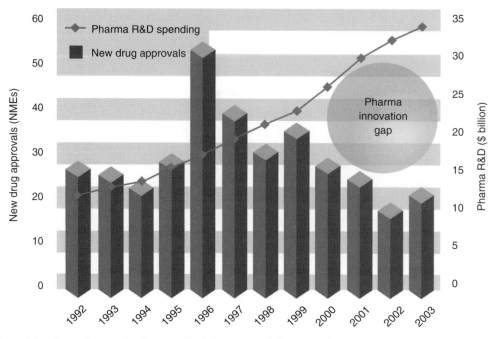

Figure 4.1   Innovation gap in pharmaceutical discovery and development.

Source: Pharamaceutical Research and Manufacturers of America (PhRMA), Burrill & Company.

genomics–proteomics era, major pharmaceutical companies typically validated a handful of new targets each year. The pace of target discovery and validation was a significant limiting factor in the creation of new drugs – especially those providing new intervention in hitherto untreated diseases. While only one part of a complex set of circumstances, the paucity of targets contributed to the innovation gap described in figure 4.1.

The types of data (as described above in the objectives of these sciences) that are extracted from genomics and proteomics offer clues toward new targets, and elucidate and validate the function of targets. Target proteins, for example, can be expressed in large quantities and then be screened for interactions against the large libraries of natural or synthetic compounds, typically proprietary to pharmaceutical companies. The molecular structure of compounds that have a preliminary promising reaction in this high-throughput screening system can be modified by chemical synthesis (aided by a system of churning out variant structures called combinatorial chemistry), resulting in new, highly targeted and efficient drugs the action of which would be so specific that fewer adverse reactions could be expected. The additional role of a related technology for matching specific drugs with specific patients to predetermine safety and efficacy for that patient – "pharmacogenomics" – has been described in preceding chapters, and will be placed in its commercial perspective later in this chapter.

As compared to the trial and error drug discovery methods of the past, the promise of the new discovery methods required competence in a wide range of specialized steps based on specific technology competence. Figure 4.2 provides a schematic of the proteomic technologies and their role in the discovery process.[1] The complex steps required recruiting of skilled scientists and technicians from a limited talent pool, and equipping them with the instrumentation needed to deliver results but without much of a basis to determine the appropriate capacity requirements or level of utilization. Companies that were in the business of drug discovery and development, therefore, had to make a "build or buy decision." Most opted for the latter (i.e., to outsource), accessing some or all of the steps in the new system of gene-based target discovery and validation. This decision, in and of itself, was a further departure (beyond in-licensing and strategic alliances) from the traditional attitude of pharmaceutical companies that the discovery and development process should be wholly in-house. Figure 4.3 describes where genomic/proteomic target discovery fits into the preclinical drug discovery process.[2] Looking at figure 4.2 and figure 4.3 together, the reader can observe the many components of this technology within the much larger scheme of discovery. Thus was set the stage for a new cohort of companies to service this need.

Strategic alliances and technology platform companies

The genomics or proteomics companies that emerged are the "technology platform companies." The underlying scientific and investment hypotheses are that each company would occupy one or more definable points in the target identification, validation, and drug discovery process using the cues provided by the sequences of genes that coded for specific proteins and the role of those proteins and their interaction in defining health and disease. Put differently, companies would provide not only new targets for drugs, but in many instances candidates for the actual drug entity for intervention as well. Such an exciting prospect captured the imagination

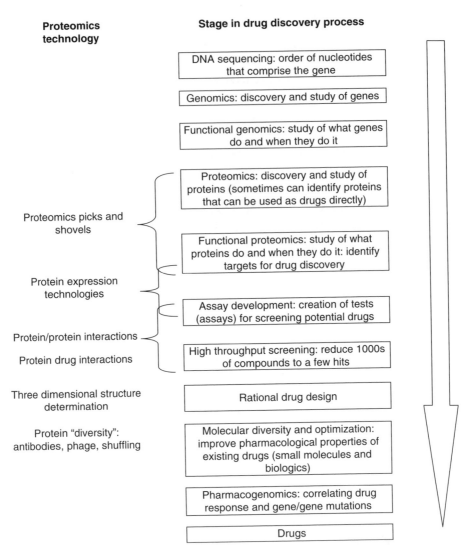

Figure 4.2 Proteomics toolbox technologies.

Source: CIBC World Markets Corporation.

of scientists, entrepreneurs, and venture capitalists, prompting a truly global proliferation of companies with initially persuasive commercial prospects. This was a turnaround from the thinking of many just a few years earlier.

Whilst the Human Genome Project was in its planning stages there was some skepticism regarding the immediate utility of the genetic information

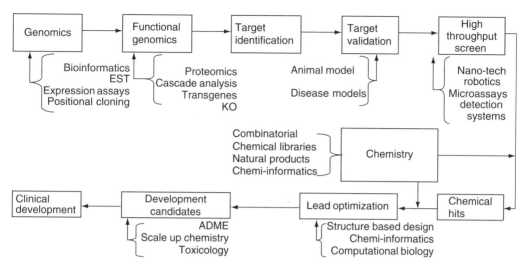

Figure 4.3   The "omics" development chain.

Source: Lehman Brothers.

to be accumulated. However, several key scientists and industrialists decided to explore the potential benefits of genomics to pharmaceutical discovery. Among the first of these was Gaithersburg, Maryland-based Human Genome Sciences (HGS) founded by two National Institutes of Health scientists, Craig Venter and William Haseltine. Their negotiations with SmithKlineBeecham (the predecessor firm of GlaxoSmithKline) and mediation provided by Frederick Frank of Lehman Brothers resulted in a partnership for genomics-driven drug discovery that was to become the model for dozens of genomics companies entering even more dozens of strategic alliances with nearly all the major pharmaceutical companies in the US, Europe, and Japan.

The primary components of this model assumed:
- proprietary accumulation of gene sequences and related patents
- licensing of those rights as a portfolio for specified disease indications, e.g., neoplastic, metabolic, neurologic diseases
- access to data developed by the platform companies when characterizing the role of particular genes in drug targeting
- bilateral participation in the discovery program on an exclusive basis within the agreed upon development focus
- revenues to the platform company in the form of up-front contract and license fees, bonus payments on the completion of milestones toward the

identification and validation of targets, and the identification of drug candidates
- typically evenly shared costs (clinical development, regulatory matters, marketing) and profits from sales in specified geography; royalty participation in the running sales of drugs brought to market by the pharmaceutical partner outside the specified geography

Since the model anticipated the likely activity and output that was expected from the platform companies, it logically became the basis for collaboration.

The HGS founders and other entrepreneurs who created technology platform companies, and the investors that supported them, expected that value would be created and ultimately realized, at the very least, through a generous annuity in the form of royalties from strategic pharmaceutical partners, or ideally, through the creation of drugs that the platform companies might bring to market directly. Historically, strategic alliances had a straightforward content. Simply stated, a biotechnology company had proprietary rights or unique capability that was of interest to an established pharmaceutical company. The parties would enter a license agreement and typically a contract to provide financial resources to the biotechnology company in order to take the products to a predetermined level of completion, whereupon the product or technology would be transferred to the pharmaceutical company. The level of royalties would be based on a variety of factors, such as the state of the technology or products when licensed, the degree to which the products could be brought to market without the need for further licensing of intellectual property from third parties, the cost of manufacturing the end product, and the market size and pricing. These arrangements, while straightforward in structure, were not trivial to manage to a point of success, but the deliverables from each side of the transaction were definable. Figure 4.4 offers an interesting breakdown of the wide range of participants in various segments of proteomic services.[3] The classification of the companies and their numbers, especially when juxtaposed against the previous figures, suggest the challenges of constructing a network of alliances.

The nature of genomic-proteomic drug discovery drove a much more ambiguous, complex, and less-definable deliverable when collaborative research and license agreements were structured between the platform companies and pharmaceutical firms. These were dictated as never before by the fundamental nature of the science and the challenges in translational research. Elucidation of specific proteins and their roles would not in and of itself define a deliverable or produce a transparent basis for the next step of drug discovery. Research scientists and their licensing executive counterparts had to allow for the uncertainty.

Category of activity	Number of companies	Various business models in category
Protein-protein interaction	> 12	Database access, reagent sales, hardware sales, drug development, collaboration and partnering, target discovery
Protein expression using 2-d gel	> 10	Contract research, licensing, diagnostic marker discovery
Protein expression using silica chips	> 5	Sale of chips and reagents
Visualization	> 5	Collaboration
Proteins expression – other	> 5	Collaboration
Protein structure X-Ray crystallography	> 5	Target discovery
Protein structure – bioinformatics	> 5	Database access, collaborations
Hardware	> 5	Equipment sales
Software: 2-d gel	> 10	Equipment and software sales

Figure 4.4   Specialty participants in the proteomics continuum.

Source: Burrill & Company and Lehman Brothers.

Proteins do not share the simple chemical nature of the genes that express them. Whereas genes can be easily cloned, studied, and screened in automated systems, gene expression analysis tells relatively little of the proteins they encode for these reasons:

- mRNA (messenger RNA – copy of a protein-coding gene) levels and protein levels are not necessarily correlated, that is, there is not a one-to-one correspondence between one mRNA and one protein
- proteins are subject to modification by other processes that affect function
- proteins have variable half-lives
- proteins function in different ways in different cellular locations
- some proteins must assemble into large complexes before they function

To compound the challenge, proteins can change geometry in different observational environments. The analytic tools must also be coordinated by sophisticated software. This is all directed to use proteomics to map out the network of biological pathways both in normal and diseased states. Protein–protein interactions are of particular importance, and the technologies to detect their associations often reside in still other companies. This landscape of capability and data in the hands of disparate parties sets not only the stage for an alliance-driven industry, but also dictates that the alliances will require far more effort on both sides in managing the process and transferring information than might be the case in a conventional license agreement.

As a consequence, licensing executives on both sides of the transaction had to build unique elements into the strategic alliances. There are, however, a few general structures that characterize major elements of most alliances between and among platform companies and pharmaceutical companies. These alliance types are profiled below.

Therapeutic area alliances

Therapeutic area alliances between a genomics/proteomics company and a major pharmaceutical company will often focus on a disease category or on diseases that emanate from a physiological cascade, such as inflammation (specifically, asthma, COPD, rheumatoid arthritis, multiple sclerosis, or inflammatory bowel disease). These arrangements typify the basic structure between a major pharmaceutical company and a discovery company. In many of the deals struck before the completion of genome sequencing, the discovery company licensed a given number of genes it expected to discover on an exclusive basis to its partner. The above-cited relationship involving Human Genome Sciences was one whereby some 100,000 genes were licensed to SmithKline. There were many intellectual property issues with the arrangement, but most telling of all was the fact that at the end of the Human Genome Project, the total of all genes was a mere 40,000 or so (the patent rights to which were owned by hundreds of companies, universities, and governments). An alliance established between Millennium Pharmaceuticals and Aventis Pharmaceuticals in 2000 in the area of metabolic disease had a more specific objective than the SmithKline–HGS arrangement, but both shared a framework for therapeutic-based alliances that typically included:

1. a discovery program for drug targets and lead compounds
   - often two-way exclusive collaboration
   - identification and selection of staffing
   - closely coordinated activity between the parties, often involving multi-sites of study and a schedule of project milestones, such as drug candidates at given intervals
   - close collaboration on the identification, validation, and optimization of the targets, chemistry, and pharmacologic formulation
   - pooling of discovery capability and work product

2. a joint development program for clinical studies, regulatory affairs, and premarketing
3. commercial agreement on
   - territories in which there is joint marketing or equal sharing of costs and profits
   - territories in which the major corporation has exclusive rights to market and sell, and the royalties and schedule of payments to be made to the genomics/proteomics company
   - territories in which the genomics/proteomics companies can either market directly or enter license or marketing agreements with third parties

Data mining alliances

Another set of alliances entail major screening programs in which the parties collaborate in the large-scale generation and screening of libraries. These are often called "data mining" collaborations. Millennium and Bayer conducted a collaboration along these lines starting in 1998 for cardiovascular disease. The fundamental sequence of events starts with the discovery of potential targets from tissues, libraries of compounds, and gene sequence and protein structure data. The screening process is automated with the goal of providing clinical candidates. As previously mentioned, figure 4.2 describes the "toolbox" of proteomics technologies applied in the discovery and development process. Generally, a goal is set for a large number of potential targets (hundreds) over several years. The established pharmaceutical company funds the screening over a period of years (in the case of Millennium and Bayer, $465 million over five years), selects a specified portion of the targets during the project, and structures a royalty-sharing scheme for drugs ultimately brought to market based on the selected targets. In a typical arrangement, the genomics/proteomics company retains the rights to the remaining targets (again, Millennium retained rights to 90 percent of the targets in its relationship with Bayer), with or without a revenue-sharing arrangement with the sponsor for products based on these targets.

Technology development alliances

Technology development alliances are a third form of strategic alliance. Figure 4.3 illustrates a rationalized but complex chain of steps in getting from genomic information to the point of clinical development. The reference to "omics" in the title is industry shorthand for the sequential role of genomics, proteomics, metabolomics, and the like. The discovery period can in and of itself take three to five years, although the original expectation was for a shorter period. The discovery process, in turn, is followed by a development period of similar length. Interestingly, figure 4.3 was developed and published not by a pharmaceutical company but by an investment bank! Figure 4.4 describes the types of companies – and their numbers – that provide technology or services along the proteomics continuum, and sheds some light on why a bank would publish figure 4.3. The investment community perpetually seeks to characterize the role of any given company within a value chain. Suffice it to say, the many specialty companies arrayed along that chain all require investment capital. The capital markets need means to assess their role in the value chain and to determine the rents that they can extract for their relative contribution to an end product. Obviously, claims on the value created are scattered among many participants.

As a further complication, without an "agent" to manage the transfer of discovery from one participant to another, there would be no product at the end of the chain. These factors form the basis for technology development alliances. In some instances, the complexity of the process has been managed by a "prime contractor," that is, by major genomics/proteomics companies such as Millennium, Human Genome Sciences, Celera, Incyte Genomics, and Hyseq. Generally, these arrangements start with a therapeutic area alliance between one of the major genomics companies and a large pharmaceutical company. In order to accomplish the full range of activity along the discovery chain, the lead genomics company assembles an alliance with one or more of the specialty companies in order to meet the objectives. In some instances a major pharmaceutical company sponsors the program, but in others the structure is a self-funded collaboration among the specialty genomics/proteomics companies. The goal of the relationship is to produce lead compounds that can either be licensed at significantly higher values and royalties to major pharmaceutical companies or brought to market by one of the specialty companies as part of their own effort to forward integrate into production and marketing. An example of this type of collaboration is a program between Millennium Pharmaceuticals and Affymetrix, where each company brings its specialized background and process technology (in the case of Affymetrix, its microarray technology) into the relationship. The purpose, in this case, is to profile transcription (the particular process by which RNA is formed from DNA). In a cross-licensing and royalty arrangement, Millennium can use the results in its other business activity, and

Affymetrix can commercialize and sell information or systems. The main advantage to this type of arrangement is that it allows the participants the ability to occupy or control a larger portion of the value chain. Again, figure 4.3 puts these issues in perspective.

Technology transfer alliances

Genomics/proteomics companies have structured a variety of technology transfer arrangements whereby the pharmaceutical partner obtains enabling technologies, sometimes for a specific set of technologies and at other times a more open-ended arrangement where new technologies flow as they are developed. The financial arrangements typically include substantial licensing and technology service fees, incentive for further development and transfer of know-how, royalties, and provisions for the proteomics/genomics companies to license other parties.

Measuring alliance performance

Given the taxonomy and characteristics of platform technology companies described above, there is the matter of success and how to measure it. According to Burrill & Company and Windhover Communications, strategic alliances are structured among pharmaceutical and biotechnology companies at the rate of several hundred each year, with an historical inventory exceeding two thousand. Industry professionals look to any number of books and courses guiding the structuring and execution of these relationships, which on the whole function at least as well as expected. The following are essentially textbook factors for determining whether or not the relationship is operationally effective:

- understanding respective goals
- establishing aggressive but realistic milestones
- preserving equal economic participation
- selecting the appropriate managerial and scientific staff on each side, and incentivizing them relative to performance of milestones
- implementing project management and information systems specific to the tasks
- rigorous reporting of progress, success, and disappointments
- regular success and failure analysis
- managing continuity after staff turnover
- mutual disclosure of developments, inventions, and findings

The measurement of productivity is another matter. Often, and especially in the life sciences, goals are set without the benefit of experience in the new field. Managements can easily make real-time adjustments, but the internal financial investments, as well as the expectations of the external financiers, are not as easily adjusted and are subject to the dilemma of expected returns within given time frames. Moreover, life sciences in general, and drug discovery in particular, begin any given program or project based on the assumption that all needed tools, intellectual property rights, capability, and so on are in hand as of the start. In practice, this is seldom the case. As gaps are discovered along the continuum, the gaps either have to be filled with internal solutions or extramural solutions. Either alternative changes the cost basis of the program and thereby the returns. In a nutshell, this has effectively happened in the genomics/proteomics platform world. The hypothesis, again, was that drug targets would be identified and validated. The assumed pace and efficiency was less valid. And the expectation that the platform companies would each enjoy a sole and privileged economic position in the drug discovery value chain was effectively wrong.

On the surface the assumptions behind the technology platform business and revenue model, and the associated strategic alliances, were reasonable, but there were several inherent flaws. The presumed basis of commerce was trumped by a variety of biological, intellectual property, and operational issues:

1. Identification of a gene sequence that encoded for a protein (a specific amino acid sequence) did not necessarily elucidate the function, or in patent terms the utility, of the related protein.

2. Establishment of the utility of a gene or genes in health or disease relied on a comparison of deviations ("polymorphisms") of the sequence(s) in the sick and the healthy presumed access to detailed multigenerational medical histories in families that struggle with given diseases (or conversely appear to enjoy health or immunity in the face of otherwise endemic disease). Longitudinal information of sufficient detail and quality rarely exists. In fact, an Icelandic company, Decode Genetics, was formed for precisely the purpose of providing information for this type of analysis. Iceland, with a relatively homogenous population, has kept detailed medical histories for many generations.

3. The function of the protein(s), or the failure of the cellular system to express the protein(s), did not necessarily characterize the related pathology or point to a means of intervention.

4. The established pathology did not necessarily result from the failure of expression of one protein (monogenic disease) but may be polygenic or, in addition, relied on the geometric configuration ("folding") of the protein(s).

5. Integration of the above required a full range of capability over several steps in the discovery continuum that translated to access to a level of capital that was frequently unattainable.

6. The filing of patent applications on genes and their utility, or presumed drug targets based on these, would not necessarily result in the issuance of a patent, or when it did that the patent would be enforceable. Specifically, would there be a basis for the owner of a patent to negotiate for participation in the royalty stream of an end product for which it provided information for one small step among dozens of other steps of varying significance?

7. The financial arrangements associated with alliances between platform companies and their pharmaceutical partners often did not provide ample revenue and profit over a long-enough time.

8. The hypothesis that overall discovery and development processes could be abbreviated adequately to provide enough cash flow for economic self-sufficiency and ultimately returns to investors within an acceptable time period proved to be largely unfounded.

Obviously, these factors created a complex simultaneous equation. But the prospect of delivering new intervention for a wider range of diseases inspired entrepreneurial energy and investment enthusiasm from both the venture capital and public capital markets. This drive toward creation, funding, and the subsequent high valuations created in the public markets has sometimes been classified as a bubble. It was not, or at least not in the sense of the bubble described previously for the early 1990s. Bubbles have no substance behind them. Platform companies had the strength of fifty years of modern biology. It was the fragmentation of capability, the disappointing pace of discovery, and the short-term inability of the companies to create an annuity from alliances or from products directly marketed that led to a loss of faith by the investment community that as of the time of this writing has not recovered. While there was some economic reward for the creation and use of tools, the anticipated cash streams from the sale of drugs based on genomic/proteomic discoveries will take a decade or two longer than expected.

The effect has been a major shift in strategy by the major platform companies to move downstream toward drug development with the goal of licensing a more valuable product to a marketing partner, or perhaps comarketing and moving toward full integration. The complexity of the genetic regulation of biological systems, of course, always exceeds the estimates of scientists and technologists and their financial patrons. This disappointment is an indictment neither of the technology nor of the role of strategic alliances in advancing and financing its use. It simply signals that the industry is ready for the next phase of the evolution of its underlying business models.

The history of technology platform companies is illustrative of the basis of the current changes in the commerce of biotechnology and the related investment focus. Such changes are occurring in real time, at a fantastic pace, during a period of major financial upheaval in the capital markets in general and in the healthcare sector in particular. Platform companies are a dramatic – but not the lone – example of biotechnology business models in transition. Participants in virtually all segments of the biotechnology sector are at this moment rethinking their fundamental business models. The strategic implications for scientists, biotechnology industry management, and their counterparts in the pharmaceutical sector are profound.

Business and revenue models: an overview

The description of the technological basis, structure, history, and strategy of platform companies is beneficial in its own right, because the emergence of these companies marks a first attempt to establish the utility of an extraordinary base of new knowledge and to translate it to an entire system for the discovery and development of drugs. The fact that platform companies have encountered obstacles in their sustainability and growth does not undermine the role of strategic alliances. It does, however, speak to a more fundamental issue: the need for biotechnology companies to respond to the changing dynamics of the industry through rethinking and ongoing reassessment of their business and revenue models. The remainder of this chapter will draw upon the experience of technology platform companies in this regard and place it within the larger, historical evolution and experimentation with these models.

Whilst the terms *business model* and *revenue model* are in common usage, they are often defined or interpreted in differing ways. In fact, the terms have an appealing "self-explanatory" ring and are therefore tossed about indiscriminately. This is especially dangerous in the biotechnology sector, where the concepts have serious implications and arguably a role and variety that are unsurpassed in any other industry. A description of the two concepts and their working definitions for this chapter are in order.

A business model of a given company is based on how and through what means it can create value from its technology or capability. The revenue model is the nature of the selling transaction through which that value is realized, for example, direct product or service sales, licensing of technology and related royalties, leasing, customer support, and so on. Classically, companies develop, manufacture, market, and sell their products to another company or to consumers (or they sell to distribution channels). Companies create value through insertion of their products or services into that point in the customer's value chain where both parties in the transaction can capture optimum value. Business models must adapt – discretely or continuously – to shifts within value chains. In the case of biotechnology, as pharmaceutical companies outsource more of the drug discovery process or fill their pipelines with in-licensed products, a biotechnology company must decide whether it will capture value by persevering with its own resources to bring products to market by itself (a fully integrated company), or must partner in some way with the pharmaceutical company through research collaboration or licensing (a research-integrated company).

From a manager's perspective, the resources of the company that define its value-added role and competitive sustainability will likely suggest whether or not the company should participate at multiple points in the value chain. The decision that arrives from this assessment, again from a managerial perspective, is the degree of vertical integration for the company. Should the company accumulate further capability in and around its point in the value chain, or should it move downstream to control more of the product development, manufacturing, marketing, and selling activities? Put plainly,

- where is/are the point(s) of greatest value creation?
- can the company participate in those points effectively?
- what resources are needed to participate?
- are those resources available?

In the biotechnology sector the resource limitations of managerial experience, scientific skill, access to intellectual property rights, and capital provide the basis for answers to these questions and are the context of business model creation and adoption.

Managers know that the capital markets historically have favored fully integrated companies, and in the case of biotechnology, companies that have proprietary rights to drug entities can raise more capital at higher valuations. Capital markets, however, have sometimes responded favorably to less fully integrated business models, as was the case early in the history of platform technology companies. When full integration is not an option for a particular biotechnology company, the option is to create maximum value by inserting its capability into that part of the discovery or development process that a pharmaceutical company decides to outsource or supplement. This results in a trade-off: the pharmaceutical company's margins decrease, but their overall discovery and development risk may be reduced while at the same time enjoying exposure to a wider range of opportunities. In parallel, the biotechnology company derives short-term revenue from development contracts (including bonuses for milestone completion) and, when a product is brought to market, some portion of the selling price in the form of royalties or transfer pricing. Such an arrangement with a major pharmaceutical company also serves as a validation of the company and its technology, thus facilitating the raising of additional equity capital. All in all, managers make business model decisions in response to changing circumstances.

Why have biotechnology business and revenue models changed? There are generally five primary motivators for change.

1. New role or importance of a given component in the processes of discovery, development, or postmarketing surveillance for usage and adverse reactions. Conversely the obsolescence of another component in the same continuum is likely to induce a change in the model, for example, the decline or elimination of traditional natural product screening required outsourcing for access to the new technologies.

2. Abandonment of part of the continuum or product line by one or more participants based on any number of factors, such as pricing issues for suppliers or a higher risk to a lower reward, such as in the case of many pharmaceutical companies abandoning their activity with drugs for infectious disease.

3. Industrial consolidation (e.g., the major pharmaceutical companies) and the resulting rationalization of research projects or product lines, thus resulting in greater competition for alliances by the biotechnology companies or in the opportunity to acquire products or projects that must be divested by the merging companies.

4. Outsourcing as an approach to reduce capital costs, achieve cost-efficiency, or improve quality (e.g., outsourcing to contract research organizations).

5. Insertion of a new process into the continuum of drug discovery (e.g., proteomics) to drug administration to the patient care system

(patient-by-patient efficacy screening using pharmacogenomics). In this instance, incumbent players must make a decision to partner, buy, or build.

6. Proliferation of new companies with similar capabilities.

Macro and micro factors affecting business and revenue models

An account of the macro and micro conditions is useful background for characterizing the past, present, and future of business and revenue models. As at the time of going to press, the biotechnology sector (four thousand or more companies globally) is within a year of entering its fourth decade. As it does so, the total historical capital infusion (some 350 billion US dollars since 1976) into the industry, including equity investments and research contracts associated with strategic alliances, is approximately six times the industry's global revenues of 56 billion US dollars in 2003. Figure 4.5 elaborates on the characteristics of the biotechnology sector at large.[4]

New annual investment has varied widely over the past decade, from lows of $5 billion to as much as $30 billion, suggesting that the 10 to 15 percent annual revenue growth rate of the industry is not yet keeping pace with new capital infusions. Figure 4.6 illustrates that the overall capital contribution to the biotechnology sector, though variable from year to year, remains strong.[5]

The capital voraciousness of basic research and development in progress, to say nothing of downstream drug discovery and development, will likely continue unabated for the foreseeable future. Currently the industry average for R&D investment is 30 percent of sales, but the vast majority of

	USA	Europe	Canada	Australia
Sales/revenue ($ billion)	58.0	7.5	1.7	1.0
Annual R&D ($ billion)	16.4	4.2	0.6	0.1
Number of companies	1,473	1,878	470	226
Number of employees	146,100	32,470	7,440	6,393
Number of public companies	356	96	81	58
Market capitalization ($ billion)	399.2	25.6	13.8	5.0

Figure 4.5   Biotechnology industry characteristics in 2004 in US $.

Source: Burrill & Company and Ernst & Young.

Public	1998	1999	2000	2001	2002	2003	2004
Public							
IPO	369	670	6,490	440	445	453	1,763
Follow-on	521	5,805	12,651	2,539	979	3,536	3,388
PIPEs	977	1,433	4,061	1,741	907	2,051	2,505
Debt	1,262	1,520	5,728	4,848	5,251	7,170	8,418
Private							
Venture capital	800	1084	2,872	2,397	2,688	2,841	3,733
Other	84	184	203	9	178	294	269
Total	**4,013**	**10,696**	**32,005**	**11,974**	**10,443**	**16,345**	**20,076**

Figure 4.6   Capitalization trends in the US life sciences industry (in $ million).

Source: Burrill & Company, *Biotech 2004: Life Sciences Back on Track* (San Francisco, CA: Burrill & Company, 2004), 351, and March 2005 update.

participants in the industry have modest sales and no profits and therefore must absorb their equity capital. Is this a financial travesty? On the whole, scientists, clinicians, and even financiers would say that this is the wrong question. They are more likely to say that the real benchmark of performance is the number of products (with sufficient patent life) in the market and products in the pipeline. Financiers would also point out that the magnitude of the ratio between capital invested and revenues is not unique to the biotechnology sector. Most major industries have similar histories in their first decades, and it is not until consolidation or business failure forces the recognition of losses in scores or even hundreds of individual industrial participants that the survivors deliver acceptable returns on equity. Here, of course, is the rub. While nearly all industries undergo consolidation after several decades in commerce, wholesale consolidation has not yet been true of the biotechnology sector, despite periods of severe financial famine. This factor begs the question: "Why?" The answers to this macro-question are also part of the story, and have a bearing on the strategy of business and revenue models.

Business and revenue models: rethinking vertical integration

Biotechnology operates within a value chain, of course, but one that has a complex interdependence within a health system that has been in the process of rationalizing its own economics. Burns and his colleagues have elucidated these changes in the *Health Care Value Chain*, and also elsewhere in this book.[6] Their work has a great relevance to our discussion, because biotechnology, as an industry, has enjoyed a reprieve from the financial realities of the larger changes within healthcare.

Biotechnology as an industry has effectively relied on the largess of strangers, particularly those wealthy individuals, venture capital funds, and financial institutions willing to accept presumed compensated financial risk over significantly extended periods as compared to nearly all other industries. The willingness to accept this risk is rooted – simplistically – in the expectation that the products of the biotechnology sector, particularly those targeting catastrophic or chronic diseases, will be enthusiastically received and promoted by health providers to the benefit of price-tolerant patients and their grudging, but nevertheless relenting insurance companies. This clearly is changing.

The biotechnology sector has also enjoyed, in a manner of speaking, subsidization from a pharmaceutical sector that has an urgent need to supplement the output of its internal discovery and development efforts with the works-in-progress and products of the biotechnology sector. The resulting transfers of technology or marketing rights offer significant advantages to both parties, as shown below.

For the in-licensee (typically major pharmaceutical companies), there is the ability to access products that have high-risk-profiles and resource intensity, and which cause a dilution of human capital if developed in-house. These arrangements serve to:

- fill a product pipeline
- complement an existing product line or therapeutic focus
- expand into a new therapeutic area
- build integrated capabilities

For the out-licensor there are the complementary advantages of:

- demonstrating to the financial markets an implied validation of technology or company capability by the partner's endorsement
- generating cash from the monetizing of under-performing or non-core assets
- using cash, in addition to equity capital, to develop more general or fungible capability (e.g., production know-how or capacity that can be used for products not under license)
- the opportunity to leverage the partner's capabilities

- access to markets generally, or in other territories
- further developed and expanded expertise (e.g., in regulatory affairs)

Figure 4.7 offers a simplified characterization of the broad categories of company definitions and their related business models. The column headings are defined as follows:

- *Period*   The approximate calendar interval during which an approach was established and executed. In most cases these are continuous. In some cases there was an interruption based on either technological or clinical experiences, replacement by alternative approaches, or dissatisfaction by the financial community.
- *Definition*   The nature of the business based on either the technology employed or the targeted intervention.
- *Hypothesis and managerial implications*   The strategic reasoning behind the business and its structure and the implications for execution.
- *Business model*   The degree of vertical integration, where:
  - "FIPCO" refers to a fully integrated pharmaceutical company where the company conducts research, product development, clinical development, manufacturing, and product detailing independently.
  - "FIPCO extended to clinical services" includes the above with the possible inclusion of some degree of clinical involvement in the administration of the therapeutic.
  - "RIPCO" refers to a research-intensive pharmaceutical company where the company conducts proprietary research and develops the products in concert with an alliance partner. A RIPCO might also manufacture the product but typically is not involved in marketing.
  - "FIDDO" refers to a newly emerging model of "fully integrated drug discovery/development." In this model, "platform" companies are building on their existing capability into development of their own products or in-licensed products, often with their own resources, but with the expectation of entering an alliance or licensing agreement with more favorable terms than an earlier stage relationship.
  - "Alliances" refers to any business relationships that might involve the licensing of intellectual property or products, or the rights to market or comarket a product. These alliances run the gamut of products as early as the discovery phase through to NDA as well as marketing.
- *Revenue model and value capture – strategy and expectations*   Reference to where in either the relationship to the alliance partner or to the purchaser/ provider link in the value chain revenue will be attained. The revenue model also anticipates sustainability based on the value add relationship

Period	Definition	Hypothesis and implications	Business model	Revenue model and value capture	Value chain positioning	Financing/investment exit options	Examples
Inception to early 1990s	rDNA/MAb products for catastrophic and/or chronic diseases	Naturally expressed proteins have accelerated regulatory pathway; less capital intense; faster to market	FIPCO Alliances for specific project or product	Rely on medium elasticity; IP ownership diffuse; art intensity* extends proprietary life; strong margins	Detail to clinician; create new category or adjunct to care	Venture capital IPO/secondary alliance revenue as supplement Exit via public markets or trade sale	Amgen Genentech Biogen Medarex Chiron Immunex Centocor
Inception to present	Service companies to biotech industry	Picks and shovels (instruments, reagents, transgenic animals, software, lab services, purification, scale-up, contract mfg.)	Product and service sales to FIPCOs and RIPCOs	Relatively short product development cycle; manageable cell cycle	Product or service providers to discovery companies	Venture capital IPO/secondary Possible alliance (not typical)	Applied Bio DNX Invitrogen Dionex
Inception through mid-1980s; resumed early 1990s to present	Immune regulation strategies for cancer and auto-immune diseases	Systems to selectively stimulate or suppress immune response; requires close clinical collaboration and new care model	FIPCO with clinical extension Alliances: limited opportunity not consistent with general pharma model with some exceptions	Rely on great elasticity; IP sole with some in-licensing; production costs high; service revenue participation unclear	Unclear. May represent a new modality of care with producer playing a role	Venture capital IPO/secondary Possible narrow sector alliance, e.g. transplantation Exit via public markets, possible trade sale	Immunogen ISIS Cephalon Genta

Figure 4.7 Representation of the dynamics of biotechnology strategies and structures and their revenue models.
*Know-how at the lab bench that extends beyond the literature and patents

Period	Definition	Hypothesis and implications	Business model	Revenue model and value capture	Value chain positioning	Financing/investment exit options	Examples
Inception to present	Drug delivery or formulation enhancement	Enhance absorption, bioavailability and effectiveness of existing drugs and enable use of large molecule therapeutics	RIPCO with contract manufacturing Alliance intensive with multiple partners	Participation in revenue stream of alliance partner; possible contract revenue	End product brought to market by the pharma partner	Venture capital IPO/secondary alliances	ALZA AIR Sepracor
Mid-1990s to present with controversy and recasting	Gene and cell therapy; stem cell companies	Various approaches of intervention using processed biological material either prepared and sold on a third party basis or administered in concert with providers	FIPCO with clinical extension Alliances: limited opportunity not consistent with general pharma model with some exceptions	Rely on great elasticity; IP sole with some in-licensing; production costs high; service revenue participation unclear	Unclear. May represent a new modality of care with producer playing a role	Venture capital IPO/secondary Exit via public markets, possible trade sale	Genovo Cellgene Genvec Osiris DNX
Mid-1990s to present with redefinition	Genomic/proteomic "platform" companies"; other drug discovery toolbox companies	Companies ally with pharmaceutical producers to discover new drug targets and candidates for clinical development	RIPCO, effectively the beneficiary of outsourced discovery; alliance intensive; multiple partners Model is moving toward FIDDO	Alliance revenues; thereafter IP driven with product royalty streams Sustainability remains unclear	End product brought to market by the pharma partner	Venture capital IPO/secondary alliance revenue Exit via public market or trade sale	HGS Millenium Celera DYAX Incyte

Figure 4.7 (cont.)

Period	Definition	Hypothesis and implications	Business model	Revenue model and value capture	Value chain positioning	Financing/investment exit options	Examples
Mid-1980s; then late 1990s to present	Specialty drug development for catastrophic and/or chronic diseases	Companies use one or more biological strategies, e.g., anti-sense or RNA interference to develop proprietary drugs	RIPCO. Possible opportunity for FIPCO in specialty indications. Alliance driven but with more leverage given large pharma company need for products	Rely on great elasticity; IP proprietary but built on core technologies owned by 3rd parties; productions costs and margins unclear	End product brought to market by pharma partner	Venture capital IPO/secondary alliance revenue Exit via public markets or trade sale	Cephalon RNAi cos. (gene messaging) ISIS Ambion Nucleonics Quiagenn Acuity
Evolving; emerged early 2000s	Digital and systems biology	Integrates advances in biology, medicine and computing to determine, characterize and validate drug targets	Evolving. Will initially resemble original model of "platform" companies. Will quickly evolve to FIDDO	Initially alliances. End products probably FIPCO extended to clinical services	End product brought to market by pharma partner	Venture capital IPO/secondary alliance revenue Exit via public markets or trade sale	IBM Life Sciences Several academic institutions
Evolving; emerged early 2000s	Evolving: personalized medicine	Integrated approach to screening, selection, modification and custom administration for needs of specific patients	Evolving. Likely to be a unique model involving discovery companies, pharmaceutical collaborators and clinical laboratories	Initially alliances. End products probably FIPCO extended to clinical services	Positioning to be determined, but will involve participation in the provider realm	Venture Capital IPO/secondary alliance revenue Exit via public markets or trade sale	Genaissance Affymetrix Probe companies ParAllele Illumina Third Wave

Figure 4.7 (*cont.*)

to the alliance partner, the purchasers or providers, as well as intellectual property factors.

- *Value chain positioning*   Reference to the place in the purchaser or provider value chain that the product is detailed and sold. FIPCOs that extend their business models into clinical services may also have a direct relationship therein.
- *Financing/investment exit options*   Reference to the most likely sources of equity capital or partnering revenue, as well as to the means by which equity investors can realize a return.

In combination with additional data points, a number of conclusions can be drawn from the assertions and comparisons described in figure 4.7. First, the prospects for creation and development of a fully integrated pharmaceutical company (FIPCO) that will compete head to head with the established pharmaceutical incumbents are limited owing to the significant costs of bringing a drug through all phases of clinical development, building manufacturing facilities, and creating a sales force. Exceptions arise in those instances where a company's products are directed at therapeutic niches with relatively few specialty physicians and limited provider sites, or for those cases where a product or service-offering falls outside the traditional pharmaceutical business model, as can be seen in the immune regulation and cell therapy models described in figure 4.7.

Second, companies created to perform research for or to sell products to the established pharmaceutical companies are in the process of redefining the discovery and development continuum from a limited position on the value chain to one that is expanded. Simultaneously, those companies are determining the levels of integration and associated revenues within that continuum necessary for sustainable business. This takes the form, where possible, of managing the manufacturing process and enjoying additional profit from the negotiated transfer price. Pharmaceutical companies, however, often resist this push for a number of reasons, ranging from the necessity to control quality to the desire to maintain the margins generally associated with manufacturing. Intellectual property issues are also a factor in this determination, for several reasons:

- The enforceability and reach of a patent on a gene sequence, even when its utility is identifiable and claimed, is not yet clear and has not been fully adjudicated at present.
- The value of the sequence *vis-à-vis* the end product is still in flux, as are other contributions to preclinical discovery and development. In those cases where a license is executed between companies for products

at the discovery stage, the aggregate royalty is averaging just over 5 percent, with up-front payments averaging $5 million. Likewise, for transactions involving those same compounds at the pre-clinical/IND stage, the royalties average 7.5 percent, with approximately $30 million in up-front payments.[7] These levels of royalties and up-front payments are not inherently parsimonious, but must cover the ownership stakes of several owners of relevant intellectual property in order to get it to that state of readiness. The share owed to the owner of the gene sequences or other key intellectual property are but parts of that royalty and may not yield cash streams for a decade or more. These are meager numbers on which to build a sustainable business.

- The royalty burden associated with biotechnology products is itself two to three times higher, on average, compared with the royalties assessed on synthetic, small-molecule pharmaceuticals. The latter generally go to market with a smaller number of patents, the main one of which is on the operant molecules as a composition of matter. By way of contrast, biotechnology products are burdened with a stack of royalties for patents owned by sundry third parties on gene sequences, therapeutic applications, processing and manufacturing methods, and a host of other patents. In combination with the higher costs of biopharmaceutical production, the gross margins are lower than with traditional drugs, and would be much lower if it were not for the price elasticity of the end products.

Third, the transfer and processing of know-how and information from the discovery entity to the development entity is neither seamless nor complete. Predictable problems surrounding differing information systems, interpretation by different teams, utility and implementation of the genetic information provided, and the like confound efficient implementation.

Suffice it to say, there is an irony here. We are at a point in pharmaceutical commerce where the incumbents are redefining their own competencies and value chain participation. As figure 4.1 illustrates, their urgent need to form a greater number of more substantial strategic alliances – effectively outsourcing discovery and development – can be met in kind by hundreds, if not thousands, of biotechnology companies.[8] But the economics of the pharmaceutical and therapeutics markets are changing and that, too, signals the need for fundamental changes in the relationships among alliance partners. The underlying assumptions in the "technology platform" model and the subsequent restructuring of the sector is a sentinel of that change.

Technological reintegration and the healthcare value chain

This chapter will conclude with cautious speculation as to how the business of biotechnology will adapt not only to its new tools, but also to the surfeit of data that it has created. The final three rows of figure 4.7 offer new models. The first of these, "Specialty drug development," is a logical and predictable outcome. It encapsulates the short- to intermediate-term business model now afoot among the major platform technology companies. It is not a foolproof strategy. It will be subject to the same risks and costs associated with clinical development generally, and will also have to deal with the clinical markets. This strategy, however, provides the best available opportunities. The established pharmaceutical companies still need products, and strategic alliances are the best approach for acquiring product rights.

The more interesting question concerns how the biotechnology sector will build upon the tools and the information that it has accumulated, and how efficiently that will translate into products to benefit human health. As to the thesis of this chapter, how will the drug discovery value chain change? Who will participate? What are the corresponding economic rewards?

The final two columns of figure 4.7 offer cautious speculation as to the role of "systems biology" and its goal of personalized medicine, that is, drugs formulated and selected for individual patient profiles. Systems biology looks at the larger picture. The tools and their corresponding business models that were the subject matter of this chapter focused on parts: genes, their proteins, cell pathways, variations, and so on. Systems biology integrates the above with mathematical and computer modeling in order to interpret data in hand and to predict the direction of future data. In the process of aggregating the elements of biological systems – genes, mRNA, protein interaction – systems biology establishes their relationship and cross-function. The goal is to establish common causes of disease, enabling the development of drugs that would target multiple disease areas.

Undoubtedly, systems biology will take life sciences to the next plateau of understanding. It begs the questions: who are the participants, and how much control will they have in the value chain? We have some hints, but it is not yet clear. Once data are assembled, informatics groups, using data belonging to yet other parties, seek patterns common to diseased samples.

The next step, most likely by still another party, moves to a laboratory for experimentation and validation. The business model challenges echo the dilemma faced by the platform companies.

The biotechnology industry has had since its origins numerous business model approaches designed to secure investment capital and strategic alliances in the short run, and a mechanism for sales and profits in the long run. Consequently, biotechnology companies have rarely achieved the status of fully integrated pharmaceutical companies and have had to find and optimize their positions somewhere in a niche in the value chain from discovery to sales. Business models necessarily evolve. Proteomic platform companies represent the embodiment of the new tools for the discovery of new drug targets and the new pharmaceuticals that would necessarily follow. They postulated that the intrinsic value of identifying and validating new drug targets would command economic rents through licensing and alliances with the pharmaceutical industry. In the process, the proteomic companies would create and sustain substantial income streams. Such value creation may yet occur, but the likely level of rewards will be modest and diluted among the many players that occupy the different steps in proteomic-based drug discovery. Hence, initial investor infatuation with proteomic platform companies has waned. If the companies can sustain themselves until their discovery agendas reach fulfillment, and if they can alter their models to participate in more remunerative segments of the value chain, then the discovery platform model will have been vindicated. The same challenge exists for the biotechnology industry in general. Genes and business models must each be reengineered.

NOTES

1. CIBC World Markets Corporation, "Proteomics Toolbox Technologies," in Burrill & Company, *Biotech 2001: Life Sciences-Genomics, Proteomics and More*, 15th edn. (San Francisco, CA: Burrill & Company, 2001), 17, fig. 2.
2. Lehman Brothers, "The 'Omics' Development Chain," in Burrill & Company, *Biotech 2001*, 19, fig. 3.
3. Burrill & Company, *Biotech 2001*, 19.
4. Windhover Communications, "Alliances statistics," in Burrill & Company, *Biotech 2004: Biotech Back on Track*, 18th edn. (San Francisco, CA: Burrill & Company, 2004), 314–323.
5. Burrill & Company, *Biotech 2004*.

6. Lawton R. Burns, *The Health Care Value Chain* (San Francisco, CA: Jossey-Bass, 2002).

7. Windhover Communications as cited in *Biotech 2004*.

8. Between 1999 and 2004 there has been a steady increase in partnering and alliance funding from pharmaceutical to biotechnology companies (in $US millions): 5,844 (1999); 6,901 (2000); 7,468 (2001); 7,496 (2002); 8,933 (2003); and 10,933 (2004). Source: Burrill & Company.

5 Mergers, acquisitions, and the advantages of scale in the pharmaceutical sector

Lawton R. Burns, Sean Nicholson, and John Evans

Introduction
M&A rationales in industrial organization theory and research
M&A trends among pharmaceutical and biotechnology firms
M&A rationales among pharmaceutical firms
The impact of M&A on the performance of pharmaceutical firms
Broader evidence on the value of size, concentration, and integration
Sources of value in the M&A process: building capabilities to enhance future performance
The future of pharmaceutical M&A and the value chain perspective on innovation

Introduction

Preceding chapters have dealt with a common set of topics: horizontal consolidation, mergers and acquisitions, the advantages of size, economies of scale and scope, diversification, and industry concentration. These topics all interrelate around the fundamental issue in industrial organization: how best to organize firms and markets in order to achieve optimal economic performance? For example, mergers and acquisitions lead to greater firm size and industry concentration, are often undertaken to achieve scale and scope economies, and can involve horizontal integration of similar firms, vertical integration of firms in adjacent stages in the chain of production, or diversification into related and unrelated industries. What is important for our purposes is that these topics all have implications for firm innovation and performance.

In this chapter we analyze the impact of these combinations on innovation and financial performance among pharmaceutical firms. Researchers are still unsure whether innovation leads to improved firm performance, or whether past performance fosters future innovation, or both. Thus, we examine the impact of industrial organization on both sets of measures. We specifically focus on mergers and acquisitions (M&As) due to the rich research literature here as well as the successive waves of M&As in the pharmaceutical sector during the past fifteen years.

Our analysis addresses several related questions. What is the value of size, scale, and M&As for pharmaceutical firms? Do such strategies help firms to develop new products? What are the challenges and opportunities created by M&As? Next, does the lens of industrial organization and its focus on the boundaries of the firm and its structural configuration provide the best perspective for understanding innovation in these firms? A different but parallel perspective suggests that firm processes within these larger, merged structures are more important for fostering increased innovation and productivity. Such processes include the generation and sharing of knowledge, the coordination of diverse specialists, the integration of different partners, and the balancing of different strategies. Can the merged structures be leveraged or exploited to improve these processes, or are they a distraction from the important process work of the firm? Finally, following on, how is the innovative activity of pharmaceutical firms tied to the larger value chain in the healthcare industry, and does a value chain view highlight important problems that pharmaceutical firms must address in their quest to improve the productivity of their research and development (R&D) arms?

The remainder of the chapter is organized into five sections. The first of these reviews the rationales for M&As, and attempts to disentangle some of the different effects of scale (firm scale, project scale, critical mass, etc.). The second section describes the historical trends in M&As among both pharmaceutical and biotechnology firms. The third section reviews the evidence on the performance effects of M&As on R&D intensity, R&D productivity, and firm economic performance, as well as the broader research evidence from the field of industrial organization on the value of size, concentration, and integration. The fourth section discusses other sources of value creation beyond the scale and structures created through M&As, such as the processes mentioned above, which serve as sources of potential advantage by means of building capabilities that can enhance future performance. The chapter concludes with a discussion of the future of M&As in the pharmaceutical sector and of the relevance of a value chain perspective for innovation in the pharmaceutical sector.[1-2]

M&A rationales in industrial organization theory and research

The academic field of industrial organization contains a rich literature on the rationales for M&As, drawn from both theoretical considerations as well as from past empirical findings. These academic rationales can then be compared to the stated rationales for M&As among pharmaceutical firms. Such a comparison can suggest the degree to which industry strategies have theoretical underpinnings that may translate into the degree of M&A success. Prior research suggests that hospital systems have failed to achieve efficiencies in their combination efforts for precisely this lack of congruence.[3]

According to industrial organization theory and research, there are several related reasons for pursuing M&As. One of the most commonly cited reasons is the achievement of economies of scale (defined as decreasing average cost as output expands). Such economies can have both production sources (e.g., the spreading of fixed costs over a larger volume of output in the combined firm, the use of more specialized and thus more productive labor, lower cost of holding inventories, improved utilization of capacity) and nonproduction sources (e.g., shared purchasing of inputs, shared marketing and promotion costs, shared research costs, etc.).[4]

Another frequently mentioned reason is economies of scope, defined as cost savings derived from the same firm producing two or more products/ services in-house compared to separate firms producing them. Thus, a combined firm can produce multiple outputs more efficiently than the premerged firms. Scope economies are a narrow form of "synergy," that is, the creation of value generated by combining complementary assets and resources of two firms that could not be generated by the two firms independently. In this manner, the acquirer can make better use of the target's assets than the target firm could do alone. Synergies are often said to exist when potential economies of scale and/or scope are achieved via a merger.

There are several other benefits that M&As may bestow beyond economies and synergies. In addition to improving the productivity of the target's assets, acquirers may discipline the managers of the target firm for not acting in the best interests of its shareholders. Firms can use the M&A strategy to speed up entry into new markets, enter new markets without expanding existing capacity and increasing the number of competitors, and enter new markets in new countries (globalization strategy). Firms may also horizontally integrate to engulf a rival, in order to reduce competitive pressures and exert potential market power on buyers downstream or suppliers upstream.

Finally, there is another set of rationales for M&As that do not necessarily bestow direct benefits. Historical evidence suggests successive waves of M&A activity are tied to rises in the stock market; firms take advantage of market upswings to (a) undertake acquisitions using their stock and its relatively high price–earnings ratio, and (b) sell their assets at peak prices. Firms can engage in M&As to protect licensed intellectual property or to access intellectual property that is otherwise inaccessible due to licensing to others. Firms can also engage in M&As due to managerial self-aggrandizement (empire-building, enriched incentives) and the mistaken belief they can manage much larger enterprises (managerial hubris). Finally, firms can pursue M&As as part of a fad driven partly by investment bankers (who have strong incentives to maximize M&A deal volumes), as well as serve a country's industrial policy by creating national or regional champions.

M&A trends among pharmaceutical and biotechnology firms

Figure 5.1 shows the number of transforming mergers or acquisitions in the biotechnology and pharmaceutical sector between 1986 and 2001, where a transforming merger is defined as a transaction where the price exceeds $500 million or the price is greater than 20 percent of the buyer's pretransaction market value. A total of 165 transforming mergers occurred during this time period, at a cumulative cost of over $500 billion.

The history of M&A in the pharmaceutical sector bears only slight resemblance to the waves of M&A activity in the wider market described above. First, pharmaceutical M&A is only a recent activity, which did not occur in bull markets prior to the 1990s. The pharmaceutical sector has survived for nearly a century as an unconcentrated industry with lots of small firms. Second, there was indeed a lull in pharmaceutical M&A activity during 1991–1993 that roughly corresponds to the recession in the economy that began in 1991 as well as to cost-cutting efforts by pharmaceutical firms, although the lull is partly explained by the need to process the first round of consolidations in the late 1980s. Third, there were additional waves of consolidation in the latter part of the 1990s that correspond with the bull market but were also driven by pipeline problems.

The decade of the 1980s marked the end of the "golden days" of the pharmaceutical sector.[5] The industry had enjoyed steady price increases in a cost-neutral environment, few competitive worries from generic competition, relatively unrestricted access to physicians by pharmaceutical sales representatives, and thus a steady growth in earnings. More hostile environmental conditions began to emerge in the 1980s and early 1990s that challenged this growth and earnings model. The Waxman–Hatch Act (1984) ushered in competition from generics. Pharmaceutical firms became more dependent on blockbuster drugs and more vulnerable to competition from "me-too"

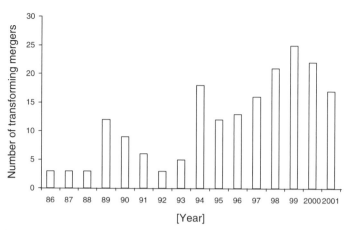

Figure 5.1   Number of "transforming" biotechnology and pharmaceutical M&A transactions.

Source: Securities and Data Corporation's Worldwide Mergers and Acquisitions database; P. Danzon, A. Epstein, and S. Nicholson, "Mergers and Acquisitions in the Pharmaceutical and Biotech Industries," unpublished manuscript, Wharton School, 2003.
Note: Price is less $500 million or 20 percent of the buying and/or selling firm's market value.

products and generics.[6] Two forms of managed care – health maintenance organizations (HMOs) and pharmacy benefit managers (PBMs) – emerged in the early 1990s, along with group purchasing organizations (GPOs) as large, organized buyers of pharmaceutical and other products. Healthcare cost containment in the private sector became a more prominent theme during the 1990s, as employers strove to contain their employee healthcare expenses. Cost containment became more visible in the public sector with the proposed Clinton Health Plan in 1993, which induced pharmaceutical firms to voluntarily hold back price increases; it was also evident in non-US countries. The recession, falling stock prices, and threats of healthcare reform scared away investors, and pharmaceutical firms made spending cuts in their R&D, sales force, and marketing budgets.[7] Finally, for some set of reasons not yet fully known, R&D productivity began to fall by 50 percent over the decade of the 1990s.

Pharmaceutical firms turned to strategies of horizontal and vertical integration as an adaptive response to these new pressures. The consolidation of the modern pharmaceutical sector began in 1987 with Roche's failed hostile takeover attempt of Sterling Drug. The first wave of mergers – including Bristol-Myers and Squibb (1989), SmithKline Beckman and Beecham (1989), and American Home Products and A. H. Robbins – were largely designed to rapidly cut infrastructure costs.[8] Such mergers created industry leaders with

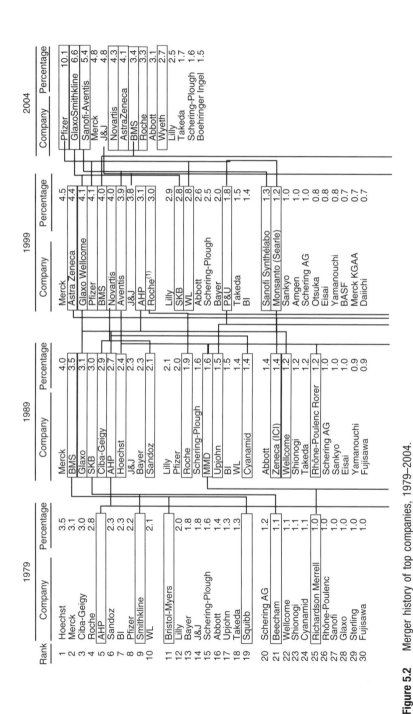

Figure 5.2 Merger history of top companies, 1979–2004.

Source: Jon Northrup Analysis, IMS Health Care Market Shares.

3–4 percent global market share. Following a quiet period between 1990 and 1993, during which the initial round of consolidation was fully processed, a second wave of consolidation began with Roche's acquisition of Syntex (1994), AHP's acquisition of Cyanamid, and the formation of Novartis from Ciba-Geigy and Sandoz (in 1996), at the time the largest pharmaceutical company in the world. The top ten companies in 1996 had a combined market share (measured as a percentage of worldwide sales) of 34 percent, up from 25.6 percent just ten years earlier.[9] Since 1998 a third (and ongoing) wave of mergers has swept the industry, driven by an exacerbation of the environmental pressures mentioned earlier coupled with dry pipelines and steep, untenable growth targets. Between 1998 and 2001 pure acquisitions among leading players became more difficult due to the rapid rise in price-to-earnings (P/E) multiples, and therefore a rise in the price of acquiring a company, across the industry.[10] Consequently, M&A activity moved almost entirely into the realm of "mergers of equals," as seen in the mega-mergers leading to the creation of Aventis and AstraZeneca (1999) and GlaxoSmithKline (2000). More recently, acquisitions have resurfaced, pioneered by Pfizer's hostile bid for Warner-Lambert (2001) and its recent acquisition of Pharmacia (2002). The top ten companies now control nearly 50 percent of the market; industry leaders have attained market shares above 10 percent for the first time (see figure 5.2).

During the same period pharmaceutical firms undertook alliances with biotechnology firms in order to shore up their sagging pipelines and to in-source R&D. These alliances picked up over the decade, along with alliances among the biotechnology firms themselves (see figure 5.3).

M&A rationales among pharmaceutical firms

The pharmaceutical sector trade literature suggests many of the rationales for M&A cited in the academic literature, but also some others. There is a clear sense from this literature that certain rationales are more adaptive and defensive in nature (particularly true for the earlier wave of M&As), such as combating cost pressures from buyers, cutting infrastructure costs, satisfying market demands for earnings growth, maintaining competitive size, and defending against acquisition. Other rationales reflect a more proactive and offensive thrust (particularly in later waves), such as diversification into new geographic markets and therapeutic areas, achieving scale and scope economies, developing competitive capabilities in R&D, and fostering disruptive

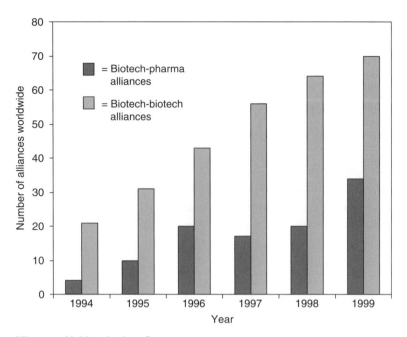

Figure 5.3   Alliances with biotechnology firms.

Source: Goldman Sachs Biotechnology Report 1999.

change. There is also the clear sense that these rationales focus primarily on cost reduction and secondarily on revenue enhancement.

Adaptive and defensive rationales

Combat increased profit pressures

The first threat to pharmaceutical sector profits was the Waxman–Hatch Act (1984), which lowered the barriers for generic entry into the market (after patent expiration for the branded drug) but also extended patent terms for many approved drugs. The reality of increased generic competition placed a concrete limit on the life cycle of a product's revenue stream and forced firms to search ever more vigorously for substantial sources of profits to replace those that were now being continually lost after patent expiry. One result of this pressure has been the increasing focus of firms on blockbuster drugs – drugs that could maximize economic return over the fixed life cycle of a drug's patent protection – leading the R&D departments of major competitors to converge on similar targets and drug classes with blockbuster potential (e.g., lower-severity conditions treated by primary care physicians such as hypertension, arthritis, etc.). This convergence of pharmaceutical focus also resulted in an increase in the number of "me-too" drugs during the 1990s, as firms could observe and imitate their competitors' R&D efforts. The branded drugs of pharmaceutical firms were thus confronted with increased competition from generic and therapeutically equivalent versions. Both sets of pressures served as an impetus for consolidation, which in turn reinforced the need to focus on larger, blockbuster products.

The early 1990s also witnessed the consolidation of intermediaries into large, organized buyers – such as HMOs, PBMs, and GPOs – along the value chain in healthcare (see figure 1.1). From 1988 to 1996, for example, HMOs doubled their penetration of employer-sponsored health plans (firms with 200-plus workers) from 17 percent to 33 percent. This growth placed additional pressure on pharmaceutical firm profits, as organized buyers negotiated large-volume discounts on drug prices, developed formularies of approved drugs, and pressured providers to prescribe generic versions or therapeutic equivalents of branded drugs whenever available. Pharmaceutical firms were also persuaded to hold down price increases during the early 1990s under the threat of the Clinton Health Plan in the United States and the proposed creation of large buying networks at state level. The period 1991–1995 saw a big decline in the price increases of pharmaceutical firms.[11]

The combination of these factors increased the perceived pressures on both revenues and life cycle durations of major branded drugs.[12] This weakened stock valuations, as evidenced by the drop in the S&P drug index between 1991 and 1994.[13] In response, pharmaceutical firms merged in order to increase their negotiating leverage with HMOs and PBMs. Mergers may also have been designed to combat the large buying groups proposed by the Clinton Health Plan. In addition to horizontal mergers, pharmaceutical firms attempted to mitigate the threat of buyer power through vertical integration into the PBM business (e.g., Merck–Medco, Eli Lilly–PCS Health Systems, SmithKline Beecham–Diversified Pharmaceutical Services), although with disastrous losses in two of these deals.[14] All three have since divested their PBM holdings.

Cutting infrastructure costs

Economic recessions, proposed governmental reforms, and price pressures from both payers (HMOs) and buyers (PBMs) placed pharmaceutical firms in a cost squeeze, which stimulated some of the early M&As. The industry was reportedly suffering from excess capacity (as much as 30 percent across its major functional areas) and inefficiencies during the 1980s, which, along with a fragmented industry and redundant cost structure, made savings possible. Pharmaceutical firms experiencing relatively large increases in operating expenses were more likely to be involved in pooling mergers (i.e., mergers of equals) in the 1986–2000 time period, perhaps as a means of cutting costs.[15] Historically, pharmaceutical firms rarely had to worry about lean infrastructure spending, enabling firms that merged from a position of weakness with subsequent overcapacity to be in an even better position to realize cost synergies. Pharmaceutical executives believed that infrastructure cost-cutting between merged firms could provide bottom-line earnings growth for two to three years after a merger's completion. In this manner, firms that historically were unable to take out costs used the merger to become more streamlined.

Infrastructure cuts could be made in R&D (close, consolidate, or sell laboratories), manufacturing (close, consolidate, or sell plants), and marketing (reduce the number of sales managers). Such cuts could improve the productivity of the remaining assets. It should be noted here that R&D is targeted as a source of short-term cost savings, not as a source of long-term productivity improvements (see below). By some estimates, up to 30–40 percent of the acquired company's cost base could be captured as earnings through infrastructure rationalization.[16] Others put the estimated savings at 20 percent of the target firm's sales. Such savings may correlate strongly with the degree of overlap in the location of the two firms' headquarters, their geographic markets of operation, product focus, and concentration of business in the pharmaceutical sector – all of which lend themselves to reductions in duplication.

Satisfy the market mandate to maintain earnings growth in the face of pipeline problems

A key objective in pharmaceutical M&A is the maintenance of earnings growth. At the same time that cost pressures from buyers developed, competition has become fierce, with multiple major players now competing within almost all major therapeutic areas. Exclusivity periods – measured as the total time from launch that a drug enjoys market dominance until a competitor (either a similar drug or a next-generation therapy) comes onto market – have shrunk from up to ten years to just one to two years, or in some cases a matter of months. Most alarmingly, pipeline productivity fell sharply in the late 1990s, with the total number of new molecular entities (NMEs) introduced each year staying essentially flat since 1990, even as spending on R&D and total revenue base more than doubled in the same time period (see chapter 2). The root causes of this productivity decline are not well known, and yet the industry has repeatedly turned to the M&A strategy as a defensive reaction. M&As may thus address some of the strategic threats (e.g., pricing pressures from payers) but be irrelevant responses to other threats (pipeline problems).

In addition to these trends, onetime shocks to a firm's revenue stream have also become an all too common headache for large companies trying to manage the market's expectations. For instance, product withdrawals due to safety concerns wiped out years of anticipated profits from such firms as Wyeth (fen-phen), Bayer (Baycol), and Warner-Lambert/Pfizer (Rezulin). Late stage clinical failures also left major gaps in firms' revenue projections. Pfizer suffered several late stage clinical setbacks bringing its blockbuster antibiotic Trovan to market, thereby restricting its ultimate value in the market; more recently, Merck lost two blockbusters in phase III trial failures (MK-0869 for depression and MK-767 for diabetes), leaving the firm in a precarious position for midterm growth. Such problems become reflected in the firm's "desperation index" (i.e., declining values of products in the pipeline).[17]

The combination of all of these factors has jeopardized the long-term stability and reliability of pharmaceutical firm revenue streams. Major gaps in revenue growth, either foreseen (e.g., patent expirations) or unforeseen (e.g., product withdrawals or pipeline failures), provide a critical challenge to management. The highly specialized sales and marketing personnel at integrated pharmaceutical firms become unproductive when patents expire and the R&D department is not able to deliver replacement products. Yet because of the scope, complexity, and long time lines of infrastructure spending on sales forces and R&D, reducing capacity to match a reduced revenue forecast is not generally an option. To stay competitive in the future, most firms believe they need to maintain the scale of their sales and science spending, no matter how difficult the present earnings challenges.

Two separate academic studies provide empirical support for this hypothesis. A study of 202 biotechnology and pharmaceutical mergers between 1988 and 2001 found that pharmaceutical firms that have a relatively old portfolio of drugs, and therefore face earnings pressure from patent expiration, are more likely to acquire another firm.[18] A second study of 160 pharmaceutical transactions that occurred between 1994 and 2001 concluded that firms with a high "desperation index," as measured by the strength of their pipeline drugs and the amount of exclusivity remaining among their marketed drugs, were more likely to merge.[19]

As a result, in the face of incredible market pressure to produce consistent earnings growth, firms turn to M&A to provide short-term fixes. M&As

provide the opportunity for accretive and external, as opposed to organic and internal, growth in earnings – and thus could theoretically keep the 15–20 percent profit margins going that pharmaceutical firms had historically enjoyed. A merger partner or an acquisition can also provide products, either marketed or in the pipeline, that are well timed to fill the revenue gaps either in the short or medium term. For example, Pfizer's unsolicited bid for Warner-Lambert allowed it to capture the full revenue stream from the emerging cholesterol-lowering blockbuster Lipitor, a drug that it comarketed. The bid was likely motivated by a period of weakness for Pfizer, at a time of dim pipeline prospects and just after the FDA had heavily restricted Trovan's use (and market potential). Lipitor provided enough revenues to smooth over both of those issues in the medium term.[20] Pharmaceutical firms discovered that buying external products (and revenues) was cheaper and faster than growing them internally.

The problem with mergers is that they beget more mergers, turning the pharmaceutical firm into a "mass-mergerer" (i.e., a serial consolidator). Mergers set off leapfrog competition in a pharmaceutical sector that used to be stable with respect to who were the market leaders. Firms adopt a strategy of "not be left behind," believing that those firms that fall in the size rankings are more vulnerable to takeover.[21] As companies get larger, the absolute value of revenues required to replace lost revenues from patent expirations and still generate double-digit earnings growth grows larger. By some estimates, the largest firms need to launch one to three blockbusters annually in order to maintain the pace of growth. So long as the pipeline productivity issue remains, satisfying the market mandate for growth will continue to require nonorganic solutions such as consolidation to help drive earnings forward.

M&As thus represent a short-term strategy and solution for firms with blockbuster drugs that are coming off patent and/or with an insufficient pipeline to replace the blockbusters.[22] Increased size resulting from past mergers and continuing pipeline problems make this strategy less tenable over time.

Maintain competitive scale and scope

Serial consolidators can be created not only by the need to maintain earnings growth but also by the competitive effects exerted by others. Common wisdom within the industry holds that sales force scale and the size and scope of R&D efforts create powerful competitive advantages for leading firms. For example, sales force size reportedly gives a pharmaceutical firm greater share of voice with the prescribing clinician and correlates with sales force productivity. Indeed, companies discovered during the 1990s that "internally copromoting" – that is, having multiple sales representatives detailing the same product to the same doctors – was very effective.[23] Not surprisingly, sales force sizes skyrocketed in the 1990s; the top forty firms added 40,000 sales reps between 1992 and 2002.[24] R&D budgets have followed suit, growing from 16 percent to 18 percent of sales between 1990 and 2000, with a peak of 20 percent in 1998.[25] In the light of this accelerated spending on sales and scientific capabilities, and as leading firms consolidate, the gap in absolute spending between the first tier and the second tier has the potential to grow exponentially, threatening to leave smaller firms missing out on the consolidation trend behind for good. Firms mentioned the danger of being the "number 12" player in the industry in terms of not attracting the best scientific talent or strategic alliance partners.

In response, second-tier players seeking a rapid way to achieve industry-leading scale have turned to consolidation, creating a series of leapfrog mergers in the 1990s with new firms setting the industry-leading standard for scale every few years. As such, the necessity of merging for scale in response to the consolidation of competitors can be seen as a catalyst for the entire consolidation trend. Examples of such mergers include Novartis (from Ciba-Geigy and Sandoz) in 1996,[26] Pfizer (after the merger with Warner-Lambert) in 2000,[27] and GlaxoSmithKline (from Glaxo Wellcome and SmithKline Beecham) in 2001,[28] each of which became the largest firm in the world at the time of the merger. The formations of Aventis[29] and AstraZeneca[30] created the second and third largest firms, respectively, at the time of the merger. Smaller mergers, such as that between Pharmacia and Upjohn in 1995, witnessed the combination of two second-tier players simply trying to maintain their position given the burgeoning might of consolidating industry leaders.[31]

Defense against acquisition

Firms with relatively weak positions make attractive takeover candidates; solid products and R&D projects can be harvested, while redundant infrastructure can be cut wholesale. For such firms, improving performance through organic growth to sufficiently block such takeover attempts is too difficult, and too slow, to provide an effective defense. On the other hand, a merger with another firm allows a corporation to maintain some semblance of control over its destiny, despite the loss of autonomy inherent in a merger. Another attractive candidate for a takeover is a firm that is performing strongly, but which has not reached sufficient scale to become too large for a takeover. These firms may also look for partners in order to avoid a fate they cannot control.

The merger between American Home Products (a large firm struggling to find growth) and Warner-Lambert (a rapidly growing firm with a hot product, Lipitor) provides an example of both types of firms seeking refuge in a mutual partnership. Unfortunately, the decision to merge came too late to save Warner-Lambert. Pfizer's unsolicited bid for the company (and its products) ultimately scuttled the deal, and Warner-Lambert effectively lost its independence.

The recent merger of Sanofi-Syntelabo with Aventis can be interpreted in the same light. Sanofi-Synthelabo, a firm with above-average R&D product-ivity and a fairly strong pipeline, represented an attractive takeover candidate for larger firms looking for new growth engines. Sanofi's merger with Aventis served several ends: to maintain Sanofi's independence, to be a European champion, to consolidate Europe's pharmaceutical sector, to be the new number three firm in the industry, and to serve France's national pride (as well as leverage Sanofi's attractive pipeline more effectively over more coun-tries).[32] In Japan, Yamanouchi Pharmaceutical Company agreed to acquire Fujisawa Pharmaceutical Company in order to battle foreign competition at home, to become the number two player in Japan, to fend off takeovers by larger global firms, and to avoid becoming a Japanese subsidiary of a foreign firm.[33] In support of these efforts, countries like France (in the Sanofi-Aventis deal) and Japan are encouraging their domestic pharmaceutical firms to combine, increase their regional scale and dominance, and avoid being battered by foreign companies.[34] (Of course, such encouragement can be misguided if it produces less competitive, merged firms that do not actively integrate to reduce costs or promote growth.)

Proactive and offensive rationales

Gain access to foreign pharmaceutical markets

Instead of (or in addition to) cutting costs and fending off price reductions, many M&As are motivated by efforts to increase revenues. For much of the century, domestic firms dominated national markets by steadily building a sales and marketing presence and by forming strong relationships with regulators and local researchers. The difficulty in building these capabilities from the ground up as a foreign entrant to an established market presented firms with serious barriers to international expansion. At the same time, the increasing value and scale of foreign pharmaceutical markets in the USA, Europe, and Japan, combined with the universal marketability of pharmaceutical products, made expansion a strategic and economic priority. The fastest way to gain access to foreign markets, therefore, was to license or buy the capabilities of local firms. Examples of mergers partially driven by this rationale were typically US–European mergers, such as those between SmithKline Beckman (US) and Beecham (UK) (1989) or Pharmacia (Sweden/Italy) and Upjohn (US) (1995). US expansion was an important motive for non-US firms given the market size, high growth, and price realizations in the US. Mergers with Japanese firms, such as that between Roche (Switzerland) and Chugai (Japan) (2002), developed to foster entry to an important market where western firms have generally struggled; however, now most western firms have a strong base in Japan and do not need an acquisition.[35]

In addition to building sales in new markets, pharmaceutical firms are also seeking to develop the image of a fast-growing and global firm. Such a perception may help attract alliance and potential acquisition partners. Global reach, combined with capabilities in rapid product launch, can also translate into a reduction of years to peak product sales and thus higher revenues.

Extend capabilities to new therapeutic areas

As firms grow, they have typically expanded the scope of their portfolio across a number of therapeutic areas. Most major pharmaceutical firms now have products in many major therapeutic areas (e.g., cholesterol, hypertension, depression, antiulcerants, diabetes, inflammation). However, this breadth results as much from the consolidation trend as from organic growth. Building up a capability in a therapeutic area, both in terms of research and development expertise and sales force presence and physician relationships, can take years or even decades. Capabilities also tend to flow from molecular innovation, which is not predictable. Clearly, in order to quickly become a player in a major market with innovative capabilities, acquisition is the fastest approach. For instance, Pfizer's merger with Pharmacia in 2002 improved its presence in immunology (by capturing 100 percent of revenues from the comarketed rheumatoid arthritis drug Celebrex as well as the next generation Bextra) and added assets in oncology, endocrinology, and ophthalmology; these products complemented Pfizer's existing strengths in cardiovascular disease, central nervous system, depression, and erectile dysfunction.[36]

Achieve economies of scale and scope in R&D, sales, and marketing

Economies of scale are believed to exist in some portions of the pharmaceutical value chain (e.g., sales and marketing) more than in others. Industry executives believe that larger commercial scale has continued to demonstrate positive marginal returns, though the magnitude of those returns has rapidly diminished. For example, "more sales representatives can call on more doctors more times," or "more representatives can sell more drugs to more doctors leading to more scripts." Larger scale may also facilitate faster product launches across larger markets, leading to higher revenues. Finally, larger scale may pose a barrier to entry by virtue of economies in SG&A; large sales force size, promotional spending, and direct-to-consumer advertising; and possibly provide some advantage in conducting clinical trials (through either greater efficiency or access to a broader network of investigators).

There is more debate surrounding the presence of economies of scale in pharmaceutical R&D, which is thus probably not a major factor driving consolidation. Many observers speculate that instead of increasing returns to scale there is a "critical mass" of research spending – a threshold level at which a minimum efficient scale is attained. This threshold level of spending allows companies to acquire key technologies and place the requisite number of bets across fixed research assets in order to achieve an adequate return on investment (ROI). This critical mass would also allow companies to adequately fund both early stage research as well as expensive, later stage development without making trade-offs between short-term and long-term spending priorities. Other observers believe that "more is better": that is, higher R&D outlays translate into placing even more bets on more projects and technologies, and thus increased odds of success. In this light, higher R&D spending is viewed as "risk management" (diversifying the portfolio of projects and the risks of any given project) rather than improved ROI.

Regardless of the above, most commentators believe that these thresholds have already been reached by most major firms – perhaps as little as $100 million in research spending, which at around 25 percent of a total R&D budget would imply R&D spending of just $400 million per year.[37] Most major players currently spend at least ten times this amount on their R&D efforts. More recently, the growing dominance of smaller biotechnology firms in developing new chemical entities (NCEs) suggests that the scale requirements of drug discovery are falling rather than rising.

There are other presumed benefits of mergers that involve economies of scale. Increased scale from a merger may allow a firm to spread the costs of acquiring any future technologies or biotechnology firms across a larger base.

Larger firms may also be better able to leverage the technology, R&D, and skill sets of these future target acquisitions. Finally, pharmaceutical firms may make strategic acquisitions of firms operating in a specific therapeutic area in order to gain scale and thereby compete with larger firms who devote a lower proportion of their R&D to this area (e.g., Eli Lilly and Novo Nordisk's efforts in diabetes). Analysts suggest that scale economies exist within (but not across) therapeutic areas, and that pharmaceutical firms can leverage knowledge across multiple states within the same disease family (narrow but deep focus).[38]

If mergers are a way to achieve optimal scale in the pharmaceutical sector, then one would expect smaller firms to be involved in more M&A activity than larger firms. In fact, larger firms, as measured by the market value of their stock and debt, were more likely to be involved in M&A in the 1980s and 1990s. Large firms apparently believe that there are advantages to growing even larger.[39]

Economies of scope may offer some ongoing advantage to larger firms. Firms that have already merged can apply the capabilities of biotechnology acquisitions across both partners. They may also enjoy a broader product line that allows them access to a greater number of physicians in the market, which may offset some of the power of organized buyers. Firms that place a larger number of bets across a number of therapeutic areas and technologies may also be more likely to create a new drug than those with a more narrow scope.

All the same, after fifteen years of consolidation, pipeline productivity continues to decline, and the extent of scope advantages for merging firms is difficult to estimate. This may be due to the fact that merging firms often cut out large groups of development projects that cannot satisfy new criteria for high potential sales; one analysis showed that postmerger firms had almost a third fewer projects in development three years after merging as their premerger baseline.[40] It may also stem from the disruption to R&D processes and projects that often result in a postmerger environment. Finally, as noted above, M&As may not even address the unknown root causes of declining pipeline productivity, but rather serve some other short-term palliative needs.

Create a competitive advantage in R&D productivity

Long-term improvements to R&D productivity, as opposed to short-term cost savings and earnings boosts, are often cited by executives at the time of a merger. Mergers are heralded as the beginning of a new research engine to drive organic growth in the future. However, such improvements have been the most elusive of all the stated benefits of consolidation. Consistently, these same companies have returned to mergers again and again in order to shore up weak pipelines and gaps in market portfolios. Serial consolidators such as American Home Products (A. H. Robbins in 1989, Cyanamid in 1994, and a failed attempt to merge with Warner-Lambert in 2001), Pfizer (Warner-Lambert in 2001, Pharmacia in 2003), and GSK (a combination of merged entities Glaxo, Wellcome, SmithKline Beckman, and Beecham in three separate transactions) have proclaimed at every juncture that their newly formed ventures would be better positioned to grow organically – and independently – for the future; yet subsequent mergers reveal still more weakness in product flows.[41]

As the R&D productivity crisis deepens, it is clear that no one has yet solved the R&D productivity problem. It may take more time than expected to assimilate the new technologies and firms acquired. In the short term, the combined earnings stream of the merged firms may provide a more consistent flow of internal funding for R&D to offset the volatile cash flows from blockbusters.[42]

Fostering disruptive change

The final rationale for M&As that we discuss is the opportunity they provide for disruptive change. As noted above, M&As are often pursued for defensive reasons to correct underlying weakness and decline in the combining firms. Mergers provide an external impetus and logic for restructuring each firm's assets that might otherwise encounter greater internal resistance. In this manner, the two firms can "start with a clean slate," conduct a company-wide review, reallocate assets to more productive areas, reengineer processes, reduce head counts, and undertake changes that neither firm could do prior to the combination.[43] Indeed, the merger event serves to justify the enormous disruption costs.[44] In this manner, merged firms may achieve the economies of scale and savings that individual firms cannot, or take out costs that the individual firm cannot. In a similar vein, M&As can be undertaken to change the "activity footprint" of a firm in order to track migration of profit pools, control profit choke points, or execute a new value proposition necessitated by changes in the economics of an industry.[45]

Summary of rationales: is there a problem here?

The above review suggests that M&As can be motivated from multiple sources. This conclusion is supported by industry surveys of pharmaceutical firms who report having multiple M&A goals: grow the core business, realize cost synergies, acquire new technologies, gain competitive advantage, generate fiscal advantage, and so on.[46] Such a phenomenon is not unique to pharmaceutical firms; firms in other industries typically have multiple objectives in pursuing M&As. It is possible, of course, that many positive aspirations are voiced to disguise underlying motivations for cost synergies (i.e., reductions).

The problem with multiple rationales noted in these other industries may also pertain to pharmaceuticals: the lack of a clear focus in the merger and the presence of conflicting agendas. In the presence of multiple goals, the intentions of the two firms (particularly if one acquires the other) are likely to diverge, if not conflict. Moreover, there may be a simultaneous (and confusing) effort to cut costs and pursue growth. Other problems that stem from multiple rationales concern the merger implementation effort – for example, the difficulty in mapping out the implementation steps due to the need to accommodate a variety of potentially conflicting interests and directions. Multiple rationales may thus prove dysfunctional during the merger transition and lead to unresolvable conflicts. Industry analysts argue that one party in clear control, with a dominant economic rationale, a simple program, great communication, and excellent execution, is the critical ingredient for M&A success.[47]

The impact of M&A on the performance of pharmaceutical firms

There is a growing body of research evidence on the benefits of pharmaceutical firm scale and M&A strategy, although it is not developed enough to test all of the rationales enumerated above. There is a fundamental difficulty, however, in isolating the benefits of M&A: pharmaceutical firms may pursue other strategies whose effects are entangled with M&A. For example, during the early 1990s Glaxo pursued horizontal acquisitions with both pharmaceutical and biotechnology firms and considered vertical integration into the PBM industry.[48] Evaluation researchers label this problem "multiple treatment interference"; economists refer to it as a statistical confound. The evidence reviewed below cannot truly disentangle the impacts of different strategies pursued simultaneously by pharmaceutical firms without first collecting data on all of the strategies and estimating competing risk models.

A further empirical complication is that mergers do not occur randomly but are chosen by managers, and firms with poor growth prospects (due to weak pipelines and/or marketed drugs at risk of losing patent protection) are more likely to engage in M&A activity.[49] This makes it difficult to isolate the impact of a merger, because firms that merge may have fared poorly even if they did nothing. Conversely, a merged firm may fare poorly compared to industry averages, but might perform better than it otherwise would have.

Finally, the researcher faces the difficulty of distinguishing limitations of the strategy of M&A from the limitations of the strategy's execution. That is, the strategy may be appropriate but the execution and implementation flawed. A later section of this chapter explores some of the important processes in merger implementation.[50]

Review of the evidence from academia and consulting firms

Relationship between scale and R&D inputs

Early research conducted across industries examined the impact of firm scale on inputs to the R&D process, such as the intensity of R&D (e.g., R&D expenditures as a percent of sales). Some researchers found positive effects of scale on R&D intensity while others found threshold effects (i.e., positive effects up to a certain level of scale, after which the effects become zero or negative). Over time, these results have been inconclusive. The literature has concluded that size has a minute effect on R&D intensity and explains little of the variation.[51] Instead, R&D intensity appears to be a function of the firm's prior cash flows and profits.[52] One study that examined mergers in all industries between 1976 and 1995 concluded that firms that merged experienced the same growth in R&D spending subsequently, on average, as firms that did not merge.[53]

In the pharmaceutical sector, consultants have likewise found no relationship between scale and R&D intensity.[54] Recent academic research has found that M&As do not lead to increased R&D expenditures.[55] Other researchers have suggested that R&D intensity may be a driver (cause) of increased size through M&A, rather than a result. Firms with higher R&D spending are more likely to engage in acquisitions as a means of diversifying their research portfolios, and use outsourced R&D to complement their internal R&D.[56] Research on corporate strategy has found that firms need the "absorptive capacity" of knowledge gained from internal R&D in order to gauge the value of potential knowledge stocks in external research programs (found in target firms).[57] An academic study of biotechnology and pharmaceutical mergers between 1988 and 2001 concluded that mergers had no impact on the growth rate of R&D spending in the first three years following a merger.[58]

Relationship of scale with R&D outputs

The vast bulk of the evidence also suggests that scale has a weak impact on various measures of R&D productivity. While larger firms may (or may not) undertake the bulk of innovative investment, they are not the source of the majority of innovations, or at least the most distinctive innovations in a therapeutic area.[59] This is obvious today from the preponderance of new pipeline drugs now being in-licensed by large pharmaceutical companies from the biotechnology sector.

Economists have found that a firm's overall R&D spending is not associated with the discovery of new drugs – measured either as the probability of success of new drug approvals (NDAs) or the number of new chemical entities (NCEs) per firm per year, although there is some evidence of R&D scale economies within a therapeutic area.[60] R&D intensity may exert a positive impact on R&D productivity, but only up to a small threshold level of investment. Over the long term R&D intensity may be a driver of firm profits.[61] Firm size may be associated with the production of knowledge, however. The overall level of a firm's research spending has been found to be associated with the number of patents in its drug discovery programs.[62] Moreover, the quality and focus of these patents (i.e., number of patent citations, smaller number of patent claims) may be positively related to the number of new product introductions.[63]

A recent study, however, does find a positive relationship between a firm's experience in conducting clinical trials, measured by the number of drugs the firm has developed independently or in an alliance, and the likelihood that a drug will successfully complete phase II and phase III trials (they find a weak relationship between experience and the likelihood a drug will complete phase I).[64] Firms that had developed twenty-five and thirty phase II and phase III drugs, respectively, had the highest success probabilities.[65] Therefore, if a firm that is below these thresholds can absorb the development experience of the acquired firm, acquisitions could improve R&D productivity.

Consultants and investment analysts have repeatedly found that firm scale has little impact on R&D productivity. In a study prepared for a large pharmaceutical firm, analysts at the Boston Consulting Group (BCG) found that firm scale in the pharmaceutical sector had no relationship with innovation productivity (i.e., more predictable flow of NMEs) or with the ability to develop blockbuster drugs more rapidly.[66] BCG analysts have also found scale to be unrelated to both the value and output of R&D.[67] Analysts at Booz-Allen report that the scale of a firm and its investment in R&D is unrelated to the marginal return on innovation investment, while McKinsey analysts find no relationship between the scale of R&D spending and return on investment (measured as the NPV of products out of research).[68] Analysts at Goldman Sachs found that three of the top five pharmaceutical firms (measured in terms of the net present value [NPV] of their late stage pipelines) scored below the global sector average in productivity (pipeline NPV divided by capitalized R&D).[69] Finally, analysts at Lehman Brothers report that average annual spending on R&D is unrelated to the number of NMEs launched, with any threshold spending effects reached early.[70]

Similarly, analysts argue that M&As have not resulted in greater R&D productivity: "The combination of two large but relatively weak players makes it more difficult to rejuvenate the now combined R&D program as it simultaneously increased the value required from new products. A $10 billion company needs a much bigger product to grow 10 percent than does a $5 billion company."[71]

There is uncertain evidence regarding the impact of M&As on project portfolios. One study suggests that larger firms are slower to terminate unsuccessful or outlived research efforts.[72] On the other hand, some analysts have reported a 34 percent reduction in development projects three years after a merger.[73] In both reports, these findings are viewed as having negative implications for R&D productivity. Indeed, some pharmaceutical firms now believe there are diseconomies of scale in research, and are experimenting with smaller organizational models (e.g., MAX teams at Aventis, CEDDS at GlaxoSmithKline).

Relationship between scale and stock price, sales, market share, and profitability

A spate of recent academic studies has reached different conclusions regarding the impact of M&As on financial outcomes. One study of 160 pharmaceutical acquisitions between 1994 and 2001 found they created positive shareholder value. The acquirer's cumulative abnormal stock market return for deals involving biotechnology or technology companies was 2.8 percent; the return for nonbiotechnology R&D firms was 4.3 percent, and the return for firms with mature products and R&D capabilities was 5.3 percent.[74] Abnormal returns were higher under certain circumstances: when the acquiring firm made equity payments to the target, when the acquiring firm had prior strategic alliance experience with the target, and when the acquiring firm had prior sales and research experience in the same therapeutic category as the target firm. The abnormal stock return methodology captures investors' perceptions of the impact of mergers at the announcement date, rather than actual performance of the combined firm following the merger.

By contrast, another study of sixty-five pharmaceutical deals (with transaction values over $500 million) between 1985 and 1996 created little shareholder value on average. Target firms experienced a positive 13.3 percent average abnormal stock market return (over a three-day window), acquiring firms experienced a negative 2.2 percent abnormal return, and the combined firm reported a positive 0.6 percent abnormal return.[75] This pattern of positive returns to investors of the acquired firm, negative returns to investors of the acquiring firm, and essentially no combined effect, is also observed in the general industry literature on abnormal stock market returns following merger announcements.[76] Some of the pharmaceutical M&A deals fared better than others, however. The greatest shareholder value was created in large horizontal mergers involving the top thirty firms and cross-national transactions; the greatest shareholder loss was generated in vertical mergers involving PBMs.

Another study of 202 pharmaceutical and biotechnology deals involving transaction values of $500+ million between 1988 and 2001 reported that mergers exert little impact on a firm's growth in sales, operating profit, and enterprise value (market value of a firm's equity plus book value of their debt) in the first and second years following a merger. For a typical pharmaceutical firm, a merger reduces operating profits by 52 percent in the third year following a merger compared to a similar firm that did not merge.[77] For a distressed firm, however, a merger increases operating profit in the third year following the merger, perhaps because of different implementation. This study highlights the importance of controlling for a firm's propensity to merge (or probability of merging). Firms with a high probability of merging (based on a firm's premerger characteristics) experience relatively slow growth in sales, employees, and R&D over the next three years regardless of whether or not they actually merge. If one failed to control for the differences between firms that do and do not merge, mergers would appear to have an even worse impact on a firm's performance.

Research conducted by consultants and analysts tends to report little financial impact of M&As. One set of researchers at BCG, for example, found no impact of M&A on ten-year shareholder returns or growth in market share. While mergers might avoid big declines in share price, they still underperformed the pharmaceutical index and suffered lower compound annual sales growth rates.[78] Another set of BCG consultants reported no impact of pharmaceutical firm size on gross margins, net margins, or ten-year total shareholder returns.[79] McKinsey consultants similarly reported no impact of firm size on shareholder returns from 1994 to 1999 and on market capitalization, and lower annual growth rates among merged firms from 1989 to 1999.[80] Consultants at AT Kearney found no association between M&A and economic returns; indeed, none of the firms in the top quartile of their overall "value creation index" (summary measure of economic returns and probable value of pipeline and marketed products) had pursued an M&A strategy at the time of their study.[81] In 1997 pharmaceutical firms that had merged had average economic returns of 1.6 percent, while the return of firms that had not merged was 7.6 percent. These consultants attribute the lower return among merged firms to lower sales growth and higher SGA expenses, intangibles, and depreciation. Finally, other studies from the same period found that M&As did not improve the market shares of pharmaceutical firms between 1992 and 1997, did not improve their market valuations during the 1990s and sometimes hurt them, and did not buffer firms from downturns in the market.[82]

Some consulting firms concur with academic studies that a pharmaceutical firm's success in generating value (e.g., development of blockbusters) is tied to its prior experience in the relevant drug category. Such experience – whether it is internally developed or externally acquired in alliances – reportedly helps the firm to devise superior clinical trials with faster speed and to incur lower costs in most phases of discovery, development, and commercialization.[83]

Relationship of scale and scope with efficiency

The academic evidence offers little information regarding the presence of economies of large scale and scope in the pharmaceutical sector. One set of researchers concludes there are scale and scope economies in drug discovery and scope economies in drug development.[84] Scope effects (e.g., the diversity of research programs) thus seem to be more evident than scale effects, suggesting the importance of internal knowledge spillovers between programs. Nevertheless, both scale and scope effects are weak predictors compared to a firm's prior research track record (e.g., past success in a therapeutic class, the accumulated stock of patents in a therapeutic program). They conclude that scale and scope effects may be small relative to enduring idiosyncratic features of a firm's organization and management of the development process. Evidence from consulting firms also suggests few economies in drug development. Firm size does not appear to promote either speed or efficiency in the conduct of clinical trials.[85]

Two other sets of researchers conclude there is only weak evidence that mergers drive cost efficiencies in pharmaceutical firms via scale and scope economies.[86] One study observes that small firm size is associated with the probability of making an R&D acquisition, suggesting that such transactions may result in some economies of scale. A second study finds that firms that merge do not experience a lower operating expense growth rate than similar firms that do not merge in the first, second, or third years following a merger.[87]

Academic evidence does point to cost efficiencies from mergers, however. Savings from horizontal mergers yield average cost reductions ranging from 11 to 29 percent of the target firm's sales. As a percentage of sales, mergers achieve cuts in administration (from 5 to 2%), marketing/sales (from 30 to 25%), in R&D (from 15 to 13%), and cost of goods sold (from 30 to 20%) – yielding an increase in operating profit from 20 to 40 percent.[88] Much of these savings result from a reduction of 8–20 percent in the combined workforce. Other analysts report consistent figures, such as an average of 11% cost savings and workforce reductions of 6–18% from M&As.[89] Workforce savings may be more difficult to achieve in friendly mergers, where no one side may be in charge, however, perhaps necessitating the search for efficiencies through additional mergers.[90] Other savings come from the consolidation, closing, or sale of R&D laboratories and manufacturing plants. However, there do not appear to be any economies of large scale pharmaceutical manufacturing – other than the utilization of excess capacity. Analysts report that firm size is not associated with the manufacturing efficiency of small molecules. There may be efficiencies in increased plant size for large molecules among the biotechnology firms, where manufacturing capacity is lacking.[91] It remains puzzling, however, why merging firms do not experience a growth in profitability if they are able to realize the costs savings enumerated above. One explanation is that the onetime implementation and restructuring costs associated with mergers may offset the cost savings.

Economies in sales and marketing may be more tangible and evident. Larger firms are able to launch drugs faster than middle-sized firms, reaching as many markets in the first year as smaller firms can reach in two years, and perhaps facilitating more global launches.[92] Having superior sales and marketing muscle also helps larger firms to in-license more effectively: on average, large firms in-license the top products and earn 15 percent more revenue per licensed product than smaller firms. There is conflicting evidence whether or not they in-license more products overall.[93] One explanation here is that there was no measurable licensing "magnet effect" ten years ago, unlike the situation today. Scale allows large firms to dominate share of voice, build larger sales forces and generate a greater numbers of sales calls per product and sales per representative.[94] This effect seemed most pronounced, again, at product launch, allowing superior rates of market uptake. It does not necessarily translate to higher levels of performance after launch. In any case, marginal returns on additional sales reps, though declining, remains positive, which is perhaps the strongest argument of all that larger sales forces do create value for leading firms.[95]

Summary of the empirical evidence: is there a disconnect with the rationales?

The findings regarding the benefits of pharmaceutical M&As presented by academic researchers and consulting firms are fairly consistent with one another. Firm scale has little relationship with R&D intensity (inputs) and, at best, a small impact on R&D productivity (outputs) – arguably the two industry value drivers. Two academic studies and the bulk of the consulting firm evidence suggest little impact of M&A on the firm's value, shareholder returns, margins, sales growth, or growth in market share. Finally, the evidence suggests there are limited economies of scale/scope in drug discovery and development, and more pronounced economies in sales and marketing. M&As do appear to help in reducing infrastructure costs in the short term.

To be sure, the empirical evidence does not test all of the hypothesized rationales for M&As presented in the earlier section. The available evidence provides limited support for the ones tested, however. For example, M&As do not improve R&D productivity; instead, low R&D productivity prompts M&As. M&As do not serve to increase either profit margins or firm earnings, although they may help to keep them stable by substituting short-term infrastructure savings for imminent gaps in product revenue streams (a hypothesis not examined).[96] Similarly, M&As do not lead to pronounced economies of scale or scope, particularly within R&D, although they may help small firms to achieve some economies and help large firms to maintain competitive scale and scope. Finally, there is no evidence one way or the other regarding the financial and performance impacts of M&As when used to foster disruptive change, provide a defense against acquisition, gain access to foreign markets, and extend capabilities to new therapeutic areas. However, based on the mixed economic track record of merged entities, it is likely that these rationales are employed as much to address strategic, organizational, political, or even personal priorities as to increase shareholder value. Thus, mergers serve to increase a firm's market share and perhaps satisfy the need to be among the leaders.

Broader evidence on the value of size, concentration, and integration

M&As are an instance of what the field of industrial organization (IO) calls "horizontal integration." The vast literature on horizontal integration reveals that the majority of mergers fail to increase the value of a firm, fail to earn back the equity capital invested within three years, and earn an average negative return of -20 percent by year four.[97] Only a fraction of firms engaged in mergers maintain their revenue growth postmerger and even fewer actually accelerate this growth. The literature on pharmaceutical firm M&As is consistent with the broader evidence.

M&As also result in larger size and greater industry concentration (smaller number of larger firms). The ten largest pharmaceutical firms accounted for 48 percent of worldwide sales in 2002, up substantially from 20 percent in 1985. The IO literature has concluded that neither size nor concentration is a strong predictor of innovation.[98] Indeed, M&As may in fact retard innovation by overemphasizing financial and systemic controls that promote greater managerial risk aversion.[99] M&A deals (or even just discussions) can also choke off the efforts of licensing departments to in-source new compounds, as well as overshadow opportunities for strategic alliances.[100] Some researchers have suggested, however, there may be an interaction effect between size and concentration – large firms are more innovative in concentrated industries, while small firms are more innovative in unconcentrated industries.[101] This relationship has not been tested in the pharmaceutical sector but is certainly consistent with the M&A rationales espoused above. Increased size can pose a barrier to entry by new competitors, a characteristic of the pharmaceutical sector for a good portion of the twentieth century until the entrance of biotechnology firms.[102]

Overall, variations in firm-level innovation may be explained less by scale and M&A activity and more by internal organization characteristics, idiosyncratic technological capabilities accumulated over time, drug development experience, past track records of R&D success in therapeutic areas, and interfirm alliances and contracts that promote complementarities between internal and external sourcing of ideas and capabilities.[103] These variations may also be explained better by execution of the M&A strategy, including both premerger and postmerger integration processes. The next section examines these possibilities.

Sources of value in the M&A process: building capabilities to enhance future performance

There is considerable research on the M&A process that impacts the M&A outcomes reviewed above. One important issue is the strategic intent of a merger. An earlier section of this chapter suggested that pharmaceutical deals may have multiple rationales. Indeed, executives from the target firm in a recently announced M&A deal that were surveyed during an executive education course mentioned several defensive reasons for the merger, particularly the avoidance of takeover by the smaller acquiring firm, but many others as well (see figure 5.4). This lengthy list suggests there has been a failure on the part of the acquiring firm to communicate a clearly articulated rationale, an omission mentioned several times by the executives. The downside is potential confusion and conflicting agendas. Moreover, as researchers have emphasized, the realization of any synergy from a combination requires a commonly shared strategic vision (clear and sometimes imposed) that serves as a continuous guide to the merger's operating plans – for example, what the synergies are and how they are to be realized.[104]

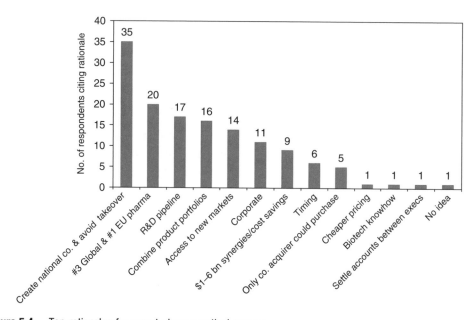

Figure 5.4   Top rationales for recent pharmaceutical merger.

This may not be as straightforward as it sounds. Executives at large pharmaceutical firms claim that roughly 50 percent of their firms' market value is comprised of the synergies between the pieces of their business. Combining these pieces with the pieces from another firm whose synergies you may not understand leads to a combined firm with a high proportion of intangible assets that have unproven productivity.

Of course, articulation of a merger's strategic intent is one part of the due diligence process. Another element is the selection of a merger partner. M&A deals are notoriously vulnerable to problems of information asymmetry (i.e., the target firm knows more about itself than does the acquirer). Deals done out of haste or for defensive reasons may short circuit the due diligence process of gathering information. Academic research suggests that access to information about the target during the preacquisition period is critical to the acquirer's success. Such access is critical in evaluating the target's intangible assets (early stage pipeline, research capabilities, and technologies) and in avoiding overpaying for them.[105–106] How is this information actually acquired? It may come through prior strategic alliances with the target, through the conduct of research that parallels that of the target, and through prior sales experience within the same therapeutic area as the product(s) that are involved in the acquisition. This prior experience helps the acquirer to better evaluate the products, technologies, and capabilities it gains from the merger, as well as their "fit" with its own portfolio of assets. However, in order for this experience to benefit the acquiring firm and to become a capability there must be management continuity and good processes of organizational learning.

On the postacquisition side, a critical capability may be the leveraging of diverse knowledge both within and across therapeutic areas in the combined firm. Such economies of scope in ideas can result from the development of several integrative devices:[107]

- cross-therapeutic knowledge repositories that capture research data and reports
- cross-knowledge networks built upon standardized and integrated information technology systems[108]
- common central reporting process to monitor the progress of clinical projects across therapeutic areas
- internal research conferences to promote idea exchange
- communities of practice that convene scientists across therapeutic areas with common interests
- cross-disciplinary teams of scientists within therapeutic areas

- within-disciplinary teams of scientists across therapeutic areas
- product strategy teams co-led by clinicians and senior marketing representatives[109]
- collaborative discovery models that improve knowledge transfers and personal interactions between different types of scientists (e.g., biologists and chemists)[110]
- parallel R&D efforts in both large molecules and small molecules
- cross-team sharing of targets and compounds
- cross-team discussions of whether compounds for initial indications that fail can be applied to secondary indications
- interdigitation between early and late stage researchers using shared financial incentives (e.g., pay research scientists out of a bonus pool based on how many new drugs they launch each year)
- decentralized control over R&D funding[111]
- parallel processing of various compounds for efficacy in different disease areas[112]
- parallel processing of adjacent steps in the pharmaceutical value chain (e.g., involvement of clinician teams in discovery, involvement of scientists in the preclinical and clinical stages, involvement of chemists in the manufacture of large molecules)[113]
- integration of certain functional areas (sales and marketing)[114]
- co-location of interdependent researchers within the firm
- co-location of R&D laboratories with external biotechnology clusters and nonprofit research institutes[115]
- teams of clinicians and scientists and mathematicians that analyze the compounds that fail in testing[116]
- teams drawing on gene-based discovery research and clinical R&D in "experimental medicine" programs[117]
- focus on learning from others inside and outside the firm rather than on trying to learn how to use new technologies[118]

Such collaboration is believed to reduce drug discovery and development times and costs, to promote serendipity in the discovery process through the free flow of ideas, and to increase a firm's stock of intellectual property.[119]

Of course, there is the empirical question of the most effective mechanisms to document and leverage the knowledge and capabilities of the firms engaged in the M&A. A long, drawn-out process is difficult to manage and keep on track. Success may hinge more on premerger planning, rapid (and sometimes dictated) integration, integration of systems across the merged firms, and often separate management of the target firm in order to preserve its intellectual capital.

Recent network research suggests two interesting caveats to these conclusions, however. First, based on research conducted in physician clinics, informal networks may be more important than the formal structural devices used to develop collaboration and stimulate consultation.[120] Second, professionals may be more willing to learn from external rivals than from internal colleagues for reasons of status and self-esteem.[121]

Postmerger integration of the firms involved in the combination may be the critical requirement for M&A success and the most important predictor of synergy realization. A major reason is that mergers must generate cost savings in order to offset the premium paid to the shareholders of the target firm as well as the costs of combination. Another reason is that the degree of interaction and cooperation between the firms may facilitate the consolidation of operations and transfer of capabilities needed to achieve any economies.

Research in industry suggests that 40 percent of mergers with a high potential for combination achieve low levels of integration.[122] One major problem is that the executives of the acquiring firm do not spend sufficient time on the postmerger integration process. Executives do not appreciate the importance of this integration process, believing perhaps that the job is done when the financial consolidation takes place. Such executives may perceive the integration process as a "cost-shaving exercise." Other common problems that detract from synergy realization include the slow speed of integration, integration of different systems for drug discovery, integration of diverse cultures, the loss of key executives and scientists from the target firm, the perception of a takeover on the part of the target firm, disruptions to ongoing operations, harnessing best practices that reside in the target, and failures to communicate merger progress throughout the organization.[123]

Solutions to these problems are time-intensive and costly. One factor that may reduce costs includes the degree of postmerger cooperation between executives of the acquiring and target firms. Such cooperation may be facilitated by prior strategic alliances and working relationships between the two firms.[124] From this viewpoint, prior alliances not only serve to foster greater access to information about the target but also provide greater familiarity with its personnel.[125]

Finally, there may be other strategies beyond mergers that confer value on pharmaceutical firms. One may be the simple avoidance of M&A and its distractions – for example, eschewing the acquisition of genomics companies as well as the automation technologies (high-throughput screening, combinatorial chemistry). There are huge disruptions and costs entailed in shifting to a genomics-focused R&D approach.[126] The payoffs from such a shift for gene-based drug discovery may be ten to fifteen years down the road, leading some critics to label it an expensive fiasco.[127]

Another strategy may be the hiring of additional drug discovery scientists ("drug hunters"), talent, and expertise on projects in order to increase the understanding of the disease and model it, to identify the right targets, and to increase the number of compounds and improve their quality.[128]

A third strategy is speed: earlier termination of unfruitful research projects and the shortening of times a drug spends in each phase of research (e.g., small-scale clinical trials using experimental medicine). Such an approach increases the number of failures, but such failures are celebrated and viewed as an important source of learning.[129] Executives at Lilly attribute their recent pipeline success to these attributes.[130]

A fourth, related strategy is greater mastery and closer integration across the internal value chain of the pharmaceutical firm – from ideation to project selection to development to commercialization.[131] This would entail a better understanding of new business opportunities (including a view of what is happening at a firm's periphery), improved valuation and governance of new research projects, balancing rigorous business decision-making with good science, efficient project management and parallel processing of tasks, and integration of marketing personnel into the prior steps.

A fifth strategy is "do more with less," that is, focus on a smaller number of compounds selected for development and reduce the number of ongoing projects (but staff them more intensively).

A sixth strategy is labeled "jumpstarting" – find new uses for existing but underexploited compounds, and reformulate existing products.[132]

A final strategy, commonly pursued today, is effective in-licensing of new products from biotechnology companies. Strategic alliances are an entire alternative strategy to M&As that require enormous managerial attention.[133]

The future of pharmaceutical M&A and the value chain perspective on innovation

The review of the literature above suggests that M&A activity has exerted little impact on R&D productivity and new innovation. Indeed, as prior chapters in this volume have made clear, the bulk of the innovation now occurring in

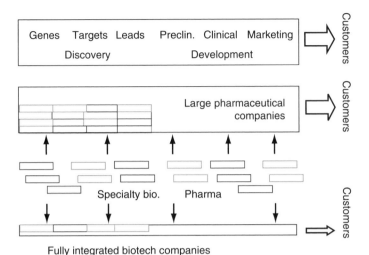

Figure 5.5   An integrating industry.

Source: Keith Dionne

the pharmaceutical market is being in-sourced from biotechnology firms using a variety of mechanisms (in-licensing, strategic alliances, acquisitions). There is a growing consensus that the task of drug discovery and development has become too complex for a single firm to handle on its own, and that it must now be accomplished through interfirm collaborative models and deals. This interdependence is illustrated in figure 5.5.

One reason for the growing prevalence of in-licensing is the consistency of the evidence that alliances improve pharmaceutical R&D productivity, contrasted with the inconsistent evidence that mergers improve R&D productivity. Several academic studies conclude that drugs developed in an alliance are more likely to reach the market than drugs developed independently by an originating company. One study that examines 1,900 compounds developed by over 900 firms between 1988 and 2000 concludes that drugs developed in an alliance have a 9.0 and 14.0 percentage point higher probability of successfully completing phase II and phase III, respectively, than drugs developed by a single company.[134] These positive effects are even stronger when the in-licensing firm has considerable experience in drug development. Two other studies arrive at similar results using slightly different samples and time periods.[135] Moreover, large firms that are successful at in-licensing products from others can offer payers and pharmacy benefit managers a broad range of products for inclusion in formularies at discounted prices.

In this manner, large firm scale leads to preference as a licensing partner which in turn leads to formulary access and thus greater sales.[136] The problem with licensing, however, is that the available pool of late stage licensing compounds is shrinking, while early stage licensing is an entirely different game.

Merger activity is nevertheless likely to continue in the pharmaceutical sector for several reasons. First, the industry is still fairly unconcentrated, leaving room for additional consolidation. Second, pharmaceutical firms continue to play a game of leapfrog using the latest merger to catapult them to a leadership position in global market share as well as to promote positive feedback.[137] Third, a pattern of mergers historically tied to swings in the stock market (evident in other industries) may become more regular in the pharmaceutical sector. Fourth, mergers in other sectors of the healthcare industry (e.g., among wholesalers and/or group purchasing organizations outside of the US) may prompt drug manufacturers to increase their size and thereby their bargaining leverage. Fifth, increasing use of pharmacogenomics to develop drugs targeted for specific genotypes, as opposed to a one-size-fits-all approach, may create stronger scale economies in drug development and sales as firms require more specialized personnel. Sixth, pharmaceutical firms may need to experiment with new business models, thus requiring them to acquire or dispose of assets (and capabilities) along their internal value chain. Seventh, cost-containment pressures are likely to accelerate worldwide. Hopefully, the potential for real cost savings will accelerate as well.

Further merger activity may also be spurred by the growing activism of payers (public sector outside of the US, both public and private inside the US), fiscal intermediaries (HMOs, PBMs), and their cost-containment efforts. Larger size and dominance in regional markets in the world may help to buffer pharmaceutical firms from public criticisms regarding rising healthcare costs and the contribution made by new drugs and their prices to those rising costs. Issues of national pride, fears of foreign takeover, and protection of domestic industries may also spur M&As, as is evidenced by recent events in France and Japan.

These considerations suggest that future value creation in the pharmaceutical sector may be tied to the broader value chain in healthcare (see figure 5.4 above), and larger firms may be better positioned to deliver value in this new environment. For example, the ability of pharmaceutical manufacturers to maintain their prices and finance their merger activity depends on the willingness of payers to continue to pay for the innovation, which itself may be tied to the ability of pharmaceutical R&D to deliver. There have already been some efforts in the US and in Europe to assess the clinical effectiveness of new drugs and that consider tying these assessments to payer coverage for the products. This is a variant of a wider movement called "pay for performance" in the provider arena, where hospitals and physicians get reimbursed or differentially reimbursed for the quality of care they deliver to patients. As part of the December 2003 Medicare Modernization Act, the US Congress barred the Medicare program from using head-to-head clinical trials to make decisions about which drugs to reimburse. Nevertheless, government officials are still calling for "practical clinical trials" (phase IV) that compare the risks and costs and benefits of alternative interventions.[138]

A similar model might be applied to the reimbursement or payment coverage for new drugs based on their cost-effectiveness. Manufacturers have already begun to make "total cost arguments" for their products (i.e., that the superior clinical benefits of their products warrant higher prices) based on their own pharmacoeconomic studies. For the purposes of credibility and public payment, however, manufacturers may have to submit their products for outside evaluation and comparison with those from rival firms. Such comparisons might include a host of diverse outcomes including symptom alleviation, health status and lifestyle improvements, workplace productivity gains, substitution for more expensive therapies, and long-term health risks.

Pharmaceutical firms might also consider how they can assist payers in their cost-containment efforts. Employers and insurers believe that prescription drug expenditures are increasing at a rate that is not sustainable: as a percentage of national health expenditures, prescription drugs are expected to climb from 10.4 percent in 2002 to an estimated 14.5 percent in 2012. Consequently, payers feel they need to protect the affordability of prescription drugs for their enrollees. Some of the measures they are considering include more rigorous cost-effectiveness analyses of new drugs, a focus on patient outcomes, innovative utilization management programs, and reference pricing.[139] Such efforts are especially likely as the newer (and relatively expensive) biotechnology drugs become available to patients.

Pharmaceutical firms must collaborate with managed care organizations on diagnostic prescribing requirements for new expensive biologics, and then agree to market within those criteria. They must also work on ensuring proper drug utilization and stringent utilization management programs to help payers with pharmacoeconomics, modeling tools for evidence-based medicine, and technology assessment.[140] Pharmaceutical and biotechnology firms may choose to partner with "specialty pharmacy providers" who physically distribute these biological products and/or support/train providers in their utilization.[141]

Currently in the US, both federal and state governments are funding demonstration programs in some of these areas in order to reduce the costs of healthcare. Pharmaceutical firms are well positioned to assist them in these efforts due to the massive amounts of information and understanding they have developed on diseases, the drug therapies applied to them, and patient compliance with those therapies. They have also developed capabilities in dealing with doctors and patients and providing them with information, which can be important to payers in terms of providing greater access and outreach to underserved populations. As is evident by Pfizer's past partnership with the State of Florida's Medicaid program, pharmaceutical firms can engage in innovative programs with payers whereby the former gains formulary benefits and the latter limits their financial risk. However, this program was recently suspended, so the trajectory of these payer–pharmaceutical partnerships is unclear.

The difficulty facing pharmaceutical firms is that there are fifty different state customers in the Medicaid program. Moreover, these customers are acutely conscious of their drug spending, since roughly half of a typical state's budget deficit ($29 billion out of a range of $50–85 billion) is spent on Medicaid drugs. Pharmaceutical firms will need to develop customized solutions to each state's fiscal problems and form partnership networks with officials, legislators, clinicians, and patient interest groups in each state. Most significantly, these customers want services and solutions, not products.[142]

On a global front, pharmaceutical firms will need to target European governments and their ministers about governmental budgets and limits on drug spending. While rationing has succeeded in holding down national health expenditures as a percentage of gross domestic product, it has also discouraged firms from launching some drugs in Europe, has delayed the launch date of other drugs, and has led to the loss of R&D jobs and their associated economic benefits to the US. It is conceivable, therefore, that European health policies have actually reduced overall welfare in those countries.[143]

There are other potential benefits from value chain alliances between pharmaceutical firms and payers. These include collaboration in the design and provision of other clinical integration programs (e.g., health knowledge access, case management), the establishment of more cost-effective clinical protocols, and the development of consumer-enabling tools.[144] Indeed, as these alliances develop and depending on the growth of the consumerism movement, pharmaceutical firms may offer more interactive information on diseases/products/treatment options, more information on disease state awareness, compliance assistance and reminders, and assistance with high-cost products.[145] Thus, manufacturers and payers may need to adopt a new, shared paradigm that focuses more on patients and less on products, focuses on helping to prevent and cure disease, reviews the innovation pipeline at its early phases and assesses how drugs generate value to patients, and cooperatively designs clinical trials that address the cost-effectiveness questions of interest to payers.[146] As part of this dialogue, pharmaceutical firms may need to recognize that not all innovative programs they pursue are worthwhile from the payers' perspective, just as payers may need to recognize that certain innovations and breakthrough products deserve fast-track approval and adequate reimbursement.

Value chain alliances with both payers and patients will increase in importance as the pharmaceutical sector shifts from a one-size-fits-all approach based on blockbuster drugs to more of a customized therapeutic approach focused on specific diseases and more narrow patient populations. In this latter model, competitive success may rely more on intimate customer knowledge and relationships, especially if the customers (physicians, patients, payers, intermediaries) exert more influence in the prescribing decision. Success may also hinge on the types of customized services pharmaceutical firms can provide these different customer segments, including information, education, and management support.[147]

In addition to value chain alliances with payers, pharmaceutical firms will need to develop traditional value chain alliances with new types of physicians and new value chain alliances with physicians. With regard to the former, pharmaceutical firms will have to supplement their marketing efforts directed towards primary care physicians with marketing efforts directed at specialists. This will be necessitated by the growing prominence of biotechnology products that target higher severity conditions in smaller patient populations that are typically treated by specialists (e.g., HIV, congestive heart failure, multiple sclerosis).[148]

With regard to the latter, pharmaceutical firms may further supplement their traditional model of drug discovery leading to new clinical treatments. For example, pharmaceutical firms may deepen their networks with academic medical center physicians and researchers in order to monitor clinical studies that lead to breakthroughs in basic biomedical sciences and improved understanding of the mechanisms involved in disease (treatments that lead to new discovery). In this manner, there can be a bidirectional flow of knowledge and learning between bench scientists and clinicians. Such physician-scientists may be essential for pharmaceutical firms' search for new drugs.[149]

There are numerous examples of such fruitful interaction. The Cleveland Clinic laboratory developed intravascular ultrasound imaging technology to study plaque build-up. Pharmaceutical firms are now using this technology to test their atherosclerosis drugs. Similarly, the paclitaxel-coated coronary stent was developed by asking physicians different kinds of questions, such as "What does the body do to these stents and why do they fail?" The answers provided by clinicians helped device makers to solve the scar tissue problem of earlier stents.[150] In addition, there is growing involvement of childrens' hospitals, universities, and nonprofit research institutes in drug discovery and early stage development (e.g., phase I clinical trials). Hospitals which conduct a minority of clinical research are expanding their research capacity and can act as new partners. Their efforts serve to accelerate the translation of new compounds from discovery into clinical use, as well as to handle some of the risks of development that pharmaceutical firms do not want to shoulder.[151]

Nevertheless, there are obstacles to deepening research ties with clinicians and hospitals. First, due to managed care pressures on their incomes, physicians are spending more time seeing patients and less time as clinical researchers. According to the Federation of American Societies for Experimental Biology (FASEB), the number of physicians listing research as their primary activity dropped six percent between 1980 and 1997. Second, a growing number of academic medical centers are blocking or threatening to block access to their physicians by pharmaceutical sales representatives. The clinical research monies they get from drug companies pale in comparison to NIH funding, while the rising costs of new drugs represents one of the fastest growing components of hospital spending.

What is not clear in these future scenarios is the value of large pharmaceutical firm size. Drug companies need to evaluate the impact of future M&As on the efficiency of their own internal value chain as well as their ability to collaborate in the external value chain in healthcare. Executives may rightly believe that larger scale provides a seat at the table and thus greater voice in any discussions with payers and consumers. However, they may also need to document how their increased scale serves to address major policy issues of importance to these other constituencies: how to reduce the cost of care (or at least contain the rise in spending), how to improve quality of care and reduce medical errors, and how to increase access to healthcare for the underserved. Moreover, given the rising cost of pharmaceuticals and their growing share of national healthcare budgets, pharmaceutical firms may need to document how their products simultaneously address two of these policy issues (e.g., cost-effective therapies).

Finally, in the face of diminishing productivity and pressures on their profits, pharmaceutical companies will be forced to manage themselves in ways that other firms now do. They will need to increase their efficiency in procurement (e.g., by consolidating purchases across their departments and regions), to automate their transaction processing, and consider outsourcing noncore functions (e.g., information technology, human resources, finance, manufacturing).[152] In this manner, pharmaceutical firms will confront whether or not they need to remain fully integrated companies and deliberate the key issue in corporate strategy: make (in house) versus buy (on the market). This issue is already on their doorstep in the form of whether to develop the capabilities of biotechnology firms themselves or partner with these firms in alliances. It is also an issue that has proven troublesome for many Fortune 500 firms, as evidenced by the massive unbundling and dediversification of their businesses in the late 1980s and early 1990s. The issue may ultimately dwarf the importance of whether or not to engage in mergers and acquisitions.

NOTES

1. The chapter deals with mergers among large pharmaceutical firms, since these have been the historical focus of academic researchers and consultants. Acquisitions of biotechnology firms by pharmaceutical firms are of growing prominence and importance due to (a) the pipeline gap in big pharma and the concentration of the industry pipeline in the hands of biotech firms, (b) the growing frequency of such acquisitions, and (c) the changing relationships between pharmaceutical and biotechnology firms over the past decade (see chapter 3 above). Future research should study these M&As as well.

2. Another important topic not squarely addressed here is the in-licensing of products and the comparative effectiveness of M&A and in-licensing. Thus, for example, the researcher might inquire whether licensing is a more effective way of enhancing performance, and whether licensing is a viable option given the industry's pipeline squeeze. There is case evidence, cited below in the chapter, that M&A can be triggered by the need to protect licensed revenue streams (Pfizer and Lipitor). The comparative effectiveness of licensing versus M&A hints at the possible need for new intermediate models of R&D such as the "orchestrator of a network of autonomous research units," which might more effectively connect intellectual property assets with infrastructure and experience without compromising entrepreneurialism. These issues are discussed towards the end of the chapter.

3. Lawton Burns and Mark Pauly, "Integrated Delivery Networks: A Detour on the Road to Integrated Health Care?," *Health Affairs* 21(4) (2002): 128–143.

4. David Besanko, David Dranove, and Mark Shanley, *Economics of Strategy*, 2nd edn (New York: John Wiley, 2000).

5. Antonio Regalado, "Drug Development's Preclinical Bottleneck," *Start-Up* (December 1997): 26.

6. Despite these pressures, pharmaceutical firms in the US performed quite well financially during the 1990s. According to Martin Reeves, continued price increases and faster roll-outs of products more than compensated for cost containment pressures and unfavorable legislation involving generics.

7. David Cassak, Roger Longman, and Antonio Regalado, "Merger Mania – Faith or Folly?," *In Vivo* (September 1996): 4–8.

8. Roger Longman, "Have Problem? Try M&A," *In Vivo* (March 1999): 59–68.

9. McKinsey & Company, "Does Market Concentration Create Market Value?," *In Vivo* (May 1998): 33.

10. Longman, "Have Problem?"

11. David Ravenscraft and William Long, "Paths to Creating Value in Pharmaceutical Mergers," in *Mergers and Productivity*, ed. Steven Kaplan (Chicago: University of Chicago Press, 2000). The decline in price escalation may be true for existing products, whereas price realizations may have escalated in the 1990s for new products (Martin Reeves, personal communication).

12. The actual impact of these pressures on revenues and patent lives is suspect. There is evidence that patent life was fairly constant during the 1990s, and that total revenues increased due to the fact that faster ramp-up of revenues (e.g., quicker roll-outs) out-weighed faster sales declines in postpatent lapse periods (Martin Reeves, personal communication).

13. Ravenscraft and Long, "Paths to Creating Value."; Susan Pulliam and Elyse Tanouye, "Drug Industry Consolidation may not be Over," *Wall Street Journal* (May 4, 1994): C1, C2.

14. Available on http://leda.law.harvard.edu/leda/data/89/cosvaldm.html.

15. Patricia Danzon, Andrew Epstein, and Sean Nicholson, "Mergers and Acquisitions in the Pharmaceutical and Biotech Industries," unpublished manuscript, Wharton School, 2004.

16. William Pursche, "Pharmaceuticals – the Consolidation isn't Over," *McKinsey Quarterly* 2 (1996): 110–119.

17. Matthew Higgins and Daniel Rodriguez, "The Outsourcing of R&D Through Acquisitions in the Pharmaceutical Industry," Emory University, unpublished manuscript, 2004.

18. Danzon, Epstein, and Nicholson, "Mergers and Acquisitions."

19. Higgins and Rodriguez, "Outsourcing of R&D." This observation complicates the analysis of M&A performance, since the sample of firms that merge is not representative of the industry overall.

20. Nikhil Deogun, Gardiner Harris, Steven Lipin, and Robert Langreth, "In Biggest Hostile Bid, Pfizer Offers $80 Billion for Warner-Lambert," *Wall Street Journal* (November 5, 1999): A1.

21. Elyse Tanouye, "Mergers will Keep Shuffling Rankings of Drug Makers," *Wall Street Journal* (March 15, 1995): B4.

22. Ravenscraft and Long, "Paths to Creating Value."

23. Martin Reeves, personal communication.

24. Amy Barrett, "Big Pharma: Getting too big for its own Good?," *Business Week* (July 29, 2002): 74.

25. "PhRMA Touts Medications' Efficacy," *Chain Drug Review* 24(9) (2002): RX2.

26. Roger Longman, "Renewing Novartis," *In Vivo* (January 2001): 17.

27. IMS Health, "Pfizer Still Ahead after GlaxoSmithKline Merger," http://www.ims-global.com/insight/news_story/0101/news_story_010104.htm, accessed 1/4/2001.

28. "GlaxoSmithKline Merger Completed as Trading for New Company Begins," *Chemical Market Reporter* (January 1, 2001), http://findarticles.com/p/articles/mi_m0FVP/is_1_259/ai_68872267.

29. Alexandre Bilous, "French and German Unions Respond to Hoechst/Rhone-Poulenc Merger," *European Industrial Relations Observer* 14(1) (February 1999).

30. Kerry Capell, "AstraZeneca: a Drug Megamerger that's Working," *Business Week* (November 15, 1999), http://www.businessweek.com/datedtoc/1999/9946.htm.

31. Thomas Burton, Steven Lipin, and Stephen Moore, "Upjohn and Pharmacia Sign $6 Billion Merger," *Wall Street Journal* (August 21, 1995): A3.

32. Andrew Sorkin, "Sanofi Makes its Bid for Aventis; it is Quickly Rejected as 'Inferior,'" *New York Times* (January 27, 2004): C1–C2; Melanie Senior and Christopher Morrison, "The Best Defense is a Good Offense: Sanofi's Bid for Aventis," *In Vivo* (February 2004): 76–82.

33. Kazuhiro Shimanura and Jason Singer, "Japanese Drug Makers to Combine," *Wall Street Journal* (February 25, 2004): A2.

34. Peter Landers, "Japan is Urging its Drug Firms to Merge, Citing Need for Heft," *Wall Street Journal* (September 4, 2002): B2.

35. "Roche and Chugai Blaze a Trail . . . but will Anyone Follow?," *In Vivo* (January 2002): 39; Peter Landers, "Merck, Pfizer Battle in Japan," *Wall Street Journal* (October 2, 2003): B4.

36. Theresa Agovino, "Pfizer Purchase of Pharmacia Brings Challenges," *Salt Lake Tribune* (April 15, 2003).

37. Rajesh Garg, Roy Berggren, and Michele Holcomb, "The Value of Scale in Pharma's Future," *In Vivo* (September 2001): 78–83.

38. AT Kearney, *Saint Joseph's University Pharmaceutical Marketing Strategy* (New York: AT Kearney, 1999); Steve Arlington, Sam Barnett, Simon Hughes, and Joe Palo, *Pharma 2010: The Threshold of Innovation* (New York: IBM Business Consulting Services, 2003); Martin Reeves, "The R&D Productivity Challenge," presentation to the New York Pharma Forum, September 17, 2003.

39. Danzon, Epstein, and Nicholson, "Mergers and Acquisitions."

40. "Troubling Numbers for Big Pharma Consolidation," *In Vivo* (July/August 2000): 2.

41. Jeffrey Dvorin, "Creating Glaxo Wellcome," *In Vivo* (March 1999): 5–16.

42. Ravenscraft and Long, "Paths to Creating Value."

43. Lawrence Fisher, "Post-Merger Integration: How Novartis Became no. 1," *Strategy + Business* 11(2nd quarter) (1998): 2–10.

44. Ravenscraft and Long, "Paths to Creating Value."

45. We thank Martin Reeves for this insight.

46. AT Kearney, *St. Joseph's Marketing Strategy*.

47. Martin Reeves, personal communication.

48. Ravenscraft and Long, "Paths to Creating Value."

49. Danzon, Epstein, and Nicholson, "Mergers and Acquisitions."; Higgins and Rodriguez, "Outsourcing of R&D."
50. The researcher also faces the challenge of measuring against the right set of metrics in the right time period. For example, the underlying problem to be addressed (e.g., high overhead cost, lagging R&D productivity) varies by historical era and by the length of payback period.
51. Wesley M. Cohen and Richard C. Levin, "Empirical Studies of Innovation and Market Structure," in *Handbook of Industrial Organization*, ed. R. Schmalensee and R. D. Willig, (Amsterdam: Elsevier, 1989), II, 1059–1107.
52. John Vernon, "Price Regulation, Capital Market Imperfections, and Strategic R&D Investment Behavior in the Pharmaceutical Industry: Consequences for Innovation," Ph.D. dissertation, Wharton School, 2003.
53. Bronwyn Hall, "Mergers and R&D Revisited," unpublished manuscript, University of California at Berkeley, 1999.
54. Jay Istvan and Roger Wolcott, "Is Bigger Really Better?," *In Vivo* (March 1996): 11.
55. Danzon, Epstein, and Nicholson, "Mergers and Acquisitions."
56. According to Martin Reeves, "it is certainly conspicuous that some of the most successful firms in the industry have engaged in acquisitions in spite of enormous and unproductive internal R&D" (personal communication).
57. Higgins and Rodriguez, "Outsourcing of R&D."
58. Danzon, Epstein, and Nicholson, "Mergers and Acquisitions."
59. Cohen and Levin, "Empirical Studies"; William Comanor, "The Political Economy of the Pharmaceutical Industry," *Journal of Economic Literature* 24 (September 1986): 1178–1217.
60. Iain Cockburn and Rebecca Henderson, "Scale and Scope in Drug Development: Unpacking the Advantages of Size in Pharmaceutical Research," *Journal of Health Economics* 20(6) (2001): 1033–1057; Elizabeth Jensen, "Research Expenditures and the Discovery of New Drugs," *Journal of Industrial Economics* 36(1) (1987): 83–95.
61. Vernon, "Price Regulation."
62. Rebecca Henderson and Iain Cockburn, "Scale, Scope, and Spillovers: The Determinants of Research Productivity in Drug Discovery," *RAND Journal of Economics* 27(1) (1996): 32–59.
63. Gideon Markman and Maritza Espina, "Patents as Surrogates for Inimitable and Non-Substitutable Resources," *Journal of Management* 30(4) (2004): 529–544.
64. Patricia Danzon, Sean Nicholson, and Nuno Pereira, "Productivity in Pharmaceutical-Biotechnology R&D: The Role of Experience and Alliances," unpublished manuscript, Wharton School, 2004.
65. It should also be noted, however, that 50 percent of the increase in costs per NDA over the 1990s has come from research and preclinical testing. The R&D productivity challenge is therefore largely an early stage phenomenon, perhaps more so than experience in running clinical trials.
66. Boston Consulting Group, "Historical Value of Size," confidential client report.
67. Martin Reeves, "The R&D Productivity Challenge," presentation given at the New York Pharma Forum, September 17, 2003.
68. Alexander Kandybin and Martin Kihn, "Raising your Return on Innovation Investment," *Strategy + Business* 35 (2004): 38–49; Amy Barrett and Kerry Capell, "Big Pharma: Getting too Big for its own Good?," *Business Week* (July 29, 2002): 74.

69. Vikram Sahu, Mark Tracey, John Murphy, James Kelly, and Kenji Masuzoe, "Tracking the 'X Factor' – Pipeline Valuations," Goldman Sachs, *Global Equity Research Report* (September 23, 2002).

70. Lehman Brothers, *Pharma Pipelines* (New York: Lehman Bros, 2002).

71. Roger Longman, "Have Problem? Try M&A," *In Vivo* (March 1999): 59–68.

72. Istvan and Wolcott, "Is Bigger really Better?"

73. CenterWatch (2000) analysis of twenty-two merged companies, reported in "Troubling Numbers for Big Pharma Consolidation," *In Vivo* (July/August, 2000): 2–3.

74. Higgins and Rodriguez, "Outsourcing of R&D."

75. Ravenscraft and Long, "Paths to Creating Value."

76. Gregor Andrade, Mark Mitchell, and Erik Stafford, "New Evidence and Perspectives on Mergers," *Journal of Economic Perspectives* 15(2) (2001): 103–120; R. Bruner, "Does M&A Pay? A Survey of Evidence for the Decision Maker," *Journal of Applied Finance* 12 (2002): 48–68; Michael Bradley, Anand Desai, and E. Han Kim, "Synergistic Gains from Corporate Acquisitions and their Division Between the Stockholders of Target and Acquiring Firms," *Journal of Financial Economics* 21 (1988): 3–40.

77. Danzon, Epstein, and Nicholson, "Mergers and Acquisitions."

78. Boston Consulting Group, "Historical Value of Size."

79. Istvan and Wolcott, "Is Bigger Really Better?"

80. Sumit Agarwal, Sanjay Desai, Michele Holcomb, and Arjun Oberoi, "Unlocking the Value in Big Pharma," *McKinsey Quarterly* 2(2001); McKinsey & Company, "Does Market Concentration Create Market Value?," *In Vivo* (May 1998): 33.

81. AT Kearney, *St. Joseph's Marketing Strategy*; see also Raymond Hill and Markus Peterseim, "Maximizing Pharmaceutical Health," *In Vivo* 17(5) (1999); AT Kearney, *A Prescription for Pharmaceutical Health* (Chicago, IL: AT Kearney, 2002).

82. Cassak, Longman, and Regalado "Merger Mania"; Jim Gilbert, Preston Henske, and Ashish Singh, "Rebuilding Big Pharma's Business Model," *In Vivo* (November 2003): 73–80.

83. Gilbert, Henske, and Singh, "Rebuilding Big Pharma's Business Model."

84. Henderson and Cockburn, "Scale, Scope and Spillovers"; Cockburn and Henderson, "Scale and Scope in Drug Development."

85. Boston Consulting Group, "Historical Value of Size."

86. Ravenscraft and Long, "Paths to Creating Value."

87. Danzon, Epstein, and Nicholson, "Mergers and Acquisitions."

88. Ravenscraft and Long, "Paths to Creating Value."

89. Carl Seiden, "Bigger is Better: Why Pharma Consolidation Makes Sense – and Will Continue," available on http://www.cpsnet.com/reprints.

90. Longman, "Have Problem?"

91. Boston Consulting Group, "Historical Value of Size"; Agarwal *et al.*, "Unlocking the Value in Big Pharma"; Ameet Mallik, Gary Pinkus, and Scott Sheffer, "Biopharma's Capacity Crunch," *McKinsey Quarterly, special edition, Risk and Resilience* (2002): 9–11.

92. Garg *et al.*, "Value of Scale in Pharma's Future"; Agarwal *et al.*, "Unlocking the Value of Big Pharma."

93. Garg, *et al.*, "Value of Scale in Pharma's Future"; Agarwal *et al.*, "Unlocking the Value of Big Pharma."

94. Lehman Brothers, *Pharma Pipelines*.

95. Garg *et al.*, "Value of Scale in Pharma's Future."

96. It should be noted that revenue growth is dependent on a few products for even the largest pharmaceutical firms. The systematic value of M&A and other strategic actions may therefore be masked by the success or demise of individual products, the firm's starting point, and the option value of its available strategic moves (Martin Reeves, personal communication).

97. Mark Sirower, *The Synergy Trap: How Companies Lose the Acquisition Game* (New York: Free Press, 1997); R. Barfield, "Creating Value through Mergers," *Banker* (July 1988): 24–25; David Ravenscraft and F. M. Scherer, "The Profitability of Mergers," *International Journal of Industrial Organization* 7 (1989): 101–116.

98. Cohen and Levin, "Empirical Studies."

99. Michael Hitt, R. Duane Ireland, and Jeffrey Harrison, "Mergers and Acquisitions: A Value Creating or Value Destroying Strategy?," in *The Blackwell Handbook of Strategic Management*, ed. Michael Hitt, R. Edward Freeman, and Jeffrey Harrison (Malden, MA: Blackwell Business, 2001), 384–408.

100. Longman, "Have Problem?"

101. Z. J. Acs and D. B. Audretsch, "Innovation, Market Structure, and Firm Size," *Review of Economics and Statistics* 71 (1987): 567–574.

102. Rebecca Henderson, Luigi Orsenigo, and Gary Pisano, "The Pharmaceutical Industry and the Revolution in Molecular Biology: Interactions among Scientific, Institutional, and Organizational Changes," in *Sources of Industrial Leadership* ed. David Mowery and Richard Nelson (Cambridge: Cambridge University Press, 1999), 267–311.

103. Richard Nelson and Sidney Winter, *An Evolutionary Theory of Economic Change* (Cambridge, MA: Harvard University Press, 1982); J. Jewkes, D. Sawers, and R. Stillerman, *The Sources of Invention* (London: Macmillan, 1958); Cohen and Levin, "Empirical Studies."

104. Sirower, *Synergy Trap*.

105. Higgins and Rodriguez, "Outsourcing of R&D."

106. The experience of some analysts seems to contradict the role of information access, however. Martin Reeves reports there is no correlation between prior knowledge of the target and deal success in biotech acquisitions. He suggests instead that many deals are undertaken to access intellectual property that would otherwise be unavailable due to licensing relationships with other firms.

107. Jeffrey Jung and Andy Wang, *Rx for Pharmaceutical Companies: Internal Collaboration is the Key to Improved Innovation* (Somers, N.Y.: IBM Institute for Business Value, 2002); Jeffrey Jung, *Creating Breakthrough Innovation during a Pharmaceutical Merger or Acquisition* (Somers, N.Y.: IBM Institute for Business Value, 2002); Gary Pisano, *The Development Factory* (Boston, MA: Harvard Business School Press, 1997).

108. Deloitte Research, *Collaborative Knowledge Networks: Accelerating Pharmaceutical R&D in the New Millennium* (New York: Deloitte Research, 2002).

109. Matthew Boyle, "Growing Against the Grain," *Fortune* (May 3, 2004): 148–156.

110. Deborah Erickson, "Amgen Moves Beyond Proteins," *In Vivo* (March 2004): 18–26.

111. Rebecca Henderson and Iain Cockburn, "Measuring Competence? Exploring Firm Effects in Pharmaceutical Research," *Strategic Management Journal* 15 (1994): 63–84;

Peter Landers, "Merck Ends Research on Once Promising Antidepressant," *Wall Street Journal* (November 13, 2003): B1, B2.

112. Amy Barrett, John Carey, and Michael Arndt, "Feeding the Pipeline," *Business Week* (May 5, 2003): 78–83.

113. Frits Pil and Matthias Holweg, "Exploring Scale: The Advantages of Thinking Small," *Sloan Management Review* (winter 2003): 33–39.

114. Thomas Gartenmann and Philippe Guy, "Rx Industry Post M&A Integration, Part I: Marketing and Sales," *In Vivo* (December 1997): 20–25.

115. Deborah Erickson, "Novartis Bucks the Trend," *In Vivo* (February 2004): 43–52; Pil and Holweg, "Exploring Scale"; Lawrence Fisher, "The New Architecture of Biomedical Research,"*Strategy + Business* 33 (2003): 58–69.

116. Thomas Burton, "By Learning from Failures, Lilly Keeps Drug Pipeline Full," *Wall Street Journal* (April 21, 2004): A1, A12.

117. Mark Ratner, "How Experimental Medicine is Affecting Big Pharma," *In Vivo* (April 2004): 59–64; Erickson,"Novartis Bucks the Trend."

118. Peter Landers, "With Dry Pipelines, Big Drug Makers Stock up in Japan," *Wall Street Journal* (November 24, 2003): A1, A7; Peter Landers, "Drug Industry's Big Push into Technology Falls Short," *Wall Street Journal* (February 24, 2004): A1, A8.

119. Henderson and Cockburn, "Measuring Competence?"

120. William Riley, Douglas Wholey, Amy Wilson, and David Knoke, "Informal Consultation in Medical Clinics: Intra- and Inter- Personal Talk," paper presented at 6th Annual Health Care Organizations Conference, Boston University, June 2004.

121. Tanya Menon, Hoon-Seok Choi, and Leigh Thompson, "Tainted Knowledge versus Tempting Knowledge: Why People avoid Knowledge from Internal Rivals and Seek Knowledge from External Rivals," unpublished manuscript, Graduate School of Business, University of Chicago, 2004.

122. Rikand Larsson and Sydney Finkelstein, "Integrating Strategic, Organizational, and Human Resource Perspectives on Mergers and Acquisitions: A Case Survey of Synergy Realization," *Organization Science* 10(1) (1999): 1–26.

123. Ravenscraft and Long, "Paths to Creating Value"; Iain Clark, "Drug Discovery – Resolving the Bottlenecks,"*Horizons*, pharmaceutical issue 1 (December, 2001); Wood MacKenzie, http://www.woodMac.com.

124. Analysts are skeptical about whether "democratic" processes of cooperation promote the success of integration in M&As.

125. Hitt, Ireland, and Harrison "Mergers and Acquisitions."

126. Deloitte Research, *Collaborative Knowledge Networks*.

127. Landers, "Drug Industry's Big Push."

128. Deborah Erickson, "Wanted: Drug Hunters," *In Vivo* (September 2003): 45–52; Gary Hamel and Gary Getz, "Funding Growth in an Age of Austerity," *Harvard Business Review* 82(7/8) (2004): 76–84; Landers, "Dry Pipelines."

129. Ratner, "Experimental Medicine"; Erickson, "Novartis Bucks the Trend."

130. John Simons, "Lilly goes off Prozac," *Fortune* (June 28, 2004): 179–184; Burton, "Learning from Failures."

131. Kandybin and Kihn, "Raising Your Return on Innovation Investment."

132. Roger Longman, "Jumpstart to Products," *In Vivo* (February 2004): 17–30.

133. Cf. Nelson Sims and Anton Gueth, "Managing Alliances at Lilly," *In Vivo* 19(6) (2001). The topic of strategic alliances (e.g., in-licensing) is too big for this chapter, and really warrants separate treatment. The topic is only briefly considered below.

134. Danzon, Nicholson, and Pereira, "Productivity in Phamaceutical-Biotechnology R&D."

135. Ashish Arora, Alfonso Gambardella, Fabio Pammolli, and Massimo Riccaboni, "The Nature and the Extent of the Market for Technology in Biopharmaceuticals," unpublished manuscript, H. John Heinz School, Carnegie Mellon University, 2000; Joseph Dimasi, "Risks in New Drug Development: Approval Success Rates for Investigational Drugs," *Clinical Pharmacology & Therapeutics* 69(8) (2001): 297–307.

136. Scott Hensley, "Biggest Drug Firm Faces Generics but has an Edge: its Very Bigness," *Wall Street Journal* (August 23, 2004): A1, A6.

137. Tanouye, "Mergers will keep shuffling Rankings."

138. Sean Tunis, David Stryer, and Carolyn Clancy, "Practical Clinical Trials: Increasing the Value of Clinical Research for Decision Making in Clinical and Health Policy," *Journal of American Medical Association* 290(12) (2003): 1624–1632.

139. Robert Seidman, "Protecting Affordable Access to next Generation Medical Solutions," presentation to the Pharma, Biotech, and Device Colloquium, Princeton, June 7, 2004.

140. Wendy Diller, "Managed Care Tackles Biotech Budget Busters," *In Vivo* (January 2004): 31–41.

141. Wendy Diller, "As Specialty Pharmacy Evolves, Biotech Companies Stay Tuned," *In Vivo* (March 2004): 53–61.

142. AT Kearney, *The State as a Customer* (Chicago, IL: AT Kearney, 2003).

143. Jim Gilbert and Paul Rosenberg, "Imbalanced Innovation: The High Cost of Europe's 'Free Ride,'" *In Vivo* (March 2004): 62–69.

144. Cap Gemini Ernst & Young, *Prescriptions for the Smart and Lean Pharmaceutical Company: Vision and Reality Survey 2003*, available on http://www.cgey.com/life.

145. Ibid.

146. Robert Galvin, "Employer's Perspective on the Role of Pharma, Biotech, and Device Sectors," presentation to the Pharma, Biotech, and Device Colloquium, Princeton, June 7, 2004.

147. Cap Gemini Ernst & Young, *Prescriptions*.

148. Brian Buxton and Robert Easton, "Blockbusters to New-Engine Drugs: The Key Industry Shift," *In Vivo* (July–August, 2003): 63–70.

149. Leon Rosenberg, "Physician-Scientists – Endangered and Essential," *Science* 283 (1993): 331–332; Elliot Gershon, "Making Progress: Does Clinical Research Lead to Breakthroughs in Basic Biomedical Sciences?," *Academic Medicine* 42 (1998): 95–102.

150. Carol Hymowitz, "The Best Innovations come from Smart Questions," *Wall Street Journal* (April 13, 2004): B1.

151. Sharon Begley, "Researchers try to cut New Path to the Pharmacy," *Wall Street Journal* (January 12, 2004): A1.

152. Anon., "Big Trouble for Big Pharma," *Economist* (December 6, 2003): 67.

Part II

Devices and information technologies

6 The medical device sector

Kurt Kruger

Introduction
Historical perspective: missteps, miscues, and misapplications of technologies
Industry analysis
Unique and defining characteristics of medical devices
Technologies
Important industry drivers
Financing and consolidation trends

Introduction

The medical device sector is by any measure one of the most attractive and profitable in all of American commerce. The broad set of products encompassed by this category span all physician specialties, touch every conceivable anatomy, and are applied to nearly every medical procedure. They range from the simplest surgical staples and sutures to complex electronic implantable devices that monitor and stimulate the heart. A cottage industry decades ago, it has consistently grown at mid-to-high single digit rates to reach over $165 billion in worldwide revenues in 2003. This total is divided between medical devices, accounting for approximately $90 billion in revenues, and commodity supplies at $75 billion.

While there are thousands of small specialized suppliers, the field is increasingly dominated by a dozen diversified franchise companies, each with extensive marketing, selling, and distribution capabilities and multiple billions of dollars in annual revenues. Three characteristics distinguish this vibrant sector: sustainable growth, high profitability, and rapid change. These and a handful of other attributes make the medical device sector unique – different from nearly all other commercial pursuits. This chapter will elaborate on these features and also on the important role that this sector has had

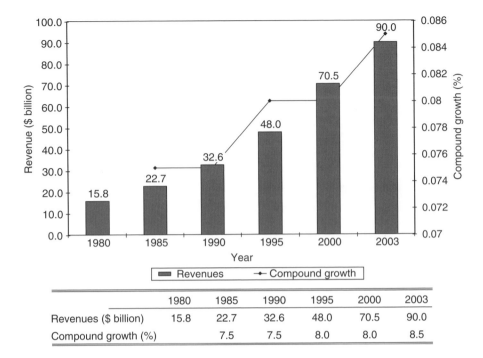

	1980	1985	1990	1995	2000	2003
Revenues ($ billion)	15.8	22.7	32.6	48.0	70.5	90.0
Compound growth (%)		7.5	7.5	8.0	8.0	8.5

Figure 6.1   Medical device industry.

Source: Analyst reports, Avamed, company reports, BBI market information.

and continues to have on the delivery of healthcare around the world. The discussion will focus on those segments within the medical products field that are the most technology-laden and have higher rates of growth, such as interventional cardiology products and implanted devices – pacemakers, defibrillators, and hip and knee replacements. The less commercially attractive, more mature and more commodity categories such as imaging equipment and hospital supplies (CAT scanners, infusion bags, gloves, and gowns) will be alluded to but will not be extensively reviewed.

Comparisons with other industries

Comparisons with other industries provide a context for the medical products sector and reveal significant differences in size, growth, and profitability. In terms of revenues, the medical device sector is considerably smaller than most other sectors. The automobile industry is multiple times larger. The revenues for the big three automobile companies, GM, Daimler-Chrysler, and Ford, in 2003 summed to $522 billion, three times the size of the entire medical products market at \$165 billion. The pharmaceutical sector is about two and a half times larger, at roughly \$492 billion. The cellular telephone industry is also much larger: the combined revenues of Nokia and Motorola alone in 2003 were \$63 billion. By comparison, the largest medical products company, Johnson & Johnson (J&J), had revenues of \$14.9 billion in 2003.[1] For what it lacks in size, however, the medical device sector makes up for in growth and profitability. It has a higher and more consistent rate of growth than nearly every industry sector, including the three that have been noted – pharmaceuticals, cellular telephones, and automobiles. To mount a decades-long record of steady mid-to-high single digit growth is rare indeed. Growth in the automobile industry has been modest and variable, with some year-to-year declines. Yet it is on the measure of profitability that the medical device sector truly stands out. The average operating profit margin for six of the larger device companies was 26 percent in 2003, twice the average operating profit rates generated by the three automakers (12%). Profitability among medical device companies also tops that of pharmaceutical companies by as much as five percentage points.

Historical perspective: missteps, miscues, and misapplications of technologies

The sector's current success is remarkable. Wafer-sized electrical devices that possess the processing power of a mainframe computer are routinely implanted in the chests of patients to treat a wide range of life-threatening heart conditions. In 2003 there were approximately 1.1 million electrical-based devices (cardiology and neuro) implanted in patients worldwide.[2] Consider the standard heart pacemaker as an example. Within the space of a few decades, the role of these electrical devices in practice has changed dramatically. At one time it was considered a risky proposition to expose a patient to the trauma of implanting the once large, clunky, and often unreliable devices, and in fact the procedure was viewed by many as a last resort. Today it would be considered unorthodox, if not an actual violation of correct medical practice, for a physician to withhold the use of these sleek, vanishingly small, and completely reliable products even for less severe heart conditions. As a testament to both the improvements in medical technology and the degree to which its use has become commonly accepted, note the recent arrival of an implanted electrical device that performs only diagnostic monitoring of a patient's vital signs and transmits this information through the skin, allowing physicians to follow disease progression and devise appropriate strategies.[3] The sector has truly come a long way.

The medical device sector was not always so successful. Its early forming was marked by many technology failures and some downright charlatanism. Medical products and technologies began a steep ascendancy in terms of acceptance and clinical impact through the 1950s, 1960s, and 1970s, yet were essentially unregulated until the passage of the Medical Device Amendments of 1976, which provided for a modest level of FDA oversight of the most life-critical devices. Even with this new regulation, however, these powerful and often hazardous technologies were used by clinicians on what could be described as an experimental basis. Electrodes were applied to the scalp in a vain attempt to treat migraine headaches. Lasers, borrowed from developments in electronics, were tried on nearly every part of the anatomy for a host of different ailments. After failed attempts to clear plaque from coronary arteries and to weld tissue during surgery (two of many misapplications), the only use that proved successful was perhaps the least likely imaginable – pointing this powerful energy source into the eyes to sculpt the cornea for vision correction.

After decades of missteps and miscues, the medical device sector has more recently entered a period of maturity and structure, in which the company participants have become self-selective, marshaling their prodigious technical capabilities to address fewer, more sensible applications. There are many implications of these changes. First, growth is sustained by the regular installments of new products that are perhaps less impactful and more orthodox than those of the past, but which are more proven and successful. Second, price behavior has rationalized as markets, companies, and products have become more homogeneous – that is fewer players offering similar products to customers that are not price sensitive. Third, profitability is maintained at above-average rates due to manufacturing scale efficiencies, evolutionary (not revolutionary) product changes, and well-developed marketing and selling channels. These positive characteristics will be discussed in greater detail below.

The history of medical device regulation

Over the last decade the medical device sector has experienced increased regulation and oversight. The most important aspect of this relates to the way in which new products are trialed, approved, and ultimately marketed. As has been mentioned, new products are the "life-blood" of this sector, and as such are the source of growth and extraordinary profit margins for device companies. More stringent regulation has most definitely increased the cost burden associated with new product development and furthermore has probably reduced new product velocity. Consider the trend toward consolidation described elsewhere in this chapter: clearly a more burdensome regulatory environment would favor large conglomerates that can readily absorb these costs, and would disadvantage smaller, capital-starved start-up companies. Here is a brief review of the history of device regulation and also an exploration of the role of regulation within the medical device sector today.

The modern-day regulation of medical devices originated in 1938 with the signing of the Food, Drug, and Cosmetic Act by President Franklin D. Roosevelt. While government regulation over the food and drugs market had existed since 1906, this act was the first to extend the FDA's authority to include medical devices as well. At first, medical devices were exempt from completing the premarket approval (PMA) process required for new drugs. Indeed, it wasn't until the passage of the Medical Device Amendments of 1976 that premarket approval requirements were extended to the realm of medical devices. Through this act, and the subsequent Food and Drug Administration Modernization Act of 1998, the modern-day system of medical device regulation was established.

Today when companies develop novel medical device products, they must adhere to a lengthy series of regulations before receiving approval to market and sell them. The level of clinical and technical data required for approval, and consequently the time to reach the market, is based on a three-tier risk classification system. Class I includes low-risk products such as tongue depressors, crutches, and scalpels, for which general controls will be sufficient to ensure safe and effective use. Class II products are of moderate risk and require additional information to establish appropriate controls. Examples include endoscopes, infusion pumps, and condoms. Class III products are defined as those that support or sustain human life, are of substantial importance in preventing impairment of human health or present a potential, unreasonable risk of illness or injury. Coronary stents, defibrillators, and tissue grafts fall into this category.

The level of technical and clinical data required to obtain marketing approval varies significantly between classes. Class I and Class II devices are not required to enter the full scale premarket approval (PMA) process but can obtain a 510(k) premarket notification instead (and many are exempt from this requirement altogether). For those devices applying for a 510(k), the requirements are far less stringent. The device is only required to demonstrate substantial equivalence (SE) to another, so-called "predicate" device that is currently on the market. These requirements can often be met through bench and animal testing alone. Most 510(k) products can reach the market within one to two years of invention. When clinical studies are required, they are typically on a far smaller scale than for those applying for a PMA. In certain cases companies themselves have elected to supplement the 510(k) with clinical trials, sometimes called a "fat-510(k)," as a way of constructing a competitive barrier to entry.

For Class III medical devices, the process is rigorous, primarily due to the required demonstration of clinical safety and efficacy. Before entering a clinical study, a new medical device must apply for and receive an Investigative Device Exemption (IDE). Upon receiving an IDE and getting approval from the Internal Review Board (IRB) of each trial site, the device may begin clinical trials. Typically, clinical trials are conducted in two or three phases. The first is conducted in a small sample of patients and is intended to demonstrate product safety. Next the company will embark on an intermediate, second phase or move directly to a large-scale pivotal trial. The second phase usually involves a larger sample of 100–200 patients and intends to establish the safety and efficacy of the device. The final, phase III trial, often called the pivotal trial, is designed to clearly demonstrate product efficacy through a large-scale, multicenter, double-blind trial. Once all three phases of clinical trials have been completed, a final PMA application can be submitted to the FDA. The agency then reviews this submission and usually convenes a panel of experts (the majority of which are physicians in practices relevant to the particular device) to vote on the approval worthiness of the product. The FDA will typically accept the panel's recommendation and make a decision that is to either grant or deny approval within three to six months of the panel date. The time required for the clinical trial, including following patients for six to nine months, or one year, after the procedure or implant can take one to two years. Then the PMA submission, the review, and the panel process can take one to two years in addition. This brings the total time to market of a Class III, PMA device to anywhere from two to four years.

The dramatic differences in cost and time in obtaining a PMA and a 510(k) create an interesting dilemma for new and established medical device companies. Applying for a 510(k) is the fastest, most effective route toward commercialization of a new device, but because it is also fast for competitors, it fails to provide any substantive barriers to entry. The PMA process, on the other hand, can give the manufacturer a competitive advantage by enabling them to more clearly differentiate the safety and efficacy of their product and to present a sizeable barrier to entry for competitors. However, the high cost of clinical trials and the potential for application rejection have important and direct implications for a company's business model and product cost economics, which can often make the risks too high.

As an illustration of the relative advantages fostered by obtaining a PMA or a 510(k), analysts have compared the historical experience of fifty-four start-up device firms going these different routes between June 1995 and July 1997: twenty firms obtaining the PMA and thirty-four obtaining the 510(k). Nearly two-thirds (65%) of the PMA firms were at the development stage, compared to only 18 percent of the 510(k) firms. The average IPO market capitalization of the two sets of firms was $185 million and $144 million, respectively. In terms of market performance, the PMA firms had an average return of 37 percent by November 1999, compared to a negative average return of −9 percent for the 510(k) firms. Forty percent of the PMA firms earned positive returns, and 15 percent earned returns in excess of 100 percent – compared to only 36 percent and 6 percent of 510(k) firms.[4] Among the "winners" (firms with products that did not fail), the returns were 172 percent for the PMA firms and 137 percent for the 510(k) firms. This is not to say that the PMA alone is responsible for the higher performance; there were strong performers in both groups, based on the commonality that they enjoyed strong clinical value and/or barriers to entry. Nevertheless, the PMA route does appear to carry a performance premium.

Industry analysis

Market size

The medical device sector accounts for approximately $165 billion in worldwide revenues per year. This includes products as different as $30,000 implantable defibrillators and ten-cent syringes. The total of $165 billion in revenues is further broken down into "medical devices" at $90 billion and general commodity supplies at $75 billion. However this discussion will concentrate on the higher-valued-added products. The major categories of medical devices, organized by anatomy or function, are shown in figure 6.2. The more attractive segments have been grouped together making up $49 billion in 2003, while diagnostics and imaging have been separated, accounting for $41 billion in revenues in 2003. The remaining category, commodities/supplies, refers to drapes, gloves, gowns, syringes, and IV infusion sets.

For reasons of size, growth, and profitability the most commercially attractive segments are orthopaedics and cardiovascular. The two engines driving the brisk growth within the $16.5 billion orthopaedics segment are spine and so-called reconstructive devices, primarily hips and knees. Spinal products, used mainly in the treatment of back pain, accounted for approximately $2.8 billion in revenues in 2003 and generated high teen growth rates.

	Revenues ($ billion)	Growth rate (%)
Orthopaedics	16.5	15
Cardiovascular	16.2	24
Ophthalmology	5.7	5
General surgery	7.7	9
Neurological products	2.2	19
Urology	0.8	12
Subtotal	*49.0*	*16*
Diagnostics	22.1	4
Imaging and other	18.9	5

Figure 6.2   Medical devices markets – major categories 2003.

Source: Analyst reports, Company reports, Advamed, Business Communications Corporation.

Reconstructive products reached nearly $7 billion in 2003 and experienced midteen growth. The cardiovascular segment is currently undergoing a growth surge, as drug-coated stents and implantable electrical devices used to treat congestive heart failure have been added to the mix. Within the $16.2 billion market for cardiovascular products revenues shown in figure 6.2, stents make up approximately $3.4 billion, defibrillators $2.5 billion, congestive heart failure devices $1.6 billion, and conventional pacemakers $3.1 billion. A breakout of particular cardiovascular product groups is provided in figure 6.3 below.

Growth in the cardiovascular area has varied considerably over the last decade. Certain new, high-growth products have a revenue magnitude that is large enough to affect overall growth as they appear and pass through the product mix. Then at other times, as products mature and new offerings are either absent or not large enough, overall growth can slow to high single digits – still an enviable rate for most industry sectors. Recent years provide an example. Buoyed by the arrival of drug-coated stents and continued strong growth in congestive heart failure, growth in devices topped 20 percent in 2003.

The use of medical technology to treat neurological problems such as epilepsy, depression, Parkinson's disease, and several types of pain is particularly compelling. This segment probably accounted for over $2 billion in 2003 and had a growth rate of around 20 percent (see figure 6.2). Medtronic pioneered this field, using technology borrowed from its extensive experience in electrical devices for the heart to address several severely debilitating neurological disorders.

	Revenues ($ billion)	Growth rate (%)
Inverventional cardiology		
Stents	3.4	50
Balloon catheters	0.8	8
Other and accessories	1.2	12
Cardiac rhythm management		
Pacemakers	3.1	6
Defibrillators	2.5	12
Congestive heart failure	1.6	60
Heart surgery, valves, aneurysm, closure	2.5	17
All other	1.1	8
Total	**16.2**	**24***

Figure 6.3   Cardiovascular product detail – 2003 revenue.

Source: Analyst reports.
*Weighted average growth rate.

Structure

According to the FDA, there are more than 20,000 companies registered as medical device manufacturers worldwide.[5] However the vast majority of these companies have annual revenues of less than $5 million. The field has become increasingly dominated by larger, diversified companies such as Medtronic, Johnson & Johnson, Boston Scientific Corporation, St. Jude Medical, Guidant Corporation, Stryker Corporation, and Zimmer Medical Holdings. These monoliths have revenues measured in billions of dollars and operate across several of the broad categories mentioned above. The top ten companies in 2003 had collective revenues of nearly $60 billion, representing roughly 66 percent of total worldwide product revenues of $90 billion. Many participate in nearly every profitable segment, such as orthopaedics, cardio-vascular, urology, and general surgery. The anatomical reach requires a tremendous breadth of skills and technologies. For instance, Medtronic's spine cage group relies heavily on an extensive understanding of metallurgy and a proficiency with the anatomy of the back, just as the company's implantable defibrillator team uses its expertise in electronic chip design and a broad knowledge of the electrical aspects of the heart. These larger companies have amassed broad technical capabilities and extensive clinical intelligence, which allows them to extend their empires and to expand the scope of their activities. In some cases, this has been the result of internal product development; in most cases, however, the extension was provided by acquisition of smaller, high-growth specialty companies. The fact that the top ten companies control 66 percent of total worldwide revenues in 2003 reflects a considerably more consolidated sector than in 1990, when the top ten companies controlled only 48 percent. This topic will be discussed in greater detail later in this chapter.

Global versus US sourcing

The medical device sector is predominately American. Close to 60 percent of all medical devices consumed around the world are produced by American companies. While there are hundreds of smaller medical device companies that operate on a local basis within the industrialized countries outside of the United States, these typically make commodity-type products such as drapes, gowns, IV bags, and other surgical supplies. Figure 6.4 shows some of the largest US medical products firms. The collective revenues of these com-panies is $64.1 billion – a figure which, when compared to the worldwide

Name	Products	Revenues ($ million)	Growth rate (%)
Johnson & Johnson*	Diversified	14,914	15.6
Baxter International	Diversified	8,916	10.1
Medtronic, Inc.	Diversified	8,570	18.2
Abbott Laboratories*	Diversified	7,335	5.1
Becton Dickinson & Co.	Diversified	4,676	10.5
Guidant Corporation	Cardiovascular	3,699	17.1
Stryker Corporation	Orthopaedics	3,625	18.0
Boston Scientific Corporation	Cardiovascular	3,476	14.0
Bausch and Lomb, Inc.	Ophthalmology	2,019	10.1
St. Jude Medical	Cardiovascular	1,933	19.8
Zimmer Medical Holdings	Orthopaedics	1,901	27.0
Alcon, Inc.*	Ophthalmology	1,586	8.1
Biomet, Inc.	Orthopaedics	1,489	15.5
Total		**64,139**	**13.5**

Figure 6.4   A selection of large US medical device companies, 2003.

Source: Company published reports.
*Revenues for these companies are for medical products and are not total corporate revenues; growth is a three-year compounded, 2001 through 2003.

consumption of medical products at $165 billion, and to outside US production of around $70 billion, suggests the clear dominance of US companies.

A review of the revenue sources of a selection of major US medical device suppliers reveals that indeed the United States is the predominant supplier to the world. A full 40 percent of the revenues of these large multinationals is derived from overseas markets. A selection of the largest US-based medical device suppliers is presented in figure 6.5, showing the geographic breakdown of their 2003 revenues.

The list of companies outside the United States that make higher value, more technologically rich products is relatively short. Furthermore, these overseas companies have disproportionately larger market shares in their respective countries and are generally not important factors on a worldwide basis. Biotronik, of Germany, has a modest participation in the worldwide market for pacemakers and defibrillators. Sorin, in Italy, part of the Fiat empire, participates in the heart valve market. Japan-based Terumo is a diversified medical products company manufacturing surgical supplies, catheters, and syringes. A selection of the large medical device companies based outside of the US is listed in figure 6.6, along with estimates of 2003 revenues.

	Total revenues (million $)	US revenues ($ million)	Overseas revenues ($ million)	Overseas mix (%)
Johnson & Johnson*	14,914	8,033	6,881	46
Baxter International	8,916	5,297	3,619	41
Medtronic, Inc.	8,570	5,999	2,571	30
Abbott Laboratories*	7,335	4,437	2,898	40
Becton Dickinson & Co.	4,676	2,363	2,313	49
Guidant Corporation	3,699	2,521	1,178	32
Stryker Corporation	3,625	2,333	1,292	36
Boston Scientific Corporation	3,476	1,981	1,495	43
Bausch and Lomb, Inc.	2,019	901	1,118	55
St. Jude Medical	1,933	1,205	727	38
Zimmer Medical Holdings	1,901	1,209	692	36
Alcon, Inc.*	1,586	861	725	46
Biomet, Inc.	1,489	1,057	432	29
Total	**64,139**	**38,198**	**25,942**	**40**

Figure 6.5   US medical device companies – overseas revenue mix, 2003.

Source: Company reports.

*Revenues for these companies are for medical products and are not total corporate revenues.

Co. Name	Location	Principal category	Revenue range ($ million)
Biotronik	Germany	Pacers, defibs	400–600
Terumo	Japan	Syringes, catheters	1,250–1,750
Sorin	Italy	Heart valves	750–1,000
Smith & Nephew	London	Orthopaedics	2,000
Fresenius	Germany	Dialysis	1,500–2,000
Synthes-Stratech		Orthopaedics	1,300
Disetronic	Switzerland	Diabetes supplies	250

Figure 6.6   Selected non-US medical device companies.

The necessary ingredients for the development of medical device companies – financial and intellectual capital, technological know-how, a supportive regulatory environment – exist throughout most of the industrialized world. It is curious, then, that the US dominates the field. Why were American entrepreneurs such as Earl Bakken (founder of Medtronic) and John Abele and Peter Nicholas (founders of Boston

Scientific) so quick to borrow from the rich outpouring of technologies from other industries and apply it to the healthcare field?[6] If anything, the regulatory environment in Europe is substantially less difficult than that in the United States. Also, every country on every continent has essentially equivalent disease prevalences, with some exceptions due to diet and genetic predisposition. Possible explanations for the national disparity are: a more specialist-dominated medical profession in the US, with a sophisticated and supportive clinical infrastructure; higher consumer demand for innovative products in the US and a reimbursement system that permits such access to them; the presence/absence of national health insurance and government rationing; social acceptance of intervening in the disease process versus fatalism in certain societies; a greater profit motive in the US owing to the structure of its system; and impediments and rigidities within European and/or Asian companies that hamper innovation. Some of these explanations are explored below.

Medtronic sells pacemakers to over 120 countries around the globe. Its fastest growing new markets include China, the Middle East, and Eastern Europe. Slowing the adoption of medical technology in certain less-developed countries has been a lack of a sophisticated clinical infrastructure and medical professionals. This is one of many reasons why medical technology consumption in some countries lags behind that of the US. However, certain technologies have been aimed at bypassing these inadequate infrastructures. Examples include pacemakers that come from the factory with fixed settings and attached lead wires that do not need to be programmed by highly trained physicians assisted by sales representatives, and minimally invasive surgical products that are used in easily constructed outpatient clinics instead of hospital operating rooms. This same leapfrog phenomenon drove an accelerated use of cellular phones in developing countries that lacked "copper wire" infrastructure. The extent to which medical technology can reach such less-developed countries points to the power of a good idea and to the remarkable adaptability and strength of the sector.

America is a heavy net exporter of medical products – it has been estimated that the current positive trade balance is $5–10 billion.[7] One source suggests that between 1985 and 2000 the medical products sector generated a cumulative positive trade balance of $60 billion.[8] Figure 6.7 shows the source and destination (consumption) of medical products by geographic region. The first column shows that US companies earned product revenues totaling $95 billion, or close to 60 percent of the total produced on a worldwide basis. The first row shows the US consumed $70 billion of all medical products, or

	Sources (read down)			Population (million)	Consumption per capita per year ($)
	US	OUS	**Total**		
Consumed (read across)					
US	65	5	**70**	288	243
OUS	30	65	**95**	5,940	16
Total	**95**	**70**	**165**	6,228	26

Figure 6.7   Sources and consumption of medical products, US and OUS, for 2003.

Source: Revenues – AdvaMed (Advanced Medical Technology Association); Lewin Group population statistics: US Census Bureau.

42 percent of this $70 billion. The vast majority, $65 billion, was "self-sourced" in the US, suggesting that the US is essentially self-sufficient.

Figure 6.7 also points to the rates of consumption of medical technology per capita per year. The United States has an outsized appetite for medical technology. The rate of US consumption at approximately $240 per person per year is around fifteen times that of the rest of the world, which consumes only $16 per capita, the price that Americans pay for a week of cappuccinos.

Implantable defibrillators illustrate the geographic disparities in medical technology utilization. Defibrillators are cigarette pack-sized electrical devices that continuously monitor a patient's heart and deliver a life-saving shock when needed. Most defibrillators now also provide several pacing stimulation modes. In other words, these devices are truly multifunctional, acting both as conventional pacemakers and as high-energy shocking defibrillators. Defibrillators cost approximately $25,000 and can be implanted on an outpatient basis in just a few hours. It has been established through scores of rigorous clinical studies that they could save hundreds of thousands and even millions of lives each year.[9] In the US alone, approximately 125,000 defibrillators (including defibrillators with congestive heart failure) were implanted in 2003. This is still only a fraction of a potential patient pool, which has been estimated at anywhere from between 500,000 to 1,100,000, representing a penetration rate of 10–25 percent.[10] The devices are expensive and require an electrophysiology laboratory for proper installation. Many countries simply do not have the necessary clinical infrastructure, and many of those that do may not have the fiscal resources. In 2003 the United States paid some $5 billion to bring this important life-saving technology to its citizens. This sum would represent one-quarter of Bolivia's GDP.[11] There are roughly 1,200 electrophysiology labs in the US and over 2,000 qualified implanting physicians. In Spain,

	US	Japan	Germany	France	UK
Defibrillators	262	10	87	18	18
Pacemakers	966	329	963	911	426
Coronary stents	4,265	994	2,500	2,000	1,000
Beating heart surgery	360	71	69	88	75
Spinal implants	760	213	366	637	174
Insulin pumps	153	2	79	67	14

Figure 6.8   Implant and usage rates per million population.

Source: Medtronic, Inc.

for example, there are 48 electrophysiology labs and roughly 85 electrophysiol-ogists. Figure 6.8 shows the defibrillator implantation rates per million popula-tion across the world. Note that the US installed 262 defibrillators per million people, a rate that is twenty-six times that of Japan and fourteen times that of France. Figure 6.8 also shows the implant rates or usage rates for a variety of other medical technology products.

Reviewing implants or usage rates points to interesting differences between products that appear to reflect the infrastructure and sophistication dis-parities across the world mentioned above. Certainly, the US leads every country in the figure, but note the differences between the more complex products that require an extensive infrastructure and those products such as stents that are simple to use and do not require nearly the same degree of capital equipment burdened infrastructure. Indeed, the US used 4,265 stents per million people, 1.7 times the usage in Germany, a much closer compar-ison than implantable defibrillators, a product type that the US used at three times the rate of the Germans. This same comparison applies to many of the countries shown. Note that France implanted only eighteen defibrillators per million, fourteen times fewer than the US. Not only does this reflect the differences in infrastructure and clinical sophistication, but also the capacity and willingness to pay. Defibrillators are the most expensive medical product shown in the figure, and are perhaps as much as ten to fifteen times more expensive than stents.

Unique and defining characteristics of medical devices

In the field of economics, especially supply, demand, and pricing theories, it is assumed implicitly that consumers of goods and services also pay for those goods and services. This is central to the study of economics. As the price of a good rises, the demand falls. The medical technology field is largely free of these laws: the demand for medical technology is either exceedingly inelastic (it does not depend on price) or is simply not subject to these principles. Additionally, economic theory suggests that "above average profits" are not sustainable, as competition will enter and drive down prices, narrowing margins and reducing profits. Here again the medical products sector does not appear to be subject to this general rule. Companies such as Johnson & Johnson and Medtronic have enjoyed above average profits, not only for several years but for several decades. Growth in nearly every other industry sector slows as markets become mature and saturated. However, in medical products, growth is sustainable because it is driven by general demographic trends, the continued prevalence of diseases, and the fact that there is a near infinite capacity for absorbing medical technology within the practice of medicine. In this section I will discuss some of the factors that make the medical device sector so different.

Separation of consumers, customers, and payers

One important economic feature of the medical technology sector and the US healthcare industry in general, but one that is quite rare in other industries, is the fact that the consumers of the products and the parties that buy and pay for these products are three distinctly different constituencies. The parties are either completely separate or only loosely affiliated; incentives are certainly not aligned. Physicians, such as interventional cardiologists, make the clinical decision to perform a procedure such as a balloon angioplasty and stent implantation, as well as the purchase decision to order the specific product and equipment needed for a procedure.[12] The physician is thus the *buyer* and the *customer*. The average cost for this procedure is approximately $9,000, comprising 4,000–6,000 dollars of equipment and the remainder for labor. The principal decision maker, the cardiologist, does not pay for the procedure and in many cases has virtually no comprehension of the product costs involved. The patient, as *consumer* of the products and services, has little say in the decision to perform the procedure and even less say in the brand and type of hardware selected.

That brings us to the *payer* for the procedure: the private insurance company or the federal Medicare payment system. While these payers have made efforts to at least monitor or in some cases adjudicate the triaging of patients into various procedures through such methods as preapproval requirements, these have had little effect. That these parties are separated from the buyers/customers and consumers and have motivations that are not only unaligned but are often directly opposed, has profound implications on the marketing tactics and price behavior of the firms operating in the medical device sector. In short, this separation between buyers/customers, consumers, and payers allows a degree of pricing freedom that is truly unusual. It is for this and other reasons that competitive pricing is a rare exception. Practitioners are motivated to provide the best care for patients and are therefore driven to select the best performing products irrespective of price. Patients are incapable of making informed decisions about both the necessity of various procedures and the selection of brands and types of hardware. Efforts on the part of the payers to limit, constrain, or group purchase (volume discount) have been largely ineffective.

This aspect of the medical device sector produces several uncommon economic benefits, including favorable pricing (covered below) and efficient channels (covered later), both of which result in high profitability. Pricing trends have been positive for decades, and there is nothing to suggest that there will be any dramatic changes in the foreseeable future. In contrast to the pharmaceutical sector, which is currently under heavy policy pressure over prices, the medical device sector is generally small enough to fly under the radar of political activist groups and policy makers. Expenditures on devices are also buried in the figures for hospital costs, and thus are not easily discerned or tracked. Further, it should be noted that medical devices by their nature are heterogeneous and resistant to administered prices. For example, implantable defibrillators and stents are bristling with features and technologies, making comparisons between brands impossible: prices vary by locations, sizes of products, feature sets, and a host of other aspects.

By contrast, the pharmaceutical sector is a more attractive target. It is larger ($492 billion versus $165 billion), prices are well understood, and products are homogeneous and relatively "featureless." Pfizer's Lipitor, the widely used statin used to lower cholesterol, can be compared to other statins on the market: doses are comparable, prices can be monitored, and restrictions can be readily imposed.

The powerful economics of clinical needs

Another feature that shapes the medical products price–consumption situation is the inestimable force of the clinical need. It perhaps goes without saying that the stunning success of the medical device sector has been fueled in large part by the tremendous need for the products that it produces. The most successful and highest revenue-generating products, such as defibrillators ($2.5 billion per year), stents ($3.4 billion per year), and even less complex products such as prepackaged sutures ($2.6 billion per year), all fulfill a clinical need and serve as useful tools that enable physicians to produce important clinical outcomes. When medical products are developed that "add value" within the clinical setting by saving time, changing outcomes, providing safety, and increasing utility, then those products will be demanded and successful business enterprises can be built around them.

Devices also play an important role in the value chain and cost continuum of care. As a patient progresses through this continuum (diagnosis, work-up, treatment), expenses stemming from labor fees and "hotel" aspects climb. By the time the patient reaches the cardiac catheterization lab, where interventional cardiology procedures are conducted, they have already consumed thousands of dollars of service fees. In the lab itself, the labor rate is truly prodigious: several technicians assist the cardiologist and monitor and record vital signs. Added to this is the compensation for the cardiologist and cardiology fellow. A well-paid anesthesiologist is also present, even though the patient is not given a general anesthetic. In addition, there is a staggeringly expensive set of capital equipment deployed: million-dollar fluoroscopes and banks of monitors sum to a sizeable financial rental cost. The cost per minute in a cath lab during a procedure is perhaps as high as $500. With this in mind, it is understandable that there would be significant demand for a medical device that would save time in such a setting or improve the outcome of such procedures. This situation also allows medical device makers to arrive at prices that are associated with the savings they generate or the outcomes they produce rather than a cost basis. Companies that market products on a performance basis, unshackled from cost-based pricing, can enjoy high gross margins and above-average profits.

Such pricing freedom was recently displayed in the market for coronary stents (the tiny wire mesh tubes used to prop open vessels). The stent market has undergone a *gestalt* shift to an improved version of an older stent technology. Conventional stents work quite well; over 1.2 million stents were implanted in the US in 2002 However, vessels containing stents often reclog, resulting in costly return visits to the cath lab for follow-on procedures. A solution to this problem sprang from the fertile laboratories within the large device companies. It was proposed that coating these wire mesh stent tubes with antiinflammatory drugs could reduce or eliminate the reclogging problem. Animal and human studies showed dramatic results and the first product, one from Johnson & Johnson, received FDA approval in early 2003. Conventional, "bare-metal" stents cost roughly $1,000 each. How would the new, improved stents be priced? Certainly a premium could be expected. In fact the pricing calculus was straightforward. The elimination of a repeat cath lab visit would save roughly $10,000 in expenses. If the rate at which the reclogs occurred was in the order of 33 percent (i.e., one-third of all patients made return visits), then the cost that this represents is (0.33) x $10,000, or $3,300 imputed to each patient. It would appear that hospitals, physician buyers, and payers would place a high value on a product that promised to eliminate or significantly reduce this expensive repeat procedure. Indeed, the first J&J drug-coated stent was priced at a significant premium to the conventional bare metal version. In fact, it bore a price that was roughly equivalent to this "probability-based" cost of a return visit. Johnson & Johnson launched its "Cypher" drug-eluting stent in March 2003 priced $3,200, a price that incidently had no connection whatsoever to its cost.

Regarding the issue of cost, it is impossible for outsiders, peering into a company's financial statements, to ascertain the magnitude of the additional production cost associated with painting the drug onto these wire mesh tubes. However, a review of the arrangements with the drug- and polymer-coating companies, including Wyeth, Angiotech Pharmaceuticals, and Surmodics, combined with some insight into the production methods involved, would suggest that this additional cost is roughly $225 per stent. (The payments made to these companies listed above probably represent only a portion of the total additional costs and may account for anywhere from $75 to $175 per stent.) It is clear, then, that the stent companies that provided this improvement benefited handsomely. The innovation caused an abrupt boost to what were already very attractive gross and operating margins carried by stents.

This is the magic of medical technology. The economic factors are forceful. Procedures and medical personnel are extraordinarily expensive. When a device can force a change in practice, save time, or reduce repeat procedures, it unleashes economic value at the critical site, the center of the cost-producing activity, and is paid accordingly. Figure 6.9 shows gross and operating profit margins for both conventional and drug-coated stents based on the operating results of J&J and Boston Scientific.

As the figure suggests, the operating margins associated with drug-eluting stents could be more than 1.7 times those of the bare metal versions – 68 percent versus 38 percent for bare metal. The comparison of the absolute dollars of profit generated is even more dramatic: coated stents may produce profits in the order of $2,075 per stent, more than five times that of the bare metal type. It is understandable, then, that the stocks of companies such as

	Bare metal stent	Drug-eluting stent
Average price ($)	1,050	3,050
Estimated cost of goods	150	375
Estimated Gross Margin (%)	86	88
Expenses – SG&A and R&D ($)	500	600
Estimated operating margin (%)	38	68
Estimated operating profit ($)	400	2,075

Figure 6.9   Stent margin analysis comparing bare metal with drug-eluting.

Source: Analysts reports, company financial reports.

	Product type	Geography	No. of reps	Revenue ($ million)	Revenue per rep ($)
Boston Scientific	All types	Worldwide	2,500	3,476	1,390,400
St. Jude Medical	Pacers/defibs	US	800	1,365	1,706,515
	Heart valves	US	100	115	1,150,000

Figure 6.10   Direct sales personnel for selected product segments and geographies.

Medtronic, Boston Scientific and Guidant are extremely sensitive to the timing and performance of each company's drug-coated stent activities. In fact, hundreds of millions in market value were lost and gained in Guidant common stock associated with the company's various missteps and successes in drug-eluting stents.[13]

Channels – direct selling

The larger, broad-based medical technology companies have well-developed direct sales forces. The majority of their sales representatives are salaried employees. The large market segments such as electrophysiology (defibrillators and pacemakers) and interventional cardiology are served by as many as 5,000 representatives, with each major participating company fielding a sales team that is roughly proportional to its market share in any particular category. Figure 6.10 shows sales force statistics for a few of the larger markets. The figure suggests that the revenue generated per "sales rep" is more than one million dollars. These statistics also underscore the tremendous selling efficiencies available within the electrophysiology space: St. Jude pacemaker/defibrillator representatives produce an eye-popping $1.7 million per sales rep per year. By way of background, pacemakers are wristwatch-sized devices that are used to speed up slow or erratic hearts, causing them to beat regularly. The more powerful, "high voltage" defibrillators, about the size of a woman's make-up box, monitor cardiac rhythms and deliver therapy jolts capable of restarting runaway hearts.

The sales forces thus play a vital role in the delivery and transfer of medical technology to the clinic. Three important functions served by these sales teams are described below.

Franchise building

A company relies on its sales force to establish and build its franchise – that is, its image and brand name. No hucksters these sales reps, indeed they are highly skilled, extensively trained medical experts that develop a close and even collegial relationship with their physician buyers/customers. Often the sales personnel will "scrub-in" and accompany the physician in medical or surgical procedures. Social involvement, sports outings, and even shared vacation holidays are not uncommon. It is no wonder, then, that doctors' views and perceptions of these companies is inextricably bound to their respective representatives. A company is known by its sales reps. So critical is the role of the sales rep in the selling dynamic that it is customary for companies to "purchase" market share by hiring an established and well-regarded sales rep in a certain territory. Sales reps hold enough sway over customers that it is possible to cause a shift in clinical practice to another brand simply by virtue of a sales rep switching allegiance to a new manufacturer. This practice occurs across many of the device specialties, but is especially common within the pacemaker and defibrillator market. Pacemaker companies such as Medtronic, Guidant, and St. Jude can dramatically increase sales in a region by hiring a sales rep or team of sales reps from one of its competitors. The economics are straightforward: an established representative is paid $250,000–$650,000 per year but may generate well over one million dollars in additional revenues. Given that these sales dollars carry 30 percent-plus operating profits, the expenditures incurred in acquiring sales personnel and the attendant market share are well worth it.

Education

The selling process for most medical products, especially for those that are technologically complex, has evolved into a true information-sharing interaction. The expression "consultative selling" is often used. The majority of doctors, at least those over the age of 35, were not exposed to today's technologies during their medical training and require instructions to correctly deploy new products. While clinicians certainly play a role in the development process, most new products and procedures are essentially invented by companies and thus require trained representatives to explain their use. As an example, pacemakers and defibrillators are installed into patients with dozens of "blank" features that must be programmed in situ, through the skin, to the particular needs of the patient. This is done with a wand held over the patient's chest connected to a dedicated laptop computer with menu-driven commands. This daunting task is usually undertaken by the physician with the sales rep close at hand serving as a guide. The reliance on the sales rep for education is exacerbated by the rapid roll-out of new products. In most segments, products are overhauled, improved, or updated on an annual basis. Furthermore, most physicians tend to spread their product selection across two or three suppliers. It is difficult enough to remain familiar with one company's model changes, but nearly impossible to be versed and trained on the product upgrades that flow from two, three, or more companies. Consequently, doctors simply must rely on the representatives for education.

Feedback – playback

Another important aspect of the field sales force is the playback of information from the clinic to the manufacturer. The sales reps, as the company's "eyes and ears," continually monitor the activities of their physician buyers/ customers and feed this information back to their product development groups. The commissioned sales rep has a direct financial incentive to increase sales. With this in mind, he/she actively solicits ideas from the clinic and then encourages his/her company to translate these ideas into products that he/she can then sell. Sales reps have no direct line reporting responsibility to R&D departments or programs within companies, and certainly do not directly administer them. However, they carry total compensation packages that are on a par with the highest-paid executives and do wield considerable power within these companies.

The orthopaedics segment is one exception to this direct selling approach. Orthopaedics companies generally use distributor networks, most of which are "inventory-taking" distributors. These small regional companies generally have half a dozen agents and carry inventories, including instrumentation, worth several million dollars. In most cases, the distributors are prohibited by the manufacturers from distributing competitors' products. However, distributors will carry product lines from other companies as long as they do not directly overlap. For instance, a distributor may carry hips and knees exclusively from Biomet but may carry casting materials from Johnson & Johnson. The manufacturers cannot exercise the same kind of control over distributors as they do over direct sales forces. Yet many of the successful practices listed above in connection with direct sales forces are also adopted by these distributors. Brand, franchise, and image-building are nearly as important to distributors, since their success is linked to the acceptance of the products they distribute. The way in which this aspect may differ in the case of distributors is the tendency on their part to promote the image and staying power of the distributors as opposed to the manufacturer. The task of educating physicians regarding product features is borne by the distributor in much the same way as it is by direct sales forces. It would appear that one important difference between direct reps and distributors comes in the category of the feedback of clinical information. Orthopaedic manufacturers make every effort to extract this critical clinical information from distributors, but the channel is probably not as efficient, fast, or effective as that between a direct sales force and their marketing and development groups.

Selling efficiencies

In contrast to most markets or industries, medical products are not purchased by consumers. Instead, they are purchased (selected) by a limited number of physicians that use the products in treating patients. Hip implants are installed in hundreds of thousands of patients in the United States each year, yet there are only 17,000 orthopaedic surgeons that perform the procedures. Similarly, there are roughly 1.5 million stents implanted each year, yet only 14,000 interventional cardiologists that make brand selections. The segment comprised of electrical devices (pacemakers and defibrillators) presents an extremely concentrated and therefore efficient market: there are roughly 550 electrophysiologists (EPs) that make brand choices for the $2.1 billion worth of defibrillators that get implanted each year in the US. Simple arithmetic suggests that each EP on average controls nearly four million dollars of defibrillators each year. If the other products used and selected by the EP are added, this product control quotient would rise to over five million dollars per year. This suggests that adding a single physician to a company's customer base could add several million dollars in revenues per year.

The concentration of buyers/customers and the associated channel efficiencies have implications for the business models of participating companies. Targeted (focused) selling campaigns, primarily carried out by the direct sales

	Medtronic[1]	Boston Scientific	Guidant	St. Jude Medical
Revenues ($ million)	9,087	3,476	3,699	1,933
SG&A ($ million)	2,801	1,171	1,199	632
Marketing expenses ($ million)	**525**	**233**	**300**	**158**
As percentage of SG&A	19	20	25	25
As percentage of revenues	6	7	8	8

Figure 6.11 Marketing expenses for selected manufacturers in 2003.

Source: Company published results and analyst's estimates.
[1]Medtronic Tables are for fiscal 2004, which ended April 2004.

forces mentioned above, are relatively inexpensive and quite effective. It is not necessary for companies to engage in inefficient and exceedingly expensive appeals to the final recipients (patients) of the medical technology. As a consequence, medical device companies can limit their selling expenses and redirect a greater portion of revenues to R&D in order to develop new products and procedures – or, in fact, can enjoy astonishingly high operating margins. Figure 6.11 shows selling general and administrative (SG&A) expenses and the break-out of marketing and selling expenses for a selection of medical device companies. The figure reveals the compelling channel efficiencies that are possible within the medical products sector: selling/marketing expenses are less than 10 percent of total revenues. Not only does this marketing efficiency allow companies to fund product development, which in turn drives growth, it also provides for higher profit margins. Indeed, the typical rates of profit generation – averaging around 25–30 percent on an operating basis – stand above those of all other segments within healthcare and across all industries as well.

Figure 6.12 shows the typical percentages for production and operating expenses – cost of goods (COGS), SG&A, and R&D – for a representative sample of device companies – Medtronic, Boston Scientific, St. Jude Medical, Guidant, Stryker and Zimmer – as well as a simple arithmetic average of these expense percentages. These rates of profit generation are truly unusual. The *net* margin (a figure that is burdened with other expenses and taxes) for the device companies was 17.3 percent, a level that is considerably higher than even the *operating profit* margins for most industry sectors, even those considered attractive and which have moderate or high growth. In fact, many industry

	Medtronic[1]	Boston Scientific	St. Jude Medical	Guidant	Zimmer	Stryker	Average
Revenues							
($ million)	9,087	3,476	1,933	3,699	1,901	3,625	
COGS							
($ million)	2,253	961	603	904	516	1,312	
Gross margin (%)	75.2	72.4	68.8	75.6	72.8	63.8	71.4
SG&A							
($ million)	2,801	1,171	632	1,199	738	1,416	
As percentage of revenues	30.8	33.7	32.7	32.4	38.8	39.1	34.6
R&D							
($ million)	852	452	241	518	106	180	
As percentage of revenues	9.4	13.0	12.5	14.0	5.6	5.0	9.9
Other expenses							
($ million)	–	143		85	–		
Operating profit							
($ million)	3,181	749	456	1,078	542	717	
Operating margin (%)	35.0	21.5	23.6	29.1	28.5	19.8	26.3
Net income							
($ million)	1,959	472	339	764	346	454	
Net margin (%)	21.6	13.6	17.6	20.7	18.2	12.5	17.3

Figure 6.12 Operating expenses – averages and selected companies, 2003.
Source: Company published reports.
[1]Medtronic's Tables are for fiscal year 2004, which ended April 2004.

sectors such as retailers or industrial supplies have *gross margins* that are on a par with the *net* margins of the device companies. Most industrial corporations have net margins that are low single digits; double-digit rates are rare. The high-teen rate shown here for medical device companies is exceptional.

Limited consumerism

In most sectors of the economy extraordinary profits are not sustainable: competition enters, prices fall, and margins are constrained. It would appear that the medical device sector is an exception and that high profit margins are indeed sustainable. The chief reason for this has to do with the efficiency of the selling channels and the unusual separation between buyer/customer (the physician) and consumer (the patient). Other aspects of high-profit generation – such as prices, sales volume, sales growth, and manufacturing expenses – may not be sustained. But the portion of profitability that stems from the efficient selling channels is durable and will persist for the foreseeable future. Central to the thesis of efficient channels is the fact that consumers do not need to be advertised to (no mass merchandising) and that physician promotion and education is efficient and relatively inexpensive. This is based on what seems to be an immutable and fundamental concept: patients cannot implant their own knees or pacemakers or stents. Physicians are critical inter-mediaries in the use of nearly all important medical technology products. Patients simply do not have the training or knowledge to make informed decisions about the brands and types of products that will be used on them and in them. Furthermore, patients cannot ultimately deploy or use the medical device. We have entered a new age of raised skepticism of doctors and medical practice; patients attempt to educate themselves on their ailments and engage in debate and discussion with physicians about their course of treatment. However, even in this new era, patients willingly give doctors free reign to choose the brands of pacemakers, stents, and defibrillators and to make procedure choices in the fields of cardiology, orthopaedics, and surgery.

A comparison with the pharmaceutical sector helps to illustrate this point. The pharmaceutical sector has been viewed as attractive, with its high rates of profit and good "visibility" (i.e., predictable and reliable future sales and earnings trajectories). For decades the large pharmaceutical companies were Wall Street favorites and consequently were accorded the highest price-to-earnings (P/E) ratios in healthcare. In recent years, however, concerns over government involvement that could affect prices and use of drugs, along with the ebbing new product pipeline, have served to reduce the attractiveness of these

	Current PE	PE in 9/99		Current PE	PE in 9/99
Pfizer	13.4	35.4	Zimmer	27.1	32.5
Bristol Myers	17.2	28.9	Medtronic	22.4	36.4
Eli Lilly	20.2	24.5	St. Jude Medical	26.4	17.2
Merck	13.7	23.5	Becton Dickinson	18.1	17.1
Schering	83.5	30.4	Boston Scientific	17.5	23.5
median	**17.2**	**28.9**		**22.4**	**23.5**

Figure 6.13 Price to earnings ratios – comparisons between pharmaceuticals and medical products companies.

Note: PE are forward-looking (on next year's earnings per share).

once loved companies. Figure 6.13 compares the current and past P/E ratios of five large US pharmaceutical companies with those of five large medical products companies. Notice that the capital markets trimmed over ten multiple points from pharmaceutical companies, to a relatively low figure of 17.2. The P/E associated with medical products companies dropped only a modest amount, easing from 23.5 to 22.4.

In addition to concerns over pricing and pipeline, there is another, potentially even more damaging problem faced by drug companies: direct to consumer (DTC) advertising. For now, DTC expenditures are only minuscule relative to total selling and administrative costs, and certainly have not constrained profit margins. However, these advertising budgets have risen dramatically from a small base, will probably continue to comprise an increasing portion of the SG&A expenses, and will chip away at pharmaceutical companies' already constrained profit margins.

Will the profit structure of pharmaceutical companies deteriorate over time to the point of resembling that of consumer products companies such as Proctor&Gamble and Gillette? Are the proud and once attractive pharmaceutical companies really consumer products companies masquerading as high-tech growth vehicles? If there is a trend in this direction, it would appear to be a slow one. That prescriptions are required for most pharmaceutical agents serves to separate the pharmaceutical sector from the broader consumer products industry. Prescriptions allow for the same sort of efficient marketing channel that benefits the medical device sector. Pharmaceutical companies can restrict their advertising and selling efforts primarily to professionals (physicians). Nevertheless, this regulatory barrier, based on the somewhat arbitrary requirement for a note from one's doctor, may not be durable. Over time, patients will become more and more empowered to choose among pharmaceutical offerings, will increasingly self-medicate and, in so doing, will draw an ever-increasing portion of the advertising expenditures. An example is the extensive DTC advertising campaigns waged by the three makers of erectile dysfunction medications: Pfizer, Eli Lilly, and Bayer for Viagra, Cialis, and Levitra, respectively. Access to these powerful drugs is gained only through prescriptions from physicians. Companies, however, have realized the importance of going beyond physicians, to make appeals directly to end consumers in order to (1) raise awareness and stimulate usage of the overall category, and (2) develop a brand preference among consumers that will can be transferred to scriptwriting physicians.

Analysts contend that the medical device sector is safe from this phenomenon affecting the pharmaceutical sector, that is, the downward shift toward a consumer products model. The fundamental difference is that drugs can be readily self-administered by consumers, while medical technology cannot. This "channel efficiency" is just one of many attractive attributes of the medical device sector that confer sustainable profitability. While it is relatively easy to imagine the transformation of the pharmaceutical sector into a consumer products industry, it is nearly impossible to conceive of the medical device sector shifting to consumer brand awareness and self-implantation.[14]

Technologies

As technologies used in medical products have improved and advanced, the role of these products within the delivery of healthcare has changed dramatically. Products have infiltrated nearly all aspects of the practice of medicine; a physician scarcely interacts with a patient without relying on some product or technology generated by the medical device sector. The success of these products in the field is based on a handful of important technologies, which will be discussed below. While the technologies have developed and matured, the companies themselves have also made tremendous progress in the way in which they marshal and deploy them. Within the hundreds of technologies that are used within the medical field today, the discussion that follows is limited to the handful that have exerted the greatest impact.

Electronics

Microprocessors have revolutionized medical practice. They are used extensively in both implanted devices and external products and equipment. Most of the advances in medical products made possible by microelectronics have paralleled those in other fields. Chips (integrated circuits) confer an increase in functions, greater automation, and of course reduced size, attributes that were a natural consequence of the pervasive sweep of microprocessors and electronics over the last few decades. However, there have been some developments in medical products in which microprocessors represent a truly enabling technology. One that is especially important from both a clinical and commercial point of view is the category of implanted electrical stimulation products: pacemakers and defibrillators. These products are imbued with decision-making powers that allow the device to respond to the ever-changing "weather pattern" of the heart's electrical activities and then respond, when necessary, with one of several different electrical therapies. The device's information-processing capabilities are staggering, and are well beyond the abilities of even the most highly trained and quick-witted physician. The human brain simply cannot synthesize the megabyte stream of information presented by a malfunctioning heart and then quickly decide on, and deliver, a suitable course of electrical therapy within the five to fifteen second time interval during which a microprocessor and charging capacitors can respond. In this way the microprocessor is enabling; the implantable defibrillator can perform functions that humans simply cannot. Not only do patients benefit by having what is essentially a "live-in" electrophysiologist, an electronic sentinel that never sleeps, they also get a function or capability that is well beyond the human limitations of even the most capable physician. Figures 6.14 and 6.15 show the dramatic increase in computing power possessed by successive generations (models) of Medtronic's implantable defibrillators over the last ten years: PCD, Jewel, uJewel (or MicroJewel), and so on.[15]

Certainly these capabilities were enabled by the miniaturized chips housed within the electrical stimulation devices. But raw computing power is of no use without the clinical intelligence that was embedded in the microprocessors. Credit must be given to the development of the expert systems, the sophisticated algorithms that were programmed into the devices that allowed them to act as superhuman physicians. The combination is awe-inspiring. The high-capacity devices provide a tableau onto which can be written the collective wisdom of decades of clinical experience across thousands of doctors and patients. Under the old paradigm a clinician could respond to an incoming patient situation with a personal algorithm that, while well intentioned, was quite limited in scope. The physician's knowledge base was comprised of personal experience with perhaps a dozen similar patients as well as best recollection of the findings of several dozen papers. Even then, the physician's processing and response could not be accomplished within the seconds that it takes a computer to respond. Compare this to the way the

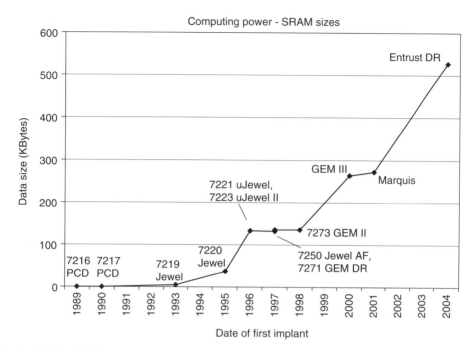

Figure 6.14 Implantable defibrillator – Medtronic's models PCD through Entrust.

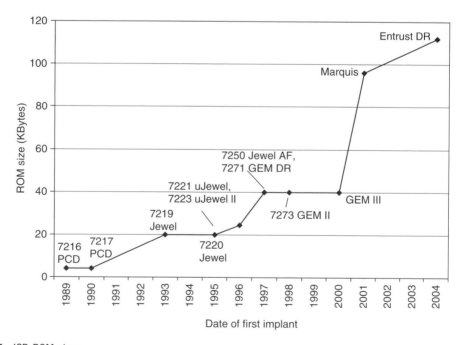

Figure 6.15 ICD ROM sizes.

"expert systems" are constructed within implanted cardiac devices. Teams of engineers and physicians can distill down the results from tens of thousands of patients, poll thousands of doctors to incorporate their "best practices," and embed them into matchbox-sized devices.

It is for this reason that this particular technological development is so important. Most other technologies and products may add value to the physician performing the procedure, they may help improve outcomes, cause less injury, or allow a faster recovery. Nearly all successful medical technologies aid doctors in their practice of medicine. However, the electronics in implanted cardiovascular devices are not just aids to doctors but essentially take on the role of the doctor.

The ensuing commercial rewards have proven to be prodigious. In 2003 those select few companies, such as Medtronic, Guidant and St. Jude, that were capable of providing this technology generated close to $7 billion from the sale of implantable defibrillators and pacemakers. Profits are also sizeable: the devices typically carry 30–35 percent operating margins. As the revolution in the practice of medicine continues – that is, the use of implanted devices to essentially carry out diagnosis and treatment that was once the exclusive province of the physician – so the companies that possess this technology may become all the more valuable and perhaps increase their already high financial ratios (price to earnings and times sales).[16]

Materials sciences

Another set of technologies that has played a significant role in recent advances in medical products is best described as materials sciences. Often overlooked because they are so broad and subtle, the developments in such areas as polymer chemistry, metallurgy, and coatings have been responsible for many important new products. The $5.4 billion interventional cardiology market (balloon angioplasty catheters, stents, and other catheters and accessories in 2003) owes its success in large part to polymer chemistry. Advances in plastics technology has allowed the manufacture of excruciatingly small catheters imbued with unusual mechanical and material characteristics. These vermicelli spaghetti-sized catheters are capable of being threaded into a patient's heart from an access point in the thigh. A tiny balloon, itself a product of sophisticated plastics technology, is located at the far end of the catheter and is inflated to open up the clogged artery. The degree to which these supple catheters have good performance in terms of maneuverability and precise control is in large part dependent on materials science, e.g., polymer formulations and extrusion manufacturing techniques.

More recently, metal mesh stents have been loaded onto these catheter conveyances to be deployed within the distant vessels. Developments in metallurgy and metal fabricating techniques have driven improvements in the performance of extremely flexible, very fine gauge wire mesh tubes. A wide variety of metals, and polymers for that matter, have been used in the construction of stents: stainless steel, cobalt, and titanium to name but a few.

Materials sciences have also shaped developments in orthopaedics. Considering the demands placed on man-made devices, it is understandable that the polymers, metals, and ceramics used in their construction are of critical importance. For instance, a knee sustains up to 750 pounds of force during a simple walk upstairs. Artificial hips and knees are expected to hold up under the wear and tear of several decades. Remember also that the body is an extremely corrosive environment for most synthetic materials.

Technological advances in orthopaedics are numerous. Scientists have found ways of compacting standard plastics-making – what is referred to as "high-density" polyethylene – that presents a nearly frictionless rubbing surface and is highly wear-resistant. Additionally, metals such as cobalt chromium and stainless steel are coated with a bone-like substance called hydroxy-apatite that induces native bone to be knitted together with the implanted device. In fact it was a revolution in materials science that prompted the recent upheaval and growth spurt in the $16.5 billion orthopaedics segment. Ceramics have become the preferred material for hip joints. While somewhat counterintuitive, it turns out that a ceramic ball moving within a ceramic cup (so called "ceramic-on-ceramic") has a wear resistance and performance that is superior to traditional metal-on-plastic combinations.

Advances in materials sciences have allowed the fabrication of implants that perfectly match the "Young's modulus" (a measure of stiffness) of native bone. This is critical to the long-term success of an implant. Conventional metal implants are too stiff and tend to "stress shield" the natural bone, causing it to atrophy and pull away from the implant.[17]

Beyond orthopaedics and cardiology, materials sciences have played a role in nearly every other medical device advancement during the past few decades; in many cases, their role has been central. Such advances include:

- lubricious coatings on the exceedingly fine gauge catheters that are slipped into the convoluted vessels of the brain in order to fix cerebral hemorrhages
- polymers from which dialysis filters are constructed that allow the fast exchange of toxins such as urea from the blood, approximating the efficiency of our kidneys
- lead wires that sense the subtle electrical weather patterns of the heart

- batteries and capacitors that power the many implanted devices, which are like sophisticated chemistry experiments that balance formulations of such substances as lithim and iodide, tantalum, aluminum oxide in just the right proportions in order to extend life of the devices and to provide life-saving electrical jolts
- pyrolytic carbon, a wonder of materials science that is extremely durable and stubbornly resists blood clotting, which is used in the construction of mechanical heart valves.

Drug–device convergence

The notion of combining the therapeutic power of pharmaceutical agents with the delivery capabilities and brute force effectiveness of medical devices has tantalized clinicians and the healthcare industry for decades. Why not deliver drugs, especially those with serious side effects, in highly concentrated doses directly to disease sites inside the body through miniaturized pumps that take their commands from patients or from implanted sensors? Indeed, could medical devices such as orthopaedic implants, heart valves, or stents be seeded, or painted, with drugs that could make them last longer, integrate with the body better, or simply have superior performance? This convergence of devices and drugs is now underway. There have been several examples of the successful combination of drugs and devices. External insulin delivery pumps, used by diabetics to maintain blood sugar levels, have enjoyed increased penetration in recent years, reaching approximately $430 million US revenues in 2003. The next stage of growth for drug–device combination products in the diabetes segment awaits the arrival of a totally implantable insulin pump that will automatically dispense insulin based on sensors capable of reading blood sugar levels – essentially an artificial pancreas. Beyond the straightforward approach of using medical devices as journeymen (simple carriers of pharmaceutical agents), the industry anticipates truly integrated drug and device products in which both aspects, drug and device, would meaningfully contribute. The whole is then greater than the sum of the parts. Two recent examples, each commercially significant, provide a view as to the clinical and financial rewards that are available. Drug-eluting stents represent a perfect example of integration. The metal stent is the primary implant, propping open the vessel and maintaining blood flow in the critical coronary artery. But the antiproliferative drug painted onto the metal mesh serves to improve the performance of the stent by stanching the regrowth of cells that would otherwise reclog the artery. The drug-eluting stent success has already been mentioned. Suffice it to say that after one year on the market this product accounted for some 75 percent of all stent implants and was likely to generate approximately $3.2 billion in US revenues in 2004.

Another example of an integrated drug–device product is the Infuse spine cage, made by Medtronic. Spine cages – hollow metal cylinders about the size of a flattened cigar butt – are wedged between two or more vertebrae in order to fuse them together as a somewhat crude, but effective way of reducing back pain. Not only must the spine be accessed by an incision in the back, a second, and often more morbid, surgery is performed to harvest bone marrow from the upper tip of one's hip bone (iliac crest). This harvested bone is tamped into the spine cage before it is implanted in the hopes of inducing bone growth and fusion between vertebrae.

The Infuse product is essentially a standard metal spine cage, but comes prepacked with bone morphogenetic protein (BMP), an extremely powerful drug (derived from biotechnology techniques) that promotes, as its name implies, bone growth. Two important advantages are realized. The drug–device combination product obviates the need for a second harvesting surgical procedure and achieves good vertebral fusion. Medtronic recorded roughly $260 million in Infuse sales in its fiscal year ending April 2004.[18] Drug-eluting stents and spine cages with bone morphogenetic protein (BMP) are just two examples of combination products that are the first in a wave of new products that serve important clinical needs by taking advantage of drugs and devices.

The powerful trend toward drug–device combinations places new requirements on medical products companies. In the drug–stent area, each of the stent makers has formed a relationship with one or a number of pharmaceutical companies in order to gain access to the various antiproliferative agents, namely, to paint onto its stents. However, these device companies must develop their own in-house competencies in working with the drug agents, namely, how to formulate them and bind them to their products, and have to develop an understanding of the so-called "release kinetics" and biologic effect. An entirely new set of competitive attributes comes into play. In perhaps what is one of the healthcare industry's great ironies, nearly every large pharmaceutical company that once held a device subsidiary has divested of it during the last two decades in order to focus on its core business. To list a few: Lilly spun out its set of cardiovascular companies as Guidant in 1994; Bristol-Myers Squibb spun orthopaedics giant Zimmer in 2001; and Pfizer divested of its Shiley heart valve division, its urological products subsidiary American Medical Systems, and its orthopaedics company Howmedica. Interestingly enough, these medical device properties were jettisoned by pharmaceutical companies just as growth and profitability was waning in pharmaceuticals and waxing in devices. At one time device divisions were a drag on a mighty pharmaceutical company's growth and margins. Today's vibrant device companies would now be powerful profit and growth contributors. Lo, how the mighty have fallen!

The revolution in drug–device convergence throws up several questions. Chief among them is which party contributes the true enabling technology: can one side survive without the other? Stents are usable without the drug coating; indeed, bare metal stents were successful for many years. But the drug is really not usable, at least in this application, without the stent. Perhaps these relative contributions can be assessed via split in-licensing fees and end product prices. Using the drug-eluting stent as an example, it is understood that Boston Scientific pays its drug supplier, Angiotech Pharmaceuticals, about $200 per stent. Boston's total COGS per stent, including this fee to Angiotech, is roughly $375, and its selling price is approximately $3,050. Clearly in this example the stent platform (along with the catheter) is the main contributor and the drug is an accessory to the product. The balance in fees and costs for wearable insulin pumps is similarly tilted toward the pump as the value-added contributor.

It would appear that for the current products envisioned in this drug–device convergence, the medical products companies still contribute the enabling technology and the pharmaceutical companies that supply the important agents are relegated to a supporting role. However, even if the device is "king" for the foreseeable future, it is still of vital importance that device companies develop drug competencies and pharmaceutical relationships – which serve as a new basis of competition. Furthermore, it seems that the new trend toward convergence of drugs and devices will drive an even greater separation between the haves and have-nots. Large companies with large and deeply resourced development laboratories are probably better able to exploit drug–device combination products. Pharmaceutical development and clinical testing are exceedingly expensive and generally have longer time horizons; these costs will be better borne by large monolithic device companies such as Johnson & Johnson, Medtronic, Boston Scientific, and Guidant. This considerably raises the "entrance fee" for the small, early stage device company. Not only must the early stage company fund the development of its own device, it must also establish arrangements with relevant drug suppliers and fund the clinical work-up and testing of the drug–device combination product. This is one of many factors contributing to the consolidation of the medical device sector.

Important industry drivers

The medical device sector, here in the first decade of the new century, appears to be as vibrant, healthy, and full of promise as ever. From an economic point of view, as noted above, the sector has matured, become somewhat more structured, and has witnessed the emergence of larger, broad-based firms. The previous section treated changes in technologies and how they may favor the larger firm while disadvantaging the smaller firm. It would appear that this trend toward a more structured sector has perhaps accelerated recently as conglomerates such as Johnson & Johnson, Medtronic, and Boston Scientific have become more dominant, controlling much of the innovation, new product development and, in fact, trends in the actual practice of medicine. One need only look to the way in which electrophysiologists treat arrhythmia patients with a quiver full of electronic gadgets and the way an interventional cardiologist uses balloon catheters and tiny metal stents, to appreciate the profound effect large companies have had on medical practice.

The shift toward a more oligopolistic form has not exerted a drag on growth, innovativeness, or profitability. Many developments continue to flow from venture-backed start-up and small, single product public companies. But perhaps an even greater number of the significant products (congestive heart failure devices and drug-coated stents, to name but two) have emanated from the handful of colossi. This section discusses these changes in more detail and seeks to identify the factors driving the device sector today. To state the conclusion up front, the prognosis for the sector is exceedingly bright: unmet medical needs are legion, the demographic trends are positive as our populations are aging, companies are harnessing the technologies effectively, and the channels required to bring products to the clinic as well as to train, instruct, and transform medical practice are well developed and extremely efficient. Analysts anticipate a continuation of profitable growth for at least the next few decades.

Sources of growth: demographics, unmet clinical needs, procedure penetration, price

Why does the device sector grow at above average rates and in a sustainable way? The multitude of factors that have driven growth over the past few decades can be simplified into four fundamental drivers: demographics, new products against unmet medical needs, procedure penetration, and price. These factors are addressed in turn below.

Demographics

The world's populations are aging. With the exception of a few countries, the age structure of the world is shifting upward. The percentage of the overall population above 65 or 50 years old is climbing. As an example, 17.3 percent of the US population in 2020 will be over 65, up from 13.1 percent in 2000.[19] Older people consume considerably more medical products than younger people. The slug of baby-boomers passing through the age strata will drive this trend in 2005 and beyond. Consider, too, that this new cohort of 65-year-olds will be even more demanding of medical products, as they are determined to stay more active and be more athletic and mobile than earlier generations. Simply put, there are more of them and their appetite for medical products is voracious. This demographic shift will probably contribute one to two percentage points of growth each year over the next twenty years.

Unmet clinical needs

Sector growth also comes about by way of using new products or new technologies to address diseases or medical needs that previously were simply not treated with medical devices. Part of the economic power of the sector is that entire hundred million dollar product lines can materialize where none existed before. The appearance of new products in a given year can imprint a new growth rate on the overall market. Consider a development in the field of vascular surgery. For decades the treatment of choice for the large and often fatal bulges in the aorta (aneurysms) was accomplished through a terribly invasive, open surgical technique. Since the open procedure, in which the bulging section of the garden hose-sized aorta was cut out and replaced by a new cloth conduit, was so dangerous, many patients elected to walk around like ticking time bombs, taking their chances that the probability associated with "death by anneurysm" may be lower than that associated with the invasive procedure. This situation set the stage for the introduction of a medical technology solution. A set of different start-up companies developed a catheter-based treatment that involved repaving the damaged roadway of the aorta by introducing a new tube-like graft through a relatively harmless access in the thigh. This so-called triple-A product (abdominal aortic aneurysm) enjoyed sales in 2003 of roughly $455 million worldwide, compared to essentially zero in 1998 ($30 million). Clearly this is an example of growth resulting from a new product that had not been invented or marketed in past years. Within the context of the total sector, the magnitude of revenues flowing from a new product such as the triple-A is small. However, it is the collection of dozens of products like the above that serve as an important contributor to growth. The new product phenomenon does vary from year to year, but on average probably adds as much as two to three percentage points to total growth. In some years there is an abundance of new, high-impact products and total growth will be above average; there are also new product droughts, during which overall growth may ebb accordingly. As was mentioned earlier, two significant new products are propelling growth in the cardiovascular segment: congestive heart failure products (cardiac resynchronization therapy at $2.2 billion) and drug-coated stents ($3.8 billion for 2004). Partly because of these new products, the cardiovascular segment was expected to experience a red-hot growth rate of around 18 percent in 2004, and in 2005 it is likely to be considerably higher than the trend-line growth of approximately 12 percent.

Procedure penetration

Another important but more subtle contributor to growth is the sweeping tendency for physicians to choose a device-based approach with greater frequency and on an ever-widening percentage of their patient base. Certainly this is a complex matter, and it would require an entire chapter to do it justice. Put simply, as medical technology improves both in safety and efficacy, and as the technology products and procedures become more accepted by the medical community, there is a tendency among physicians to use more. To a man wielding a large hammer, everything looks like a nail. If a physician sees 500 patients a year, perhaps 10 percent or fifty patients would receive a given medical product, perhaps a hip implant or coronary stent in the case of a cardiac patient. Because of this acceptance and penetration factor, this same physician, if presented with a similar set of patients in a new year, would apply that medical product to 20 percent or one hundred patients. This is an exaggerated case for the purposes of illustration; however, this factor, in a more modest magnitude, is at work driving several percentage points of growth each year in medical products. Utilization rates of most medical technologies, especially the more successful ones, rise each year. Given that underlying disease conditions do not change dramatically from year to year, the unit growth of devices such as pacemakers, defibrillators, and stents is a direct manifestation of this penetration phenomenon. The US consumed roughly 530,000 stents in 1997, or 0.2 percent of the population. In 2003, with only a modest rise in population, US stent consumption rose to 1.3 million, representing a penetration rate of 0.5 percent, more than two times the rate of five years earlier.

Pricing

Pricing can also affect growth, either as a propellant or as a drag. Over the past few decades pricing trends have generally been favorable in the medical products sector. New products carry higher prices and tend to buoy overall prices as they pass through the product mix. In the case of more mature markets such as pacemakers, new products loaded with additional features have helped to at least maintain prices. In fact, the average price of a pacemaker sold in the US has remained remarkably steady at around $5,000 for the last five years, and prices have risen modestly from the early 1990s. An earlier section referred to the price increases instituted by makers of drug-coated stents, namely a tripling price for the new version. The defibrillator-like devices used to treat congestive heart failure were priced at $30,000–35,000, a significant step up from the $22,000 for conventional defibrillators. However, the new devices contained nearly the same electrical components.

Several factors contribute to positive pricing trends. For one, products are not selected on the basis of price. It is almost inconceivable that a surgeon would select an off-brand mechanical heart valve in order to save a few dollars. Because of this, companies do not tend to compete on price.

However, pricing is of greater importance in the orthopaedics market segment. Certainly, knee and hip implants are brilliantly fashioned, contain dozens of special features, and are made to the highest standards keeping in mind that they are designed to last a lifetime. However, there is a perception that the product offerings of most of the large orthopaedics suppliers are quite similar in use and function. Perhaps it is because of this that pricing in orthopaedics has exhibited shifts and swings across the years. In the early 1990s concerns about healthcare costs and the threat of national healthcare reform brought about a period of modest decline in hip and knee implant prices. This downward trend reversed itself in the late 1990s, and average prices have been on the rise ever since then, somewhere in the range of three to five percent in each year. This pricing environment has contributed to the high-teen revenue growth exhibited by large orthopaedic companies during the period.

Rising importance of channels

Because the activity of selling medical technology to the clinic is so highly remunerative, the access way or conduit to this profit-making action could be likened to the goose that lays golden eggs. With this in mind, it is understandable that companies would invest in franchise-building activities such as the funding of clinical programs, sales force development, education, and physician entertainment. Indeed, these activities appear to be on the rise. Once a large company has built efficient conduits into the clinic, then a variety of products can be merchandized through them. Technology and product performance is important, but so is the franchise necessary to market them. A typical growth cycle will illustrate this point. A young company may reach a certain size and level of recognition entirely on the basis of introducing a clinically significant new product or procedure. Having done that, it will begin the task of building a marketing channel or conduit to ensure that it can sell future products. These next generation products are almost never as significant as the earlier ones that helped to form the company's reputation. The channels or conduits into the clinic are similar to a club membership – the fees are expensive, but once they are paid the membership provides access to a continual flow of profits. Companies recognize this feature to their great success and ignore it at their peril.

An example of an astute understanding of the importance of franchise and conduit was the fierce patent scuffle between an up-and-coming balloon angioplasty company, SciMed Life Systems, and ACS (now Guidant) back in the early 1990s. Mid-sized SciMed was gathering tremendous momentum, taking share in the high-growth, high-profit angioplasty market. ACS, embarrassed by this upstart, cried foul, claiming that one of SciMed's catheters infringed a critical patent. The courts ruled in favor of ACS. Now to the point of this example: instead of proscribing SciMed from this segment, ACS charged an extraordinary royalty (30%) but allowed SciMed to practice the patented feature – a move that could be likened to giving (selling) your enemy the keys to the city. SciMed recognized the value of developing a conduit, paid what was a usurious price, and went on to build a tremendous franchise. SciMed, now housed within Boston Scientific, is the leading seller of interventional cardiology products (catheters and stents).

This is not to suggest that companies, once they build franchises, intentionally allow product performance to decline and use marketing to push inferior products to the clinic. Certainly, large franchise companies such as Medtronic and Johnson & Johnson strive to develop and offer the very highest performance products. However, it appears that these companies balance their energies, efforts, and expenditures, supporting both product development but also marketing and franchise building. By investing in their franchises, large companies can help ensure their continuation and survivability.

Financing and consolidation trends

Consolidation premise

The once highly fragmented medical device sector continues to consolidate. Not long ago most companies specialized in one anatomical segment or clinical specialty, such as cardiology or general surgery, or had one category of technological weaponry, such as electronics or polymer chemistry, to bring to bear on the clinic. In fact, these smaller, nimble, and innovative companies produced most of the high-impact products that continue to occupy the growth segments of the market. This has changed. Specialization, once an advantage because it allowed companies to successfully fulfill the highly discriminating demands of the clinic, has all but become a disadvantage. Size, scale, breadth, and heft have become increasingly important bases of competition. The fixed cost components of participating in the medical device sector, including R&D efforts, regulatory requirements, and clinical trials, have risen dramatically. The prospect of leveraging and streamlining these sizeable expenditures across a larger corporate structure has been the impetus for many of the recent acquisitions. This current section reviews the medical device sector from a broad financial or economic perspective in order to consider funding and business combinations. This includes a discussion of merger and acquisition (M&A) activities as well as a look at the role of the capital markets with respect to public financings (initial public offerings or IPOs).

M&A activity during the last decade

Figure 6.16 suggests a gradual upward sloping trend toward consolidation. The number of company combinations, both large and small, has risen during the last five or six years. In 2003 there were approximately thirty-three mergers, up

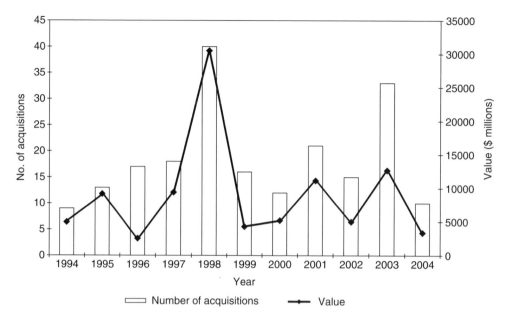

Figure 6.16   The number of acquisitions and their value.

from fifteen in 2002 and twenty-one in 2001 and nearly twice the annual average during the early part of the 1990s. The value of these combinations in 2003 was more than $12 billion, up from the trend line but well under the extraordinary year of 1998 when transactions topped $30 billion.

The combinations in 2003 included several in the orthopaedics segment, among them Zimmer's $3.2 billion acquisition of Centerpulse (née Sulzer Medica). Syntheses-Stratec, the Europe-based orthopaedics powerhouse specializing in trauma products, was active in acquiring two properties at a collective value of nearly $1.3 billion. The positive economic trends within the orthopaedics segment – strong pricing, positive demographics, and deepening procedure penetration – brought the larger companies to market to buy smaller technology-based properties, especially those that provided access to the fast growing spine segment. Indeed a full third of all combinations in 2003 were in the orthopaedics sector.

This pick-up in acquisition activity in orthopaedics followed a structural rearrangement of the larger orthopaedics properties in 1998. In that year two of the largest hip and knee implant companies found new owners: broad-based DePuy was added to Johnson & Johnson's strong knee implant business; and Howmedica, which had perennially struggled under the tutelage of drug giant Pfizer, was sold to Stryker, forming the largest implant supplier.

As 1998 came to a close, what had been the top five players, controlling 55 percent of worldwide orthopaedics revenues, were now reconfigured as the top three orthopaedics companies – J&J, Stryker, and Zimmer (then housed within Bristol Myers).

In years past it was the cardiovascular segment that figured heavily in mergers and acquisitions. However, combinations within this sector in 2002 and 2003 were small and somewhat inconsequential. The diagnostics segment was relatively more active in M&As in 2003. Abbott, in an effort to stimulate growth, bought the so-called "point of care" blood gases company i-Stat. Roche, the diagnostics giant, bought the assay company IGEN and the diabetes treatment company Disetronics for $1.2 billion and $900 million, respectively.

Concentration ratios

The upturn in the number and size of acquisitions has brought about a corresponding change in the concentration ratio of the medical device sector. In 1990 the ten largest companies accounted for less than one-half (48%) of total worldwide revenues. As top companies have started exhibiting growth rates that are considerably higher than the overall market, this has naturally led to higher concentration ratios, partly as a result of internal development but also as the simple result of acquisitions. Each time Johnson & Johnson, Medtronic, or Boston Scientific acquired an independent company, its revenues were brought within the confines of the large conglomerate. As can be seen in figure 6.17, the concentration ratio has risen to a point where the top ten companies now control roughly two-thirds of total sales.

	1990	1995	2000	2003
Top ten companies[1]	15.7	25.9	42.2	59.2
Total market revenues				
($ billion)	32.6	47.9	70.5	90
Concentration ratio (%)	48	54	60	66

Figure 6.17   Concentration ratios – a consolidating industry.

Source: Company published reports.
[1]The top ten companies are: J&J, Baxter, Medtronic, Abbott, B-D, Guidant, Stryker, Boston Scientific, Bausch & Lomb, St. Jude Medical.

M&A cycles

While it appears that the medical device sector is undergoing a broad, and seemingly inexorable, consolidation trend, there have been cycles and fluctuations over the past ten years. This ebb and flow of merger and acquisition activity is related to two principal factors. First is the timing of the strategic initiatives on the part of larger consolidators such as Johnson & Johnson, Medtronic, and Boston Scientific. The second factor is the pace of initial public offerings (IPOs) and the tone or receptivity of the capital markets.

Timing of corporate strategy

There are two examples of where corporate strategic initiatives have impacted M&A activities. Note that the number of combinations in any given period is small and therefore easily affected by the efforts of one or two companies. If a corporate buyer enters an acquisition phase prompted by its slowing growth or by virtue of having reached a certain size and scale, then this activity itself may cause a perturbation in the overall number of combinations in any given year. Medtronic underwent an aggressive acquisition strategy in 1998, acquiring five companies representing a value of $8 billion, roughly 30 percent of Medtronic's premerger capitalization. Medtronic had already diversified away from pacemakers and defibrillators and into other cardiovascular areas in the early 1990s, but it was this 1998 move that found the company moving far afield, entering orthopaedics for the first time by acquiring Sofamor-Danek for $3.5 billion. Medtronic's buying spree, combined with selected acquisitions by Boston Scientific, Guidant, Johnson & Johnson, Tyco, and Stryker, made 1998 a record year: forty combinations with a value of more than $30 billion.

Boston Scientific went through a similar build-out in 1995 when it bought five companies for $1.2 billion. Three of these five properties were languishing recent IPOs – EP Technologies, CVIS, and Heart Technology, minted in 1993, 1992, and 1992, respectively. Boston's activities alone exerted a significant effect on the M&A level in 1995, contributing nearly half the number and value of that year's crop.

Pace of IPOs

Public financings have been an important source of funding for medical products development. Indeed, during the last decade approximately 6.5 billion dollars have been raised by medical device companies going public.

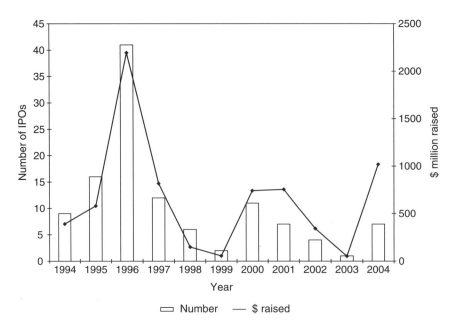

Figure 6.18   Medical products initial public offerings.

The size of offering, the number of offerings, and the nature of the companies have varied dramatically during this period. As can be seen in figure 6.18, 1996 was a boom year: forty companies went public, raising over two billion dollars.

A surfeit of recently minted early stage public companies with sagging stock prices can attract corporate buyers and stimulate acquisitions. In fact, the peaks in M&A activity during the last decade – 1998 and 2003 in particular – directly follow surges in IPOs by two to three years. Clearly these factors are interrelated: corporate buyers are active when the capital markets are less receptive to early stage companies. Just the opposite occurs when the capital markets are sanguine and bid up the prices of early stage companies, making them unattractive to corporate buyers causing a slowing in merger activity. During such times funding for these small, capital-starved companies was readily obtained through IPOs.

The surge in IPOs

Many reasons conspired to cause the surge in IPOs depicted in figure 6.18. For one, investors had been treated to some extraordinary successes in the medical products category during the early part of the 1990s, and the capital markets had developed quite an appetite for medical technology. Successes were achieved in both the established, seasoned public companies and in the small, newly minted public companies. Shares of US Surgical, the maker of surgical instruments, experienced an astonishing price rise as the company invented and then directly benefited from the "less-invasive surgery revolution." US Surgical's stock tripled in value twice in the early 1990s. Medtronic returned a compounded 46 percent per year to investors during the first three years of the decade, as it found itself squarely in front of the several powerful trends in cardiovascular products, including the increased use of implantable defibrillators.

These successes produced an environment in which average valuations for medical products companies rose to dizzying heights, and dozens of start-up companies with little more than a product concept found good receptivity in the capital markets. Of the more than forty companies that went public in 1996, only two, Fresenius Medical, a German-based leader in kidney dialysis equipment, and DePuy, the orthopaedics implant company, were established and had meaningful sales levels. Nearly all other IPOs in the class of 1996 had products that were untested in the clinic and had yet to generate sales. Examples of these capital-needy start-up companies include CardioGenesis, which raised $60 million to fund clinical trials and development of a laser used to fire holes in the heart to stimulate growth of new vessels and consequently improve perfusion. Later the product was found to be ineffective and the company, and its once impressive market value, essentially disappeared. Biofield, in breast cancer detection, and Integ, in blood glucose sensing, raised $20 million and $28.5 million, respectively, for ideas that ultimately failed in clinical trials. However, not all early stage IPOs during the year failed. Stent maker AVE (Arterial Vascular Engineering), which raised $105 million in 1996 at a market value of $678 million, was a spectacular success as a public company until it was later acquired by Medtronic in 1998 for $3.75 billion – tracing an annual compounded valuation increase over those years of 135 percent.

The surge in public offerings in 1996 was followed by a sharp decline in the following year, as investors attempted to sort out the value and the prospects of the properties in which they had invested. Most companies disappointed with respect to the clinical utility of their products, regulatory approval timing, market acceptance, and of course sales ramp. Most had business plans that called for measurable sales (in the range of $5–10 million) to be reached by 1998 or 1999. It became clear in 1997, the first year after the IPO, that these levels of sales would not materialize and would be delayed for at least two years. In the case of the frank failures – those cases in which the product simply did not work in the clinic – the sales goals and business plans had to be completely reconfigured. This cast a pall over the medical technology sector: investor sentiment changed, valuations dropped, and the capital markets became less receptive to any new offerings. Indeed, into this difficult environment only twelve companies went public in 1997, raising only $800 million. The bulk of the money raised was from a well-established orthopaedics company, Sulzer Medica, which raised $550 million. The public markets tightened even further in 1998 and 1999, with a steady decline in both the number of offerings and the amount raised.

Public offerings rebounded modestly in 2000, when eleven companies went public, raising nearly three-quarters of a billion dollars. This brings to mind the adage "once burned twice shy." By this time, the capital markets were more selective and discriminating, and consequently funded companies that were more established and did so at more modest valuations. Two examples of well-established, substantial companies within this crop are Wilson Greatbatch, the pacemaker battery supplier with a thirty-year track record, and American Medical Systems, the urology products company that had operated for over a decade as a subsidiary of Pfizer. Operating history, relevant sales levels, and solid profitability were all key components for capital market receptivity. Indeed, Greatbatch had revenues in 2000 of $98 million and American Medical Systems, $100 million.

Reasons for combinations

Whether or not combinations are part of a broad strategic thrust or are more isolated and opportunistic, the specific reasons for each transaction tend to fall into a few general categories. This section explores the rationales of buying growth, leveraging channels or operations, and technology–anatomical combinations.

Buying growth

The larger, broad-based companies generate annual sales in the multiple billions of dollars. In order to maintain low-to high-teen growth rates – a requirement imposed by investors or by company management – these companies must generate hundreds of millions of new sales each year. Core products and self-invented products, even in moderate growth markets such as congestive heart failure or spine treatments, are in some cases not capable of registering growth rates in the teens, especially when diluted by a company's slow growth product segments. The acquisition of small product categories and new technologies can add tens to hundreds of millions in annual revenues and thus tick up overall growth by as a much as a percentage point or two. While at first blush this may not appear significant, consider that a two percentage point change in Medtronic's corporate growth objective, from 15 percent to 17 percent, accompanied by an assumed P/E ratio change of two points, would increase the company's market value by roughly $2.4 billion. Furthermore, most of the successful large companies have exceedingly high rates of profit generation and throw off correspondingly high amounts of cash that can be used to fund acquisitions to ensure continued strong growth. It is to this phenomenon that the conglomerates owe their continuity or sustainability of growth.

Embedded within the data in figure 6.16 are several examples of acquisitions that fit into this category. One of the more successful examples is Medtronic's $3.5 billion purchase of the spine products leader Sofamor Danek in 1998. During the last four years Medtronic's base sales growth, excluding Sofamor

Danek, would have been approximately 13 percent. The cardiovascular conglomerate allowed Danek to operate with great autonomy, and it flourished under its new parent, posting an annual top-line growth rate of roughly 30 percent during this period. While Danek is considerably smaller than Medtronic (comprising a little more than 10% of its sales base), it was large enough and fast-growing enough to add perhaps as much as three percentage points to Medtronic's total corporate growth rate, lifting it to a respectable 16 percent from a base of 13 percent. Similarly, in 2001 Boston Scientific acquired its way to growth with its purchase of IVT, a maker of angioplasty catheters that had, at the time, higher top-line growth rates than Boston.

Leverage distribution channels

Large broad-based companies have established and efficient distribution channels. Start-ups have attractive innovative products but have underdeveloped means of bringing products to the clinic. This disparity has, if anything, been exacerbated in recent years as the medical device markets have matured and become more structured, with higher barriers and agency costs. In times past most product innovations, whether they be high or medium impact, could serve as the basis for an entire company to be formed. SciMed Life Systems, the angioplasty balloon company, existed for nearly a decade as an independent before being acquired by Boston Scientific in 1994. Ventritex had singleness of purpose, daring to be a stand-alone implantable defibrillator company in a market dominated by the giants Medtronic and Guidant. This Sunnyvale, California upstart generated peak annual sales of $125 million and became a well-followed Wall Street darling. Ultimately Ventritex was purchased by St. Jude Medical, but it did enjoy several years as an independent company.

While both of these innovative companies were fated to be acquired, they still serve as testaments to a time when technology-driven independent companies could survive and in fact flourish on essentially one or two product innovations. As mentioned earlier, this has now changed. In the current environment, unless the innovation is truly spectacular, the single product company must move with haste to align itself with, or be acquired by, a larger conglomerate capable of providing distribution channels. The capital markets reflect this change too. The public markets are less receptive to early stage, single product companies – either the company simply cannot go public, or it can only do so at unattractive valuations (discussed below).

Several acquisitions in the last two years serve as examples of early stage companies that were acquired by market channel companies before going public. In the orthopaedics segment, Link Spine, Spinal Concepts, and Spinal Dynamics were acquired before going public by Johnson & Johnson, Abbott, and Medtronic, respectively. In the cardiovascular segment, both Percusurge, the "downstream protection" device company, and Atrionix, the atrial fibrillation treatment company, were acquired by Medtronic and Johnson & Johnson, respectively, without going public. In an earlier time, these five companies would most likely have enjoyed gestation periods as public companies of at least two to five years before being acquired.

Technological/anatomical combinations

Often larger or well-established companies will undertake acquisitions or combinations in order to fill gaps in their product mix. Guidant has found itself chasing acquisitions as a way to accelerate its participation in the drug-coated stent market. Its aborted acquisition of the Cook Group and its completed acquisition of Biosensors were both aimed at bringing forward a coated-stent product to supplement its very strong position in the bare metal stent market. Boston Scientific added a critical technology component to its cardiology product set when it acquired Schneider in 1998. Already a leader in balloon catheters, Boston purchased Schneider so that it could add a subtle but important feature – so-called "rapid exchange" – to its products.[20] In 2003 Edwards, the leading player in conventional tissue heart valves, broadened its product set with the acquisition of PVT (Percutaneous Valve Technologies), a company that provides a heart valve repair treatment administered through less invasive catheter approach.

In addition to the already mentioned acquisitions undertaken for the purpose of adding a technology or related product set, there are also several examples of situations in which companies have used acquisitions to extend their anatomical reach. Medtronic, the leader in cardiovascular products, has, through acquisitions, broadened into many new anatomies. First it ventured anatomically northward to ears, nose, and throat with its acquisition of Xomed in 1999. Looking anatomically south, it has built a burgeoning involvement in urology, partially through acquisition; its purchase of VidaMed, a maker of devices to treat prostate enlargement, in 2002 is the latest example.

Increased scale, scope, or geographic reach

The increasing importance of size has already been commented upon. The sharp rise in the fixed cost elements such as regulatory requirements and clinical trials have been noted. Indeed these changes have fueled the trend toward consolidation. All business combinations result in a size increase; however, few acquisitions are undertaken primarily for the purpose of increasing size and scale. Nevertheless, a few that occurred during the last decade should be noted. Orthopaedics giant Zimmer, with annual revenues of $1.4 billion in 2002, added nearly $1 billion in revenues when it acquired Centerpulse in 2003. It could be said that Swiss-based Centerpulse provided Zimmer with some European marketing strength, but it would appear that Zimmer's primary objective was to bring its sales base and market share in line with the leaders: Johnson & Johnson and Stryker. Boston Scientific's aggressive build-out in 1995, when it acquired five companies contributing more than $200 million in revenues (close to 20% of Boston's base revenues at the time), was also done in part for purposes of increased size and scale.

Conclusion:
public market activity and its impact on innovation

The attractiveness of the medical device sector has much to do with its sustainable growth. Over the last decade the sector has experienced rates of growth in the mid-teen range – a level that is more than twice that of the overall economy. Naturally these rates represent an average of slow-growing products combined with several newer product categories that exhibit considerably higher rates. A portion of these higher-growth products is generated by early stage start-up companies. The trends identified in this section – continued consolidation and the ebbing of IPOs – may portend of a reduction in new product flow and with it a lull in the overall growth rate of the sector. If the capital markets continue to tighten and restrict investment to established companies with significant sales levels, and furthermore if the larger oligopolistic companies obtain a significant portion of their growth by way of combinations with other medium-sized firms, then how will smaller, innovative firms that are capable of inventing the unusual break-out products be funded? As noted above, there has been a reduction in the number of medical technology IPOs during the last ten years. It remains to be seen whether or not the changes in capital markets and the continued trend toward consolidation will serve to reduce innovation within the sector, or alternatively, whether the larger, deeply resourced companies are capable of conducting effective product development of their own. Will their efforts be as fruitful as those that were once carried out by the dozens of small, early stage companies that were readily funded by the capital markets?

In considering these trends in the sourcing of innovation, it may be helpful to review the source of some of the recent growth drivers in the cardiovascular arena. The two most important of these are drug-coated stents and CRT (cardiac resynchronization therapy) devices for congestive heart failure. Drug-coated stents have transformed the slow-growing $2.2 billion bare metal stent market into a total category (bare metal and drug coated) that was likely to top $5 billion in 2004, up from $3.4 billion the year before. CRT devices have similarly shifted the implantable defibrillator market from $1.8 billion in 2001 to a forecasted total market of $4.7 billion in 2004. Both of these innovations were birthed by large conglomerates: attribution for drug-coated stents is generally given to Johnson & Johnson and Boston Scientific, while CRT was developed by the pacemaker and defibrillator giants Medtronic and Guidant. This would suggest that indeed the development programs within large companies are capable of generating the growth-imbuing, breakout products that have been the cornerstone of the sector.

NOTES

The author wishes to thank Nathan Kelley for his research assistance in preparing this chapter.

1. Johnson & Johnson's revenues refer to medical products excluding pharmaceuticals and consumer products.
2. Estimates for implants in 2003 were compiled from analyst reports from Banc of America Securities, Morgan Stanley, and Lehman Brothers. Cardiology products include implantable defibrillators, devices for congestive heart failure and pacemakers – collectively 1.1 million implants. Neurology implants, primarily for pain, epilepsy, and Parkinson's disease and other movement disorders sum to approximately 40,000.
3. Medtronic's first implant of a diagnostics-only implantable device, called the Chronicle, was in 1998. The device, which measures hemodynamic performance, was used extensively in several clinical trials in 2001, 2002, and 2003. At the time of writing FDA approval has not been granted.
4. Rob Faulkner, "Go Where the Value will be," presentation to the Wharton School, December 1998.
5. FDA/CDRH (Center for Diagnostics and Radiological Health) factsheet, available at http://www.fda.gov/cdrh.
6. Earl E. Bakken founded Medtronic in a garage in northeast Minneapolis, Minnesota in 1957; John E. Abele founded Medi-tech, Inc., later named Boston Scientific Corporation, in Watertown, Massachusetts in 1965; Peter M. Nicholas partnered with Abele in 1978.
7. MDDI Reports, (Medical Device and Diagnostics Industry), available at http://www.devicelink.com/mddi.

8. Medical Technology Industry Overview, Report 1, The Lewin Group, March 24, 2000.
9. Clinical studies that have shown survival benefits for patients that received implantable defibrillators in comparison to those patients on conventional drug therapy include: MADIT – Multicenter Automatic Defibrillator Implantation Trial (1996); AVID – Antiarrhythmics Versus Implantable Defibrillators (1997); MUSTT – Multicenter UnSustained Tachycardia Trial (1999); and MADIT II (2001).
10. Analyst reports from Banc of America Securities, Morgan Stanley, UBS, and Lehman Brothers.
11. Bolivia's GDP given as $21 billion. see http://www.phrasebase.com/countries.
12. Balloon angioplasty is a common technique in which a spaghetti-like tube is threaded into a blocked artery in the heart in order to expand and clear the blockage; in the vast majority of cases a wire mesh tube, called a stent is delivered and implanted at the same time as a way to prop open the vessel.
13. Shares of Guidant stock went from $70 to $29 per share between the period October 2000–July 2001, at a time when the company suffered significant setbacks in its efforts to enter the coated stent market. One setback involved a potential acquisition of Cook Corporation as a way of gaining access to the so-called Taxus drug coating.
14. One rare exception is Stryker's recent television advertising campaigns for its hip implants using the endorsement of famous implant recipients, such as the professional golfer Jack Nicklaus.
15. All generations (models) starting with PCD (pectoral cardioverter defibrillator) treat ventrical defibrillation. Models with the AF suffix also treat atrial fibrillation, while models with the DR suffix add on pacing capability.
16. Based on closing prices on September 2, 2004, the price-to-earnings ratios (twelve-month trailing) for implantable device companies Medtronic, St. Jude, and Guidant were 30.2, 34.6 and 30.9 respectively.
17. Stress shielding refers to the tendency for the implant, since it is stiffer than native bone, to shoulder most of the force burden and therefore to cause the native bone to weaken from inactivity.
18. Analyst at Piper Jaffrey.
19. Social Security Administration.
20. Rapid exchange catheters incorporate a special design to allow a convenient exchange, or replacement, of the angioplasty balloon catheter while keeping the narrow guide wire in place.

7 The healthcare information technology sector

Jeff C. Goldsmith

Introduction to information technology

Healthcare information technology (IT) is expected to be almost a $100 billion business worldwide by 2005, comparable in scale to a Latin American economy.[1] It is also an industry in transition, from early applications which supported batch processing of financial transactions to sophisticated, artificial intelligence-assisted real time clinical process control. This chapter will discuss the size and organization of this important sector, review the major applications developing in healthcare information technology, and also look at the barriers to adoption and use of these important technologies.

Over the next decade, of all technologies that affect the healthcare experience, information technology holds the greatest potential for yielding positive changes for patients and their families – more rapid and accurate diagnoses, fewer medical errors, and less wasted time from duplicative information requests in the treatment and payment process.

While overall IT spending faltered in the wake of the collapse of the Internet bubble, healthcare IT spending has continued growing in the United States, and is expected to accelerate due to pressure from payers to improve clinical quality and outcomes.

Year	Total HCIT spending (US) ($ billion)	Annual growth rate (%)
2001	34.1	n/a
2002	35.7	4.7
2003 (e)	38.6	8.1
2004 (e)	41.6	7.8
2005 (e)	44.6	7.2
2006 (e)	47.9	7.4

Figure 7.1   Growth in healthcare IT spending.

Source: Gartner Dataquest (August 2003); "In Unforgiving Times, the US Healthcare Market Boosts IT Spending, 2001–2006," executive summary by Geraldine Cruz (August 13, 2003).

However, even at its current levels, healthcare IT spending in the US represents only about 2.5 percent of overall health expenditures, a percentage which is less than half of that in other industries such as financial services or retailing.[2] Healthcare IT spending is likely to grow at a near double digit rate for at least the next decade worldwide (see figure 7.1).

Why has progress in healthcare IT been glacial?

It is fashionable to bemoan the primitive state of information handling in health services. Indeed, it can be argued that information technology applications lag behind those in other sectors of the modern economy – financial services, retailing, and manufacturing – by as much as a generation. This is not the result of willful incompetence on the part of vendors and health services managers, however. Automating healthcare services is the most demanding application set in the modern economy, because health services are that economy's most complex product.

The enormous difficulty in adapting modern information technology to health service organizations may be attributable to the sheer complexity of these organizations. According to Peter Drucker, the modern urban hospital may be the most complex organization in human history. In its vain attempt to track and capture healthcare activity on a microscopic level, the modern health insurance firm may not be any less complex.

There is more variability and uncertainty at the point of service in healthcare than in any other economic activity. There is no inventory of standardized health services; rather, they must be customized at the point of care on a "just in time" basis. There is, as John Wennberg has shown us, tremendous variation in physician response to diagnostic uncertainty from case to case, village to village, and county to county.[3] And finally, more stakeholders (i.e., health professionals) collide at the point of service than in any other process or service in the economy.

In this collision lies the potential for anarchy. Each profession has a unique view of its centrality to the care process, its own private language, its own worldview, which includes barely concealed disdain for other health professionals, and, until recently, its own information system. In many hospitals, this may mean that an individual patient may have as many as a dozen distinct records, scattered across the hospital's many clinical and administrative departments. This fragmentation of health information domains mirrors the inherent fragmentation in the care process itself, regardless of the financing mechanism.

In the United States, one must overlay upon this complexity the additional burden of billing for each individual unit of service to a bewildering array of private insurance (health maintenance organization, preferred provider organization, point of service) and government payers (Medicare, Medicaid). Because health services are paid for on a piecework basis, healthcare payment in the US generates tens of billions of transactions annually, enswathing the care process in a blizzard of partially automated but still largely paper-driven transactions.

Current technology has limited the automation of clinical care

The inherent complexity both of care processes and of healthcare organizations has generated technological demands which, until recently, outstripped the capacity of hardware and software to capture and rationalize clinical services. Assembling healthcare data in a data repository has been possible for decades; organizing and extracting that data rapidly in a format that enables clinicians to use it has been a daunting technical challenge.

Healthcare computing requires the use of large, complex databases, which, in turn, requires not only capacious data storage but also nimble and flexible database management utilities. To extract and deliver information from these databases requires powerful servers and high-capacity, transparent data networks. Latency of system response (e.g. the length of time between executing a command and the system's response) has been a major barrier to physician and nurse acceptance of clinical applications. So has the so-called graphic

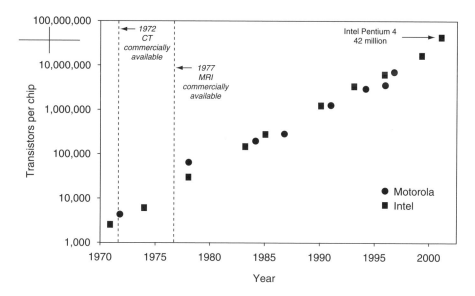

Figure 7.2 Moore's Law: transistors per microprocessor.

Source: San Jose Mercury News.

user interface (GUI), the face the system presents to the user. Until the advent of Windows, manipulating clinical data required mastering an arcane language of computer commands, a steep barrier to adoption for busy clinicians. Even the Windows-based screens of healthcare IT systems have tended toward clutter and complexity, a further barrier to easy adoption.

The ability to integrate diagnostic and therapeutic applications at the point of care also required those processes to be digital. Up until a very few years ago, radiology, cardiology, and tissue pathology were disciplines tied to interpretation of images rendered in film and located, often, in the dank basements of hospitals and clinics. As these diagnostic modalities migrate from film to digital format, the information locked within them becomes easily storable and readable, and is moveable literally anywhere in the world. It can also be embedded in a patient's digital clinical record, where it can be retrieved and viewed as needed from multiple locations.

Almost forty years ago Gordon Moore, a founder of Intel, issued what has become the central self-fulfilling prediction in the semiconductor world: that the computing power of a microchip would double every eighteen months with the price held constant (see figure 7.2). This remarkable technical dynamic has enabled stunning gains in the productivity of computer manufacturing and concomitant improvements in the capacity of computing hardware.[4] Less dramatic but sustained progress has been made in reducing the cost of computer memory, disk storage capacity and network band width.[5] While this progress in cost reduction has led to the emergence of an infrastructure capable of executing healthcare solutions, the cost of clinical informatics software remains a barrier to adoption in less developed countries as well as less affluent areas of the United States. This is because of the confounding effect of the cost of building and installing software. A number of years ago, Nathan Myrvold, then chief scientist at Microsoft, declared that "software is a gas – it expands to fill the available storage space." As disk storage and random access memory have become more affordable, software engineers have succumbed to the temptation to fill this capacity with features and functions to attract users and technical reviewers. This has certainly been the case in healthcare software, leading to cumbersome products that are difficult and expensive to maintain. Vendors have, until relatively recently, avoided the creation of new system architectures, relying instead on interfaces to link older, less capable applications together.

Cost-reducing technological advances seem poised to balance out costly software development and installations and make the resulting applications more affordable. This is an area where the Internet will eventually make a huge difference, providing a low-cost public infrastructure for supporting distributed computing applications through technologies such as application service provision (ASP). This will be particularly important for physicians in solo and partnership practice, for safety net hospital and clinic providers, long-term and chronic care providers, and others who lack the resources to support complex IT applications directly.

Cost-reduction opportunities for health-related software include the ability to configure and install software by using wizards, the ability to remotely host and maintain applications in centralized servers rather than care sites, and the outsourcing of engineering and code development to lower-wage regions of the world. Technological advances are conspiring to close the gap between the economic and the functional demands of healthcare users and the applications to meet those needs.

Healthcare IT market structure

The single defining feature of the healthcare IT market worldwide is fragmentation. Unlike the pharmaceutical sector, where the top ten firms accounted for roughly half of all pharmaceutical sales in 2002, no single vendor of healthcare IT software, consulting or data management services, has more than $2 billion in worldwide healthcare revenues.[6]

Healthcare IT applications and services firms traditionally develop in cycles. When private equity is plentiful and capital markets are receptive to relatively small-scale initial public offerings, start-up healthcare IT firms sprout like mushrooms in a damp forest meadow. When they reach a certain scale of enterprise ($50–200 million), they are absorbed into larger firms seeking to grow through acquired revenues and accreted earnings.

In the past decade HBOC (now part of McKesson), Web MD, IDX, Quadramed, and iSoft, a British firm, have all sought to roll up healthcare applications into a single integrated IT platform. Eventually, however, when growth through acquisition subsides, these firms must not only continue to grow organically, but must invest aggressively in new engineering in order to integrate the acquired applications. Along the way, faltering sales momentum leaves firms vulnerable as prey for larger acquiring entities.

The acquirers tend to be concentrated in cash-rich, slower-growth firms with a healthcare presence. Equipment manufacturers such as General Electric and Siemens have sought a presence in healthcare IT by acquiring software firms to complement their diagnostic imaging businesses. For these large, integrated manufacturers, the pressure to acquire rapidly growing firms increases as growth in their core manufacturing and service businesses slows.

Thus, Siemens, which manufactures radiology equipment, purchased Shared Medical Systems, a pioneer in distributed computing applications for healthcare providers in 2001. In 1999 Shared Medical Systems reported $134.4 million in hardware revenues and $1.1 billion in service and system fees before its acquisition by Siemens.[7] This grew to a reported $1.86 billion by 2003 from Siemens Medical Solutions (see figure 7.3). Similar pressures in drug distribution led McKesson to acquire the rapidly growing healthcare IT software firm HBOC in 2000, which reported $1.14 billion in 2003 information technology sales.

In both cases, the acquiring firms have attempted to leverage their substantial presence in two key, data-intensive parts of the hospital – radiology and the pharmacy – to sell software for the rest of the hospital. In all three cases (including GE), embedding healthcare software applications inside a complex, multidivisional firm makes it virtually impossible to track healthcare IT sales, engineering investments, margins and other performance data, in turn complicating the analysis of market shares and return on capital invested in IT of competing multidivisional firms.

At the time of writing, it is far from clear that these diversification strategies have paid off economically. Hospitals and health systems remain

Rank	Company	2003 revenue*	US location
1	Siemens Medical Solutions	1858.4	Malvern, PA
2	McKesson Information Solutions	1139.0	Alpharetta, GA
3	WebMD	964.0	Elmwood Park, NJ
4	Cerner Corporation	839.6	Kansas City, MO
5	Misys Healthcare Systems	467.0	Raleigh, NC
6	IDX Systems Corporation	399.2	Burlington, VT
7	Per-Se Technologies	334.5	Atlanta, GA
8	TriZetto Group	290.3	Newport Beach, CA
9	Medical Information Technology (Meditech)	270.8	Westwood, MA
10	PeopleSoft	260.7	Pleasanton, CA
11	Eclipsys Corporation	254.7	Boca Raton, FL
12	3M Health Informations Systems	216.0	Murray, UT
13	Keane	176.3	Melville, NY
14	Epic Systems Corporation	160.0	Madison, WI
15	QuadraMed Corporation	125.1	Reston, VA

Figure 7.3   Top healthcare software application providers.

Source: Modern Healthcare (May 17, 2004): 17.
*$ million

highly fragmented, and having a large presence in the pharmacy or the radiology department has not been a guarantee that enterprise-wide solutions have credibility with the senior managements and physicians whose endorsement is required to make an IT vendor selection decision. It is also not clear that there is synergy between equipment manufacture and servicing and healthcare information technology, even as the output of diagnostic imaging, laboratory, and other instrumentation becomes increasingly digital.

The largest freestanding, "pure play" healthcare IT software firm, Cerner, was predicted to generate a little less than $1 billion in revenues in 2004. Its two principal, publicly traded competitors, IDX and Eclipsys, and two privately held competitors, Epic and Meditech, are less than half as large. QuadraMed and iSoft are perhaps one-quarter as large.

Of the overall US healthcare IT market, 75–80 percent of system sales are for financial (e.g. billing) software and systems, while the remainder is for clinical applications. The fact that billing and collection remains a deeply troubled management function in hospitals and physician organizations, despite the heroic level of IT investment, may speak as much to the inability to implement complex solutions as to the quality of the software itself.

Clinical applications are rapidly growing as a share of IT spending, and seem likely to represent as much as one-third to a half of all software spending, as healthcare providers move to adopt the electronic medical record and computerized physician order entry (CPOE). As of 1998, fewer than 5 percent of US hospitals had a fully implemented computerized physician or clinical order entry system in place.[8]

Outsourcing/systems integration

With a few notable exceptions, firms that supply IT management to healthcare providers and payers, or that offer systems integration consulting, do not also supply proprietary software to the industry. According to Gartner, outsourcing in IT represents more than a $20 billion market in the US alone, a number that is expected to grow by 15 percent per year for the next several years. Within the healthcare industry, Frost and Sullivan estimates that roughly $4.2 billion was spent on outsourcing IT activities in 2002.[9]

This estimate, however, may include part of the cost of systems integration. Larger organizations that contemplate, for example, installing an electronic medical record with computerized physician order entry (see below for description) may opt to hire an outsourcing firm to install the software and build interfaces between this software and their legacy systems. As much as 45 percent of revenues attributed to outsourcing may represent systems integration (e.g. custom programming and installation).[10]

During the 1990s systems integration was one of the most rapidly growing areas of the IT consulting business. Systems integration represented a $64.5 billion segment of the IT consulting business in 2002.[11] Major actors in systems integration include IBM Global Services, Computer Sciences Corporation, Accenture, Cap Gemini, and First Consulting. As outsourcing became a logical avenue of growth for these firms, they came into competition with Electronic Data Systems and Perot Systems (established by the original founder of EDS, Ross Perot). And as with healthcare software, the services market is highly fragmented, with no single actor accounting for more than 15 percent of the total market share.

Major healthcare IT applications

Healthcare IT spending in the next decade will be driven by emerging application sets that will reshape both clinical services and administration.

These include the electronic medical record (including physician/clinical order entry), diagnostic radiology picture archiving and communication systems (PACS), remote clinical management systems both for hospitalized and ambulatory patients, customized consumer-directed health insurance plans, and real time claims management and payment systems.

The electronic medical record: the point of convergence

The most important IT application in healthcare is the so-called electronic medical record (EMR). For more than three decades healthcare informatics specialists have sought to replicate in electronic form the paper chart that has been the central focus of the patient care process in hospitals and physicians' offices. Digitizing this chart, and creating mechanisms for calling it up in diverse care settings – the exam room, the operating suite, the patient room in hospital – has been a complex technical challenge.

In order to make the electronic record usable at the point of care, it has been fused with CPOE systems. CPOE systems embed clinical decision-making capacity (the ability to order medications, diagnostic procedures, or clinical interventions) in the electronic record, enabling a physician or nurse to respond directly to changes in a patient's status. This process is enhanced by a computerized decision support system (CDSS), which audits physician orders and flags decisions that may place the patient at risk for adverse events.

That this application lies at the core of medicine's future is best validated by the decision of the Ministry of Health in Great Britain to devote nearly $6 billion (£4.3 billion) to digitizing the clinical information systems of the UK National Health Service.[12] In the United States, installing the clinical informatics systems to enable CPOE may cost as much as $30–40 million for a large hospital, and may require up to 4–5 years of implementation time.[13] Installing the software is a highly complex process, whose cost may exceed the software license cost by as much as four- or fivefold.

To date, despite pressure from payers and employers to implement CPOE, the road to implementation by healthcare providers has been exceedingly rocky. The best publicized failure was that of the Cedars-Sinai Medical Center in Los Angeles, which encountered stiff physician resistance to their CPOE system and had to retreat in the face of this opposition.[14] CPOE fundamentally changes both the clinical process and the division of administrative responsibilities within a healthcare organization. The change management challenge in organizations with poor medical staff relationships or weak buy-in by the administrative and nursing staffs is substantial. As with financial systems, the ability to implement solutions is as much or more constrained by organizational weaknesses as it is by the state of the software itself.

Historical milestones on the path to CPOE

There have been several milestones in progress toward an "intelligent" clinical record. Informatics specialists at the University of Indiana's Regenstreif Institute, Intermountain Health Care, and the Peter Bent Brigham Hospital in Boston built different versions of the electronic record, integrating electronic ordering into the record system beginning in the mid-1970s.[15] In Intermountain's case, the system generated passive alerts informing the care team of drug allergies, contraindications for ordered therapies, and required those ordering care to acknowledge and either amend the order or override the system's alert. This software, which the 3M Corporation marketed as the HELP system, was commercially available by the early 1980s.

In the mid-1980s researchers at George Washington University took another important step. They built decision support tools to help care teams in intensive care units to predict the likely survival of patients based on their presented conditions and the care interventions given. This system, called APACHE, was the first commercially available product to predict patient outcomes based upon extensive analysis of patient responses to care.[16]

These early systems were handicapped by some of the technical constraints discussed earlier, particularly inadequate database management utilities and nonfriendly user interfaces. They also required manual entry of clinical information from diverse sources that were not connected to the record system. To make the chart a living document requires wiring it to the sources of new information about a patient, which are rapidly becoming digital. Everything learned about a patient – from their genetic "fingerprints" to their lab and radiology results, as well as their vital signs and medication orders – must flow to their record in a timely and organized fashion and create new decision points in the care process.

However, the most exciting technological advance is not merely connecting the record to these converging streams of digital clinical information. Rather, it is wrapping all of this information in a decision-making framework that guides a care team in making effective clinical decisions. Rapid advances in medical knowledge are being translated into clinical decision support systems – artificial intelligence adapted to medical care decision making.

These decision support systems can help a care team and a patient to understand the implications of care decisions – medications, clinical interventions, and so on – for a patient's health, and also help structure the decisions a care team makes. Medical knowledge is directly presented, in easily accessible form, at the point of medical decision making.

At some point in its evolution, the "intelligent" electronic medical record is no longer a "record" – that is, a passive, historical document reflecting decisions made in the past about a patient and their consequences. Rather, the "record" pivots on a temporal axis, and faces forward – framing the decisions a care team should make to improve a patient's health. When fused with physician or provider order entry (CPOE), the electronic "record" becomes somewhat akin to the navigational system in an airplane – assimilating current information about a patient's position with what is known about their trajectory and the likely consequences of care decisions.

Computerized physician order entry systems have been shown to markedly reduce not only adverse drug events but also other forms of medical error.[17] It is a function of the ability of CPOE systems to audit and evaluate the quality of physician ordering decisions and bring potential risks of a given order to a physician's attention prior to executing the order. Less obviously, these systems save scarce resources by reducing the duplication of diagnostic tests and by improving the throughput of patients whose treatment requires the coordination of complex diagnostic and therapeutic decisions.

Constraints on CPOE adoption

Intelligent clinical record systems incorporating CPOE remain constrained by the current state of medical knowledge, particularly the relative paucity of clinical effectiveness studies that evaluate the consequences of care decisions for a patient's health. Updating this knowledge base will be a continuing cost challenge to the vendors of these systems.

These clinical management systems are also constrained by the various data needs of multiple users – for example, in medication decisions between the prescribing physician, the nurse charged with administering and monitoring the medications, and the pharmacist who must compound and deliver the medications. Each actor has a unique set of data needs and a unique set of decisions that must be made based upon the data presented. Failure to resolve these issues can leave a patient exposed to communications breakdowns, which result in medical errors such as those that killed *Boston Globe* reporter Betsy Lehman several years ago at a prominent Boston cancer treatment facility.[18] Resolving this latter issue is a complex engineering and human factor challenge for software engineers.

As mentioned earlier, implementation of CPOE remains constrained by a daunting array of organizational and resource issues. CPOE requires digitizing not only a patient's medical record but also connecting the diagnostic resources of the hospital or health system to that record. The substantial cost and complexity of installing the infrastructure required to support CPOE is both an economic and administrative barrier to adoption of this tool. Not all institutions or practices have the capital resources or IT support staff to effect the transition. Transition will also be a challenge to national health systems, whose capital budgets compete with governmental resource demands outside of healthcare, which in turn are affected by the economic conditions and fiscal policies of the sponsoring governments.

Leadership is also an essential ingredient to making a transition. It is senseless to digitize all of a hospital or physician group's current order sets, or to reproduce processes made necessary by paper- or telephone-based ordering and verification. Reordering clinical work flows and eliminating unnecessary steps will reduce clerical employment and alter the boundaries around traditional professional franchises. This process has significant change management and "political" implications, and cannot be delegated to IT vendors. Hospitals and health systems with weak leadership or with poor relationships with physicians and nursing staffs will have great difficulty reaching consensus on appropriate clinical protocols and work flow schemes.

In the United States there is the real prospect that wealthy hospitals and physician organizations may make the digital transition a decade before less fortunate organizations, and that hospitals may make the transition long before its private practicing physicians, many of whom practice in small-scale practices and who lack both the capital resources and the time required to install and operate new systems. Hospitals that wish to help their physicians make this transition will face a variety of legal constraints, including fraud and abuse laws and laws governing the transfer of resources from nonprofit to for-profit uses. There is a substantial and complex public policy agenda associated with leveling these resource gradients, and in assuring the adoption by physicians of these tools.[19]

Diagnostic applications

Output from major diagnostic resources will become digital over the next decade, and data from laboratory and radiology facilities will enter the "record." Diagnostic applications are not distinct from other elements in the digital surround of patient care; increasingly, diagnostic radiology and tissue pathology is information technology, and visual images traditionally captured on film or on slide will become digitized.

Clinical genetics

As information about a patient's genetic makeup becomes more plentiful and useful for guiding care decisions, a digital means of manipulating and interpreting genetic information will become incorporated into a patient's record. Genetic variation in pathogen response to treatment will be an important component of the management of infectious disease and cancer treatment.[20] Genetic information will also be needed not only to assess the immune competence of patients, but also the variation of individual patients' abilities to metabolize drugs. Genetic variation in the metabolism of drugs may hold the key to predicting and avoiding adverse drug reactions.[21] The gathering of this information will be tied to semiconductor-based clinical microarrays. Analysis of the implications of this information for patient treatment will become part of the clinical decision support process.

The increasing relevance of genetic information, both on pathogens and on patients, to clinical decision-making will heighten the importance of how institutions safeguard the privacy and confidentiality of patient records. This issue was not anticipated when the US Congress passed the Health Insurance Portability and Accountability Act (known as HIPAA) in 1996. Patients will not permit genetic testing unless they can be assured that only those individuals involved in their treatment have access to the information, and that genetic information will not be used to discriminate against them in the clinical environment or the workplace.

Digital radiology

Hospitals and physician groups are installing infrastructure to route and store digital images from radiological examinations that will be integrated into patient care and billing systems. The systems employed are called PACS (Picture Archiving Communication and Storage). PACs enable hospitals and clinicians to dispense with radiology film and rely instead on digital records of examinations as the basis for diagnostic evaluations. When wedded to the broadband Internet, PACS systems enable radiologists to practice "anytime and anywhere" that images can reach them. As of 2003, the estimated figure for PACS revenues in North America was roughly $1.0 billion. Projection for 2004 was $1.16 billion.[22]

PACs systems were made possible by early and aggressive efforts by the radiology community to create digital data and messaging standards that permitted images from different hardware platforms to be communicated and stored efficiently. This standard, DICOM, made it possible for networks to form among institutions with different radiology equipment, or inside institutions with multiple hardware vendors.[23] Laboratory equipment vendors are poised to implement a similar data standard.[24]

The confluence of digital radiology and broadband Internet connectivity have abolished the geographic constraints upon diagnostic radiology practice, and have enabled radiologists in India or Australia to interpret images forwarded to them from London or New York "overnight." It has also enabled academic radiology departments to extend their consultative reach into remote geographic areas where radiologists may not even be able to practice.

Manufacturers of radiological equipment have sensed that digital radiology has blurred the boundaries between hardware manufacture and clinical software. Indeed, the most advanced data management applications in medicine are in high-technology imaging modalities such as magnetic resonance imaging (MRI) and computerized tomography (CT). As a consequence, radiological equipment manufacturers such as Siemens and GE have diversified into clinical software, seeking to consolidate a highly fragmented field, and offer applications which both link to their hardware and extend their corporate reach into clinical areas that are not hardware dependent. This diversification was mentioned earlier in the discussion of healthcare IT market structure.

Remote monitoring/management of patients

Traditional patient care has involved taking physical custody of patients and providing hands-on monitoring of their condition. This has involved intervening in clinical crises and remaining involved until a patient has stabilized. However, an increasing amount of care in hospitals has involved monitoring patients at risk for some form of catastrophic medical event (cardiac arrest, breathing crises, etc.). Hospitals have introduced whole subcategories of beds (observation beds attached to emergency rooms, telemetry beds for cardiac patients, etc.) to monitor the unstable patient.

For two decades hospitals with 24-hour cardiology coverage have monitored patients in remote locations (smaller hospitals, clinics, etc.) through electrocardiograph (EKG) signals transmitted through telephone lines. These connections have permitted evaluation of changes in patients' heart rhythms and also communication with the remote care team to intervene when rhythm changes threatened a patient's health. Cardiologists have also allowed patients with aberrant heart rhythms to return home with Holter monitors, which record several hours of heart rhythms for later analysis and possible intervention.

These applications are on the verge of enabling an entirely new business for healthcare providers: the location-independent monitoring (and management) of unstable patients. Advances in biometrics, that is, the monitoring of patient physiological signs and characteristics, will enable large numbers of unstable patients to be monitored from remote locations for a wide range of clinical conditions. These conditions include cardiac instability, diabetes, asthma, congestive heart failure, chronic obstructive pulmonary disease, chronic pain, and Alzheimer's. Those individuals being monitored will span the acuity spectrum: from critically ill patients in hospital intensive care units to the frail elderly living at home or in assisted living facilities.

Biometrics technology has enabled a wide range of conditions to be monitored continuously by increasingly affordable sensor arrays. These sensors can monitor a wide range of physiological conditions: heart rhythm, temperature, blood pressure, blood sugar and oxygen, breathing, physical location (indoors or outdoors), gait, and physical orientation (standing, lying, falling). In the near future, sensors will be able to detect smells (including infections) remotely, as well as evaluate by machine interpretation voice stress and the content of speech.[25] Sensor arrays can also be integrated with real-time two-way voice communications with the subject being monitored via wireless connections.

Sensor arrays can be deployed with remarkable flexibility to accommodate the mobility of a "patient" (a term which applies inaptly to the well but unstable person outside of the institution). They can be worn as part of garments or wristbands, or can be incorporated into a patient bed or room, or into a living environment such as a home or apartment. The latter applications are being explored by a consortium of investigators working on the so-called "Smart House" – an intelligent monitoring system capable of maintaining unobtrusive surveillance of the health status of fragile persons in their homes, including not only health indicators but also whether a person is eating, opening the medicine cabinet, or sleeping[26] (see figure 7.4).

A California-based company, CardioNet, has incorporated a wearable three-lead EKG monitor with wireless technology to build a real-time cardiac

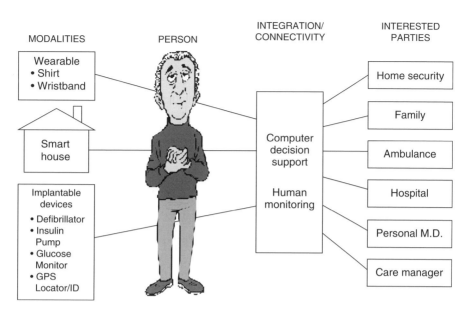

MODALITIES PERSON INTEGRATION/CONNECTIVITY INTERESTED PARTIES

Figure 7.4   The emerging healthcare safety net.

Source: Health Futures, Inc.

monitoring system for patients with unstable heart rhythms. The technology incorporates two-way live voice communication with a wearer, enabling an operator to determine if a wearer is experiencing pain and possibly to coordinate emergency medical intervention. During 2002 the firm, in collaboration with the region's cardiologists, deployed a monitoring network across metropolitan Philadelphia that enabled patients across a region to be monitored outside a hospital, creating a "virtual" telemetry system.[27]

Most remarkably, sensor arrays can be integrated with microprocessors and wireless technology into implantable devices such as pacemakers or insulin pumps, which not only monitor and medicate patients continuously but are also capable of storing and sending information about a patient's status to a monitoring station as well as responding to external signals redirecting the intervention (e.g. resetting the pacemaker or altering the dosage of insulin).

Companies such as Medtronic and the Cordis division of Johnson & Johnson are developing "intelligent" implantable devices for virtually every organ system in the body, which can continuously monitor and intervene to stabilize patients who are at risk of acute illness. The demand in the US for implantable medical devices will increase nearly 11 percent annually to

$24.4 billion in 2007. Favorable growth will continue due to upward trends in medical conditions and patient activity, changing patient treatment approaches and technological advances.[28]

It is possible to monitor and direct the care of intensive care patients from remote locations. Hospitals in the United States are under pressure from payers and employers to shift clinical management of intensive care patients from independent attending physicians to hospital-employed specialists who do nothing but care for critically ill patients. Intensive care specialists have been shown to dramatically lower length of stay, mortality, and variation in clinical resource use of intensive care unit (ICU) patients. The problem is that far fewer intensivists are being trained than would be required to effect this staffing change across the full spectrum of US hospitals.[29]

A technology originally developed at Johns Hopkins University incorporates remote physiological monitoring, video surveillance, voice communications between remote intensivists and the nursing staff in a target ICU, and an "intelligent" patient record into an intensive care monitoring system. This technology has been called the eICU, and in alpha tests permitted a single intensivist to monitor and manage over forty ICU patients in three remote locations from a single monitoring station.[30]

The firm that developed the technology believes that it will scale up to enable a single intensivist and intensive care nurse team to monitor as many as two hundred ICU patients from a remote location. They also believe that with appropriate adaptation, the same suite of applications could be used to remotely manage operating suites, cardiac telemetry and step-down ICU units, and 24-hour observation units attached to hospitals' emergency rooms.[31]

Telepresence technology, facilitating direct communication by providers from remote locations, may enable two-way remote physician visits. A California-based firm, In Touch Health, has built a robot physician extender incorporating infrared sensors, a moveable video screen, two-way voice and video communication, including a video camera directed by a joystick. The camera can focus not only on a patient's face, but also on the affected parts of their body.[32] Patients seem to enjoy the idea of a real-time personal connection with a physician, even if the physician is not in the same room.

Remote patient monitoring is presently an emerging market filled with small firms seeking to develop autonomous, free-standing applications with proprietary monitoring systems. Each emerging company must also develop its own network of physician users, depending on the specialty involved – cardiologists, pulmonary disease specialists, and so on. This will prove uneconomical as the number of competing monitoring applications reaches a certain level.

Eventually, the proliferation of remote monitoring modalities will require consolidation of monitoring functions and the creation of software conventions which integrate patient telemetry signals into the intelligent clinical software maintained by hospitals or large physician clinics. Monitoring of unstable or at-risk patients will become integrated with disease management applications, and will become a substantial business independent of inpatient or outpatient services.

Payer applications

The principal purpose of the HIPAA legislation of 1996 was to provide continuity of insurance coverage for individuals who had lost or changed jobs. However, it also contained significant changes in privacy policy for confidential medical information for providers and health plans. This in turn had profound implications for the handling and transmittal of information. Finally, HIPAA contained provisions that standardized administrative procedures in the management of electronic medical claims.

The administrative simplification provisions of HIPAA impose significant mandates on health insurers by standardizing coding schemes and data formats for medical claims. To comply with HIPAA, health insurers needed to rework their software for managing claims, at a cost estimated at close to $15 billion.[33] The federal Department of Health and Human Services estimates that HIPAA regulations in the healthcare industry will result in $29.9 billion in benefits over the following ten years. HIPAA provides a rationale for some health insurers to digitize their claims management process and to harmonize their claims systems with emerging broadband Internet connectivity.

The back end of health insurance information systems in the United States were until recently a nightmarish agglomeration of partially computerized paper-based claims systems. The sheer volume of transactions boggles the mind, and by itself constitutes a formidable argument in favor of a national health insurance system. In 2001 American health insurers processed over 6 billion claims for payment, and tens of billions of other transactions related to claims (eligibility determinations, referral authorizations, etc.).[34]

According to Faulkner and Gray, only 18 percent of HMO claims and 45 percent of commercial insurance claims were even submitted electronically as late as 1999.[35] The vast majority of claims had to be processed manually because of incomplete or inconsistent data, and communications back to providers were almost universally driven by paper or telephone, requiring resubmission of the claim. While it costs pennies to process a clean claim electronically, manual processing of a defective claim can cost insurers as much as $50.[36]

Providers in turn have had to employ vast numbers of clinically literate workers, many of whom have nursing backgrounds, to manage the flow of claims and feedback on claims from insurers. (Simultaneously, American providers were experiencing double-digit vacancy rates for nursing personnel in direct patient contact positions.[37])

Electronic submittal of medical claims has a more than two decade-long history in the United States. Submittal media have included magnetic tape and dedicated high-capacity telephone lines, such as T-1 lines. However, only recently has it been possible for electronic claims management to be truly interactive. The advent of broadband Internet connectivity has revolutionized the medical claims management business by providing an affordable, public infrastructure capable of reaching into physicians' offices as well as hospitals.

The late 1990s witnessed an attempt by an aggressive and well-capitalized start-up firm to build an Internet clearinghouse for medical claims. For a brief moment, it seemed possible that this firm, Healtheon (now Web MD), could have created a ubiquitous web-based medical claims management system.[38] However, a combination of software engineering problems and resistance by health insurers to surrendering their direct linkage to their provider network scuttled the firm's plans. Web MD continues to have a major foothold in physician office software, and in more traditional electronic data interchange medical claims management.[39] Nevertheless, regional claims clearinghouses that employ broadband Internet connectivity are cutting both provider and insurer medical claims costs in New England, the Pacific Northwest, and other parts of the country.[40]

Internet connectivity will do much more than help restructure medical claims management. It will also help health plans develop new relationships with their subscribers.[41] Health plans have been limited in their ability to interact with their geographically dispersed membership through mail or telephone communication. With growing consumer access to the Internet, health insurers have been able to create personalized web portals for their subscribers, which give them access to information about their benefits and enable them to make appointments and to have email connection to their physicians. Kaiser and Group Health of Puget Sound were early and aggressive adopters of this approach. The Internet has also provided health plans with an interactive and affordable platform for launching disease management/health improvement initiatives with their subscribers.

Consumer-directed health plans – an IT intensive new health insurance product

Web-based decision support tools are at the core of an emerging product for health plans – the consumer-directed health plan. Rather than providing all their employees with the same coverage, consumer-directed plans enable the employee to identify their family's specific insurance needs, determine the amount of insurance they are likely to require, and select both premium contributions and cost-sharing alternatives that match their needs. Consumer-directed health plans feature "personal spending accounts," which may roll over from year to year and which represent money that consumers can save if they are more conservative in their use of health services and medications (see figure 7.5).

By helping to disentangle the pure "casualty" insurance and "service benefit" portions of their health coverage, consumer-directed plans provide financial incentives for employees and their families to manage their own health. Information technology can not only help employees track their use of "personal spending" accounts in real time, IT applications can also provide dual use debit/credit cards to debit their personal spending accounts, and when the funds in personal accounts are exhausted, charge the patient share

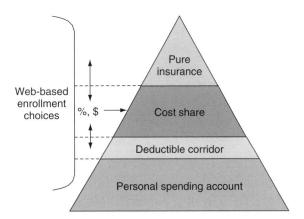

Figure 7.5   Consumer-directed health plans: a primer.

Source: Health Futures, Inc.

of subsequent health costs. Providers benefit by being paid directly rather than via a sixty- to ninety-day (costly) billing process.

Many US observers predict rapid growth in this IT-enabled model of health coverage. Early experience with this approach suggests that consumer-directed plans, appropriately implemented, can cut the rate of increase in health benefits costs by half or more.[42] Forrester Research believes that 2.7 million Americans will be covered by such arrangements by the end of 2005, less than 2 percent of the more than 160 million Americans covered by private health insurance.[43]

Barriers to adoption include the unwillingness of employees to consider increases in cost-sharing, regardless of the impact on their monthly premium contribution, resistance by labor unions and lack of understanding of the concept and mechanics by insurance brokers and corporate benefits managers, and paternalism on the part of corporate benefits managers reluctant to surrender control over benefits design to their own workers. The easing of health cost growth could slow the adoption of this IT-intensive approach, even as health insurers reap the benefits of incorporating digital technology into their core business.

Outsourcing information technology installation and management

Outsourcing is not a new phenomenon in healthcare. When the United States government implemented its Medicare program in the mid-1960s, the Department of Health Education and Welfare outsourced claims processing for care to the elderly to the nation's Blue Cross plans, who functioned as "fiscal intermediaries" for the federal program. Beginning in the 1970s, US hospitals outsourced management of their housekeeping and food services programs to firms such as ServiceMaster and Sodexho. Hospitals and payers were traditionally reluctant to outsource their core administrative functions, even if they were not functioning optimally.

In information technology, the groundwork for outsourcing was laid early with the growth of modern computing. In the early 1970s mainframe computers were sufficiently expensive and difficult to operate that most providers and smaller payers could not afford to own their own. In the early days of mainframe computing, two firms gained large footholds in medical claims processing through time-sharing. These were Shared Medical Systems in the hospital financial systems market and Electronic Data Systems in the state government-run Medicaid market. Both firms employed batch processing to speed claims' processing and management, communicating with their customers first through magnetic tape and subsequently through expensive, high-bandwidth dedicated telephone lines such as T-1 lines.

As hospitals and payers merged into larger and more complex enterprises during the 1990s, the challenge of integrating diverse legacy administrative and clinical computing systems into enterprise-wide models created intense demand for "systems integration" consulting. Systems integration became the fastest growing segment of the management consulting industry during the 1990s. And as IT vendors offered new suites of clinical software, including the electronic medical record (EMR) and computerized physician order entry (CPOE), so systems integration became more complex.

Some categories of healthcare workers such as database managers became increasingly scarce, and hospitals in particular faced growing personnel shortages in their information technology departments at all levels. Consulting firms such as Accenture, First Consulting, Cap Gemini Ernst Young and Computer Sciences Corporation thus began offering to operate hospital and health insurer IT departments as part of their systems integration packages. They competed for this rapidly growing business with firms such as Electronic Data Systems and Perot Systems, which grew into outsourcing from the claims processing side.

Outsourcing got a big boost from the broadband Internet, which enabled IT vendors to create so-called "thin client" models of computing. Instead of installing 25 million lines of complex systems code under the desks of every healthcare worker, "thin client" architecture enabled workers in an organization to access system software operated in remote data centers through a web browser. This technology is known as "application service provision" or ASP.

Instead of data processing taking place within a complex network of servers inside the client institution, complex applications are maintained by the outsourcing firm in their own data centers. Clinical and financial data flow in a continuous and highly complex matrix of loops between the client institution and the outsourcing firm. It is far cheaper and easier to maintain, upgrade, and troubleshoot software in proprietary data centers than it is in the vast, city-like mazes of large provider sites. ASP has had a very slow takeoff in healthcare, as providers and their IT professionals have been reluctant to surrender control of their data and software licenses, and the applications themselves have been slow to develop.

Outsourcing IT applications was expected by Gartner to be more than a $20 billion business in the United States economy by 2005. Outsourcing in healthcare IT has grown at a 15 percent rate, double the rate of IT systems spending, since 2000, suggesting that the increasing complexity of IT applications in healthcare is promoting an outsourced model. IT will be only one of a suite of core administrative functions outsourced in health systems.[44]

The same broadband connectivity that has promoted ASP and remote hosting of clinical and medical claims management will also promote the outsourced operations of business office functions, human resources, and supply chain management. As was discussed earlier, the ability to digitize diagnostic information will make the outsourcing of some clinical services, particularly diagnostic radiology, intensive care, and clinical laboratory services feasible.

Conclusion

Robust investment in clinical informatics solutions seems likely to accelerate in coming years, as pressures from private and public payers for improved clinical performance and efficiency increase. Those expectations will translate into political support not only for public investment in healthcare information technology, but for increased regulatory efforts to assure interoperability and compliance.[45]

Healthcare providers can expect pressure to alter their traditional bricks-and-mortar and equipment capital spending priorities to make room for clinical information technology investment. Boards, managements, and clinical leadership will find that incorporating digital technology into their service offerings is their most significant management challenge in the next decade. Healthcare workers will find that IT will help to reduce the amount of time consumed in clerical and administrative activity. Health professionals will also find that IT systems will grow in sophistication and that they will assist professionals in remaining current with the evolving state of medical knowledge as well as with new uses for technologies and drugs.

Consumers will notice significant changes in their relationship to the health system as IT applications broaden and gain widespread acceptance. They will find easier access to medical knowledge and to care provision. As the capacity of health systems to monitor health status independent of provider sites grows, so patients in need will be freed from the need to visit providers or to be admitted to care within institutions in order to receive help. A health system available twenty-four hours a day and seven days a week is within realization. Health insurance will also change; it will become essentially transparent and interactive. Subscribers will find that IT applications not only enable them to customize their coverage to their unique needs, but they will also find assistance and guidance in managing their health risks through disease management programs that reach out to them through Internet connectivity and intelligent voice interfaces.

Healthcare will become less obtrusive and more sparing of the time both of patients and families and of those who care for them. Information technology will lower barriers to access to medical knowledge and consultation, dramatically lowering the access gradient for medical knowledge both regionally and worldwide. Health services will become "more intelligent," context-aware, and better woven into the fabric of human life. These advances will come at a substantial economic cost to health systems, both in acquisition and in learning to use the complex new tools. How effectively the investments generate returns for healthcare organizations and health economies will depend in large measure on how effectively and thoughtfully the powerful tools are taken up, used, and implemented.

NOTES

The author wishes to thank Gilbert Gimm, a doctoral student at the Wharton School, and Anita Gupta for providing invaluable research assistance in preparing this chapter.

1. Executive summary by Suresh Gunasekaran, "Market Forecast: Healthcare Industry, 2000–2005," *Gartner Dataquest* (April 25, 2002).
2. Phelps Manatt and L. L. P. Phillips, "Spending our Money Wisely: Improving America's Healthcare System by Investing in Healthcare Information Technology," Health Technology Center (April 2003), available on http://www.nhii.org/Docs/HealthTech_MonographV2.pdf.
3. J. E. Wennberg and M. M. Cooper, eds., *The Dartmouth Atlas of Health Care* (Chicago, IL: American Hospital Publishing, Inc., 1998).
4. R. J. Gordon, "Does the New Economy Measure up to the Great Inventions of the Past," *Journal of Economic Perspectives* 4(14) (2000): 49–74.
5. F. Lecureux, "New Perspectives on Computer Concepts," *Computer Architecture*, chapter 5, available on http://gaia.ecs.csus.edu/~lecureux/power01slds/04ch5–98/sld036.html.
6. "Healthcare: Pharmaceuticals," *Standard & Poors Industry Survey* (December 11, 2003): 7.
7. Shared Medical Systems, Company Annual Report (10-K), 2000.
8. D. F. Doolan and D. W. Bates, "Computerized Physician Order Entry Systems in Hospitals: Mandates and Incentives," *Health Affairs* 21(4) (2002): 180–188.
9. V. Subramany, "US IT Outsourcing Markets for Healthcare," *Frost and Sullivan Research Report* (December 8, 2003).

10. George Yurek, Perot Systems, telephone interview, November 2003.

11. "Computers: Commercial Services," *Standard & Poors Industry Survey* (January 15, 2004): 5.

12. "NHS Seeks Extra £2bn in IT Funding," *Financial Times* (November 29, 2003).

13. Doolan and Bates, "Physician Order Entry Systems."

14. J. Morrissey, "Harmonic Divergence. Cedars-Sinai Joins Others in Holding off on CPOE," *Modern Healthcare* 34(8) (2004): 16.

15. E. H. Shortliffe, L. E. Perreault, G. Wiederhold, and L. M. Fagan, *Medical Informatics: Computer Applications in Health Care and Biomedicine*, 2nd edn (New York: Springer, 2001).

16. W. A. Knaus, "APACHE 1978–2001: The Development of a Quality Assurance System Based on Prognosis: Milestones and Personal Reflections," *Archives of Surgery* 137(1) (2002): 37–41.

17. Doolan and Bates, "Physician Order Entry Systems."

18. L. K. Altman, "Top Hospital's Blunders Blamed in Big Overdoses; One Cancer Patient Died; Another Hurt," *Houston Chronicle* (March 24, 1995).

19. J. Goldsmith, D. Blumenthal, and W. Rishel, "Federal Health Information Policy: A Case of Arrested Development," *Health Affairs* 22(4) (2003): 44–55.

20. C. Arnst, "New Cancer Weapons Strut their Stuff," *Business Week Online* (May 10, 2001), online article retrieved 11/20/2002 From http://www.businessweek.com/technology/content/may2001/tc20010510_835.htm; M. S. Hirsch *et al.*, "Antiretroviral Drug Resistance Testing in Adults with HIV Infection," *Journal of the American Medical Association* 279(4) (1998): 1984–1991; J. Durant *et al.*, "Drug-Resistance Genotyping in HIV-1 Therapy: The VIRADAPT Randomized Controlled Trial," *Lancet* 353 (1999): 2185–2199; H. Z. Ring and D. L. Kroetz, "Candidate Gene Approach for Pharmacogenetic Studies," *Pharmacogenomics* 3(1) (2002): 47–56.

21. J. Brockmoller *et al.*, "Pharmacogenetic Diagnostics of Cytochrome P450 Polymorphisms in Clinical Drug Development and in Drug Treatment," *Pharmacogenomics* 1(2) (2000): 125–151; K. A. Phillips *et al.*, "Potential Role of Pharmacogenomics in Reducing Adverse Drug Reactions: A Systematic Review," *Journal of the American Medical Association* 286(18), (2001): 2270–2279.

22. Antonio F. Garcia, Industry Analyst, Medical Imaging, Frost & Sullivan, personal correspondence, May 2004.

23. Shortliffe *et al.*, *Medical Informatics*.

24. CDISC Laboratory Standards, online information retrieved 4/2/2004 from http://www.cdisc.org/standards/.

25. Robin Felder, Director of Medical Automation Research Center, University of Virginia, telephone interview, February 2003.

26. A. Eisenberg, "A 'Smart' Home, to Avoid the Nursing Home," *New York Times* (April 5, 2001).

27. CardioNet, "CardioNet Closes $18.5 Million Financing Round," online press release (2002) retrieved 1/2/2003 from http://www.cardionet.com/pr_03_09_02.html.

28. Report by the Freedonia Group, "Implantable Medical Devices to 2007 – Market Size, Market Shape, Market Leaders, Demand Forecast and Sales," October 2003, available on http://www.Freedoniagroup.com/index.html.

29. D. C. Angus *et al.*, "Caring for the Critically Ill Patient. Current and Projected Workforce Requirements for Care of the Critically Ill and Patients with Pulmonary Disease: Can we

Meet the Requirements of an Aging Population?," *Journal of the American Medical Association* 284(21) (2000): 2762–2770.

30. M. J. Breslow *et al.*, "Effect of a Multiple-Site Intensive Care Unit Telemedicine Program on Clinical and Economic Outcomes: An Alternative Paradigm for Intensivist Staffing," *Critical Care Medicine* 32(1) (2004): 31–38.

31. Brian Rosenberg, Medical Director, VISICU, telephone interview, February 2003.

32. Associated Press, "Remote Robot Provides Medical Care to Patients," PDF format *USA Today* (June 18, 2003).

33. Cost estimated from AHIP and Gartner data; Gartner Reports, W. Rishel, "HIPAA Survey: Cost Estimates Down, but Fewer Expect ROI" (June 2003).

34. Faulkner Gray, *Health Data Directory, 2001 Edition* (New York: Faulkner Gray, 2001).

35. Faulkner Gray, *Health Data Directory, 2000 Edition* (New York: Faulkner Gray, 2000).

36. Christine Malcolm, Computer Sciences Corporation, personal communication, June 2000.

37. American Hospital Association, "In Our Hands: Helping Hospital Leaders Build a Thriving Workforce," AHA Workforce Commission report, January 2001.

38. M. Lewis, *The New, New Thing* (Harmondsworth: Penguin, 2001).

39. K. Southwick, "The Nine Lives of WebMD," *Medicine on the Net* 10(6) (2003): 1–6.

40. F. Jossi, "Transaction Processing," *Healthcare Informatics* 20(2) (2003): 72–75.

41. J. C. Goldsmith, "Internet and Managed Care, a New Wave of Innovation," *Health Affairs* 19(6) (2000): 42–56.

42. J. C. Goldsmith, "Consumer Directed Health Plans: The Emerging Template for Private Health Insurance," *COR Healthcare Market Strategist* 1 (October 2003): 17–20.

43. B. J. Holmes, "Consumer Directed Health Plan Leaders Poised for Growth," Business View Brief, Forrester Research (July 22, 2003), online article retrieved 5/11/2004 from http://www.forrester.com/ER/Research/Brief/Excerpt/0,1317,16035,00.html.

44. Frost & Sullivan, "Healthcare IT Outsourcing to Swell," online press release retrieved 5/11/2004 from http://medicalinformatics.weblogsinc.com/entry/6696037503747793.

45. Goldsmith *et al.*, "Federal Health Information Policy."

8 Healthcare innovation across sectors: convergences and divergences

Lawton R. Burns and Stephen M. Sammut

The twin towers: invention and adoption
Common business models
Strategic resources, capabilities, and key success factors
Technological convergence across sectors

The twin towers: invention and adoption

All of the sectors analyzed in this volume face the same dual challenge: the invention of new technology and assuring its long-term clinical adoption by customers. These challenges are neither easy nor inexpensive.

For many of the sectors, the technology and the underlying science have encountered the same phenomenon as other technology development in other endeavors, namely convergence of many skills. Pharmaceutical and biotechnology firms – long accustomed to both random discovery and synthesis of bioactive chemicals or recombination of known active proteins – are now relying on genomic and proteomic foundations for drug discovery. These new sciences are just the first steps in the long process of drug development wherein tools such as bioinformatics must be integrated. As companies in the sector pursue new avenues of discovery and development, and as the associated costs spiral ever upward, healthcare systems throughout the world seek to rationalize care and lower overall costs. The industry has the added burden, therefore, of demonstrating the economic advantages of new drugs, thus giving rise to yet another new discipline, pharmaco-economics.

At the same time, the sectors must increasingly conduct their R&D activities with an understanding of multiple technologies. Pharmaceutical and biotechnology firms must embrace not only genomics and proteomics, but also the more traditional technologies that are chemistry-based. Platform-based firms are constrained to advance beyond their circumscribed technological base to incorporate development and delivery capabilities. Device firms have migrated beyond electronics to encompass various materials sciences and information systems, and information technology (IT) firms have begun to combine their products with imaging and broadband capabilities.

The increasingly complex milieu of discovery and development has the added challenge of satisfying the needs of an aging and more health conscious community of patients. Physicians, therefore, must remain current with new technology as never before and must determine how the new therapies can be incorporated into their practice in such a way that payers exerting increasing levels of control will approve.

To a great extent, the firms are built on the intangibles of their intellectual capital and the ability to harness and coordinate it across different therapeutic areas and research programs. Not surprisingly, several of the sectors rest heavily on the *art* of discovery and the vagaries of trial-and-error experimentation.

Intellectual property law in the developed nations has always been the foundation of pharmaceutical economics, wherein companies could depend on a limited monopoly for their patented synthetic compounds. There are many factors conspiring to the resulting hegemony in each therapeutic area for both traditional pharmaceutical companies as well as biotechnology companies. These factors merit review in this summary chapter, because the fundamental business strategies will be affected by a sea change in intellectual property regimes and necessary new approaches to managing intangible property.

Historically, the discovery and development of a new compound was the effort of each company. A company had sole ownership of a chain of patent blockades for each compound from lab bench to the scaled-up synthesis for production. The drug discovery and development intellectual property inventory has grown increasingly fragmented, however. The proliferation of competent university technology transfer programs and the global emergence of research-driven biotechnology companies – now in the thousands in the US, Europe, India, China and Taiwan, Singapore, South Africa, Brazil, and former Warsaw Pact countries – has produced a patent landscape that requires a dozen or more technology licenses for each product brought to market, with a resulting layering of royalty obligations and consequent reduction of profit margins. These factors are compounded by the concerted efforts of developing countries to secure products at affordable costs for their health-stressed populations. The pharmaceutical companies acquiesce with deeply discounted or donated products, only to find that black markets in those countries emerge and export the same products at below market prices to the developing world, thus undermining attempts at health equity. And the industry is cast as avaricious and must, therefore, address issues that now extend from the challenges of drug development through commerce to unprecedented issues of ethics and morality. There is a cruel irony here; the industry's contribution to human health over the last half-century is inestimable and the professionals in the industry pride themselves on their commitment to doing good while doing well. The controversy, however, will not be soon resolved.

The invention of new technology and the securing of proprietary rights to assure a return on investment are only half of the equation. The other half is its successful commercialization and adoption by customers and buyers – ideally as a new standard of care. The challenge here varies, depending on the sector. Some sectors have succeeded largely due to their commercialization efforts, such as the pharmaceutical sector's development of large sales forces and sophisticated marketing techniques. But pharmaceuticals' success here has been financed by two decades of strong earnings that are not enjoyed by other sectors such as the still emerging biotechnology sector, where scarcely two dozen companies of thousands globally have achieved profitability. In contrast to pharmaceuticals, biotechnology firms have spent more of their revenues on R&D activities as compared to 15 percent to 20 percent spent by the pharmaceutical sector (although in absolute numbers the R&D spending of the largest pharmaceutical companies rivals the cumulative spending of the greater than 300 US publicly traded biotechnology companies).

Given the cumulative losses referred to in chapter 3 and the mere handful of successful products, biotechnology companies have not enjoyed the financial slack to invest in both R&D and the infrastructure for commercialization, such as detailing forces and advertising. This limitation has largely condemned the majority of biotechnology companies to retreat from being fully integrated pharmaceutical companies (FIPCOs) to the model of research-intensive pharmaceutical companies (RIPCOs). While it is the case that biotechnology firms from their origins worked with pharmaceutical firms, for example, Genentech's collaboration with Eli Lilly for the development of recombinant human insulin, the pace and absolute number of joint commercialization efforts with pharmaceutical firms has moved markedly upwards.

The issues above have a curious metric expressed in the capital markets. Burrill & Company has tracked the market capitalizations of the entire group of public biotechnology companies against the combined market capitalization of Merck & Company and Pfizer. Over the decade the ratio of market capitalizations has been in the range of 0.7 to 1.1. In other words, the public markets value the commercial infrastructure and FIPCO model of established pharmaceutical companies (despite their challenged product pipelines) far more than the research pipelines (over 350 products in clinical trials) of the biotechnology industry as a whole.

As described in chapter 4, platform technology and IT firms face the issue of strained resources and severely decreased market capitalization, largely because the bulk of firms in these sectors are smaller, entrepreneurial start-ups that have focused heavily on new genomic and proteomic approaches to drug discovery only to find that the required array of technologies and skills is so fragmented that their point in the value chain cannot extract sufficient rents from the pricing of pharmaceuticals to sustain their business models.

Across the five sectors characterized in this book, medical device firms are best positioned to deal with the two challenges of innovation and commercialization. Companies such as Medtronic, Guidant, and several operating companies of Johnson & Johnson have a documented stream of innovative products – often revolutionary in terms of less-invasive life-saving intervention – and a strong history of earnings to finance product development and commercialization activities. Device companies are not immune from the changing nature of intellectual property regimes, but their use of and reliance on patents differs from the pharmaceutical industry. Each product line is often covered by scores of patents often controlled by each company – for example, the patent blockades assembled by each of the above cited participants in the balloon angioplasty and vascular stent business.

Until the early 1990s pharmaceutical firms enjoyed a growth rate in earnings the pace of which began to decline with the downturn in drug productivity. Like pharmaceutical firms, device companies market their products directly to physicians. Unlike pharmaceutical firms, device firms enjoy a shorter and less costly regulatory path and far more efficient marketing channels by virtue of dealing with a small number of specialists with high volumes in a given therapeutic area (as opposed to marketing to a large number of primary care physicians). There are also other differences in the marketing dynamics. The most successful devices over the last two decades have created new procedures that carry fees for physicians and hospitals that drive sustained adoption. Patients have clearly been the beneficiary of the new technologies, as well as the national health care bill, as the number of open heart and renal calculi surgeries have declined dramatically with the introduction of less-invasive procedures.

Less tangible is the relationship between device company detailers and their physician customers. Here there is a far greater two-way dialog whereby companies are fed with a continuous stream of new ideas or ways of improving their products. While there are advantages to participation in the medical device sector, it is also the most competitive and litigious sector. Entry into the market is enormously difficult, but when successful, the younger companies are rewarded with extraordinary acquisition deals. For example, Medtronic acquired Minimed, with modest sales for over $1 billion. Why? Minimed had technology for blood glucose monitoring that was an important key to Medtronic's product strategy in diabetes. In similar manner, Johnson & Johnson paid $14 billion for ALZA, which had only $1 billion in sales. Why? ALZA's drug delivery and controlled-release technologies, which had been utilized largely through a network of alliances with pharmaceutical companies, would provide J&J's divisions with dramatic proprietary means of delivering their own drugs. To close the circle, J&J incorporated ALZA technology into the coating of vascular stents with antirestenosis factors.

In contrast to the more definable commercial environment and fully integrated business models of the device sector, both platform technology and bioinformatics firms seem less well positioned to deal with these dual challenges. Each sector faces difficulties in developing new technology that is dependent on integration with other technologies (including change management in the case of biotechnology and healthcare information systems) to be useful. This need to integrate among companies conspires against a privileged and patent-protected position in the value chain; the demonstration of problem-solving capabilities to end users is lost in a morass of complexity and competition.

Biotechnology firms pursuing drug discovery and development seem to occupy an intermediate position on the spectrum. While in the past they certainly experienced challenges with both innovation and adoption, they are emerging as the solution to the productivity problems faced by pharmaceutical firms in terms of developing new, innovative products. As chapters 2 and 3 noted, the majority of the promising drug candidates of the future are being sourced from the biotechnology sector. Moreover, given the novelty of the new therapeutics emerging from the companies addressing hitherto untreatable debilitating diseases that affect smaller patient populations, such as rheumatoid arthritis (monthly costs for the new drugs exceed $1000), and given the current ambiguity of market entry of "biogenerics," these firms have thus far faced much lower pricing resistance from payers than do the makers of synthetic pharmaceuticals that have focused on chronic diseases that affect large portions of the population. Nevertheless, a major challenge going forward for the biotechnology companies will be the integration of genomic-based technologies into the practices of physicians.

Common business models

Another convergence evident across sectors has been the pursuit of common business models. Many of the sectors have undergone rapid transitions in their business models toward fully integrated companies. Biotechnology and platform technology firms are both migrating away from a strict focus on research toward the inclusion of drug development and commercialization activities. In this manner, they are striving to achieve the FIPCO model already prominent in the pharmaceutical sector and among the large medical device firms. One obvious driver of this trend is the need to confront the dual challenges of innovation and adoption discussed above and ultimately to enjoy higher price-earnings multiples and thus a lower cost of equity capital.

Another common business model has been growth via mergers and acquisitions (M&As). Across the sectors, firms have used M&A in an effort to leapfrog the competition, facilitate convergence of complementary technologies, increase their attractiveness as a strategic partner (e.g., for licensing in pharmaceuticals), diversify into new therapeutic areas (e.g., pharmaceutical firms, device firms) or new complementary technologies (e.g., IT firms), or to achieve scale economies (whether real or imagined). Several of the sectors adhere to a belief in the value of large scale in their operations. Evidence from chapter 5 questions the presumed benefits, at least among pharmaceutical firms. There is unpublished evidence that M&As among medical device firms also do not translate into abnormal stock returns.[1]

The M&A model has also been utilized to sustain growth rates in increasingly large firms that have found it difficult to grow organically. This is particularly true for those sectors with proportionately larger amounts of public equity and thus great pressures for quarterly earnings. M&A satisfies the demand for earnings growth by pooling the earnings of the merging firms and rationalizing R&D programs, general and administrative costs, and detailing costs, thus forestalling or dampening the need for internal, organic growth.

The M&A model is also another common strategy used in dealing with a fragmented market structure. A merger has the effect of reducing the number of competitors by one. As Porter's "five forces" analysis (see chapter 1) suggests, mergers reduce market rivalry and potentially lessen price competition, thereby increasing the ability of incumbent firms to earn above-average profits.

The chapters in this volume suggest that most sectors have fragmented market structures, that is, lots of competitors with small market shares.

This is clearly true for biotechnology firms, platform technology firms, and IT firms. The pharmaceutical sector has undergone a decade of consolidation and become more concentrated than before; however, no single firm enjoys greater than 10–11 percent market share. The medical device sector is the most consolidated of all, with three very big players in what the author of chapter 6 describes as an oligopoly. Nevertheless, all five sectors are quite innovative, lending further confirmation to the observation in chapter 5 that the market structure of an industry does not seem strongly correlated with the innovativeness of the firms within it. It is possible, of course, that all of this M&A activity might diminish innovation by virtue of erecting entry barriers to the industry and/or by consuming the attentions and energies of incumbent firms. In keeping with the Porter paradigm, fewer major players means fewer companies with which to partner biotechnology companies, thus tilting the economics of alliances in favor of the larger incumbents.

In addition to the fragmented sectors, most of the market sectors examined here are modest in size relative to pharmaceuticals, but are expected to grow significantly over the next few years. Worldwide, the sales of pharmaceuticals were pegged at nearly $500 billion in 2003, compared to $56 billion for biotechnology products and $75 billion for devices, and were estimated at $100 billion for IT in 2005.

Strategic resources, capabilities, and key success factors

The strategic management literature (in particular, the resource-based view of the firm) places a heavy emphasis on strategic capabilities as keys to competitive advantage. These capabilities are based on combinations of "resources" and "routines" that are unique to a firm. Resources can be both tangible (capital, balance sheet strength, physical plant, and equipment) and intangible (intellectual capital, reputation, innovation potential, employee motivation, culture). The routines are processes for coordinating the resources in productive ways (e.g., harmonizing social and technical systems, teamwork, and other integrative mechanisms) that other firms find difficult to do or emulate.

Resources

What are the strategic resources in the sectors examined here? Based on the prominence of risk, capital, and long cycle times in many of these sectors, the amount of *financial resources* is clearly important. Firms that generate high earnings, such as pharmaceutical and device companies, can rely on their own internal cash flows to finance R&D, rather than be subject to the vagaries of private equity and the IPO marketplace. In addition to being more predictable, cash flows provide lower cost capital. Such cash flows have been found to be associated with higher levels of R&D investment in the pharmaceutical sector. In the other sectors, by contrast, firms tend to be smaller start-ups in continuing need of capital to grow.

Scale is another, related resource of importance. Scale enables a firm to develop geographic scope in its marketing and commercial activities: for example, sell its products more broadly, target more customers and do so more intensively. Scale also improves the attractiveness of a firm as an alliance partner, and thereby provides an advantage over other firms in accessing new technologies and products from smaller firms.

Established and efficient *sales channels* might also be considered an important resource for competitive advantage, partially by serving as a barrier to entry to smaller firms. Many of the products and technologies discussed in this volume are marketed to physicians and other providers. Like the sectors discussed here, these buyer markets are fragmented and not centrally accessible. Large sales forces with detailed understanding of the clinicians being targeted and historical relationships of support are typically required for success.

There is, finally, a subtle concept in the resources literature, and that is the notion of fungibility of resources, as distinct from the concept of "ambidextrous" companies described below. The term basically means the ability of a firm to apply a resource or capability in one area of its business to another, thereby accelerating development of new business activity or achieving greater production economies across a firm. The mechanics of fungibility vary greatly from one sector to another, but biotechnology has a version of fungibility that a few companies in the sector discovered early in the history of the industry. For example, the aforesaid relationship between Genentech and Eli Lilly meant that Genentech would abandon the insulin market to Eli Lilly, the dominant provider of the soon-to-be obsolete porcine insulin but also the controller of relationships with internists and diabetologists. The arrangement, however, had the obvious benefit of providing Genentech with critically needed cash. The less obvious benefit was that Lilly effectively financed the development of Genentech's know-how for production and scale-up (major issues for biopharmaceuticals in the 1980s) that could be used across its pipeline of products. Lilly's knowledge of regulatory matters and its credibility with the Food and Drug Administration also promoted the creation of standards for the evaluation of recombinant products, with Genentech and Amgen (to say nothing of the public) being the major beneficiaries.

Organizational routines and capabilities

Beyond these resources, there are a series of organizational routines and capabilities that seem critical for success. One important routine is the ability to *manage knowledge* across a firm's silos (the distinct departments or organizational enclaves for portions of the discovery, development, or marketing processes) and projects, both within and across therapeutic areas. The leveraging of knowledge and the insights thereby gleaned produce one set of the synergies expected from diversification efforts. This is no easy task, as professional firms in other knowledge-intensive industries (e.g., medicine, academia, consulting) have discovered.

Firms in the pharmaceutical, device, and IT sectors nevertheless appear to rely on these presumed advantages as one justification for their diversification activities. As chapter 5 describes, the activity requires a host of *integrative mechanisms* to bring together individual expertise, departmental silos, scientific disciplines, development projects, and stages in the internal value chain, namely, research, development, manufacturing, marketing. A cardinal principle of management theory has long held that the degree of internal differentiation within a firm must be matched by the requisite amount of integration across laboratories, operating units, and divisions – another spin on the concept of fungibility. Diversification thus necessitates integration.

Executives and managers in the firms profiled in this volume face some daunting prospects here. First, diversification is often pursued via M&A strategies. The qualitative evidence on M&As suggests that top executives – until recently – place heavier emphasis on the merger transaction than they do on postmerger integration. Failure to attend to the latter will diminish the prospects for achieving any synergies, assuming that the synergies were honestly assessed during merger planning.

Second, integration is time-consuming, meeting-intensive, and difficult work. It also affects the power equation among executives and requires the emotionally wrenching problem of reducing staff and closing plants. While it may be a cynical observation, senior executives often address the impact of mergers on the issues of shared power among the same senior executives following the actual merger. Executives at lower levels are often left to fend for themselves. These are among the reasons why top executives often delegate integration to lower level executives or engage outside consultants to develop – and sometimes implement – rationalization plans. Outside consultants are often used to study and rationalize R&D projects and product lines in order to comply with the requirements of antitrust authorities. Evidence from the strategy literature suggests, however, that integration activities and efforts to retain the intellectual capital from the firm acquired are the two most important predictors of M&A success.

Third, the literature on corporate diversification is mixed, at best. Diversification, of course, is definable only on a case specific basis. On the one hand, companies can diversify, essentially augment, a product line by adding new drugs that fit into a detailing call pattern to the same physicians. On the other hand, diversification can take the form of adding entirely new lines of business, albeit in the same industry, justified on the basis of a portfolio approach to risk mitigation. The pharmaceutical sector has had a curious history of this latter type of diversification. During the 1970s many of pharmaceutical companies redefined themselves as broad human care companies and diversified into diagnostics systems and services, medical devices, hospital supplies, laboratory instrumentation, dental and optomology products, over-the-counter pharmaceuticals, nutritional supplements, and even cosmetics. It is hard to establish technological synergy between surgical instruments and lipstick. This human care conglomeration did not work, and the companies systematically began divesting all nonpharmaceutical businesses. Perhaps the only company in the industry to achieve successful diversification is Johnson & Johnson. The basis of their success is a topic for another large book, but suffice it to say, their operational and marketing insight is managed across the corporation, and the company is disciplined to know when it can win and when it cannot. Why does J&J sell toothbrushes but not toothpaste?

Diversification is often pursued and justified, therefore, for reasons of scope economies. The underlying assumption, however, is that each functional unit is sufficiently linked to other units in ways that they can equitably share the economies. Integration of new systems often interrupts the status quo of transfer pricing among departments and the related margins for those departments. Again, not to be cynical, but managerial compensation and promotion are determined by each unit's performance. Units and divisions within corporations compete, and the pharmaceutical sector is not an exception to this dynamic. In fact, the managerial structure of the pharmaceutical sector differs from other industries. True profit and loss responsibility exists at only the highest levels of a corporation. At lower levels there is virtual profit and loss responsibility for the product and brand managers. The other operational silos, such as discovery, development, and manufacturing, are cost centers. In cases where scale economies are effectively a zero-sum game, senior management cannot assume cooperation among divisions unless the compensation standards are revised. This may explain why firms that pursue "related diversification" do not necessarily perform better than those that pursue "unrelated diversification." Instead, the literature suggests that some modicum of diversification is correlated with firm performance, but not with excessively high or low levels.[2]

Another key capability is *portfolio management and optimization*, as alluded to in the discussion of M&A. This is clearly a major issue facing the pharmaceutical sector today: specifically in which new products should a company invest, and which existing products should be milked, further developed, or divested. The participants in the medical device sector confront these issues differently from the pharmaceutical sector; their decision points are sharper by virtue of more rapid changes in marketing performance and technological substitution. The device sector will confront these issues more frequently, given the number of emerging and unexplored clinical areas outlined in chapter 6.

A key capability in portfolio management and optimization is factoring two sources of uncertainty: market uncertainty (is there a market?) and technical uncertainty (can the firm deliver?). These two types of uncertainty parallel the two key challenges discussed at the beginning of this chapter. As a solution to this dual management problem, strategy theorists as well as industry practitioners have relied on real options reasoning rather than on net present value calculations. In the real options approach, firms distinguish among the available technological opportunities available to them, manage them differently, and then learn from them for purposes of the next round of investments. The real options framework has the additional benefit in this industry of forcing the formulation of process milestones that have the effect of establishing decision criteria and the mitigation of financial risk by portioning the development process into predefined stages.

For example, Ian MacMillan of the Wharton School has devoted considerable effort to studying how firms decide among technological opportunities which ones to fund and staff.[3] In an analysis of a medical device firm, he first identified the current portfolio of investment projects along the two types of uncertainty. He found that the grid was overcrowded with more projects than the firm could staff or finance, and overly invested in highly demanding, new platform launches. Such a situation is typically found in other firms and industries. To correct the problem, he has developed a grid of five strategic options for firms to consider based on these two types of uncertainty: enhancement launches (add new attributes to existing platform – low on both types of uncertainty), new platform launches (medium uncertainty), positioning options (can fail on the dimension of technical uncertainty), scouting options (can fail on the dimension of market uncertainty), and stepping-stones (can fail on both technical and market dimensions). The problem then becomes one of strategic allocation of finite resources across the five options. The solution MacMillan develops is to identify a separate resource pool for each type of option, recognize that each type has its own timing pattern, and then allow competition for resources among opportunities within (but not across) option groups. In concert with executives in the semiconductor industry, MacMillan argues that strategic allocation of resources is the key task of entrepreneurship.[4]

In a similar vein, some pharmaceutical firms are refocusing their R&D efforts on a smaller number of projects and therapeutic areas. In effect, they are dediversifying – and thereby recognizing some of the problems of diversified activity noted above. In combination with this more focused approach, they are also developing multidisciplinary and multifunctional silo teams on a global basis to coordinate product development, along with smaller groupings of people. In effect, they are also recognizing the importance of integrative mechanisms and the value of small scale (e.g., as found in the biotechnology sector) for innovation.

Another key capability is the *management of strategic alliances* and collaborations along the value chain. The chapters in this volume suggest that success in the pharmaceutical, biotechnology, and platform technology sectors all hinge on alliance formation and performance. Perhaps this observation should sound the alarm. As numerous management scholars have pointed out, alliance formation and performance is a behavioral science skill – and as such is more art than science. Indeed, one scholar has likened it to dating.[5] It should thus not be surprising that the success rate with strategic alliances in industry (roughly a 50 percent "instability rate," defined as an unplanned and premature change in alliance relationship status) parallels the success rate of marriage. And even marriages that endure are not necessarily happy ones!

The strategic literature informs us as to the critical ingredients for a successful strategic alliance (echoing some of the ingredients mentioned in chapters 2 and 3). To reiterate one of the themes above, alliances are knowledge-creating networks. Their success depends heavily on processes of knowledge creation and management, organizational sharing and learning, conflict resolution, and trust building.[6] Perhaps even more importantly, like the M&As discussed in chapter 5, alliance success hinges on due diligence in selecting the proper partner up front.

The management of collaborations is also implicit in efforts to make M&As work. There is a growing body of qualitative evidence on the postmerger processes that need to be in place, particularly those that serve to retain the human resources talent in the acquired firm and to merge the different cultures of the merger partners. Both factors have been identified as key contributors to M&A success or failure.[7]

Another important capability mentioned in chapter 1 and reiterated in several forms throughout the volume is *managing the balancing act*. In addition to managing the dual challenges noted at the outset, smaller start-up firms (e.g., in the biotechnology, platform technology, devices, and IT sectors) must balance their R&D investments with maintaining sales momentum to thus avoid becoming the target of acquisition by a larger competitor.

At a more conceptual level, the innovation literature has suggested the need to balance a firm's short-term focus on earnings and operating efficiency with a long-term focus on research, discovery, and experimentation. Innovation scholars argue that "ambidextrous" firms – firms that can simultaneously pursue these two, contrasting orientations of "exploitation" and "exploration" – are more likely to succeed.[8] The ambidextrous approach requires two different types of change processes (short-term adjustments versus long-term adaptations), goals of change (maximize economic value versus develop firm capabilities), methods of planning (programmatic versus emergent), targets of change (structure/systems versus culture), directions of change (top-down versus bottom-up), methods of change (imitation versus experimentation), and scales of change (small scale versus large scale).

This balancing act will prove difficult for most firms. The ambidextrous approach requires two different mindsets not likely found in the same executive. Thus, firms need an executive team with both mindsets in some balance. Moreover, most firms may not have (or do not perceive they have) the luxury to pursue the exploration side, given Wall Street pressures for short-term earnings growth. Exploration may also be inhibited by CEO compensation packages and incentives from the Board, the tendency to outsource strategic planning to consultants, the short tenures of CEOs, the tendency of CEOs to subscribe to programmatic change methods, and the associated tendency to deemphasize local level experimentation in large firms.[9]

Perhaps the most important capability that will be required in the future is "*affordable innovation*" as described in chapter 2. Following the value chain perspective, producers across all sectors may confront a payer community that is increasingly activist in documenting the value (price for quality) of the products they pay for. There are already signs of this in Europe for both pharmaceutical and device products. There have been rumblings of this developing in the US, although a recent attempt to tie head-to-head clinical performance of drugs to Medicare reimbursement was scuttled (revised approach may emerge, however).

The pressures here for affordability and performance are keenly felt in the IT sector, where the costs of replacing legacy systems are enormous. They are also growing in the pharmaceutical sector, given the need to monitor drug reimportation and track and recalibrate reference pricing on a real-time basis. Pressures for more affordable products have been slower to develop in the biotechnology and device sectors, partly because the cost of devices is often submerged in payments to hospitals, partly because of the stunning clinical benefits afforded by some of these technologies, and partly because of the lack of alternative therapies and generics. Manufacturers should expect greater payer scrutiny of the ⌐   ᶠor their products, however, as the technologies diffuse to thᴄ   n and as reports surface about their actual cost. Suᴄᴸ   ɔming from the organized buyers of these   ɜ organizations).

Tecʜ   **ors**
___

                                        in the belief that each sector must have a
                                        e chapters have illustrated several areas
                                        the different sectors are penetrating
                                        "recombining" with one another to
    ᶤ   vider and consumer. This has been
    cᴄ   ʜ show how pharmaceutical and
    mᴄ   ⌐ɪngly interdependent in solving the
    biot   ⌐ʊ adoption. These chapters, along with chap-
    twin   ⌐ɴow drugs and devices are being combined in new
    ters 5·   ⌐w devices can be used to transport biologicals to local targeted
    treatmᴄ areas in the human body; how imaging technologies can help researchers correlate biological changes with disease, provide hard endpoints to diseases, and guide implantation of surgical devices; and how broadband connectivity can communicate patient diagnostics to remote providers.

As noted in the introductory chapter, there are several barriers to growing convergence, and some of them are alluded to above. First, producers may eschew products with convergent technologies if they entail smaller markets than those they currently target. For such products, the innovation comes at the expense of widespread adoption. Second, convergent products may require the harmonization of different business models, cultures, and customer orientations among firms contributing to these products. As we have argued above, such harmonization is already a challenge in M&As and strategic alliances that has not yet been successfully mastered. Third, convergence may require firms to develop a wider value chain perspective, which is not common in the healthcare industry in the US.[10] This volume seeks to address this myopia.

We should point out that we have been speaking of convergence in technologies, not necessarily convergence of markets or sectors. Some discussion of the latter is in order, however. Almost all biotechnology firms (with the exception of Amgen and Genentech) and platform technology firms (with the exception of Millennium Pharmaceuticals), as cited in chapter 4, are quite some distance from developing into FIPCO-model pharmaceutical firms, but there is movement in that direction. By contrast, medical device firms are not likely to become pharmaceutical firms, even if the success of drug-eluting stents diffuses to other drug–device combination products.

To the degree that sectors actually converge, one might hypothesize what competitive dynamics might occur. The history of the convergence between the telecommunications and computer industries provides some evidence.[11] Analysts anticipated that sector boundaries would become vague and blurred, the core competencies of traditional suppliers would be challenged, and firms from adjacent markets would be enticed to enter the industry as firms accumulated competencies in those markets. In fact, the convergence did not occur as expected for many of the reasons discussed in this volume. First, the presumed economies of scope from joint production were lower than expected, while the scale economies and large size of incumbents remained important advantages. Second, as discussed in chapter 5, it is difficult to make cross-firm therapeutic alliances work (let alone cross-industry market entry) when the acquiring firm does not have an historical track record in the therapeutic area and "absorptive capacity" – that is, the ability to absorb and leverage the acquired knowledge into its own technical core.[12] Third, large firms are subject to inertia that reduces their ability to deal with changes in their technological cores. Indeed, the work of evolutionary theorists suggests that firm behavior is more predictable and routine than innovative, leading to the well-known "success breeds failure" syndrome. Thus, technological convergence at the market level did not play out at the firm level.

There is another reason why convergence among sectors may not occur. The production of useful knowledge has become so specialized and professionalized that firms (and perhaps sectors too) have limited abilities to grasp and absorb it all. The range of relevant disciplines to a firm's innovative processes has expanded both in terms of the breadth of disciplines and the depth of knowledge within each one.[13] Thus, the knowledge boundaries for the emerging convergent technology innovations identified above stretch way beyond a firm's production boundaries. Firms using multiple technologies to make products need to have knowledge in excess of what they need for what they produce. This imbalance is required to cope with imbalances caused by uneven rates of development in the technologies (pharmaceuticals versus biotechnology) on which they rely and with unpredictable product-level interdependencies.[14] Moreover, the knowledge and product domains evolve in different ways.[15] For these reasons, firms draw their organizational boundaries more tightly than they do their knowledge boundaries.[16] To manage the discrepancy, they rely on the many types of strategic alliances discussed in this volume. Alliances allow them to benefit from the advantages of both specialization (scale economies) and integration (coordination). This is the more likely scenario for the future in the producer side of the healthcare industry.

NOTES

1. Robert DeGraaff, unpublished dissertation, Wharton School, 2005.
2. Robert M. Grant, *Contemporary Strategy Analysis* (Oxford: Blackwell, 2002).
3. Rita Gunther McGrath and Ian MacMillan, *The Entrepreneurial Mindset* (Boston, MA: Harvard Business School Press, 2000).
4. Andrew S. Grove, *Only the Paranoid Survive* (New York: Doubleday, 1996).
5. Rosabeth Moss Kanter, "Collaborative Advantage: The Art of Alliances," *Harvard Business Review* 72(4) (July/August, 1994): 96–107.
6. Andrew C. Inkpen, "Strategic Alliances," in *Handbook of Strategic Management*, ed. Michael Hitt, R. Edward Freeman, and Jeffrey S. Harrison (Oxford: Blackwell, 2001), 409–432.
7. Mitchell Lee Marks and Philip H. Mirvis, *Joining Forces* (San Francisco, CA: Jossey-Bass, 1998).
8. Michael Beer and Nitin Nohria, eds., *Breaking the Code of Change* (Boston, MA: Harvard Business School Press, 1998).
9. Cf. Stefan H. Thomke, *Experimentation Matters* (Boston, MA: Harvard Business School Press, 2003).
10. Lawton R. Burns, *The Health Care Value Chain* (San Francisco, CA: Jossey-Bass, 2002).

11. Geert Duysters and John Hagedoorn, "Technological Convergence in the IT Industry: The Role of Strategic Technology Alliances and Technological Competencies," unpublished manuscript, Maastricht University, 1997.

12. W. M. Cohen and Daniel Levinthal, "Absorptive Capacity: A New Perspective on Learning and Innovation," *Administrative Science Quarterly* 35 (1990): 128–152.

13. Q. Wang and G. N. Von Tunzelmann, "Complexity and the Functions of the Firm: Breadth and Depth," *Research Policy* 29 (2000): 805–818.

14. Stefano Brusoni, Andreas Prencipe, and Keith Pavitt, "Knowledge Specialization, Organization Coupling, and the Boundaries of the Firm: Why do Firms Know More than they Make?," *Administrative Science Quarterly* 46 (December, 2001): 597–621.

15. G. N. Von Tunzelmann, "Localised Technological Search and Multitechnology Companies," *Economics of Innovation and New Technology* 6 (1998): 231–255.

16. Brusoni *et al.* "Knowledge Specialization."

Index